TOWERING ABOVE HARLEM

Towering Above Harlem

Geographies of Race and the
Power of Elite Institutions

Steven Gregory

Edited by Elizabeth Chin

NEW YORK UNIVERSITY PRESS
New York

NEW YORK UNIVERSITY PRESS
New York
www.nyupress.org

© 2025 by New York University
All rights reserved

Please contact the Library of Congress for Cataloging-in-Publication data.
ISBN: 9781479831371 (hardback)
ISBN: 9781479831388 (paperback)
ISBN: 9781479831418 (library ebook)
ISBN: 9781479831401 (consumer ebook)

This book is printed on acid-free paper, and its binding materials are chosen for strength
and durability. We strive to use environmentally responsible suppliers and materials to the
greatest extent possible in publishing our books.

The manufacturer's authorized representative in the EU for product safety is Mare
Nostrum Group B.V., Mauritskade 21D, 1091 GC Amsterdam, The Netherlands.
Email: gpsr@mare-nostrum.co.uk.

Manufactured in the United States of America

10 9 8 7 6 5 4 3 2 1

Also available as an ebook

CONTENTS

FOREWORD

ARLENE DÁVILA

It is an honor to share a few words about the brilliant book of a dear friend who is no longer with us, and unable to interact with its readers. Many who knew Steven Gregory or read his work will recognize his intimate ethnographic style, finely tuned attention to detail—from how people talk to their mannerisms—and his uncanny ability to link the seemingly mundane to micro-spatial political-economic processes and trends.

For those encountering Steven's work for the first time, without the pleasure of having met him, I'd like to focus on what I imagine he would want people to know about him and his work before embarking on this journey.

Firstly, readers should be aware that Steven Gregory was a proud African American/Black scholar and critic. He approached research and writing through an uncompromising, critical, anti-racist lens. Urban studies and anthropology, as disciplines, have traditionally been among the whitest fields. Steven's positionality is fundamental to his approach, critiquing urban studies dominated by capitalism rather than racial capitalism—a term he didn't use, being more of a traditionalist/classicist. Yet his understanding of capitalism was intrinsically tied to racialized class exclusion and dispossession, making class inequality impossible to understand without centering racism and race. Readers are in for a foundational resource that explicates why urbanism cannot be understood without a rigorous racial analysis and why geography is intrinsically tied to racial and class-inflected hierarchies.

On the traditionalist/classicist point, Steven eschewed fads and trends, turning his eye to classical, foundational resources. His analysis is an example of the longue durée he exposes in this book, engaging with scholars, thinkers, and activists across historical fields with rigor and nuance. He loved history and archives—and felt that they were essential to any understanding of political economy, and of power. The more things change, the more they stay the same is a key lesson of this book, as well as how history can be a powerful tool to uncover long-standing patterns and new techniques of dispossession.

Steven was a cheerleader of the disenfranchised and the poor, someone who truly loved the "popular" and popular classes. His critique of institutional elites associated with Columbia University and other peer institutions, spanning real estate, government, public health, academia, and media, is uncompromising. Readers will find vivid examples of how institutions of power converge to create inequalities, serving as a call to action for activists, scholars, and community members to fight institutional elites and a model of how we should adopt similarly uncompromising positions when documenting institutions of power, even those that employ us.

Steven was also an activist and a critic of fake news and media propaganda in all shapes and forms. He was genuinely incensed over the erasures of power and race fostered by the national news, and this sentiment informs this work, which can also be seen as a guide and handbook to decipher how institutional elites operate to create misinformation, and to make oppression and dispossession seem natural and even necessary.

Steven was a humanist at heart, and his ethnographic practice was characterized by deep respect and political engagement. He wanted readers to feel and imagine being part of the scenarios he describes, as stakeholders in the game alongside anyone else on these pages. This is why his previous books were so praised and so useful in the classroom, and why he would be delighted when this new work is used in classrooms to train and inspire new budding ethnographers.

Steven was also an artist. He was a skilled photographer, and his camera was his prop everywhere he went. He used it to break the ice and as an extension of his notes, but also as an act of love toward his friends, and to show respect and uplift the communities he worked with. This book does not have as many pictures as Steven would have liked—his archive is greater than represented. But I encourage readers to look closely at the pictures in the book, to notice people's faces and reactions of hope, anger, and despair, and to pay attention to how the structures of new buildings seem to squash and take over the landscape—and how all these visual cues reinforce the central arguments of the book.

Steven was a genuinely generous teacher, mentor, and friend. He uplifted, supported, and brought joy to everyone around him, and he was truly loved by colleagues, students, and friends. He was a cheerleader and optimist who hated injustice everywhere. Approach these pages with the reminder to never lose hope.

EDITOR'S NOTE

ELIZABETH CHIN

The first question might be, "So why does this book have an editor?" It is certainly unusual for a book like this one, a piece of research and scholarship undertaken by a single author. The reason is that Steven Gregory was in the final stages of completing revisions on this work when he died, suddenly and unexpectedly. My task has been to make some of the changes it was clear he had planned to do, to bring the length of the manuscript down, as Steven had discussed with his editor, and to do all of this in a way that does justice to the importance of the project, and with respect for Steven's aims and vision.

The editing was guided by two peer review reports, and by Steven's own response to them. Academic books, like academic articles, typically go through a peer review process in which the manuscript is shared with experts (whose identities are usually kept confidential) who offer their comments and critiques. The author answers with a "response letter" that defends some choices, while laying out changes that they will make in response to their peers' recommendations. In typical form, Steven defended some choices with panache. One reviewer wondered about the larger relevance of the study, and in particular, the parallels to the University of Chicago, with its own storied (and equally sordid) history of strategically racializing its geography and dispossessing the people who lived there. With characteristic directness and a mastery of the tiniest details, Steven wrote that because at the time Columbia's sociology department consisted of only one person who espoused eugenicist notions of evolution, it was virtually impossible that their scholarship had any truck with the Chicago school of sociology, which rejected those ideas. More importantly, in the next passage, Steven framed why he was uninterested in a national, comparative project:

But I am not telling a national or comparative story of *university* expansions; my focus is on a constellation of diverse institutions and their specific interests and relationship to Harlem and other working-class communities. . . . Moreover, a central focus of my manuscript is the evolution of the Morningside Heights/Harlem interface and conflict in relation to *geography* over the longue durée, which makes my case, in many ways, distinct from the more episodic expansion of Chicago or the University of Pennsylvania.

The response letter also sketched a comprehensive and important role of "the growing body of literature on Black geographies, such as the work of Katherine McKittrick, Clyde Woods, Jodi Rios, Rashad Shabazz, as well as Brandi Summers." As he prepared to bring the manuscript to completion, Steven particularly wanted to "foreground black geographies as a field throughout the text, beginning with the Introduction, and then engage and cite the work of these scholars where relevant, particularly in Chapters Four, Seven, and the Epilogue." These edits, no doubt, would have involved more than a sentence or two, and, moreover, were going to involve integrating key terms and ideas throughout the manuscript. I am in agreement with one anonymous reviewer, who wrote, "I would hold that only Gregory could tie these things together as he envisioned." Accordingly, in addressing the work on Black geographies, I have added as little writing as possible; the only new paragraph I have added to this book is a very short one on Black geographies in the introduction. In an effort to signal his plan for this literature to have a presence throughout the book, I have added references to those authors whom Steven mentioned above, particularly in chapters 4 and 7 and the epilogue, as he had planned to do. Following his own general practice, and to minimize my own intrusion, the references are brief and self-explanatory.

Like Steven, I am an anthropologist of North America, and a great deal of my work focuses on Black life in the urban United States. Steven and I ran into each other at conferences and occasionally had a drink together, and we knew and admired each other's work. We shared a commitment to social justice and a disdain for elitism. I also came to learn that he had an annoying tendency to begin sentences with needless openers like "nevertheless" and "although." He was maniacal about detail, except when it came to providing all the details in bibliographic references. Each day as I cut and then cut some more, I begged his forgiveness. A long section on the Tenderloin district, for example, was important to him, largely, I believe, because it includes key material on the economics and sexuality of women of color, as well as paying attention to the livelihoods and political insecurity of late nineteenth-century Chinese immigrants, topics the data did not allow him to address elsewhere. But the Tenderloin is not in Morningside Heights, nor is it near Manhattanville or Harlem. Taking my cues from his own stated goals in tracing "the evolution of the Morningside Heights/Harlem interface," my edits were always aimed at pruning away material that, while valuable, was ancillary to the central purpose he articulated.

This book focuses on the institutions making up what Steven Gregory called "the American Acropolis," to show how the elites who created those institutions—perhaps most notably Columbia University itself—used politics, policy, academic knowledge, prestige, and technologies of knowledge to create a shining city on a hill. Located atop a plateau in Morningside Heights, Columbia, Riverside Church, and other institutions were sited majestically and strategically, enjoying views, good drainage, and defensible geographic and social isolation from the woes and ills of poverty, disease, and urban unpleasantness. Identifying and controlling what Steven calls "the constitutive outside" were integral to this process, and over the longue durée the geography and people of Manhattanville, Harlem, and surrounding areas were studied, educated, and enumerated. Theories about their intelligence, their health, and their ability to be American were developed and disseminated. The constitutive outside was also defined through the erection of spite fences, the razing of slums, and the forcible takeover of land through eminent domain. Columbia's status as an agent of dispossession is one of the primary themes of this book. Columbia University, as an institution and as the home of influential academics, educators, and researchers, was, from its very beginnings, dedicated to rising above, setting itself apart. What Steven Gregory makes clear over and over again is that generations of professors, educators, and researchers were instrumental in producing knowledge designed to keep the constitutive outside out. His scrupulous accounting is also an act of calling for accountability. To what degree can an Ivy League institution truly consider itself to be excellent when it has xiv | EDITOR'S NOTE

destroyed the lives, livelihoods, neighborhoods, and thriving cultures of its neighbors? What responsibility do we as scholars—even with the best of intentions—have to the people we study, particularly when our work is used to justify their denigration, their surveillance, or their removal? While he never directly raises these questions in his own analysis, his position is clear: we must take responsibility for what our work does out there in the world.

With its interdisciplinary methodology, Steven's book follows in the legacy of Du Bois's *The Philadelphia Negro*. Moreover, like *The Philadelphia Negro*, this book is a masterpiece astonishing in its scope and vision. Among the many important aspects of this book is its ethnographic approach to historical materials. Anthropologists are notorious for an obsession with kinship, interrogating the ways in which family making (or denial) entwines with power and politics. Drawing from archives, newspapers, secondary sources, and interviews, Steven extensively documented the close ties between members of the elite, using his ethnographic skills to show how their membership in organizations, presence at meetings, letters to politicians, donations to charities, and intermarriages constituted a web of connections that was simultaneously social, political, and institutional. This material, taken together, amounts to a forensic social ethnography worthy of its own recognition. Yet the abundance of byzantine details left many passages so stuffed with names, dates, and locations that they threatened to burst at the seams. In many cases I have snipped or culled such details that, while true, fascinating, and important, were not ultimately necessary to the argument at hand.

Steven's approach to analyzing and interpreting census materials is also deeply ethnographic. The early census methods and documents allowed for the identification of individual census enumerators, and also allowed for a reconstruction of their daily work. Chapter 2 is built around this ethnographically oriented census analysis. In the section "A Day in the Life of a Census Enumerator," Gregory takes us through one census enumerator's day, describing in cinematic detail the brick-fronted tenements, the apartments, and the people who lived there. In some ways similar to the ethnographic vignette that opens so many anthropological works, this chapter takes the stuff of everyday life as the ground upon which the main theoretical themes are introduced and put to work. The power of Steven's method is especially notable as he follows a man named William Lynch across more than twenty years of census records, raising questions about racial categorization and the state, the African diaspora, and more. I left much of this specific narrative intact to demonstrate the acuity of Steven's methodological approach to census data, so often reduced to dry numbers and charts. In the original manuscript, he made use of this technique in several places, including in the section on the Tenderloin. These incredibly detailed, rich, and critically incisive sections could not ultimately be included, but they constitute a singularly impactful example of historically grounded ethnography, and deserve to be reckoned with methodologically and theoretically on their own terms.

Steven's rage against elitism vibrates in every word. Though he worked at Columbia University, he was never of it. His people, the people he claimed, and the people he worked in solidarity with, were the everyday people of Washington Heights and Harlem, the gas station owners, the tenant activists, those whose voices he privileges. Ultimately, as he reflected in the book's epilogue, this book is about rights to the city, the rights of the not-elite to live and breathe and cross the street, raise their children, tell jokes, sit outside a café and have a smoke and a shot of rum. The shadow cast by those who believe themselves to be better and above, up there on the Morningside plateau, threatens to stifle or even suffocate what Steven defends so fiercely. This book shines a light into that shadow, an indictment of the ways that elites make worlds for themselves, justifying their exceptionalism by defining those around them as less-than.

As Steven finished the book's epilogue, COVID-19 had transformed a collective sense of rights and responsibilities, exposing the degree to which the right to the city is also, as he underscored, a matter of life and death. Today, the processes charted in this book are more relevant than ever.

Introduction

One brisk morning in February 2009, a neighbor told me about a rally taking place later that day at Floridita, a Cuban-owned restaurant at the corner of West 129th Street and Broadway in West Harlem. Floridita was a popular, affordable restaurant that attracted ethnically diverse customers. The rally had been organized by Columbia University's Student Coalition on Expansion and Gentrification and was being held, among other things, to protest the imminent closing of the restaurant, pursuant to the university's plan to expand its Morningside Heights campus into a seventeen-acre area of West Harlem known as Manhattanville.

The university's $6.7 billion expansion plan called for the acquisition and demolition of all but three Columbia-owned buildings in the project's footprint and the construction of a state-of-the-art campus over a roughly thirty-year period. Columbia had been buying properties in Manhattanville for over a decade, and in 2004 purchased the squat building that housed Floridita, an Eritrean social club, and three other commercial tenants. On July 18, 2008, the Empire State Development Corporation, the New York state agency charged with promoting economic development, approved the university's expansion plan and, after determining that Manhattanville was suffering from conditions of "urban blight," cleared the way for the exercise of eminent domain—that is, the state appropriation of private property with compensation but without the consent of property owners.

The use of eminent domain was a lightning rod for community opposition. Most critics recognized Columbia's right to buy property and expand its campus, but opposed the university's demand for exclusive control of the project's seventeen-acre footprint and expected use of eminent domain. The university maintained that the research conducted at its new campus would serve a public purpose—directly, by researching cures for illnesses such as Alzheimer's disease and providing employment, and indirectly, by helping to usher in a knowledge-based economic future.

I arrived late. About fifty people, most of them Columbia students, had gathered inside Floridita; its owner, Ramon Diaz, treated them to lunch. When I arrived, the crowd was spilling onto the street. Some carried signs reading, "Good Neighbors Respect their Neighbors" and "Hasta la Floridita siempre!" a wordplay on Che Guevara's famous sign-off in his last letter to Fidel Castro, "Hasta la victoria siempre!" (Ever onward to victory!).

The protest took the form of a walking tour of the seventeen-acre project site, led by three community activists who had been staunch opponents of the university's expansion: Nellie Hester Bailey, president of the Harlem Tenants Council, a tenants' rights organization; Vicky Gholson, a member of West Harlem's Community Board 9, which had opposed the campus expansion plan; and Mario Mazzoni, an activist working with the Coalition to Preserve Community, a community organization that had been formed in 2003 to resist the campus expansion.

Once the crowd had gathered on 129th Street, Gholson raised her bullhorn, directing the group toward a gas station located further along the triangular-shaped block. The station was one of two in the area owned by Gurnam Singh and his wife, Parminder Kaur, Punjabi immigrants from northern India. The couple had started the Manhattanville businesses twenty-five years earlier (T. Williams 2008b). In 2009 Singh was one of two property owners who had refused to sell to the university. The second holdout, Nick Sprayregen, owned Tuck-It-Away, a self-storage company that occupied three large buildings within the proposed footprint.

The crowd gathered around the gas station's office, where Singh, a stately, bearded man of forty-seven, was standing. He listened as Bailey recounted the history of the conflict over the expansion and summarized what she believed were its negative consequences. Singh took the bullhorn and explained that, although university officials had offered to relocate the couple's gas stations, it would take years to reestablish the businesses elsewhere. The gas stations enjoyed ideal locations, attracting taxi drivers who often ate at Floridita.

We stopped at a large self-storage facility, a booming barbeque restaurant, and two recently renovated apartment buildings. Gholson, Bailey, and Mazzoni situated each site in time and space, challenging the state's finding that the area was blighted and the university's characterization of

Rally at the gas station of Gurnam Singh, February 2009. Photo by author.

the area as an "obsolete," former manufacturing district. At a car repair shop, Mazzoni paused and raised his bullhorn. The repair shop was bustling with activity. A half dozen or so mechanics looked on with curiosity. "This is a good example of the kind of business that Columbia says is blighting the area. But this repair shop provides good jobs and provides a service that people in the community need. Why should Columbia, using the threat of eminent domain, have the power to decide what the needs of this community are? Or determine which jobs and businesses are valuable and worth saving?" The protesters gathered around Mazzoni shouted in agreement.

Bailey then reached for the bullhorn. "This didn't all start today. For years and years, Columbia and the other institutions on the Hill have been buying up property in Harlem and in Morningside Heights, and evicting Black and brown people from their homes." Bailey spoke about the university's campaign during the 1960s and 1970s of purchasing rooming houses and apartment buildings in Morningside Heights in order to evict their predominantly low-income African American and

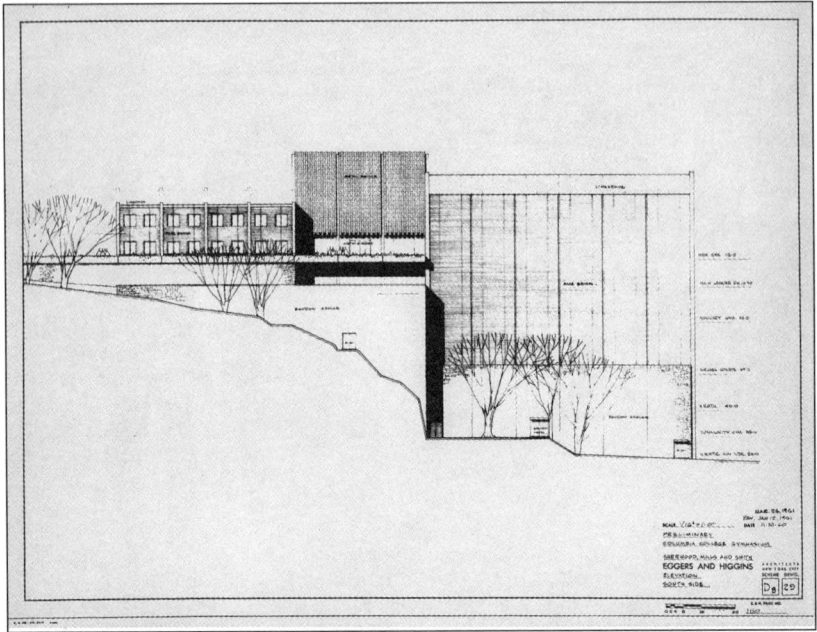

Section drawing of Columbia University's proposed "vertical gymnasium," by the New York architectural firm Eggers & Higgins. Courtesy of the Columbia University Archives.

Puerto Rican tenants. Gesturing toward Morningside Park, less than a mile away, Bailey spoke of Columbia's plan to construct a gymnasium on public parkland in Harlem, a plan defeated by community-based and student activists in 1968.

Bailey witnessed many of these struggles. She had cofounded the Harlem Tenants Council in 1995 and, as its director, had been advocating for tenants' rights in the greater Harlem area, in her own words, "to counter displacement and homeless caused by gentrification and the illegal actions of landlords against poor and working class tenants" (Bailey 2008:232). A civil rights activist since college, Bailey had worked as a tenant advocate with the Columbia Tenants Union, an organization that had been cofounded in 1973 by her husband, Bruce Bailey. Bruce Bailey, a graduate of Columbia College, had been radicalized during the 1968 student rebellions and, soon after, had joined the Progressive Labor Party. In 1989 Bruce Bailey was murdered and his dismembered body found in plastic garbage bags in the Bronx. No one was ever arrested for the horrific crime; his wife and associates surmised that it had been the landlord of one of the buildings that Bailey was organizing (Bailey 2008; Raab 1973; Guttenplan 1989:4; Hevesi 1989). The contested Manhattanville campus expansion in 2009 was the latest chapter in a history of racialized class exclusion—one that, if successful, would project the boundaries and influence of the university and its allied institutions north of West 125th Street and deep into West Harlem. Nellie Bailey's comments rooted the present controversy in a long history of institutional expansion and racial dispossession that was materialized in the landscape of the present. Longtime residents of Harlem and elsewhere often referred to this constellation of institutions in Morningside Heights as "the Hill." For their part, since the late nineteenth century, institutional elites in Morningside Heights and their supporters have referred to the plateau as the "American Acropolis," celebrating the area's separation, or "vertical secession," from surrounding working-class communities (Graham and Hewitt 2012).

Beginning in the late nineteenth century, religious, educational, and other nonprofit institutions were established in Morningside Heights, a

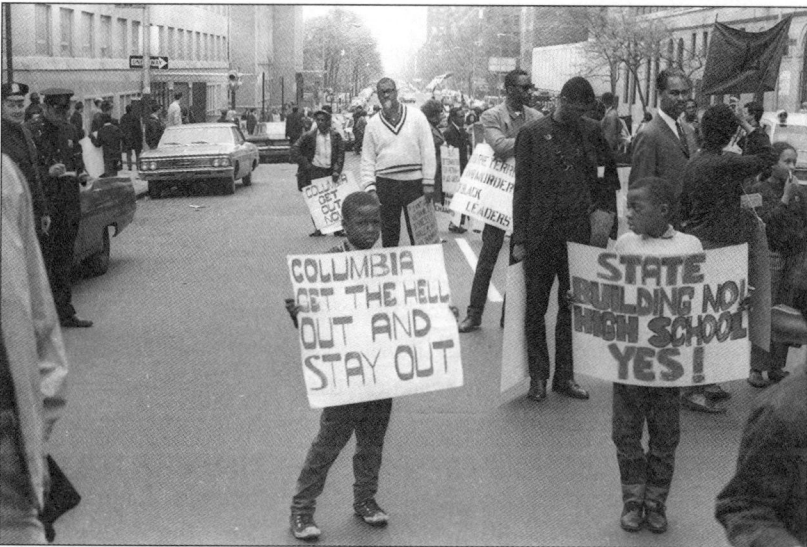

Protesters near West 115th Street, picketing Columbia University's presence in the Harlem community, 1968. Photo by Lee T. Pearcy.

plateau elevated some one hundred feet above the surrounding neighborhoods of Manhattanville, Harlem, and Manhattan Valley. The plateau was
set apart from surrounding areas by geography: a steep cliff of Manhattan schist along Morningside Park formed its eastern border with Central
Harlem; the Hudson River its western limit; and two valley depressions
to the north and south formed symbolically potent and, at times, politically charged boundaries with West Harlem and Manhattan Valley, respectively. Bailey's gesture toward Morningside Park referenced not only
Columbia University's aborted effort during the 1960s to build a gymnasium, but also a potent racialized border along the park that for decades
had separated, both physically and symbolically, Morningside Heights and
its nonprofit institutions from Central Harlem and its people of color. This
history of racialized class inequality and exclusion had been sedimented
over generations in the area's architecture, ordering of buildings, and street
patterns, as well as in its racial and economic geography, rendering all of
it spatiosymbolically charged. This landscape of power consisted of iconic
buildings, institutional clusters of land use, topographical features, and
polysemous social boundaries, all of which signified and cross-indexed
deeply layered meanings, memories, and struggles.

The relationship of academic knowledge to other domains of knowledge is a central and consistent focus of this book. Throughout, I trace
ways in which emergent forms of social scientific knowledge were put to
use in the interest of the American Acropolis. Examining the contested
history of racialized class exclusion and dispossession over the longue
durée, this book addresses the various ways in which institutional elites
on the Hill, associated with Columbia University, Teachers College,
the Riverside Church, and other peer institutions, have both imagined
and secured the boundaries separating the American Acropolis from
its "constitutive outside"—the working-class immigrant and racialized
populations of surrounding neighborhoods (Laclau and Mouffe 1985).
As in the most recent campus expansion, these boundaries were secured
through a spatial politics directed at acquiring and controlling the uses
of real property. But these boundaries were constituted through a variety of discourses and practices, associated variously with the real estate
industry, government, public health authorities, the press, and perhaps
most importantly, academic disciplines. These discourses and practices
articulated hierarchical distinctions—ethnic, racial, class, temporal—

that set apart the civilization-building mission of the American Acropolis from its racialized constitutive outside.

This spatiosymbolic terrain was also polysemous, with many social identities and differences constitutive of, and interpellated through, this spatial order. As Henri Lefebvre put it, "Groups, classes or fractions of classes cannot constitute themselves, or recognize one another, as 'subjects' unless they generate (or produce) a space. Ideas, representations or values which do not succeed in making their mark on space, and thus generating (or producing) an appropriate morphology, will lose all pith and become mere signs, resolve themselves into abstract descriptions, or mutate into fantasies" (1992:416–17). By examining the contested formation of the American Acropolis order over the longue durée, I highlight continuities and regularities in discourses and practices of development and conflict. Development and conflict have shaped the interrelated histories of Morningside Heights, Harlem, and other surrounding, predominantly Black and brown neighborhoods. The policies of racial exclusion and dispossession pursued by elites on the Hill, by private real estate interests, and by municipal authorities have been resisted by tenant associations and other community-based organizations. During the Depression era, anti-eviction campaigns were organized by the Harlem Tenants League, a tenants' advocacy group founded by Black communists. In the 1950s, the Manhattanville-based Committee to Save Our Homes worked to stop a university-sponsored urban renewal project. In 1968 campus activists joined with the Congress of Racial Equality, the Student Nonviolent Coordinating Committee, and other activists based in both Harlem and Morningside Heights to successfully oppose the construction of the university's gym in Morningside Park. Thus space is materially and symbolically constructed and experienced, in what Margaret E. Farrar conceptualizes as a perduring spatiosymbolic order.

The longue durée approach advanced by Fernand Braudel and the *Annales* school emphasized the coexistence of a plurality of temporalities and structural patterns of historical development. As Christopher Tilley noted, time is "subjective and made up of different rhythms: some short, some medium, and some very long indeed, which intermingle and criss-cross. . . . The past is always a material presence and we are always surrounded by things of the past that, in fact, are constitutive of that present" (2017:6). While that past was present in the memories and embodied experiences of Bailey and other long-term residents, it was also present in the built environment, continuing to exert influence on how people inter-act with and move through the urban landscape, constitute themselves as subjects, and imagine and experience their relations with others.

Attending to the coexistence of multiple temporalities over the longue durée makes it possible to consider the effects that perduring structural factors, most notably geography (Braudel's *tres longue durée*), have had on shorter-term events (*événements*) and clusters of events, in spatiosymbolic terms. For example, the elevated geography of the plateau has exercised a strong influence over time on both the development of the Heights (e.g., its infrastructure, patterns of land use, and economy) and how elites imag-ined the American Acropolis as a cloistered community, engaged in the fashioning of American civilization set apart both spatially and temporally from the working-class immigrant and African American populations and industries on their margins and beneath them. This vertical seces-sion, real and imagined, has been pursued by institutional elites through policies aimed at fending off incursions of poor and working-class people of color into the Heights and shoring up the latter's borders with nearby communities, notably Harlem. This vertical contrast between the Hill and the valley has been constitutive of perduring spatiosymbolic boundaries rendered potent by racial and class difference.

The growing body of literature on Black geographies underscores the de-gree to which this vertical secession "also illustrates how metropolitan space and local governance are critical instruments in the remaking of the mod-ern racial state and processes of subject-making (and subject-unmaking)" (Rios 2020:2). In setting the American Acropolis apart, elites necessarily created boundaries, thus "spatializing blackness," as Rashad Shabazz argues in the case of Chicago rendering the landscape both carceral and ideologi-cally charged (2015). Katherine McKittrick argues that because geographic presence is founded on ownership, itself equated with whiteness, Black-ness is "ungeographic" (2006). This point is especially relevant to chapter 5, where efforts to develop a cordon sanitaire attempted racial containment through racial improvement and property ownership. This spatialization leveraged policy, practice, and social scientific knowledge to erect material boundaries that were also powerfully polysemous and contested.

As Braudel succinctly put it, "Each 'current reality' is the conjoining of movements with different origins and rhythms. The time of today is composed simultaneously of the time of yesterday, of the day before yesterday, and of bygone days" (Braudel and Wallerstein 2009:182). Black geographers remind us that these bygone days necessarily include the plantation, segregation, and carceral logics among other forms of spatialized racial violence (Shabazz 2015; Woods 2017). In 1968, when opposition to the university's gym in Morningside Park reached a crescendo, this vertical contrast and politics of secession became the lightning rod for community and campus-based activism. The gym's vertical design proposed a community gymnasium at grade with Morningside Park, and a second, much larger gym over a hundred feet above, on the plateau, with a separate entrance for the Columbia community. Harlem activists soon dubbed the separate and unequal design the "Jim Crow gym." The proposed gym secured and expressed a symbolically laden geographical divide, spatially materializing a perduring racialized class division. The short-term conjuncture of social processes and events associated with the defeat of the gym project must be understood in relation to societal and institutional interactions with geography that have taken place over the longue durée: Harlem's effort to defend public parkland, the rise of the civil rights and Black Power movements, and the 1968 student rebellion at Columbia coexisted with and expressed conflicts extending back in time to the late nineteenth century.

Recognizing the coexistence of multiple temporalities and the socially constructed nature of time also focuses attention on the discourses and practices through which space-time relations are actively produced and reproduced (Rios 2020; Tilley 2017). The American Acropolis was viewed by Hill elites as a privileged and future-leaning landscape, embedded within the linear and universal temporality of Western modernity. By contrast, the areas inhabited by working-class people of color were seen, in the language of real estate appraisers and urban planners, as "obsolete" remnants of a superseded past. Moreover, the residents of these areas were depicted as unevolved, lacking in socio-moral development, and thus ill-equipped to coexist with urban modernity. In the early 2000s, as Columbia University sought to realize a future based on innovation, it did so in part by using eminent domain to render residents "ungeographic," in McKittrick's terms: obsolete, and unable to participate properly in the future.

If nineteenth-century social evolutionism placed normative whiteness within a modernity geographically sited at the American Acropolis, the twenty-first-century spatiotemporal ideas wielded by Columbia in its bid for expansion were remarkably unchanged. From the nineteenth century into the present, the constitutive outside of the Acropolis, blighted and deviant, was understood by elites as full of racialized others incompatible with modern urban life, a conceptualization that denied "coevalness" to racialized populations and the spaces they inhabited (Fabian 2014). Imagining and materializing varied space-time distinctions was the project of interrelated entities ranging from the university itself to the private real estate industry, government authorities, and philanthropists. The techniques of knowledge and the research produced by historians and social scientists at Columbia were crucial to the power and legitimacy of these distinctions.

Social exclusion and dispossession are materialized in the spatiosymbolic order, augmented and naturalized by the production of knowledge by academics whose techniques, studies, and publications integrated biopolitics, policy, and statesmanship. In focusing on elite social and private institutions in the city's many and evolving forms of and justifications for social exclusion and dispossession, this book demonstrates that the right to the city for *all* matters. It is this historically layered relationship between geography and racially and class-inflected spatial and temporal discourses and practices that is the focus of this book. These space-time divisions, their attendant cultural expressions, and patterned spatial practices and relations that they have produced have persisted over generations, continuing to shape urban landscapes today. Social exclusion and dispossession are much more than theory. They are also matters of life and death.

The Structure of This Book

Chapter 1 examines the founding or relocation of religious, cultural, educational, and other institutions to the Morningside plateau beginning in the late 1880s. The plateau's remoteness made it a suitable location for charitable institutions, such as the Bloomingdale Insane Asylum and Leake and Watts Orphan Asylum, and for the mansions and summer homes of the affluent, seeking relief from the congestion of lower Manhattan and its outbreaks of cholera, yellow fever, and smallpox. Over a few decades, these charitable institutions were replaced by a constellation of nonprofit, civilization-building institutions.

Grant's Tomb in Riverside Park served as a critical symbolic anchor for imagining and assembling the American Acropolis. Grant's funeral and the lengthy construction of his tomb focused public attention and private investment on the Upper West Side, elevating the city's status as a center of political culture and American civilization beyond, if not in spite of, its reputation as a commercial juggernaut. The Episcopal Diocese of New York began construction of the Cathedral of St. John the Divine in 1893 on land purchased from the Leake and Watts Orphan Asylum; by 1900, Columbia College, St. Luke's Hospital, Barnard College, and Teachers College had all relocated to the plateau.

If the elevated topography and the natural barriers of the Morningside plateau provided the opportunity to assemble a center of American civilization removed from the industries, social conflicts, and cultural dissonance of poor and working-class districts, the Manhattanville Valley facilitated the converse. In chapter 2, I trace Manhattanville's development as a multiethnic poor and working-class community during the course of the nineteenth century. I focus on how the area's geography and location shaped its economic development as an entrepôt, transportation hub, and industrial suburb. This course of development, in turn, shaped the composition of Manhattanville's largely immigrant labor force, patterns of land use, and environmental conditions.

Incorporated as a village in 1806, Manhattanville was laid out along the 125th Street Manhattanville fault line valley, which cuts a channel through the rock ridges forming Morningside Heights and Washington Heights to the north. This prime location offered at-grade access to the Hudson River and its river-borne commerce, which increased with the completion of the Erie Canal in 1825. The contrast in elevation between the plateau and the fault line valley below led not only to differing patterns of investment and land use, but also to a social geography, repeated in other American cities during the nineteenth century, that counterposed upland, affluent areas of industrial cities to lowland, working-class slums, or "bottoms," which, due to their marshy conditions, poor drainage, and inadequate sewerage, were vulnerable to a host of infectious diseases.

Knowledge about the inhabitants of Manhattanville and the conditions in which they lived was produced through investigative technologies that gained authority in the nineteenth century, including population censuses, sanitary surveys, and charity organization studies. Research in the emerging social sciences also contributed to this knowledge base. Despite differences in their purpose, methods, and intended use, these investigative technologies consistently contrasted what were perceived as the deviant dispositions and conduct of low-income, ethnically and racially marked communities with the putative norms of white native-born society. I examine how knowledge of the valley and its diverse population was constituted through two normalizing technologies—the 1865 sanitary survey of Manhattan, made by the Citizens' Association of New York, and the 1900 federal census of population. These defined, surveilled, mapped, and policed unhealthy environmental conditions and deviant identities, modes of conduct, and domestic arrangements against the putative norms of middle-class white native-born Americans.

In chapter 3, I consider how this growing body of knowledge about the poor and working classes emerged within the context of a political culture shaped by industrialization, immigration, and the migration of African Americans to northern cities from the South. It also informed the development of sociology at Columbia and the pedagogy and practice of the Speyer School and Settlement, an experimental school created in Manhattanville by Teachers College in 1903. I focus on Howard B. Woolston's sociological study of Manhattanville, based on research conducted while he was employed at the Speyer School. Woolston was among the first generation of sociologists trained at Columbia by Franklin H. Giddings and, along with several of his peers (e.g., Thomas J. Jones, John P. Clyde, and William Ogburn), conducted sociological field research in New York City. I explore what Albion Small called the "fatal antithesis" in Woolston's text between the speculative theoretical framework of his mentor, Giddings, and Woolston's own empirically based fieldwork (Small 1896:296). I then consider how this knowledge shaped the pedagogy and settlement work of the Speyer School, whose program of "social education" was aimed at constituting disciplined citizens, productive workers, and docile subjects willing to accept subordinate stations in the industrial political economy. The sociology of Woolston, like the work of sanitarians and census officials, sought to define and assess how immigrants and Black people deviated from a putative white native-born norm; the Speyer School set out to domesticate and correct those deviations.

As Woolston was conducting his study of Manhattanville, Harlem was undergoing a profound demographic transition that rearticulated the spatiosymbolic relationship of the American Acropolis to its northern neighbors "along the color line," as Du Bois put it. The variegated, hierarchical racial categories that Woolston catalogued—the Irish, Germans, Hebrews, Native-White Americans, and Negroes—would be steadily reduced through spatial politics, popular culture, and the social sciences to a binary distinction between whites and non-whites. In chapter 4, I examine the transformation of Harlem from a predominantly white middle- and upper-class area into the political and cultural mecca of Black life. My focus is on the specter of a "Negro invasion" and efforts to draw the color line and shore up the emerging category of "whiteness." Spatiosymbolic and epistemic distinctions produced through spatial practices, popular culture, and the formation of the social sciences framed Blackness, as a zone of abjection, peopled by unevolved pseudosubjects, against whiteness, as a normative—albeit heterogeneous and unstable—category of ontological privilege.

This overdetermined and polysemous boundary, as Du Bois foresaw, was the central problematic of the twentieth century, governing the spatiosymbolic relations between the Acropolis and the racialized communities on its margins, and in chapter 4, I examine the multi-sited constitution of this racial boundary through the spatial practices of the real estate industry, the visual and lyrical iconography of the "urban coon" and Black "dandy," and the work of social scientists still under the sway of social evolutionism. Karin Knorr Cetina conceptualizes these relationships as mutually constitutive, "transepistemic fields of action" (Knorr Cetina 1982). In examining the Dunning School of southern historiography at Columbia, I stress the way the development of social science itself was transepistemic, inseparable from the realms of real estate and popular culture, emergent spatiosymbolic meanings, and their constitutive space-time making practices. Finally, I explore the manifold ways in which Black activists and organizations contested these space-time making practices and attendant spatiosymbolic order. These range from the transgressive business practices of Harlem-based Black realtors, such as Philip A. Payton, to the cultural activism of vaudeville performer Bert Williams, to the research and activism of the Du Boisian school sociologist George Edmund Haynes, a key founder of the Harlem-based National Urban League.

In chapter 5, I examine the efforts of John D. Rockefeller Jr. to establish and preserve a white cordon sanitaire around the celebrated Lincoln

School, a Rockefeller-funded Teachers College experimental school, which relocated to West 123rd Street from the Upper East Side in 1922. At the same time, Rockefeller financed the construction of the Dunbar Cooperative Apartments in Harlem to demonstrate the profitability of privately financed middle-income housing. Another goal was to instill in its Black tenant-owners the virtues of responsibility, pride in homeownership, and morality, which he and others believed they lacked. While the cordon sanitaire was intended to stem the tide of Black settlement west into Morningside Heights, the Dunbar Apartments served as a model for constructing racially segregated middle-income housing that could contain the rising Black middle classes within Harlem amidst increasing civil rights activism and urban unrest, exemplified by the 1935 Harlem riot.

During this period, Rockefeller also financed the construction of International House (1922) and the Riverside Church (1930) in Morningside Heights. For its founders, the towering, neo-Gothic cathedral was to be a symbol of and instrument for unifying Protestantism under an ecumenical banner and modernist theology, and for reconciling religion with an increasingly secular humanism. Rockefeller's philanthropic investments in the Heights were seen to be future-leaning and universal, thus reiterating the spatiotemporal distinction between the Acropolis and its constitutive outside. In contrast, his real estate ventures in Harlem were aimed at preserving racial segregation, emphasizing the ontological particularity of Blackness and its spatiotemporal incompatibility with modernity. I demonstrate how this racialized distinction shaped, if not overdetermined, the efforts of the Riverside Church and other institutions on the Hill to engage surrounding communities of color through outreach efforts aimed at providing educational, recreational, and other social services.

In chapter 6, I focus on the efforts of institutions on the Hill to arrest and reverse the post–World War II incursions of Black and Puerto Rican populations into Morningside Heights by using biopolitical strategies of containment and racial dispossession, and wielding urban redevelopment tools. The 1943 Harlem riot, triggered by the police shooting of a Black soldier, contributed to a "moral panic" among majority-white Hill elites focusing on the putative threat posed by Black and brown youth (Hall et al. [1978] 2013). This alliance established the Manhattanville Neighborhood Center, located in the building formerly used by the Speyer School. Although its founders claimed that the center's purpose was to engage

Manhattanville's residents in defining and addressing neighborhood needs, it did not. Instead, social workers at the center deployed biopolitical techniques, informed by psychiatry, to transpose socioeconomic problems and structural inequalities faced by Manhattanville residents into personal problems. Poor housing, unemployment, under-resourced schools, and other issues were not the outcome of structural inequalities, but rather the result of cultural and psychological deficits.

This alliance of some nine key institutions on the Hill also created an urban redevelopment organization, Morningside Heights, Inc. (MHI), to develop and implement plans for reversing the alleged spread of urban blight and undesirable residents. After the passage of the Housing Act of 1949, MHI sponsored the construction of a middle-income cooperative housing complex that led to the eviction and dislocation of over two thousand largely Black and Puerto Rican households. I argue that these practices of racial dispossession, akin to policies pursued in settler colonial societies, were predicated on the construction of people of color living in the area as irredeemable and disposable; as *homines sacri*, existing in a "state of exception" beyond the shelter of citizenship (Agamben 1998). In short, the institutional elites of the Acropolis would simultaneously prosecute strategies of biopolitical containment, intended to control Manhattanville's population by providing palliative social services, and exercise sovereign "slow violence" aimed at racial dispossession (Nixon 2011). Both strategies relied on the constitution of racialized others whose presence was viewed to be incompatible with the privileged, normative landscape of white modernity.

In chapter 7, I continue this examination of racial dispossession as Columbia and its MHI partners, through an aggressive and protracted campaign of property acquisition and institutional expansion, demolished or rehabilitated much low- and moderate-income housing stock, evicting thousands of tenants, and repurposing that real estate for institutional expansion and student and employee housing. I demonstrate how these practices of racial dispossession relied on perduring tropes of Black urban deviancy, reminiscent of nineteenth-century constructions of the "urban coon." Academic portrayals—Staley Elkins's "Sambo thesis," for example—cast the area's Black and brown people as criminal, vice-ridden, and unproductive transients who were incompatible with white middle-class modernity and the civilization-building mission of the American

Acropolis. These policies of racial exclusion and dispossession found both status and legitimacy in the epistemological order of the academy.

Finally, I examine resistance by tenants associations and by an assortment of largely Harlem-based organizations, activists, and public officials, culminating in the 1968 "crisis at Columbia." I argue that this crisis, by linking community and campus-based opposition to the policies of racial exclusion and dispossession pursued by Columbia and its peers, shattered, if only temporarily, the illusion of the American Acropolis as a unifying and universal singularity. Race erupted as *the* issue cutting across the imagined spatiotemporal frontier that had divided the elite institutions of the Morningside plateau from their constitutive outside, while exposing the hypocrisy of elite gestures to principles of democracy, liberalism, and racial equality.

In the epilogue, I return to the Manhattanville campus expansion (under construction during the writing of this book) and consider continuities and regularities in elite discourses and space-time practices that have perdured over the longue durée. I examine how, in the interest of a major expansion plan, Columbia University once again constructed Manhattanville as an obsolete, "blighted" manufacturing area, visually and physically isolated from neighboring communities, thus gaining control of the project's footprint through eminent domain. In place of Manhattanville's moribund, static, and visually obscure "past-present," the university offered a state-of-the-art, "transparent" campus, where glass architecture and pseudo-public plazas welcomed Harlem residents, with scientific research ushering in a radiant future of "smart growth" and innovation. As it had done in its pursuit of urban renewal during the 1950s and 1960s, Columbia was able to override Harlem residents and their representative institutions by harnessing the powers of city and state agencies and elected officials. As in earlier decades, the racialized populations of Manhattanville and Harlem, as Frantz Fanon put it, had "no ontological resistance" in the eyes of the elites and institutions of the American Acropolis.

1

Making the "American Acropolis"

Just as none of us is outside geography or beyond geography,
none of us is completely free from the struggle over geography.
—Edward Said

Man is the product of the earth's surface.
—Ellen Churchill Semple

A Shining City upon a Hill

In the spring of 1887, George MacCulloch Miller was walking along
Fifth Avenue in Manhattan when he happened to glance down West
111th Street and notice the steep cliffs rising from Morningside Park to
the plateau above. Miller, a founding trustee of the Cathedral of St. John
the Divine, had been searching for a site for the proposed Episcopal
edifice—one that would rival the recently completed St. Patrick's Cathedral. When Miller showed the location to Henry Codman Potter, the
Episcopal bishop of New York, both men agreed that the Heights were a
potential "American Acropolis"—a national center of religion, learning,
and culture that could rival the great cities of Europe (Nelson 1916).

The appropriation of the Athenian Acropolis as "a free floating, disembodied signifier in Western thought" was common in late nineteenth-
century US political culture—one that drew a contrast with the
monarchical and absolutist traditions of Europe (Loukaki 1997:306). The
idea of the American Acropolis was not merely a metaphor. Bounded
by the Hudson River on the west, the cliffs rising above Morningside
Park on the east, and Manhattanville Valley (West 125th Street) on the
north, the plateau's elevated topography has been imagined to insulate
Morningside Heights from what Columbia University architect Renzo
Piano called the city's "quotidian freneticism" (Piano 2017:22). A *New*

Postcard depicting the completed construction of the Cathedral of St. John the Divine from Morningside Park, 1903–1904.

York Times editorial celebrating the relocation of Columbia College to Morningside Heights in 1892 characteristically linked the plateau's spatial remoteness to the conditions necessary for cultivating the arts of civilization, asserting a distinction between the latter and the "material strife" and poor and working-class populations associated with industry and commerce.

> The new quarter will be a great and conspicuous center of civilization, a city set on a hill and devoted to the things of the mind, where it will remain an impressive monument to those engaged in the material strife that will go on below it. (May 12, 1892)

The *Times* editorialist recognized that the topography naturalized an ontological hierarchy, with "things of the mind" on the plateau and those "engaged in the material strife" below. This hierarchy was vertically stratified in space and buttressed—indeed, defended—by the lay of the land. The closing decades of the nineteenth century witnessed the founding or relocation of a constellation of nonprofit institutions to the plateau: the construction of the Cathedral of St. John the Divine (1887);

the relocation of Columbia University and Teachers College (1894), St. Luke's Hospital (1896), and Barnard College (1897) from sites in lower Manhattan; and the construction of the tomb and memorial of General Ulysses S. Grant (1897).

This chapter examines the relationship between verticality and social hierarchy, both as a power-laden, sociospatial ordering of the urban landscape and as an ideology for ranking human differences. I argue that the plateau's topography aroused and provoked power-laden discourses and epistemological commitments grounded in culturally shaped constructions of landscape. These, in turn, naturalized dominant relations of power and prestige (see Gandy 2002). Archaeologists, geographers, and others have emphasized the degree to which topography is actively fashioned and reworked "in relation to differing social and political agendas, [and] forms of social memory" (Tilley 2006:8; B. Bender 1993), and how the material attributes of a given landscape, in turn, influence and constitute human subjectivity and agency (Bennett et al. 2017). Researchers have also attended to the capacity of topography to provoke meanings and effects that, though culturally mediated, are often unanticipated by human subjects.

By attending to human-nature relations, I do not minimize the significance of human agency, politics, and culture (*pace* Fowles 2010). Rather, I argue that a rigorous analysis of how humans engage with, adjust to, and marshal materiality to purposeful and culturally mediated ends within historically contingent conditions provides a critical and nuanced analysis of the constitution of political interests, antagonisms, and relations of power. As Karl Marx famously put it, "Men make their own history, but they do not make it as they please; they do not make it under self-selected circumstances, but under circumstances existing already, given and transmitted from the past" (Marx 1963:15). And for Marx—a student of preeminent geologist Johann Steininger—those circumstances were material *and* ideological (Clark and Yusoff 2017). I examine varied forms of political struggle and resistance that emerged as the plateau's institutional elites sought to harness geography and assert control over the built environment, bringing them into conflict with the real estate industry, working-class communities, and others.

Geographers in particular have focused attention on what Nigel Clark has termed the "politics of strata"—that is, how human interactions with the earth's vertical strata have contributed to the structuring of power relations and the exercise of domination (2017; cf. Weizman 2007; Elden 2013). Clark argues that this constitutive, sociopolitical role, exercised vertically, precedes the temporal horizon generally associated with the Anthropocene thesis, suggesting that "all social and political formations are implicated with specific geological formations" (2017:214). Stephen Graham and Lucy Hewitt have argued that Anglophone critical urban research has mostly neglected verticality, privileging the horizontal in urban spatial analyses (2012). This "flattening" of spatial discourses and imaginaries, they contend, risks neglecting the vertical and "volumetric" qualities of cities and urban life that shape the experience of urban space and form, and the organization of social relations and political power. As Andrew Harris has argued, we must examine how "the vertical and horizontal are mutually implicated and produced" (2015:602). Attending to the volumetric qualities of cities focuses attention on above- and below-ground infrastructure, processes of vertical secession through, for example, vertically stratified or "capsular" residential and corporate developments (Ayoub 2009).

I argue that the imagining and construction of the American Acropolis were strongly influenced by this politics of verticality. Elites of the American Acropolis imagined vertical secession as a condition of possibility for cultivating the arts of civilization, and they also exercised their dominance over surrounding working-class communities below. This politics of space sought to preserve the social secession of Morningside Heights, symbolically and physically, from surrounding communities. Attending to this politics of verticality proves key to understanding the structuring of power relations and social antagonisms, and their reproduction over the longue durée.

I begin by examining how the geography of the Morningside plateau shaped its development prior to the spate of institution building in the 1880s. I then turn to three iconic development projects: the construction of the tomb and memorial of General Ulysses S. Grant, the Cathedral of St. John the Divine, and the campuses of Columbia University and its affiliated colleges. I demonstrate how each project marshaled verticality as a means of asserting the symbolic eminence and the heterogeneity of the logics, discourses, and practices deployed in securing their secession from nearby, predominantly immigrant, working-class areas.

The Lay of the Land

In his foundational study of Morningside Heights, architectural historian Andrew Dolkart identified three interrelated factors that hampered the area's development in the nineteenth century. "Geology," Dolkart noted, "was the key" (1998:2). Whereas the cliffs abutting Morningside Park obstructed entrée from the Harlem Plain, the high bluffs overlooking the Hudson limited the plateau's access to river-borne commerce. On its northern boundary, where the plateau dropped to the floor of Manhattanville Valley, a manufacturing center and working-class community known as Manhattanville had prospered since the early nineteenth century. This northern boundary became a focus of anxiety and action for institutional elites as Harlem took shape in the early twentieth century.

Not surprisingly, the plateau's geography influenced the development of its infrastructure. For example, railroad development on Manhattan's Upper West Side had bypassed the Morningside plateau in favor of the flat Harlem Plain to the east. Although a freight rail had operated along the Hudson River shoreline since 1851, the plateau's elevation made it inaccessible for much of the West Side. The transportation needs of the plateau were served by horse-drawn streetcars, converted to cable power in the 1880s, until the opening of Interborough Rapid Transit Company's Broadway-Seventh Avenue subway in 1904.

The plateau's lack of accessibility and remove from the city made it suitable for the siting of asylums, orphanages, and other curative institutions, which not only required ample space, but were also considered to be nuisances, unsuitable for more populated areas of the city (Schweik 2009). In the case of the Bloomingdale Insane Asylum, nineteenth-century medical views on mental illness stressed the curative effects of the natural environment and held that patients benefited from bucolic settings removed from congested, poorly ventilated, and vice-ridden areas. These factors tended to push insane asylums, orphanages, and other curative institutions to the rural margins of the city. However, private real estate interests had long argued that the Bloomingdale Asylum undermined the area's potential for profitable development and posed a nuisance to residents and businesses (Dolkart 1998). By the 1880s, the opening of the Ninth Avenue El and skyrocketing land values on the East Side primed the Morningside plateau for real estate speculation and development (Stabler 1905).

Another "nuisance" hindering West Side development was the shanty settlements across the rocky ground of the West Side from 59th Street to 125th Street. In the 1880s, city officials and property owners prosecuted a campaign to remove the estimated 2,500 shanties, evicting residents and razing their homes (*New York Herald*, May 20, 1880). Rising property values spurred owners and speculators to bear the costs of the rock blasting and grading necessary to improve the land for more profitable uses. Many of those evicted resettled north of 125th Street and in New Jersey, while others were forced to abandon "the freedom of squatter life for the bondage of the tenement houses below Fifty-ninth St." (*New York Tribune*, May 19, 1880). These shanty settlements, along with others located in low-lying, swampy areas of the Harlem Plain, would remain a thorn in the side of elite-driven development efforts on the plateau and in adjacent areas (Rozenzweig and Blackmar 1992).

The Death and Internment of the "Savior of the Union"

Wherever General Grant's body lies, that is national ground.
—Samuel Clemens (a.k.a. Mark Twain)

On July 23, 1885, Ulysses S. Grant, commanding general of the Union Army and ex-president, died at Mount McGregor, New York, where, diagnosed with inoperable throat cancer, he had withdrawn to write his memoirs. Grant's legacy as savior of the Union made him the very embodiment of postbellum national reconciliation and a national hero, equal in stature to Washington and Lincoln (Waugh 2005). Siting Grant's Tomb in Riverside Park was an important political and symbolic event in the plateau's development, focusing public attention and private investment on the Upper West Side, and raising the city's status as a center of American political culture.

Within hours of the announcement of Grant's death, New York Mayor William R. Grace telegraphed his family at Mount McGregor, offering to provide a burial site in one of the city's public parks. After considering a number of locations, the Grant family agreed with Mayor Grace that the heights of Riverside Park would, in the mayor's words, "vie in beauty and fitness of location with the famous statue of Germania on the Rhine" (in Balch 1885:580). Grace's reference to the Niederwalddenkmal,

towering above the Rhein in Hesse, Germany, was telling: the Nieder-
wald monument memorialized the unification of Germany and founding of its empire under Wilhelm I in the wake of the Franco-Prussian
War (1870–1871). Similarly, Grant's Tomb served as a powerful symbol
of American postwar reconciliation and a tribute to US imperial am-
bitions. On the heels of the American naval victory over the Spanish
squadron at Santiago de Cuba in 1898, a flotilla steamed up the Hudson
to Grant's Tomb, where triumphant warships fired salutes. The passing
in review of the battleship *Texas*, sister ship of the ill-fated USS *Maine*,
was filmed by Thomas A. Edison.

In 1886 the *Century Magazine* published a lengthy essay on the
planned monument, arguing that, like the Niederwalddenkmal, Grant's
final resting place offered a unique opportunity for national commemoration. The essay's author, Richard Watson Gilder, directed the reader's
attention to the significance that the project shared with its German
counterpart:

> We misconceive the [Niederwalddenkmal] if we think of it as a record
> of German conquest abroad, or of Prussian conquest in Germany. It is
> a record, rather, that the various peoples of Germany, so long disunited,
> bitterly antagonistic, actually at war among themselves, and so recently
> forced together by the strongest sword, had now accepted the brother-
> hood into which it had compelled them, and so cordially accepted it as
> to desire a permanent—that is, a great artistic—expression of the fact.
> (Gilder 1885:953)

Clearly, Gilder had misconceived the Niederwalddenkmal, for the brotherhood that it celebrated did not embrace German Jews, Poles, and other
ethnic minorities any more than Grant's Tomb would venerate the wartime sacrifices and equality of African Americans. Nevertheless, Gilder's
essay suggests the degree to which the project of building Grant's Tomb
was understood as a spatiosymbolic act of nation building, one that
raised the unfinished landscape of the plateau to the national political
and cultural stage. Moreover, like its German counterpart, the tomb's
location on a high bluff overlooking the Hudson River was well suited
for a monument intended to project its meanings above and beyond its
local context.

DEDICATION OF THE MEMORIAL TO GENERAL GRANT IN NEW YORK: THE 7TH REGIMENT PASSING THE MONUMENT.

Dedication of the memorial to General Ulysses S. Grant in New York, 1897.

Vertical elevation has long been associated with power, knowledge, and authority. Since the mid-nineteenth century, the increased utilization of ballooning (and, later, powered flight) for military, scientific, and photographic purposes gave rise to an "aerial" perspective and imagination that established the scopic conditions for a modernist gaze—one that was heroic, utopian, and elitist (Morshed 2004; Dümpelmann 2014).

Grant's Tomb looked down upon Manhattanville's factories and tenements in the valley below. Manhattanville's location along a fault line valley below Morningside Heights shaped elite perceptions of its working-class residents and the conditions in which they lived. An 1865 sanitary survey, conducted by the Citizens Association of New York, revealed that the opening of streets and grading of building lots had disrupted the valley's natural water courses and drainage system, resulting in the creation of pools of putrid standing water, marshy ground, and waterlogged basements and privies. During the nineteenth century these poor sanitary conditions led to outbreaks of malaria, yellow fever, diphtheria, and other infectious diseases; these outbreaks were often attributed to the alleged racial and ethnic dispositions of the immigrant poor and non-white groups. The author of Manhattanville's sanitary survey contrasted its insalubrious topography with the healthy, elevated, and well-drained topography of Morningside Heights (Rodenstein 1865). Verticality and the premium that it assigned to elevation, therefore, also played a role in elite fears of contagion, and the discourses and practices of public health reformers.

The selection of Riverside Park—or New York City—as Grant's final resting place drew sharp criticism from newspaper editors, public officials, and citizens across the nation. In a vitriolic editorial, the nativist-leaning *Chicago Daily Tribune* challenged the very "Americanness" of the city and its motley populace: "New York has always been a plague spot on the body politic. It is the most un-American and un-National city in the United States" (July 30, 1885). This representation of New York City and Riverside Park as un-American—a sentiment linked to its large population of immigrants, commercial orientation, as well as uncertain loyalty to the Union during the Civil War—did not go uncontested. In 1886 the renowned historian and magazine editor Martha J. Lamb published a ten-cent pamphlet, *The Guide for Strangers to General Grant's Tomb*, which provided a brief history and description of the park along with instructions for traveling to the tomb by elevated railroad, ferryboat, and horse-drawn trolley. Lamb's description of Riverside Park emphasized the landscape's patriotic pedigree. "Here came Washington," Lamb wrote, "the great 'Father of our Country,' to inspect the situation when the British were in hot pursuit in September, 1776; and nearby was fought the Battle of Harlem Heights, in which American soldiers won their first victory over the trained warriors from Great Britain" (1886:4). In her descriptions, historical events and their protagonists were woven into topography, narrating the past as a presence in the landscape.

On July 29, 1885, as Grant's temporary vault was being constructed in Riverside Park, a lightning bolt struck an oak tree within yards of the site. Visitors flocked to collect leaves and splinters from the shattered tree as souvenirs (Kahn 1980). On the very next day, a bolt of lightning struck the cottage at Mount McGregor where Grant's body lay in repose, extinguishing the electric lights and prostrating two army officers "with such violence that the blood flowed freely" (*New York Tribune*, July 31,

1885). Although the *Washington Post*, for one, rejected mystical explanations of the events, it indexed the uncanny coincidence to a lightning strike that allegedly had occurred on St. Helena as Napoleon lay on his deathbed (August 16, 1885).

Throughout the vault's construction, scores of "relic hunters" carried away stones, bricks, wooden slats, and other construction materials, defying park police and bribing stonemasons for the much sought-after glazed interior bricks. According to a *New York Times* article, these relic hunters "would converse with the workmen or the park policeman, or with anyone who would discuss any matter relating to Gen. Grant. The pockets of such persons were bulging with bits of brick and little packages of earth and sand, and of twigs from the neighboring trees" (August 3, 1885). In the name of guarding public decency and respect for Grant, the police waged a campaign against hawkers, many from nearby Manhattanville, who sold the relics and other goods in Riverside Park.

These "idiosyncratic acts of commemoration" highlight the unpredictable agency of materiality and the quotidian way landscapes are sensuously entwined with human subjectivity and agency (Schramm 2011:11). Although the meanings, affect, and associations that the relic hunters drew from their acts of commemoration remain obscure, the latter constituted a process of sacralization, "wrapping transcendence" in the mantle of materiality (Leone 2014:49). These vernacular acts of appropriation and commemoration also provide evidence of the variety of ways in which subaltern groups engage with, inflect, and contest elite practices of vertical urbanism (cf. A. Harris 2015). The lightning strike at Riverside Park suffused the foliage, soil, and terrain of the tomb site and environs with an aura of sanctity, setting it apart from the mundane spatial order of the city.

Grant's funeral, held in New York City on August 8, 1885, was a unique spectacle. Grant's body lay in state for two days at City Hall, where it was viewed by as many as 250,000 people (Blight 2002). Twenty-four black horses hauled the catafalque carrying Grant's body north along Broadway to muffled drumbeats and a solemn dirge. The procession stretched for over three miles. It was estimated that, from any point along the route, it took up to five hours to pass and that 1 to 1.5 million people witnessed the event—roughly the population of Manhattan in 1885 (Kahn 1980; *Baltimore Sun*, August 10, 1885).

Grant's funeral boosted property values on the Upper West Side, spurring the development of municipal services and infrastructure. The funeral was a powerful, symbolic event—a carefully choreographed ritual of national reconciliation, if not rebirth. Christopher Tilley has argued that parades, carnivals and other public spectacles engender and crystallize structures of feeling among their participants (2006:14). Frederick Dent Grant, the general's son, had asked Mayor Grace to include two Confederate generals—Simon Buckner and Joseph E. Johnson—among the pallbearers. Commentators stressed the funeral's importance as an event realizing national reconciliation; full-page newspaper accounts celebrated the easy fraternization between Union and Confederate veterans. Like the relic hunters' impromptu acts of commemoration, Grant's funeral imbued the plateau's landscape with national and transcendent significance, and the plateau came to be seen as a fitting site for crafting a unifying, postwar American civilization.

Materializing the Trinity

In 1887, two years after Grant's funeral, the trustees of the Cathedral of St. John the Divine agreed to purchase the property owned and occupied by the Leake and Watts Orphan Asylum, situated on the ridge overlooking Morningside Park. The *Real Estate Record and Builders' Guide* attributed the low price paid for the property to the fact that it was marred by large masses of rock, and that some of the orphanage's trustees were also affiliated with the Episcopal Church (November 12, 1887:1413). In fact, the president of the orphanage's board of trustees was the Reverend Dr. Morgan Dix, who held overlapping institutional roles as rector of Trinity Church, a powerful Columbia College trustee, and a member of the board of the new cathedral. This web of associations likely facilitated the sale of the orphanage property to the Episcopal Church (rather than piecemeal to private developers), and the clustering of affiliated institutions on the plateau. It had been Bishop Potter's ambition to create a constellation of church-affiliated institutions on the plateau, as church chronicler Edward Hall later emphasized:

> On Morningside Heights, in the City of New York on ground consecrated by the blood of our forefathers in the War of Independence, stands a trin-

ity of institutions which represent with singular completeness the three-fold nature of man: Columbia University, which ministers to the Mind; St. Luke's, which ministers to the Body; and the Cathedral of St. John the Divine, which ministers to the Soul. (1922:11)

The siting of the cathedral on ground consecrated by the plateau's history and, more compelling at the time, by the national spectacle of Grant's funeral and interment spurred public interest and private investment in Morningside Heights. The plateau's elevated "natural beauty," together with widely disseminated proclamations of the area's destiny as a center of American civilization, encouraged real estate interests, politicians, and others to redouble their efforts to lobby for the removal of the Bloomingdale Asylum. The ensuing conflict, pitting property owners and local Tammany Hall politicians against a patrician elite, became a struggle over the meanings and organization of this vertical urban landscape.

In 1888 the Morningside Park Association (MPA), an ad hoc group of property owners with holdings near the asylum, challenged its tax-exempt status, arguing that public economic hardship and inconvenience had resulted from the refusal of New York Hospital, the asylum's proprietor, to allow street openings across its land. The two grievances were linked: the asylum had been granted exemption from the city's 1811 grid plan based on its status as a charitable hospital; any attempt to open streets across its property required a change in that status. I maintain that the terms of the contest took shape in relation *and* reaction to the materiality of the landscape. The plateau's topography was an actant in the conflict, resisting, deflecting, and channeling the efforts of subjects to encode its matter.

In its memo to a Senate committee in February 1888, the MPA argued that the asylum was operating as a private hospital for the purpose of profit, rather than being a charitable institution entitled to tax exemption. Moreover, the MPA maintained, "the governors of said asylum keep closed the streets through their grounds to the great injury and annoyance to the public" (New York State Legislature 1888:232). The MPA's case for the asylum's removal expressed late nineteenth-century anxieties concerning urban growth and planning in rapidly developing industrial cities. As Susan Schweik has pointed out, urban crowding, poverty, and rampant mendicancy prompted many municipalities to pass ordinances restricting the public appearance of persons deemed unsightly due to physical disability, disease, racial phenotype, or other characteristics (2009). These "ugly laws" banned the unsightly from, in the words of Chicago's exemplary 1881 ordinance, "streets, highways, thoroughfares, or public places" on hygienic, moral, and aesthetic grounds (quoted in Schweik 2009:1).

In the case of the Bloomingdale Asylum, the MPA maintained that the presence of the insane blighted the West Side and checked the improvement of surrounding properties. If the abstract symmetry of the grid plan offered an idealized visual order—"a God's eye view," as James Scott put it—then the public presence of the insane, like the shanty settlements, tenements of Manhattanville, and other sensory obstructions, rendered its rationality and visual order illegible (1999:57).

The conflict between the MPA and New York Hospital was in no small measure a struggle over the substance and meaning of topography and its relationship to urban culture and progress. To be sure, MPA members stood to benefit from higher property values tied to street openings, just as the hospital's governors would from preserving the integrity of their holdings. But economic and other interests do not thicken in a vacuum, nor do they, a priori, explain the agency of social actors. Rather, the actions of both parties must be understood within a complex and unstable agentive field, one in which materiality can disrupt as much as enable the fabrication of place.

The tyrannical horizontalism of the grid plan was highlighted at the Senate hearings in a curious exchange between New York Hospital's legal counsel, John Cadwallader, and Kiliaen van Rensselaer, the vice president of the West End Association, a powerful property-owning group promoting the area's development.

Cadwallader cross-examined van Rensselaer:

Q. You don't seriously mean to be led by Mr. Olmstead to say that any carriages ever would go from Morningside Park up to Riverside Park at One Hundred and Sixteenth street; don't you know that the grade is 100 feet, a straight wall of rock?

A. Yes; but if the street was opened, that would be all graded down.

Q. Graded down to what—Morningside [Park]?

A. From Morningside to Riverside.

Q. Why, it is a hundred feet there—A straight wall of rock!

A. Well, I don't know; they will overcome it in some way.

(New York State Legislature 1888:45)

Cadwallader's incredulity and van Rensselaer's befuddlement underscore the incongruence between the flat cartographic grid and the material doggedness of the terrain, and the degree to which verticality and the horizontal are mutually constituted. The volumetric *thingness* of the cliff, that "straight wall of rock!," disrupted the grid's logic, just as it seemed to naturalize the cloistered precincts of the asylum and the privileges of its elite governors.

The materiality of the rock formation, far from having a stable, ontological essence, existed in a shifting relational field of human actors, topographical features, entities, and events, as Christopher Witmore has argued in a comparable case (Alberti et al. 2011; see also Law 2009). It was precisely the irreducibility of the rock formation to this unstable relational field that accounted for its capacity to provoke unanticipated meanings, actions, and consequences. For the hospital's governors, the wall of rock was a polysemous bulwark against the mundane world of commerce, conflict, and social differences. For the MPA, it was an all-too-familiar obstacle to the imposition of a grid rendering the landscape flat, uniform, and fungible—"a form of currency," as Scott put it (1999:58).

In fact, Dwight Olmstead, the MPA's attorney, had devoted his life's work to land transfer reform, a movement that he summarized in an 1886 article: "It is sufficient here to remark that the direction of modern reform is toward simple titles to land, its general distribution among the people, free holdings, and in opposition to entailments and permanent settlements" (1886:7). It was precisely the question of entailments that was at the heart of the MPA's dispute: the Society of the New York Hospital had been granted its original charter by King George III in 1771, and its tax-exempt status and exemption from the grid had been repeatedly upheld by the state legislature. These restrictions flew in the face of the laissez-faire economic ideology and interests of Olmstead and other West Side property owners.

A graduate of Columbia College Law School, Olmstead was a partner in the law firm of Tracy, Olmstead & Tracy. A speculator in West Side property, Olmstead also served as the president of the Land Transfer Reform Association, and of the powerful West Side Association, founded in 1866. Olmstead's spearheading of the MPA's campaign against the asylum was, more than likely, motivated both by his short-term interests as a property owner and by an abiding commitment to rationalizing the city's real estate industry—to rendering the urban landscape transparent and divisible into identical, abstract units that could be efficiently circulated through indefeasible contracts. This "way of looking," as Julian Thomas has put it, had roots in the linear perspective of Western landscape painting that took hold during the Renaissance and that "allowed land to be looked on as a commodity disengaged from hereditary patterns of tenure, able to be bought and sold at will" (1993:24).

On April 4, 1889, the Society of New York Hospital auctioned off eighty-nine lots of its approximately thirty-five-acre holding on Morningside Heights to private investors. The lots sold were south of the asylum's main buildings and therefore did not significantly compromise its spatial integrity or the possibility of selling the remainder of the estate intact to nonprofit, culture-building institutions. The lots were subject to restrictive covenants proscribing "noxious, dangerous or offensive" trades, and relegating apartment buildings to the avenues. The cross streets, the covenants stipulated, "shall only be first class private dwelling houses of brick, or stone, with roofs of slate, tin or other metal or any fire proof material, and not less than 4 stories in height, and designed for the occupancy of a single family each" (in Rosner 1982:181).

David Rosner has suggested that the hospital's governors used restrictive covenants to prevent working-class immigrants and the industries that employed them from locating on the vacated asylum property (1982:172). However, as Dolkart has pointed out, restrictive covenants were already in use across the West Side. In fact, Olmstead's West Side Association had approved articles of covenant in 1880, binding its membership, "their heirs, and assigns" to restrictions on noxious commercial and residential land uses (New York Herald, April 4, 1880).

For the governors of New York Hospital and their institutional peers, the use of restrictive covenants was a necessary but insufficient condition to achieving their purpose. The governors were less interested in conserving an antiquated social order than in reinventing that order by converting topography into new and authoritative forms of social, cultural, and "spatial capital" (Centner 2008; cf. Bourdieu 1986). Like the educational, religious, and cultural institutions that would follow, they aimed to spatially edify a unifying vision of American civilization, thus valorizing elite claims to power in an ethnically diverse city, governed by a corrupt yet relatively inclusive "politics of spoils" (T. Bender 1987). Put another way, the edification of the American Acropolis was an effort to retool and shore up the city's elites in the wake of civil war, immigrant-driven industrialization, and the coming of age of US imperial expansion. As with the siting of Grant's Tomb and the cathedral, the plateau's vertical extension as a defensible space of social secession was essential.

The intent of the cathedral's trustees to take optimal advantage of the cliff-top site generated considerable controversy. In their guidelines to competitors in the contest held to choose an architectural design, the trustees stipulated that the cathedral be oriented to the north so that its front facade would face south on 110th Street. This orientation would have presented an unobstructed view of the towering cathedral from both rivers and from the "commercial city sprawled at its feet" (J. A. Strong 1990:51). This conflicted with the medieval tradition of locating the apse (the vaulted recess containing the altar) at the eastern, rather than northern end of the cathedral's axis. In the end, the trustees complied with the tradition of the eastern apse.

Geology imposed its own constraints. The winning Heins & La Farge design adopted the east-west orientation. As excavation proceeded in the spring of 1893, engineers discovered that the land under the cathedral's planned crossing and tower was honeycombed with subterranean springs and pockets of decomposed mica schist. Because of these foundation problems, ongoing design modifications, and unending financial difficulties, the crossing tower and spire were never built (J. A. Strong 1990).

The Coming of a University

On February 26, 1892, Seth Low, president of Columbia College, addressed its alumni to rally support for the acquisition of an eight-acre site on the asylum property. Columbia College had acquired the option to buy the parcel for $2 million from the governors of New York Hospital only the year before. In his speech, Low highlighted the suitability of the site, marshaling the icon of the citadel-like Acropolis and triangulating the planned campus to the tomb and cathedral:

> With the Grant Monument completed, with the projected cathedral in its place, with Columbia fitly occupying the proposed site, every visitor to New York, from our own country or from abroad, would visit this plateau as the most notable part of the city. . . . Not to go into details concerning the site, I may yet say that it stands upon the summit of an acropolis, with the river on the west and a precipice upon the east. It is fairly accessible only from the north and south. (*New York Tribune*, February 27, 1892)

The devil was in the details, and Low's narrative deferral is perhaps an indication of the difficulty of linguistically constituting a heterogeneous assemblage of social-cum-material actants. The idea of the Acropolis was polysemous and malleable; it was *doxa*, which "goes without saying because it comes without saying: the tradition is silent, not least about itself as a tradition" (Bourdieu 1977:167).

By the 1870s, Columbia College had outgrown its midtown Manhattan campus. The campus's environs had developed into an upper-class residential district and, with the opening of the Grand Central Depot in 1871, were thought unsuitable for an academic environment. Moreover, during the presidency of Frederick Barnard, the trustees had come under increasing pressure, internally and externally, to expand the curriculum beyond the classics (traditional preparation for careers in law, medicine, and the ministry) to include professional training that was useful to the middle classes, and disciplines that would transform the college into a research university along the lines of the German *Humboldtsches Bildungsideal* (T. Bender 1987)—changes requiring considerably more space.

In 1891 Low formed a committee to examine the college's relocation. It considered three options: fragmenting the campus at various locations in lower Manhattan; removing the campus to the countryside; or finding a suitable site for a contiguous campus elsewhere in the city. At one of its first meetings in December 1891, Low's committee assigned John B. Pine, the influential clerk of the board of trustees, to "prepare and submit to the Committee a statement as to the legal status of 117th, 118th and 119th Streets between Amsterdam Avenue and [Broadway]" (Minutes of the Committee 1891). The committee wanted assurances that the asylum property, once purchased, would remain exempt from street openings. Although Pine's inquiry found that the exemption remained in force, in February of the following year, State Senator George Plunkitt, a powerful Tammany Hall politician, introduced a bill to the legislature proposing the opening of 115th through 120th Streets, which included the intended Columbia campus (*New York Herald*, March 1, 1892). However, under pressure from Mayor Grant and others, Plunkitt's bill was amended to exclude the Columbia campus, clearing the way for the purchase of the Bloomingdale Asylum tract.

The "island" plateau seemed to offer the best of both worlds: a campus within the city, yet insulated by topography from the hubbub of commerce and the social dissonance of nearby slums. In 1892, following secret negotiations with New York Hospital, Columbia secured the option to purchase the Bloomingdale property. Teachers College, anticipating an affiliation with Columbia, purchased a twenty-acre site on 120th Street even before the latter's purchase had been finalized (Cremin et al. 1954). In February 1895, the trustees of Barnard College followed suit and executed an option to buy a New York Hospital plot west of Broadway.

One year after Columbia's purchase, Low and the trustees protested the Manhattan Elevated Railway Company's proposal to construct elevated railroads along Amsterdam Avenue and the Boulevard (Broadway). "An elevated railroad," they argued, "constructed in either of these avenues will, therefore, be in immediate proximity to the college, and will not only offer a most serious interference with the educational purposes of the college, but it will be destructive of the imposing architectural effect which it is hoped the new buildings will produce" (*New York Tribune*, March 24, 1893). Although the trustees were primarily opposed to elevated railroads (in contrast to an underground "subway," which came later), their anxieties regarding a disruption of the college's "educational purposes" and "imposing architectural effect" reiterated the vertical hierarchy afforded by the plateau's seclusion, and of the threats, sociocultural and infrastructural, to its spatiosymbolic order and integrity.

Low and the trustees agreed in 1893 on an architectural plan proposed by Charles McKim, a partner in the firm McKim, Mead & White, in the style known as "monumental classicism," best exemplified by Low Library, whose design was influenced by the domed Roman Pantheon—a long-valued symbol of the greatness of classical civilization—and the Baths at Caracalla. Breaking with tradition, McKim situated the library, instead of the chapel, at the center of the campus (Dolkart 1998).

Faced with substantial difficulties raising funds for the first phase of construction, Low announced in May 1895 that he would donate up to one million dollars of his personal fortune for the library as a memorial to his father, who had died two years before. In December 1895, the cornerstone of Low Library was laid in a private ceremony and, in the following year, a public dedication of the campus was held to coincide with the laying of the cornerstones of Schermerhorn and Fayerweather Halls. With Columbia's unbroken campus secure, other nonprofit institutions soon followed suit, including Barnard College (1897), the Jewish Theological Seminary (1903), Corpus Christi Roman Catholic Church (1907), the Union Theological Seminary and the Julliard School of Music (1910), International House (1924), and the Riverside Church (1930).

Women in the Shadows

The making of the American Acropolis was also a deeply gendered project, one that institutionally marginalized women for generations. The struggle for coeducation at Columbia, which led to the creation of Barnard as a women's college in 1889, has been well documented (see Farrell 2009; Miller and Meyers 1939; Rosenberg 2004). My focus here is on the development of Teachers College, which, established by women, was a key source of programming and curricular initiatives that engaged nearby poor and working-class neighborhoods through educational, social welfare, and other community services. These initiatives, addressed in subsequent chapters, often challenged the insularity of the American Acropolis and the spatiosymbolic order promulgated by its overwhelmingly white, male, and elite leadership. In these community-based efforts, women provided the labor and, more often than not, the initiative and leadership.

One year before the cornerstone had been laid for Low Library, Teachers College opened for classes, following the completion of its first building on 120th Street in 1894. It had been provisionally chartered by the

State Board of Regents in 1889 as the New York College for the Training of Teachers, but its origins reached back to the founding of the Kitchen Garden Association (KGA) by a group of prominent New York women in 1880. As a philanthropic organization, the KGA sought to promote "the domestic industrial arts among the laboring classes, by giving to the children of the same, and to such others as might be deemed desirable, gratuitous instruction in household arts" (Commission on Industrial Education 1889, 232). The prime mover in the KGA was Grace Hoadley Dodge, an affluent evangelical Presbyterian and the granddaughter of one of the founders of the metals and mining firm Phelps, Dodge & Company; her father, William Earl Dodge Jr., was a partner in the firm and the donor of Columbia College's Earl Hall in 1902.

Dodge began her charitable work in 1876 as a volunteer with the industrial schools sponsored by the Children's Aid Society (CAS). Members of the Dodge family were major contributors to CAS schools, lodging houses, and other charitable projects. CAS's industrial schools were intended to address the educational needs of poor children who were beyond the reach of both the public schools and CAS's Free Schools due to language barriers, income-earning activities, or other circumstances associated with poverty.

Students in the industrial schools received basic primary school instruction and training in practical skills, such as sewing, carpentry, and cobbling. Volunteers, typically upper-class women like Grace Dodge, assisted the paid teachers and were also valued for their role as exemplars, imparting middle-class morality, discipline, and other putative virtues upon the children of the poor (Katz 1980).

Dodge developed an interest in the work of Emily Huntington, a Connecticut-born mission worker, who was among those promoting the teaching methods of the German pedagogue and philosopher Friedrich Froebel (1782–1852). Froebel's ideas and educational work laid the foundation for the international kindergarten movement, finding support among advocates of women's rights since it placed female kindergarten teachers at the center of educating children for citizenship (Allen 2017).

Froebel's philosophy and methods found fertile ground in the postbellum United States, particularly in urban areas experiencing unprecedented levels of poverty, having absorbed large numbers of foreign immigrants and African American migrants from the South. Low-income households were believed to be too unstable, ignorant, and preoccupied with economic survival to properly socialize their children before they entered the public school system. This problem was more pressing in the case of immigrant households, where linguistic and cultural differences were perceived as barriers to assimilation. Moreover, many children did not attend school at all because their labor was necessary for the household economies of working-class families. Froebel's kindergarten approach legitimated the intervention of trained middle- and upper-class professional women in working-class households during a phase of childhood development hitherto considered private.

The kindergarten movement shifted the pedagogic focus in the education of the poor to what Froebel termed the voluntary "self-activity" of children learning among their peers. Eschewing the Christian doctrine of original sin, Froebel stressed the realization of the child's innate potential by adopting modes of play and symbolic gifts linking psychological "inner states" to external actions. For example, wooden blocks were used in play to demonstrate the relationship of parts to the whole, and diversity to harmonic unity. "Thus," Anne Taylor Allen wrote, "kindergarteners described their classrooms as microcosmic models for a new ideal of citizenship that reconciled individual freedom with public responsibility" (1988:29). In heterogeneous, postbellum New York City, the need for this reconciliation, political as much as cultural, was believed to be pressing.

Adopting Froebel's methods to industrial training, Huntington advocated teaching domestic skills to young girls through use of miniature household utensils along with songs, exercises, and play. Huntington termed this approach the "Kitchen Garden method" of domestic education. Dodge believed that this domestic education would not only prepare girls for their roles as mothers and household heads, but also, as Esther Katz noted, "offer a successful way of channeling these girls away from unskilled jobs in shops and factories, where she held the moral and physical climate was dangerous, and toward paid domestic work in 'respectable' homes" (1980:40).

In 1884, working in concert with thirteen women employed in carpet and silk factories, Dodge founded the Working Girls' Society, which provided space for women to meet, socialize, and attend lectures and classes on topics ranging from cooking and sewing to foreign languages, elocution, and typing. The society offered a circulating library, reading room, and lecture hall, and encouraged "practical talks" on topics deemed to be relevant by the society's dues-paying working women. The society also retained a female physician. Echoing Froebel's emphasis on coopera- tive self-guided activities as a means to individual self-realization, the Working Girls' Society was self-governed and self-sufficient. Departing from the top-down approach of the previous generation of philanthro- pists, Dodge argued that privileged women "owe it to their laboring sis- ters" to strive toward "not working *for*, but *with*" them (in Robertson 2007:11). Attendance at the society's clubrooms grew from 5,500 in its first year to 9,364 in 1888. Finally, in 1886, Dodge was appointed, along with Mary Nash Agnew, as the first female members of the city's Board of Education.

In 1884 Dodge recommended to the KGA's board of managers that the group expand its mission to address the vocational needs of boys and older students, as well as promote industrial education in public and private schools. With Dodge's urging, the board voted to dissolve the KGA and create the Industrial Education Association (IEA) in its place. The new organization's mission was broadened "to provide instructors for schools and classes, and, if necessary to train teachers" (*New York Times*, March 8, 1885). Dodge and the IEA also hoped to extend its pro- grams to southern states and to the education of the Black freedmen. Dodge supported the work of Booker T. Washington at Tuskegee and later supported the White Rose Industrial Association, founded in Man- hattan in 1897 by the African American writer, philanthropist, and for- mer slave Victoria Earle Matthews (Robertson 2007).

To bolster the authority and influence of the IEA, Dodge and her colleagues reorganized the association's governing structure. Dodge recruited prominent men to serve as "honorary members" of the IEA, including William E. Dodge Jr., Charles Loring Brace, Frederick A. P. Barnard, Abraham S. Hewitt, Seth Low, and Bishop Henry Codman Pot- ter. General Alexander S. Webb, a decorated Civil War veteran and the president of the College of the City of New York, was elected to the largely figurehead position of president; Dodge served as vice president tasked with day-to-day matters. By 1887, 4,383 students were attending IEA in- dustrial education classes (Katz 1980). The IEA also offered teacher train- ing and created a model school for demonstrating Froebel's methods.

The IEA's rapid growth led Dodge to believe that the organization needed a full-time, salaried president with educational credentials, who could strengthen its role in teacher training and expand its influence and fundraising capability. With a $10,000 donation from George W. Vanderbilt, the IEA embarked upon a search for a "hands-on" president, settling on Nicholas Murray Butler, a twenty-five-year-old newly minted PhD. After graduation, Butler had embarked upon a one-year *Wanderjahr* in Europe, returning to his family's home in New Jersey in 1885 with the hope of securing a teaching appointment at his alma mater. However, despite the enthusiastic support of Columbia's president, Frederick Barnard, who described him as an "indubitable genius," the trustees rejected Butler's appointment due to a lack of funds. After teaching philosophy for a year without a salary, as a replacement for his ailing mentor, Alexander, Butler was hired as a fellow and assistant in the Department of Philosophy, Ethics and Psychology in 1886 (Rosenthal 2006).

In his autobiography, Butler traced his interest in educational matters to Barnard's efforts in the early 1880s to create a department of history, theory, and practice of education along the lines of the emerging sciences. The trustees and faculty of the college greeted Barnard's proposal with skepticism. "A department of education," Butler wrote, "seemed as strange and as odd as a department of aviation would have been!" (1939:177). Butler accepted the IEA's presidency in 1887, although not without conditions. Butler explained to Dodge and the IEA that he would accept the position only on the condition "that the whole movement . . . be converted from a philanthropic enterprise into one for educational advancement and reform" (1939:181). Butler's desire to transform the IEA, renamed the New York College for the Training of Teachers, from a philanthropic organization focused on the education of working-class people and teacher preparation, to a professional teacher training college seems at first to be consistent with Dodge's own vision of the IEA's expanding mission. However, the distinction that Butler insisted on between philanthropy and that which was of "academic interest" relegated the pedagogical insights and reforms, as well as commitment to addressing the varied educational needs of poor and working-class people that had been championed by the IEA women, to the feminized margins of purportedly more academically rigorous professional teacher training.

By 1890, the School for the Training of Teachers had outgrown its building at 9 University Place in Greenwich Village—a building that Dodge had rented at her own expense. Butler, who had been privy to Columbia's negotiations with New York Hospital for the Bloomingdale Asylum property, advised the college's trustee George Vanderbilt to purchase an adjacent property on West 120th Street. With the support of Vanderbilt, the school, renamed Teachers College (TC), purchased the twenty-lot site on West 120th Street, days before Columbia's purchase had been made public (Cremin et al. 1954). However, TC's building campaign soon ground to a halt due to financial troubles. Dodge, who had become the college's treasurer, raised $100,000 between March and July of 1894, enabling the completion of TC's Main Building. Dodge also anonymously donated $400,000 for the construction of a Household Arts Building, later renamed Grace Dodge Hall (Katz 1980). With its campus established on Morningside Heights, the college's trustees pursued affiliation with Columbia.

In 1892 the chairman of TC's board, William Appleton Potter (brother of Bishop Henry C. Potter), submitted a proposal for a merger to Columbia's board of trustees, who rejected the proposal, in part because they viewed coeducation as injurious to Columbia's aspiring reputation as a university. Moreover, schools for observation and practice were "a distinct anomaly in the work of the university" (in N. Butler 1939:185).

Columbia's rejection of the Potter consolidation plan institutionalized a boundary that was profoundly gendered and class-inflected. This distinction—an epistemic boundary with far-reaching consequences—would also be drawn in sociology between its "practical" and "scientific" branches. Received orthodoxy, masquerading as scientific rigor, marginalized the efforts of Dodge and other women who made efforts to engage in progressive reform. Indeed, this orthodoxy dismissed oftentimes innovative theory and its practical application. The lines had been drawn, insulating the college and greater university from more substantive, positive, and enduring engagements with surrounding communities. Unsurprisingly, it was women who spearheaded, in the words of Grace H. Dodge, "not working *for*, but *with*" the nearby communities of Manhattanville and Harlem.

2

Manhattanville Valley, Constituting the Outside

The most fundamental condition that determines the welfare of a social group, is the number and character of its
members. The mass of the population decides the relation
of the people to their habitat, as well as the extent and complexity of their organized activities.
—Howard B. Woolston, 1909

In the fall of 1904, Howard Woolston embarked upon a two-year study
of Manhattanville, the working-class community and manufacturing
district located on the northern border of the Morningside plateau along
the Manhattanville fault line valley. Woolston, a student of Columbia
University sociologist Franklin H. Giddings, set out to apply his mentor's inductive method to the study of Manhattanville's racially and
ethnically diverse, predominantly poor and working-class population.
Influenced by the work of social reform-minded researchers, Woolston
believed that empirical studies of communities such as Manhattanville
could generate the expertise needed to redress the pressing problems
facing rapidly growing and diverse industrial cities (Woolston 1909).

Woolston's study was originally conceived as part of a larger, comprehensive study of neighborhood conditions sponsored by the Speyer
School and Settlement. Founded in Manhattanville in 1903 by Columbia-
affiliated Teachers College, the Speyer School sought to inculcate moral
character, discipline, and the virtues of responsible citizenship in its
working-class students, many the children of immigrants. Pedagogy and
curriculum stressed practical education in the industrial and domestic
arts, hygiene, and physical training. These were intended to foster self-
control, manual dexterity, and discipline—knowledge, skills, and modes
of conduct believed to be essential to producing a disciplined, docile,
and culturally assimilated citizenry and labor force. Woolston worked
at the Speyer School while conducting his study of Manhattanville, and

viewed his research as contributing to "a scientific program of social education" (1909:6).

Manhattanville, with its tenement and shanty housing, its racially and ethnically diverse residents, and their unskilled and semiskilled occupations, was the "constitutive outside" against which the American Acropolis and its civilization-building mission was imagined and spatially secured (Laclau and Mouffe 1985). As discussed in chapter 1, the elites associated with the still-expanding constellation of educational, religious, and cultural institutions on Morningside Heights constructed the Acropolis via an "exclusionary matrix," as Judith Butler put it, creating an elite, normative space, suitable for the multifaceted fabrication of civilization, while casting surrounding working-class communities as zones of abjection, characterized by social deviancy, pathology, and unassimilated cultural-cum-racial differences (J. Butler 1993; see also Kristeva and Lechte 1982). The stark contrast in elevation between the Morningside plateau and the Manhattanville fault line valley below led to differing patterns of investment and land use, and also a new social geography, repeated in many American cities during the nineteenth century, where upland, affluent areas were counterposed to lowland, working-class slums, or "bottoms" (Moga 2020).

Dominant land-use thinking in the late nineteenth and early twentieth centuries was influenced by plant ecologists and other Darwinist frameworks that stressed interspecific competition and ecological succession (Valverde 2011; M. Davis 1999). From this perspective, the spatial segregation of economically, racially, and ethnically distinct populations and supposedly incompatible land uses into "natural areas" was regarded as both natural and normative, and found authority in the social sciences still under the sway of social evolutionary theory and scientific racism (e.g., Wirth 1925:188; Park and Burgess 1925). Howard Woolston's evocative "bird's eye" visual description of Manhattanville as located in a depression "between two peaks of higher learning" suggested a conflation of geographical elevation with enlightenment, and also indexed spatialized oppositions between the normal and pathological, the orderly and disorderly, the universal and particular. The spatial practices that secured and sustained the vertical secession of Morningside Heights from surrounding poor and working-class communities were informed and legitimated by knowledge produced through a variety of novel investigative technologies, including population censuses, public health surveys, and the emerging discipline of sociology. These technologies similarly contrasted the supposedly deviant and pathological traits and conduct of racially and ethnically marked working-class areas to the putative norms of native-born middle- and upper-class communities. As Michel Foucault noted, the new political anatomy that arose through disciplinary power was the result of a "multiplicity of often minor processes, of different origin and scattered location, which overlap, repeat, or imitate one another, support one another, distinguish themselves from one another according to their domain of application, converge and gradually produce the blueprint of a general method" (1995:138). And it is these interrelations and epistemological congruities among these various investigative technologies and their disciplinary functions that are the focus of this chapter and the next.

I begin by tracing Manhattanville's nineteenth-century development as an industrial working-class community, focusing on how location and geography shaped its development as an industrial center, entrepôt, and transportation hub. This, in turn, shaped the composition of Manhattanville's predominantly foreign-born labor force, patterns of land use, and environmental conditions. I then examine how two key normalizing technologies—the 1865 sanitary survey of New York City and the 1900 federal census of population—constructed knowledge about Manhattanville and its heterogeneous population. These instruments encoded putative norms of white native-born American society, to define, surveil, and map deviant and pathological environmental conditions, modes of conduct, social identities, and domestic arrangements (Canguilhem 1991). These investigative distinctions solidified boundaries between the normal and the pathological, between the elites of the American Acropolis and its constitutive outside.

Geography, Industrial Development, and the Spatial Production of Difference

If the elevated topography and the natural barriers of the Morningside plateau provided the opportunity for assembling a center of American civilization removed from the poor and working-class districts, Manhattanville's location facilitated the converse. Incorporated as a village in

1806, Manhattanville was laid out along the 125th Street Manhattanville fault line valley, which cuts a channel through the rock ridges forming Morningside Heights and Hamilton Heights to the north. Most of the shorefront along the Upper West Side was at high elevation; Manhattanville was the only practicable point of access to the Hudson River north of 72nd Street.

The new village was also situated along the Bloomingdale Road, the principal north-south thoroughfare during the early nineteenth century, linking lower Manhattan to the north of the island and the Bronx. Moreover, Manhattanville's location along the fault line valley made it a key transshipment point east to the town of Harlem. Since the Dutch period, this path linked the Hudson River and Manhattan's Upper West Side to Nieuw Haerlem on the East River (Riker [1881] 1904).

Incorporated by merchant landowners Jacob Schieffelin, Thomas Buckley, and Jacob Lawrence, Manhattanville developed as an important entrepôt, transportation hub, and center of manufacturing. Manhattanville's founders were also interrelated through marriage, business dealings and, in the case of Buckley, Lawrence, and landowner Joseph Byrd, membership in the Society of Friends.

In 1806 Adolphus Loss, the city's surveyor, laid out the village on a street grid roughly in alignment with the valley floor. This grid conformed to the natural drainage channels along the fault line valley, allowing water runoff from the surrounding heights to flow southeast along the main streets. However, the city's 1811 street grid imposed an arbitrary east-west axis, ignoring the valley's natural drainage system. Just as the geography of the Morningside plateau had enabled an elite politics of vertical secession, the 1811 street grid disruption of Manhattanville's natural drainage system led to outbreaks of cholera, malaria, dysentery, and typhoid. These in turn gave rise to a geography of risk that conflated environment and disease with the putatively innate racial and ethnic attributes of the poor and working classes. Geography played a critical role in the process of class formation and in the spatialization of racial, ethnic, and class identities and antagonisms.

By 1813, wool was being manufactured in Manhattanville, and the *Columbian* assured its readers that "there is no doubt that Manhattanville cloth will equal that of any in the United States" (June 2, 1813). The development and expanded use of water-powered textile mills, grist mills, sawmills, tanneries, and iron foundries during the first half of the nineteenth century fostered the growth of industrial suburbs in the Northeast in proximity to mill dams and similar sources of water-power (Muller and Groves 1979; Seely 1981). The manufacture of wool and other commodities in Manhattanville was also promoted by a number of measures taken by the New York state legislature. Trade embargoes during the Napoleonic Wars led to a severe shortage of consumer goods in the United States. Beginning in 1808, the state legislature created mechanisms providing financing to farmers to acquire pedigreed sheep and boost textile manufacture. Entrepreneurs were encouraged to seek incorporation to manufacture a variety of commodities, including glassware, iron implements, paint pigments, and textiles, many of which were manufactured in Manhattanville (Seavoy 1972).

The completion of the Erie Canal in 1825 dramatically increased commercial ship traffic at Manhattanville's port. This increase in riverine commerce highlighted the need for a more direct route from the Hudson to the East River, Long Island Sound, and the Atlantic ports. During the 1820s and 1830s, a canal linking the Hudson and East Rivers had become both practicable and pressing (Pessen 1985). In 1826 the city's Common Council approved the Harlem Canal Company's plan to excavate a sixty-foot-wide canal linking the Hudson River at Manhattanville to Hurl Gate on the East River near 108th Street. Although construction began, the project was abandoned, possibly a casualty of the financial crises of the 1830s (Hermalyn 1983). In 1834 the city inspector recommended that large sections of the canal be filled in, as the water collecting there was "extremely injurious to the health of the neighborhood" (*New York American*, October 17, 1834:6). The completion of the Hudson River Railroad in 1851 secured Manhattanville's importance as a critical transit hub in northern Manhattan, linking river, rail, and road transportation.

In 1832, paint and pigment manufacturer Anthony Tiemann and his son, Daniel, moved their business from 23rd Street in lower Manhattan to Manhattanville (Swackhamer 1858). Rising property values and inadequate space in their urban centers incentivized manufacturers like Tiemann to relocate to the urban periphery, where land was cheap and plentiful, and where worker housing could be built nearby (Muller and Groves 1979). In 1833 Daniel F. Tiemann assumed control of the family business. Tiemann, who served as mayor of the city from 1858 to 1859, built his factory on a bluff overlooking the Hudson River. His enterprise required considerable space for storing raw materials, grinding pigments, and producing lead carbonate, the toxic powder used to make white lead-based paint. Additional space was needed for mixing operations and for the stabling of horses. By 1858, the D. F. Tiemann & Company Paint & Color Works stretched over forty building lots and employed 120 workers, predominantly German-born (Swackhamer 1858). Other industries followed, taking advantage of Manhattanville's location and new sources of immigrant labor. In 1851 Bartow Van Voorhis and Russell H. Hoadley founded the Manhattan Iron Works Company along the Hudson River between 142nd and 146th Streets. Burning anthracite coal, the firm imported iron ore from Lake Champlain via the Erie Canal, producing pig iron for foundries and mills (American Iron and Steel Association 1880).

Workers generally lived within walking distance of their jobs since the cost of streetcars was prohibitive. The 1880 federal census enumerated clusters of wool sorters and other mill workers, many born in England, residing in adjacent brick tenements on Manhattan Street, near D. F. Tiemann's factory. For example, thirty-year-old wool sorter Charles Stanley lived with his wife and three children in an apartment near Twelfth Avenue. The Stanley household also housed a boarder, twenty-five-year-old Lilly Stubs, who worked at Butler's mill as a wool spinner (US Census Bureau 1880).

By the Civil War, Manhattanville was a prosperous manufacturing center and commercial entrepôt, and well into the twentieth century it remained an important distribution center for meat, milk, and agricultural produce transshipped from the Hudson Valley. However, its largely unplanned industrial development gave rise to slum conditions for its poor and working-class population. Poor infrastructure, unregulated housing construction, and weak, often corrupt municipal oversight and regulation created intolerable conditions. During outbreaks of infectious disease, these slum conditions forcibly confronted elites and the middle classes, who used new research technologies to spatialize their anxieties about class, ethnic, and racial difference.

Plotting Disease, Disorder, and Difference: The 1865 Sanitary Commission Survey

In 1864 Louis A. Rodenstein, a German-born physician, conducted a survey of sanitary conditions in Manhattanville. The first empirical study of the district and city, it examined population, industry, infrastructure, and housing conditions. Rodenstein had been one of the founders in 1862 of the Manhattanville Dispensary, a hospital located at 131st Street and Amsterdam Avenue. Rodenstein's father was the rector of St. Mary's Episcopal Church in Manhattanville; in 1861 Rodenstein married D. F. Tiemann's daughter, Sarah Cooper, the great-niece of the industrialist, inventor, and philanthropist Peter Cooper (*Deaf-Mutes Journal* 1915).

The study was sponsored by the Citizens Association, a private organization formed in the wake of the city's 1863 draft riots to reform city government and promote policies improving conditions in poor and working-class areas. The city's elites had been alarmed by the widespread violence and rioting and believed that good government reforms aimed at eliminating political corruption and sanitary reforms directed at ameliorating the living conditions of the dangerous classes were essential to preserving a social order that was increasingly threatened by a "politico-sanitary menace" (Curtis 2002:512). Among its founders were some of the city's wealthiest merchants, lawyers, and real estate tycoons, including John Jacob Astor Jr., August Belmont, and Peter Cooper. The city's population—its hygiene and health, productivity, and potential for deviant and disorderly conduct—had become the subject of pressing interest and concern for the city's economic and political elites.

Sanitary reform, as a biopolitical strategy and technology, was directed at the population as a whole. The health of each individual, integrated into the family, the labor force, and the population, was essential for the productivity—and reproductivity—of labor, the ability of the population to consume goods and services, and the maintenance of social order. Sanitary reform in New York City was spearheaded by John H. Griscom, a physician, city inspector, and member of the association's Council of Hygiene and Public Health. In 1844 Griscom developed a plan to safeguard the city from diseases associated with poor sanitary conditions. Griscom's goal was to establish a public health department independent of the city's system of political patronage, one that also legitimated the professional expertise and authority of trained physicians (Woods and Chi 1986). By the latter half of the nineteenth century, health and hygiene were viewed as central to American identity and modernity. Public health authorities were granted sweeping powers to surveil and regulate city infrastructure, private property, and population, serving as proto-urban planners (Peterson 1979).

By 1865, there was a general consensus among physicians and public health officials that infectious diseases such as typhoid fever, cholera, and diphtheria were associated with place-specific environmental factors, such as poorly drained, marshy land, cesspools, accumulations of waste, and congested and poorly ventilated tenements. However, prior to the maturation of germ theory late in the century, it was not known whether filth and poor sanitation *caused* diseases or rendered people more susceptible to them (Szczygiel and Hewitt 2000; Whooley 2013). Rodenstein, like many, believed that "miasmas," the noxious fumes emitted by decaying organic matter, sewage, and standing water, were responsible for the outbreak and transmission of infectious diseases. Emanating from urban slums, miasmas posed a hazard to the greater city—an invisible and transgressive threat frequently conflated with the supposedly weak moral character and racial and ethnic habits and dispositions of slum dwellers.

To correlate abnormally high rates of disease with specific environmental conditions, nineteenth-century sanitary reformers adopted the techniques of medical topography, plotting clusters of disease morbidity and mortality in "dot maps." As a visual representation of disease in space, dot maps provided public health officials evidence for reforms targeting specific localities and populations. Owen Whooley, writing on nineteenth-century efforts to understand cholera in the United States, noted, "The cholera dot maps were arguments in visual form, and the argument they sought to convey was that there was a relationship between disease and some local factor" (2013:118). Those local factors included the inhabitants of the areas surveyed; the resulting medical topographies scientifically legitimated the argument that the racial, ethnic, and class differences, ranked by the social evolutionists, were pathological, unassimilable, and in need of containment.

Investigators had to demonstrate that the clusters of disease morbidity and mortality exceeded the "normal death rate," itself a problematic concept tied to what could be defined as abnormal and, therefore, preventable through spatially targeted sanitary surveillance and intervention (Whooley 2013). As Lennard Davis has pointed out, this notion of normalcy implied a theory of moderation or self-control; sanitarians and other public health officials frequently associated infectious diseases with the putative characteristics of slum dwellers, such as excitability, overstimulation, noisiness, and excess (L. Davis 1995). Drawing parallels between the human body and the wider body politic, officials saw the abnormal disease rate, visualized in dot maps, as evidence of societal instability and unrest.

Rodenstein was particularly alert to the impact that the ongoing opening of streets, rock blasting, and the grading of the terrain were having on Manhattanville's natural drainage system, resulting in large pools of standing water, marshy ground, and waterlogged basements and privies. Although Manhattan Street, the main east-west thoroughfare, had been macadamized—that is, covered with crushed stone and a binding layer of stone dust—its gutters did not drain. Manhattanville's founders had pointed to potential drainage problems when they made their appeal to the Common Council to have its main avenues exempted from the 1811 grid plan. Although the exemption had left sections of Manhattan Street (West 125th Street) and Lawrence Street (West 126th Street) intact, the rest of the area was remapped to conform to the 1811 grid. Rodenstein emphasized the dire sanitary consequences of laissez-faire development in Manhattanville:

> Where an incipient city defaces Nature, and deprives it of its own provision for restoring the equilibrium of its disturbed elements . . . ; there we find the habitats of malarious fevers, and the undertaker's great marketplaces for little coffins. (1865:340)

Advances in the medical sciences had contributed to sanitary discourses and theories that viewed the unobstructed movement of air, water, and people through the city as indications of the circulatory health of nineteenth-century cities (Gandy 2002). This "sanguine mechanics," as Richard Sennett put it, had roots in the revolutionary discoveries of the seventeenth-century English physician and physiologist William Harvey concerning the operation of the heart and circulatory system (1996). From the seventeenth century on, these circulatory discoveries informed urban planning. "Planners sought to make the city a place in which people could move and breathe freely," Sennett wrote (1996:256). From this sanguinary perspective, congested, poorly ventilated tenements, unflushed cesspools, pools of standing water, and inefficient infrastructure were analogous to a human body's blocked veins and arteries, impaired respiration, and inability to eliminate waste. These circulatory impediments, many believed, generated transgressive excesses that threatened middle- and upper-class areas of the city in the form of miasmas. Poor urban circulation also impeded the functioning of capitalist free markets and political security.

Rodenstein was most alarmed by the still intact remnants of Manhattanville's aborted 1826 canal project. As the district's main avenues were extended north and graded, Rodenstein observed, they intersected with the aborted canal trench, where they formed block-long bodies of stagnant water. Rodenstein warned,

> As surely as the summer sun makes its appearance, so surely do remittent and intermittent fevers rise in the miasmata from the green surface of those stagnant pools, and afflict the people who live around them. (1865:337)

In compiling data on Manhattanville's history, population, and occupations, Rodenstein observed that Manhatanville's population was predominantly Irish and German. Most inhabitants were unskilled and semiskilled: stable hands, laborers, servants, factory workers. The densest concentration of population, tenements, and shanties was found north of Manhattan Street along the Old Bloomingdale Road and in the earliest settlement, known as Pig Alley, a reference to the pigs kept by Irish laborers. This class- and race-inflected social geography was common. Popular or slang neighborhood designations associated with lowland areas, such as "the flats," "hollows," and "bottoms," were used synonymously with racialized slums, connoting not only swampy and poorly drained environmental conditions, but also the abject populations and undesirable land uses that occupied them (Moga 2020). For example, prior to the rise in popularity of the term "ghetto," low-lying Black settlement areas were often disparagingly referred to as "Black bottoms" (Haynes 1913).

A plate taken from E. Robinson's 1884 atlas shows a concentration of largely wood tenements and shanties. The map shows that many of these wooden structures were still aligned along Manhattanville's defunct 1806 grid, an indication of their age, condition, and disconnection from the area's few sewer lines. Although Rodenstein did not shrink from faulting developers and landlords, he was not above associating poor sanitation and health with the innate dispositions of the immigrant poor. Commenting on the difficulties faced by physicians when administering to Manhattanville's population, Rodenstein observed,

> They are chiefly Irish and Germans of the lower class, and the evils we
> have to encounter arise partly from the moral dispositions of these two
> groups. The Irish, with their proverbial carelessness, will act utterly heed-
> less of medical advice; neglect and absolutely expose their children to
> inclement weather in winter, or the vertical rays of the sun in summer.
> The Germans, on the contrary, can never be careful enough; closed, over-
> heated rooms, feather beds above and beneath them, and exclusion from
> the fresh air they deem essential to the treatment of their sick. Of the
> two evils I prefer the Irishman's carelessness; for the patient has at least
> a chance of getting fresh air while, among the Germans, I have known
> patients to be actually smothered to death. (1865:342)

As the first comprehensive study of Manhattanville, the 1865 sanitary survey contrasted the disease-prone habitats of the poor and working classes with those of elites: the former were constituted as spaces where the natural order had been disrupted; the latter were imagined to be spaces of health, moderation, and normalcy. The institutions then occupying the plateau—the Bloomingdale Insane Asylum and the Leake and Watts Orphan Asylum—were, in theory and by design, places for the recuperation of normality amidst nature, undisturbed by industry, commerce, social differences, and conflict.

This medicalized topography, contrasting normal and pathological, uplands and "bottoms," affluent and poor, and native-born whites and the racially and ethnically marked, influenced discourses and strategies of development of the American Acropolis well into the twentieth century. The semantic genealogies of such vague and polysemous concepts as "urban blight," the "plague of poverty," and the "pathology of ghetto life" that have since animated the discourses of social scientists, public policy makers, and the mass media have their foundations in the racialized conflation of poor and working-class communities with disease, deviancy, excess, and contagion as systemized by the sanitarians.

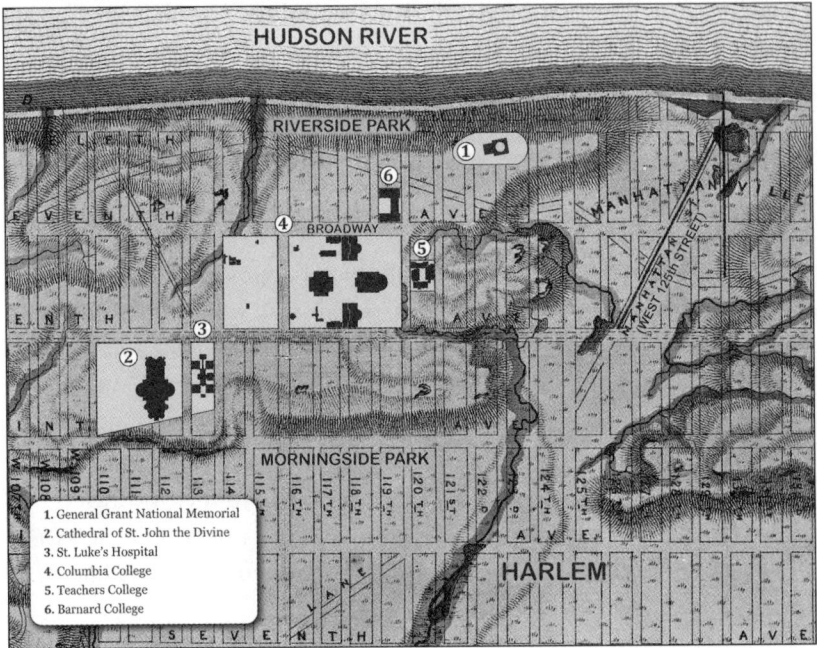

Detail of Egbert Viele's 1865 sanitary topographical map, with an overlay of the institutions present on the plateau in 1897.

Making the Population: The 1900 Federal Census of Population

"What is your name?" asked the enumerator.
Mr. Cassidy thought for a moment and then said: "There can be only one answer to that, so far as I can see; me name is James P. Cassidy."

"What is your relationship to the head of the family?"
"Ah, now," said Mr. Cassidy, "that's not so easy, Ye see, I'm the head of the family meself, and so I can't say all in a minute what relation I am to meself. I'll have to think about it."
—"Cassidy and the Census"

By 1880, the United States had experienced what Ian Hacking has called an "avalanche of printed numbers," and nowhere was this more apparent than in the evolution of the federal census (1982). For example, in

1870 the census asked 156 questions, including information on agriculture and manufacturing. By 1880, that number had increased to 13,010. Between 1870 and 1890, the number of published volumes of census data increased from five to thirty-two (M. Anderson 1988). Francis A. Walker, the economist and statistician who was appointed superintendent of the 1870 federal census, greatly expanded its scope and instituted the publication of the *Statistical Atlas*, which provided a synopsis of national demographic trends accessible to a variety of nonspecialized readers. Walker's administration introduced detailed color maps illustrating population densities and their spatial distributions, and he prepared maps for subgroups, such as Blacks and whites, native-born and foreign-born. These maps, like those of the sanitarians, spatially visualized representations of politically charged social differences.

In the late nineteenth century, the purpose of the census shifted and expanded to monitoring the state of American society as a whole. Earlier in the century, census data had been primarily used by politicians, but later census data was sought by business associations, social reformers, the press, and academics. The introduction of electronic enumeration machines in 1890 made it possible for statisticians to swiftly make complex cross tabulations of population data. Universities began teaching courses in the emerging "science of statistics," and trained statisticians viewed themselves as possessing increasingly more sophisticated and authoritative interpretations of data (M. Anderson 1988).[1]

By 1880, census data revealed that half of the US labor force worked in manufacturing, transportation, services, and other non-agricultural occupations, and much of this labor force lived in rapidly growing cities. In northeastern cities, many of these urban workers were new immigrants: between the 1840s and 1860s alone, 6.6 million European immigrants had settled in the United States, the majority in urban areas (M. Anderson 1988). By 1900, 37 percent of New York City's population was foreign-born, while New York, Chicago, and other urban areas of the northern United States were beginning to receive the first waves of the Great Migration of African Americans from the southern states.

These trends alarmed many politicians and commentators who viewed the immigrant-driven growth of cities and the ascendancy of an industrial working class as a threat to the character and stability of American society. Nativists, such as census superintendent Francis A.

Walker, stoked fears that immigrant-fed urban populations were increasing at a rate that outpaced that of native-born whites (M. Anderson 1988). Nativists and supporters of eugenics sounded the alarm that the native-born white population was in danger of committing "race suicide"—a term coined by sociologist Edward A. Ross—if its birth rate remained low in the face of continued immigration and the expansion of the African American population (Ross 1901).

While the sanitary survey mapped the abnormal occurrence of disease in order to identify pathological habitats and conduct, the census identified deviant social identities, household arrangements, and livelihoods by imposing normalizing categories, procedures, and judgments onto the enumeration process. An investigative technology of population, the census served not merely to describe but also to actively discover "the secrets of demographic processes and to render them susceptible to management" (Curtis 2002:516).

In this section, I examine the Manuscript Population Schedules of 1900—the handwritten enumeration sheets prepared by census takers in the field—to provide a snapshot of Manhattanville's heterogeneous population, the organization of its households, and the livelihoods of its residents in 1900 as viewed through the political technologies of the state (see Barrows 1973, 1978). I examine how census enumerators attempted to render legible and quantifiable the social identities and complex living arrangements of poor and working-class people at a time when the latter were being increasingly subjected to the surveillance and discipline of public and private authorities at home, at school, and at the workplace.

As Evelyn Ruppert noted, census taking implicated its subjects in a reflexive practice of "recognising oneself as a member and part of a population that is connected to myriad practices involved in the formation of a political subjectivity" (2008:2); these practices of subjectification did not go uncontested. I examine conflicts and disputes occurring between census enumerators and their subjects regarding the conduct and categories of enumeration, and identify critical areas of judgment and classification that proved problematic in the field. By examining these zones of contention and resistance to the normalizing logic, categories, and practices of the census, I hope to shed light not only on the urban architecture of biopower at the time, but also on the unruly livelihoods, domestic arrangements, and forms of self-identifications that constituted the infrapolitics of everyday life in diverse poor and working-class communities.

The population census was an aggressive and intrusive investigative technology that gave largely white, native-born, and male enumerators unfettered entrée into people's homes, and required—by force of law— that they present themselves, their domestic relationships, and their economic livelihoods in a manner that conformed to the normalizing logic, categories, and judgments of the enumerator. Censuses of population, along with the vital statistics compiled by sanitary surveys, the research of sociologists and reformers, and other investigative technologies were involved in both the constitution and classification of identities as socially recognized and lawful, and in the generation of actionable bureaucratic categories for state surveillance, regulation, and intervention (Ruppert 2008).

The 1900 census improved the accuracy and comprehensiveness of the enumeration process. For the first time, people seeking employment as census enumerators were required to take a written examination intended to identify qualified enumerators and reduce political patronage in hiring. Once the enumerators were hired and trained, their daily work was checked by a supervisor, or "special enumerator," who, when necessary, went into the field to audit, amend, or complete the census taker's enumeration schedules. Also for the first time, census enumerators were provided with detailed maps of their districts that plotted the locations of all buildings and monitored the enumerator's daily progress through the enumeration district.

Poor and working-class immigrants had reason to be wary of census enumeration. Only months following the passage of the Chinese Exclusion Act, the US Congress passed the general Immigration Act of 1882. The first comprehensive immigration law passed by Congress, the 1882 act defined the categories of foreigners who were deemed to be undesirable for entry, prohibiting the immigration of "any idiot or any person unable to take care of himself or herself without becoming a public charge" (in Szajkowski 1978:291).

The 1882 act and subsequent legislation also established an intrusive and widespread system of surveillance, investigation, and deportation of undesirable noncitizens already in the United States. The 1885 act rendered undesirable immigrants who had been living in the United States for less than one year subject to deportation. Because the 1900 census solicited data on literacy, employment, citizenship and nativity, age, and length of residence in the United States, it would have provoked fear, suspicion, and resistance among recent immigrants, particularly those who were unemployed, infirm, institutionalized, and viewed as political radicals. It is unclear whether census enumerators actively reported undesirable noncitizens to immigration authorities for investigation and deportation, but given their roles as temporary federal officials, they had the authority, access, and contacts to do so. Moreover, census enumerators routinely called on police and other public authorities to assist in gathering information and securing compliance of households.

According to press accounts, certain census questions provoked more indignation and resistance than others. Census officials often complained that enumerators encountered difficulties with female respondents when they were asked to provide personal information, such as age, marital status, and occupation. Failure to comply with a census enumerator was made a misdemeanor, punishable by fines up to one hundred dollars—an exorbitant sum in 1900. Census enumerators were issued badges emblazoned with the words "United States Census 1900" to shore up their authority, and those who encountered resistance were instructed to seek the assistance of law enforcement. Moreover, enumerators had the legal right to enter every dwelling in their district with or without the occupants' consent (US Census Bureau 1900).

For example, on June 18, 1900, forty-year-old Evelyn Allen, a live-in housekeeper for a Harlem woolen merchant, was arrested by deputies of the US marshal for refusing to cooperate with enumerator Joseph Eintracht. The *New York Times* reported,

> According to [Eintracht] she made no objection to answering the questions until he asked her whether she was married or single. Then, Eintracht claims, she appeared very indignant and asking, "How dare you?" opened the door and shoved him out. Other efforts to get the questions answered were unsuccessful, and he was finally compelled to get a warrant. (June 19, 1900:9)

One can only speculate as to the reasons for Allen's indignation. Many women (and men) regarded the marriage question and others as too personal to be posed by anyone, let alone a stranger and government official; or Eintracht might have been rude and disrespectful. Given that the census recognized only legal and heteronormative unions, among working-class women like Evelyn Allen, the question about marriage may have seemed like a normative judgment on their morality and respectability. Allen, who was accompanied to court by her employer, was released without fine, but only after she answered the marriage question.

Eintracht also had an altercation with Rebecca Hunter, a forty-seven-year-old native-born woman living in an apartment at 50 West 119th Street and referred her for arrest. According to Eintracht, Hunter had thrown him out of her home and threatened to shoot him if he returned (*New York Times* 1900b:9). At her arraignment, Hunter testified that Eintracht had been "ill mannered" and that he had collected false information. Hunter testified that she was a "woman of influence," and that her boarders would vouch for that fact. Eintracht's enumeration schedule indicates that he visited on June 14, recording her as the "head of family" and her occupation as "keeping boarders." Also in Hunter's household were her two teenage daughters and four single, unrelated women, born in Ireland and in their twenties. Eintracht enumerated the occupations of the four Irish women as servants. However, Eintracht also classified their relationship to Hunter as that of servants, despite the fact that she was taking in boarders. In fact, Eintracht enumerated no boarders at all; this is probably why Hunter, accompanied by the four Irish women, declared in court that her boarders would vouch for her (US Census Bureau 1900c:22).

It is unlikely that a working-class woman who took in boarders would employ four servants; Eintracht's classification suggests that he was reluctant to accept Hunter's self-reported occupation as "boarding keeper" and/or suspected something unseemly. Perhaps Eintracht had imposed a normalizing logic on a household that he either could not or would not make sense of: the presence of Hunter, two daughters, and four female boarders in an "unmanned" household might have raised Eintracht's suspicions about moral impropriety or sex work, prompting Hunter's assertion that she was a woman of influence.

Census enumerators were instructed to only record occupations for women and children who were engaged in "gainful labor"—that is, labor remunerated with a regular, monetary wage. Given that many poor and working-class women earned income doing residence-based piecework or were engaged in informal economic activities (e.g., vending, laundering, providing room and board to lodgers, and providing childcare), the question of occupation for women, married or unmarried, was prone to the misinterpretation, caprice, and sex/gender biases of the overwhelmingly male enumerators.

Only one Joseph Eintracht was enumerated in New York County at the time of the 1900 census. This twenty-four-year-old single man lived in the household of his Austrian-born father, a merchant, at 1486 Fifth Avenue in Harlem, then a middle-class district. As a middle-class, white, and native-born man, Eintracht would not have been immune to the prejudices of his gender, class, and nativity regarding the domestic organization, gender roles, sexuality, and livelihoods of poor and working-class households, particularly those headed by women. Moreover, the enumeration process granted interpretive authority to enumerators, empowering them to overwrite or, better, interpellate middle-class, heteronormative, and deeply gendered roles and relationships (US Census Bureau 1900c:13).

Working-class, immigrant, and African American women in particular had more serious and potentially life-damaging concerns with census enumeration. Widows and unmarried women were especially vulnerable to deportation as a result of the 1882 Immigration Act and subsequent legislation because of low wages; in the case of household-based and other informal work, their labors and earnings were often not recognized by census enumerators and other public officials (Brown 2017). Consequently, women were at far greater risk of being deported as public charges. Moreover, immigrant exclusion legislation, beginning with the 1875 Page Act targeting Chinese women, judged female sex workers and women suspected of immoral or disorderly conduct as subject to deportation.

Just months before the beginning of the 1900 census on June 1, Lillie Devereux Blake, the writer, feminist, and veteran of the fight for co-education at Columbia, published a petition in the *New York Times*, advocating the hiring of women as census enumerators. Dismissing the excuses given by census officials that women would be endangered when faced with the hostility and noncompliance of the public, Blake sarcastically wrote,

> It is certainly far more agreeable to the homemaker in high or humble life to be questioned by one of her sex rather than, as it has been humorously put, "to be busy about your work in an old wrapper, and then have a man come with a warrant of law to ask you how old you are." In such cases a masculine enumerator might "make residents angry," and in the interests of men and for the sake of their comfort, I would urge that they not be exposed to such dangers, but that throughout the resident districts women alone shall be employed. (March 22, 1900:3)

In response to Blake's letter, a *Times* editorial conceded that women could do enumeration, "not merely as well as it would be done by men of equal ability, but much better," given that it was often the women of the household who provided information to enumerators. However, since enumerators were generally selected on the recommendation of members of Congress, the editorial reasoned, the latter would have to be persuaded to nominate women (March 25, 1900:22). Although some women did work as enumerators in 1900, often to canvas orphanages, mental hospitals, and similar institutions, most women employed by the federal census entered the manuscript data onto punch cards or operated tabulating machines.

Another fraught normative census category was "head of family." Enumerators were required to designate one household member as its head, and then classify the relationship of each member of the household to that head—as "wife," "child," "boarder," and so forth. Since this designation was not a measure of the economic contribution of the family head, it presupposed male authority and, as a result, typically subsumed the economic contributions of the designate "wife" as "keeping house," even when the male family head was unemployed.

An analysis of an African American family living in a tenement on West 131st Street in Manhattanville in 1900 exemplifies this structural concealment of women's labor. Fifty-four-year-old James Goodlett, a native of South Carolina, worked for the Department of Highways as a "rock man," an unskilled and low-paying occupation. James lived with his forty-nine-

year-old wife, Christina, a son, an adopted daughter, and nine male boarders. Christina's occupation was enumerated as keeping house. However,
it is likely that Christina's occupation was that of boardinghouse-keeper
and that her work involved keeping the lodgers fed and supplying them
with clean clothes and linens. Rent paid by boarders was crucial to the
household; enumerating her as keeping house concealed the financial importance of her work (US Census Bureau 1900b:4).

Tracking the family's progress over the next decade shows just how
important Christina's economic contribution was. By the 1910 census,
the Goodletts had moved to New Rochelle in Westchester County,
where they owned a home at 131 Main Street. In 1910 the "Instructions
to Enumerators" clarified the occupational classification of women who
performed paid labor in the household (US Census Bureau 1910a:34).
Christina was enumerated as "self-employed" in the "employment office" field. James reported his occupation as "fish peddler." The Goodletts
employed a servant and were providing lodging to nineteen male and
female boarders, ten of whom were employed in domestic service. Seven
of the other boarders were children under the age of four. None of the
young lodgers were classified as relatives of the Goodletts or carried the
surnames of the adult boarders (US Census Bureau 1910d:9B).

With a total of twenty-six boarders, it is likely that Christina was
working out of her home as an employment agent for Black workers,
whom the couple may have also lodged. Christina appeared in New
Rochelle city directories, between the years 1905 and 1914, as operating a "colored employment agency" at her Main Street address. W. E. B.
Du Bois described similar employment agencies in Philadelphia during
the 1890s: "They conduct lodging houses and, in some cases, boarding
houses in connection. . . . Their business is to act as agents for persons
desiring servants, and to guide unemployed persons to situations; for
this they charge a percentage or fixed sum out of the wages. They also
often serve as homes for unemployed servants, giving them board and
lodging, sometimes on credit" (1899:118). The Goodletts were also likely
providing lodging to the young children of working or otherwise absent parents, an option that was preferable to committing children to
orphanages as "half-orphans"—that is, children placed in orphanages as
a result of parental illness or other reason preventing full-time parental
custody (L. Harris 2004).

James Goodlett's occupation as a rock man and, later, as a fish peddler could have accounted for the family's economic mobility. And it is more than likely that Christina Goodlett had been doing a lot more than keeping house in 1900. Based on her activities in 1910, it is reasonable to conclude that the Goodletts were providing their nine boarders in 1900 with not only room and board, but also laundry services and assistance in finding employment and permanent housing—services that would have been in demand for newly arrived African American migrants from the South.[2]

It is important to situate the census as a technology of population within wider structures of power and governmentality. Deeply gendered domestic categories, such as "keeping house," "family head," and "servant," interpellated normalized middle-class ideals of the family, misreading and overwriting labor performed in the household. More broadly, the household labor was being differentiated from extra-residential, factory work. For example, in 1892 the New York state legislature amended the factory law to make it illegal for residence-based workshops to employ persons who were not members of the immediate family. This restricted lawful tenement work to the nuclear family, sharply differentiating it from wage labor or "gainful employment" performed in factories, which could be regulated by inspectors. In 1893 further legislation required family workshops producing textiles and other goods to be licensed and inspected (*New York Times* 1903). The supposed purpose of this legislation was to improve conditions in tenement-based sweatshops, but by enforcing a sharp, often untenable distinction between "family workshops" and wage labor performed outside the home, the laws also undermined the ability of working-class families—women in particular—to maneuver within the economy. Moreover, the legislation also strengthened and enforced the division of labor between devalued women's work in the household and men's gainful employment in the factory.

A Day in the Life of a Census Enumerator

On the opening day of the 1900 census, Alexander Lockwood began his work on enumeration district 611, a roughly four-square-block area of Manhattanville. Enumerators in 1900 were expected to work ten-hour days and complete their work within two weeks of the June 1 start date. Census enumerators were typically hired to canvas the districts in which they lived, since they would have already had some local knowledge of their home districts. In this section, I follow Lockwood's progress on the first day of the census as he enumerated forty-five households along West 130th Street between the Hudson River and the Boulevard (now Broadway). Tracking the progress of one enumerator provides the opportunity to not only present a worm's-eye view of Manhattanville's population in space, but also to consider how one enumerator serially interpreted schedule data across ethnically and racially diverse households. Manuscript schedules also included the street names, house numbers, and the order in which households were visited, allowing reconstruction of an enumerator's route and work on any given day.

Lockwood began at the Hudson River piers at West 130th and 131st Streets, documenting the households of four ship captains. West 131st Street was the terminal of the Fort Lee ferry, which provided passenger service across the Hudson to New Jersey and the Manhattanville Station and freight facilities of the New York Central Railroad (US Census Bureau 1900b:1). Fifty-five-year-old Otto Brink captained the *Algonquin*, docked at West 130th Street, probably the Clyde Steamship Company's cargo steamer, which operated on the Great Lakes and along the Atlantic Seaboard (Caledonian Research Trust 2023). Brink lived on board with his wife and their six-year-old granddaughter. Lockwood visited three other boats, one of which was captained by a Black man from Central America, who was married to a native-born white woman.

West 129th Street was the site of one of Manhattan's seven recreation piers, established during the 1890s to provide summer respite for tenement dwellers. By day, the covered piers were dominated by women with children, many of them teenage girls who were paid to babysit the children of their neighbors (*New York Times* 1905:5). Private franchises sold beverages, ice cream, and other foods. In the 1890s, philanthropist and merchant Nathan Straus (co-owner of the city's two largest department stores, R. H. Macy & Co. and Abraham & Straus) established pasteurized milk stations at the piers to supplement the nutrition of poor children—a plan later adopted in other American cities (Straus 1917).

Although police and black-clad matrons enforced a ban on dancing, alcohol consumption, and "love-making," the piers were a popular entertainment venue for poor and working-class families. Newspapers were quick to comment on the young working women, or "rowdy girls," who were said to chew gum and "walk around the chairs of the long promenade until they saw somebody they knew." The Docks Department banned ragtime music from the piers in 1902. The *Tribune* applauded the prohibition, describing ragtime as an "inane and dreary negro music . . . ground out by Tenderloin composers." Although the *Tribune* conceded that tenement crowds would not be pleased by the likes of Richard Wagner, it insisted that there were other musical varieties that would not be "a deliberate debouching and deterioration of their tastes" (May 25, 1902:8).

Lockwood then crossed Twelfth Avenue to enumerate the north side of West 130th Street. He would have walked under the nearly completed Manhattanville Viaduct, which linked Morningside Heights to Hamilton Heights. The first residential building he enumerated was a small brick building at 651 West 130th Street. John Connolly, a forty-four-year-old grocer and butcher, headed the household. Born of Irish parents, Connolly had emigrated from Scotland in 1880. Sarah, his wife, had emigrated from Ireland in the same year. Of the six children she had birthed, only three survived. The Connollys' three daughters were attending school. Unsurprisingly, Lockwood did not record an occupation for Sarah Connolly, although she likely co-operated the family's business. The Connollys employed a young Irish woman as a live-in clerk (indicating that the business was in the residence); two brothers of Irish descent were boarders, a seventeen-year-old apprentice and a "horseshoer."

Lockwood continued east along West 130th Street, enumerating a handful of wood frame and brick buildings housing families of New York-born men of Irish and German descent employed as stablemen, teamsters, and blacksmiths. At 637 West 130th Street, as chance would have it, Lockwood enumerated his own household. Lockwood, a stonemason, was born in Jersey City in 1856 to Irish immigrants. Ella, his wife of twenty-three years, was native born and had given birth to five children, three of whom had survived. Lockwood had been raised in the town of Saugerties in Ulster County, New York. At the time of the 1870 census, Lockwood's father was employed as a farmer but also worked with his two sons in the town's bluestone quarry—a sedimentary rock that was used for street curbing and paving, and for window and door sills. Given Lockwood's experience and skills as a bluestone mason, Manhattanville would have been a promising place to settle (US Census Bureau 1900b:1).

Lockwood continued along West 130th Street, enumerating a string of brick buildings. Behind them was the Manhattan Dye Works, a wool and cotton dying factory where Lockwood's next-door neighbor was employed as a "dye man." Next, Lockwood enumerated the household of Thomas Collins, a forty-four-year-old policeman who lived in a building sandwiched between the city's Department of Street Cleaning's stables and a sawmill.

Just before quitting for the day, Lockwood approached a row of four tenements—615 through 609 West 130th Street. The buildings were three-story, pre-law brick structures built before 1884, each divided into twelve apartments.[3] The typical floor plan included a room with windows facing the building's front or rear, and one or two small, dark, and poorly ventilated interior rooms. Households tended to use the windowed room as a parlor, workshop, and/or sleeping space for boarders, and the interior rooms as bedrooms. A coal-burning stove, used for both cooking and heating, was typically located in the windowed room or, if space allowed, in a small interior kitchen.

On the ground floor of each tenement, the two front apartments on either side of the entrance brought the highest rents and were often rented as commercial spaces for saloons, barbershops, dry goods stores, sewing shops, and other businesses. Some tenement basements housed oyster cellars, where oysters were sold with beer or "stale ale." Many tenements had "tramp rooms," typically located in their cellars, equipped with makeshift bunks and coal-burning stoves, rented by the day. Lockwood would not have counted transients stopping there. At 615 West 130th Street, Lockwood enumerated ten German, Italian, and Irish households, totaling forty-two persons. Compared to tenements in congested areas of lower Manhattan, this was low density. Frank Conway, an Irish immigrant, lived in one apartment with his wife, Rose, seven children, and a niece. Forty-four-year-old Conway worked as a "rock man," drilling, blasting, and removing rocks—much in demand in 1900 as road beds and building lots were being excavated and graded. Conway's two oldest sons worked as sweepers for the nearby Department of Street Cleaning; his nineteen-year-old daughter was a saleswoman. John and Catherine Heimes, New Yorkers of German descent, occupied another apartment along with three school-aged daughters and two boarders, both skilled tradesmen: a German cornice worker and an Irish brick mason. Heimes, a teamster, had been unemployed for two months prior to Lockwood's visit.

The same building was also home to three households of Italians, all of whom had immigrated in the 1890s. Benigno Clementi, a laborer, arrived in the United States in 1892; his wife, Vincenza, and infant son followed in 1898. Enumerators were instructed not to ask respondents for assistance in spelling their names to avoid embarrassing or antagonizing illiterate people; Lockwood recorded the surname of another household, a young couple and infant who had immigrated in 1898, as "Scharamee-treeni." The couple had taken in two Italian men as boarders: one a laborer and the other a gas "lamp lighter." All members of the three Italian families were illiterate (US Census Bureau 2023).

Although many single working men and women lived in private residences as boarders, others lived permanently in low-cost hotels. John Ryan, a seventy-nine-year-old Irishman who had immigrated to the United States in 1849, owned a hotel on West 130th Street near Twelfth Avenue. (Lockwood enumerated Ryan's hotel later in the week.) Ryan lived in the hotel with a son, daughter-in-law, and four school-age grandchildren. Ryan provided lodging to his six employees (bartenders, cooks, and porters), and to forty male boarders, all but four of whom were Irish immigrants. All but one of Ryan's boarders were single, and most worked as unskilled laborers, except for a dozen men who worked as conductors and motormen for the Third Avenue Railway Company.

Ryan's establishment was a "Raines Law hotel," a class of hotels that spread throughout the city after the passage of the Raines Law in 1896. Proposed as a temperance measure, the law prohibited saloons from opening on Sundays, usually their busiest day and the sole holiday for most working people. The law exempted saloons that were located in hotels, which led George Chauncey to conclude that the law's main purpose was to suppress working-class male socializing (1995). To meet the letter of the law, saloonkeepers converted their establishments into hotels by constructing or subdividing rooms. By 1906, city officials estimated that 1,200 of the 1,400 certified hotels in Manhattan and the Bronx were Raines Law hotels. Ryan's hotel-saloon met the needs of largely single working-class men for affordable lodging near their workplaces, as well as for socializing.

Lockwood would have experienced few transcription problems at his next stop, a tenement building at 613 West 130th Street with ten African American households. Thirty-year-old Virginia-born Charles Leftwich lived at 613 with his wife and four children, two of whom were attending school. Leftwich was a rock driller but had been unemployed for a year. Seven other male family heads from Virginia, also laborers, lived in the building and had been unemployed for two to three months. Lockwood listed no occupations for their wives, but their work, no doubt, was economically crucial. Henrietta Haley, a forty-year-old native New Yorker, lived in an apartment with her adopted son and a white boarder, William Von Eiff, a German immigrant and baker. Lockwood recorded Haley's occupation as "boarding house keeper." Haley's German boarder was uncommon, since white people generally refused to live in buildings that housed African Americans. Given the composition of the household and the presence of only one boarder, one suspects that the category "boarder" was used to designate non-kin who did not fit the census's underlying normalizing logic, such as common-law marriages and other non-heteronormative relationships. Lockwood encountered two interracial married couples in his district, living in otherwise all-Black buildings—Black men married to Irish immigrant women. And, as elsewhere in the city, the increasing presence of Black people in white districts often incited animosity and violence from white residents and the police.

On August 2, 1901, for example, a riot erupted on West 130th Street between Twelfth Avenue and Broadway after a white man assaulted a Black woman. According to the *New York Times* account, Mrs. Jennie Williams, a personal attendant, was on her way to the Fort Lee ferry terminal at 129th Street to meet her employer. A white street sweeper, James Grant, encountered Williams on 130th Street and, as the *Times* put it, "objected strenuously to having a negress on the same side of the street with himself" (August 3, 1901). Grant struck Williams across the back with his broom and the latter cried for help. Black people poured into the street to defend Williams and were confronted by a mob of white men. A riot ensued. Police and their reserves were called out from the West 125th Street station. The *New York Times* provided a vivid account of what the police found upon their arrival:

> Just at this juncture two shots were fired and the police, drawing their clubs, charged the mob and fought their way to its center. A negro named George Jackson of 611 West One Hundred and Thirtieth Street was standing in the midst of the crowd with a revolver in his hand. Another negro, Samuel McLain of the same address, was lying on the ground with a dangerous cut in his head. He had been hit with a shovel by Patrick Conway of One Hundred and Thirtieth Street and Amsterdam Avenue, another street sweeper. Four negroes were found with a large beam, which they were using as a battering ram against the whites. This weapon did great execution.

The police dispersed the mob and arrested two Black men and two white men (including Grant) and recovered several razors and revolvers from the scene of the melee.

Lockwood had enumerated the Conway household the year before. Jennie Williams and two of her defenders lived at 611 West 130th Street, a building that had been all-white the year before. Grant, her white attacker, lived across the street in a large tenement that had housed only one Black couple in 1900. African Americans and Black immigrants were moving into buildings that only the year before had been exclusively or predominantly white. This pattern of "Negro invasion," white violence, and white flight characterized Black settlement in greater Harlem and elsewhere in the ensuing decades.

Finally, Lockwood enumerated the household of sixty-nine-year-old William H. Lynch, who lived at 613 with his African American wife, two teenage children, and two boarders. Lockwood enumerated Lynch's occupation as janitor, probably of the building in which he lived. Lynch's son worked as a bicycle repairman and his daughter as a servant. Lockwood recorded Lynch's race as Black and his place and year of birth as Ireland in 1830. The birthplace of his father was also recorded as Ireland and that of his mother, Africa (US Census Bureau 1900b:1).

Curiously, and in contrast to his enumeration of other immigrant households, Lockwood provided no immigration information for William Lynch, such as his year of arrival or whether he was an "alien" or naturalized citizen. This is an interesting anomaly. Lockwood might have been disbelieving of or confused by the identity of a Black person whose place of birth was Ireland. Moreover, since mixed racial categories had been dropped from the 1900 census in favor of a white/Black binary in keeping with the "one-drop rule," Lockwood might have found it challenging to reconcile a Black racial identity with a hybrid ancestry and complex migration history. Lynch was, as a result, denied both an ethnicity and migration history.

The mixed-race categories of mulatto, quadroon, and octoroon were first introduced in 1850, part of the effort of census officials and statisticians to produce increasingly differentiated data on population. Christine Hickman, analyzing commentaries published in the *Congressional Record*, has suggested that these hybrid categories also provided data to consider and debate pseudoscientific racial theories, such as the theory of mulatto or hybrid inferiority and infertility—claims relevant to assessing, for example, the vitality of plantation labor (1997). By 1900, the post-Reconstruction triumph of Jim Crow in the South and the hardening of the color line elsewhere had trumped such concerns, and the one-drop rule was categorically asserted.

The Lynch family reappeared in the 1910 federal census living at 322 East 127th Street. Lynch, then eighty-one, was enumerated as a "travelling salesman" of dry goods, living in an apartment with his wife and granddaughter. The schedule of questions in 1910 was the same as in 1900, but the racial categories were modified to include "mulatto." In 1910 the enumerator did provide Lynch's immigration and citizenship status: Lynch had emigrated to the United States from Dublin, Ireland, in 1832 at the age of two and he was a naturalized US citizen. The 1910 enumerator also classified his race and that of his wife and grandchild as "Mu," for mulatto (US Census Bureau 1910b:7B).

In 1920 the census found Lynch as a ninety-one-year-old widower, living alone at a new address on West 127th Street, now working as the caretaker of a private house. In the race column, the enumerator entered "Black." It is unclear whether this was the enumerator's assessment or Lynch's own. As in 1900, the birthplace of Lynch's mother was recorded as "Africa," next to which the enumerator had written "O.C.," perhaps short for "overseas colony," and perhaps at Lynch's prompting. The 1920 census schedule included the "mother tongue" of household members and their parents. The mother tongue of Lynch and his parents was recorded as "French," suggesting that the latter had lived in French colonies.[4]

Lynch's enumerative profile over a twenty-year period presents not only an intriguing narrative of the mobility of Black people throughout the African diaspora, but also an instructive example of how the census, as a normalizing technology, selectively elided Lynch's migration history and hybrid identity, and objectified a racial identity that was no more than a power-laden effect of the dominant racial order. Lynch was not legible within the logic and categories of the census. To constitute the category "Black," enumerators had to exclude variations, instabilities, and ambiguities in the system of racial classification, as in the wider social order. For people of African descent, race trumped both ethnicity and mobility.

Race, Language, and Culture: The Paradox of the "Black Irishmen"

If the juxtaposition of William Lynch's race, ethnicity, and nativity had conflicted with the binary logic of racial classification, the unstable or slippery relations among race, language, and culture were also a subject of anxiety, fascination, and irony in the press. Around the turn of the century, a spate of articles appeared in the city's newspapers disclosing cases of ethnically Irish Black people. In 1906 the *New York Tribune* reported that Patrick Jackson, a "coal-Black Irishman," had been brought before a magistrate at the Tombs Police Court for having knifed a "Florida coon." The incident occurred when Jackson attempted to board the steamship *Algonquin* in lower Manhattan and was accosted by a Black crewman, James Brown. When Brown gave the Black Irishman "some jaw," it was reported, the latter pulled a knife. "Yer Anner," Jackson declared in court, "he put his hand to strike me an' I hit him first. I'd be the queer Irishman if I didn'." Irish brogue or not, the judge ruled against Jackson. The *Tribune* noted that the "Black Corkonian" was fluent in Gaelic, which he used to converse with an Irish policeman in the courtroom (October 17, 1906:15).

In another case, the pistol-wielding Black cook of a schooner docked off City Island was reported to have chased its white captain and crew into the ship's rigging after they mocked his Irish stew. "Why a 'nigger' couldn't make an Irish stew anyhow," the ship's Scottish mate reportedly told the police. "But I'm an Irish 'nigger,'" retorted the Black cook. "Ain't my name O'Neill? I know more about an Irish stew than any Scotchman that ever lived." The Black Irishman was charged with felonious assault (*New York Tribune*, August 28, 1909:7). Although the Irish origins of both Black sailors is plausible, as William Lynch's case demonstrates, the narration of these suggests that the racial distinction between the Irish and people of African descent was unstable and slippery. If, as William Mahar has written, minstrel songwriters frequently "turned to Irish materials when creating stereotypes of American Blacks," then the narratives of the Black Irishmen secured the reverse: Black skin could be harnessed to heighten the cultural-cum-racial difference of the Irish vis-à-vis American society at a time when Irish immigrants' grip on whiteness was still tenuous (1988:15). These narratives mustered and reiterated prejudices against the Irish as "the Blacks of Europe," also calling into question the conflation of race, language, and culture that was advanced and reiterated through the pseudoscientific constructions of racial type espoused by eugenicist Madison Grant, Columbia sociologist William Ripley, and Howard Woolston. For if a Black man could speak Gaelic or make Irish stew, then all that remained to differentiate one from the other was skin color.

This latter possibility is supported by an 1891 report in the *New York Herald* entitled "Born White, but Now a Mulatto," which chronicled the case of an Irishman whose skin had turned "almost Black" (May 16, 1891:6). The report tells the story of a fifty-year-old Irish man who had been admitted to a Manhattan hospital suffering from a severe case of jaundice. In six months, Henry Welch's skin had darkened from "the shade of a typical Italian," to as "yellow as a Chinaman," to "the coloring of a quadroon"— the progress of his illness narrated as if to recapitulate the ranked racial categories of the social evolutionists. Welch had become, to adopt a metaphor of the time, a "smoked Irishman" (Ignatiev 1995). Troubled more by his skin color than by his liver, Welch sought a medical cure. While in the hospital, Welch visited a nearby restaurant and, when its waiter ignored him, slammed his fist against the table. "Now stop that and light out!" the restaurant's proprietor rebuked. "We don't serve colored people here." Undeterred, Welch replied, "O'im white as yisself. Can't you tell a white man when you see one?" Apparently not: Welch was kicked out.

Although, the Irish in particular would have been likely targets for racial crossover angst and amusement, non-Irish Black ethnicities also captured the imagination of journalists and their readers. A 1905 *New York Times* article entitled "Black Fraulein Hales Scotch Negro to Court" tells the story of John Manton, who was summoned to the Harlem Police Court by his common-law wife, Henrietta Tuite, for breach of promise. The article dwells on the astonishment of the Virginia-born magistrate when told that Tuite had been born in Düsseldorf, Germany, and her beau in Kilmarnock, Scotland. "Bless my soul," the southerner quipped, "I thought I knew everything about colored folks!" As in the earlier narratives, the reporter clumsily transcribed fragments of ethnic dialect, presumably to authenticate the ethnic identities of the Black subjects and heighten the irony. By pointing to the judge's Virginian origins and puzzlement, the report suggested that *even* a white southerner was ill-equipped to sort out the city's racial and ethnic complexity—a complexity that such accounts suggest required greater vigilance, disaggregation, and policing (June 23, 1905:7).

As investigative technologies, both the 1865 sanitary survey and the census contrasted the identities, livelihoods, and living arrangements of the city's poor and working-class immigrant and Black populations with a putative white middle-class norm, which was claimed to represent mainstream American society. These technologies, popularized in the press and in the culture at large and infused with scientific authority by the work of academics and statisticians, sharpened the contrasts and divisions, both spatial and socioeconomic, between middle- and upper-class districts of the city, such as Morningside Heights, and ethnically diverse and racialized working-class areas like Manhattanville. In sanitary surveys, abnormal rates of disease morbidity and mortality were evidence, imbued with the authority of statistics, not only of insalubrious environmental conditions, but also of the allegedly innate characterological traits and pathologies of subaltern immigrant and racialized groups. At a time when environmental determinism and Lamarckian theories of the heritability of acquired traits still held considerable sway, sanitary surveys played a critical role in class and racial formation and in the constitution of perduring and hierarchical racial geographies and symbolic economies.

In the next chapter, I consider how this data regarding Manhattanville's population and its underlying dichotomous logic, differentiating the normal from the pathological, informed the sociological research of Howard B. Woolston and the pedagogical theory and practice of the Speyer School and Settlement. Under the mentorship of Franklin H. Giddings, sociology students at Columbia were encouraged to do field research using, at least in theory, the inductive method. Woolston conducted a study of Manhattanville building on data from both the 1865 sanitary survey and the 1900 federal census, also informed by his mentor's sociological theories and nativist and racist dogmas. The turn of the twentieth century was a critical period in the development of the social sciences. An examination of the emergence of sociology at Columbia and of Woolston's monograph provides the opportunity to explore the constitutive tension between theory building and empirically based research in a discipline still indebted to social evolutionism and scientific racism.

Woolston's research was conducted while he was employed by the Speyer School and Settlement, an experimental or "laboratory" school established by Columbia-affiliated Teachers College. The Speyer School enrolled Manhattanville's poor and working-class students—many the children of immigrants—providing training in the industrial and domestic arts, hygiene, and physical education. The aim was to craft disciplined, culturally assimilated, and docile citizens willing to accept subordinate stations in a hierarchical class structure. An examination of the Speyer School and Settlement's pedagogy and practice provides the opportunity to consider how sociological research and knowledge produced through public health surveys, the census, and other investigative technologies were brought to bear on the practical problem of assimilating the "outside" that had been constituted by the American Acropolis.

3

Power/Knowledge and the Crafting of Citizens

When Howard Woolston arrived at Columbia in 1904 to pursue his PhD, its sociology program was a relatively independent department within the Faculty of Political Science, headed by Franklin H. Giddings, considered by some to be one of the founders of modern sociology. The fledgling department developed out of an ambition to wed sociological research, guided by statistics, to Progressive Era social reforms aimed at addressing the social problems associated with rapidly growing cities. Laissez-faire industrial development, coupled with European immigration and an equally dramatic influx of African Americans from the Jim Crow South, heightened fears of racial, ethnic, and labor conflict and unrest, underscoring for many the challenge of assimilating both populations to a normative ideal of American society and the evolving needs of capital. As an emerging discipline struggling to define itself and achieve a footing in academia, sociology was confronted with demonstrating its relevance to the social issues of the day (Morris 2015).

Woolston, a student of Giddings, spent his first two years at Columbia serving together with his wife, Florence Guy (a settlement teacher and editor of the suffragist journal the *Woman Voter*), as director of night classes and neighborhood work at the Speyer School and Settlement—a Teachers College experimental school in Manhattanville (Kennedy and Woods 1911). Woolston's dissertation, "A Study of the Population of Manhattanville" (1909), was based largely on research conducted while working at the school. Woolston was both sociologist and settlement worker; in addition, his department's aspiration to combine theoretical training with practical experience in charity and reform organizations influenced his work. Woolston's study, then, offers the opportunity to consider the mutually constitutive relation between the development of sociological theory and methods, and Progressive Era politics surrounding urban inequality and social differences. If, as I will demonstrate, Woolston's study produced a social taxonomy that cataloged the supposedly race-

and ethnicity-linked traits of Manhattanville's diverse population, traits deviating from a putative American norm, then the Speyer School and Settlement's pedagogy and strategy for community engagement offered a comprehensive program of action to correct such deviations and make good citizens.

As Stephen Turner has pointed out, the key figures in the development of the social sciences at Columbia—notably, Giddings, John Burgess, and Richmond Mayo-Smith, a pioneer of statistical analysis—were part of a closely knit network that encompassed representatives of charity and reform organizations, government offices, such as the US Census Bureau, and professional and quasi-professional associations, including the American Statistical Association (Turner 1991). For example, Franklin Giddings served on the boards of the Charity Organization Society and the University Settlement House and, from 1923 to 1930, was an influential member of the advisory council of the American Eugenics Society. This chapter examines the relationship between the development of sociology and the wider political and socioeconomic context within which it emerged during the Progressive Era. As Pierre Bourdieu put it, "The sociology of science rests on the postulate that the objective truth of the product—even in the case of that very particular product, scientific truth—lies in a particular type of social conditions of production, or, more precisely, in a determinate state of the structure and functioning of the scientific field" (1975:19).

By the mid-1890s, Columbia had transitioned from being a relatively small college with schools of the arts, law, and mining, to a university offering graduate training and advanced degrees in the social sciences. The first steps had been taken in the 1880s, when the board of trustees adopted a proposal prepared by political scientist John Burgess to create a school of political science in order to prepare students for careers in public service (R. Wallace 1989). Columbia's social science curriculum focused initially on political economy and statistics, given the expertise and interests of the school's key faculty members, Burgess and economists Mayo-Smith and R. A. Seligman. By 1891, support had grown for the teaching of sociology proper and for the creation of a chair in sociology.

A key supporter of both the creation of the university and the development of the social sciences was Seth Low, who became president of Columbia in 1890. Low, a reform-minded Republican politician with a background in philanthropy, had served as the mayor of Brooklyn between 1881 and 1885. As mayor, Low had implemented important reforms, such as the desegregation of Brooklyn's public schools and the introduction of the Civil Service Code to reduce political patronage in municipal hiring. As president of Columbia, Low advocated strengthening ties between the university and the city, establishing university affiliations with Union Theological Seminary, the American Museum of Natural History, and the settlement movement, and serving as president of the University Settlement Society. Although Low left Columbia in 1901 to become mayor of the consolidated city of New York, his support of the social sciences and Progressive Era reforms had a considerable impact on the development of sociology at Columbia and, perhaps to a lesser extent, the university's relationship to the city (R. Wallace 1989).

Giddings was hired as professor of sociology in 1894 and, soon afterwards, occupied the nation's first endowed chair in sociology. In a report to the trustees in that same year, the Faculty of Political Science articulated a three-pronged mission for a department of the social sciences, emphasizing the application of scientific knowledge to pressing social problems. Offering instruction in sociology, political economy, statistics, and other related fields, the department also engaged students in field research and established ties to charity and reform organizations where advanced students, such as Howard Woolston, could gain practical experience. These reform groups had pioneered the "social survey" as a methodology for gathering data on social problems, such as the conditions in tenements and factories. Finally, teaching and fieldwork were to be enhanced through the establishment of a statistical laboratory that would generate and analyze data and serve as a resource for students, independent researchers, and reform organizations (R. Wallace 1989).

During its formative years, sociology grappled with the tension between achieving intellectual authority through the scientific pursuit of general laws and the Progressive Era's mission of practically addressing social problems (Calhoun 2007). For Giddings and his students, this tension took the form of an incongruence between a commitment to inductive research methodology, the model of the social surveys produced by charity and reform organizations, and general theory building and testing by deduction—what W. E. B. Du Bois critically described as "metaphysical wandering" (2000).

Franklin Giddings had begun his career as a journalist, during which time he developed an interest in political economy, statistics, and sociology. Although he had attended Union College in Schenectady, New York, Giddings left before graduating, and the postsecondary school degrees that he later received (including his A.B.) were all honorary. Despite his lack of formal academic training, Giddings began reading the classic authors in political economy. In 1886 he resigned from his job at the *Springfield Union* newspaper to found his own publication, *Work and Wages*, which addressed current topics in political economy and, as Dorothy Ross put it, "offered workers condescending advice on the proper uses and abuses of labor organizing and warnings that the unemployed were 'defective' working people" (1991:127–28). After publishing a number of articles in academic journals, Giddings secured a position at Bryn Mawr College in 1888. While there, Giddings was hired to lecture in sociology at Columbia during academic years 1891–1892 and 1892–1893 in support of the efforts of Low, Burgess, and Mayo-Smith to establish a stable, independent footing for sociology within the Faculty of Political Science. In 1894 he was appointed professor of sociology (R. Wallace 1989).

Consciousness of Kind

The dominant voice of sociology at Columbia from the mid-1890s through the 1920s, Giddings argued that the elementary form of social consciousness and organizing principle of society was "consciousness of kind," a condition that results when any conscious being "recognizes another conscious being as of like kind with itself" (Giddings 1896:17). Giddings believed that during the evolution of society, social aggregates formed as populations adapted, biologically and behaviorally, to a given environment in similar or parallel ways. These collective behavioral responses to social needs and interests gave rise to expressions of "like-mindedness." Alternatively, "impressions of unlikeness," Giddings maintained, produced "psycho-physical disturbance" (1896:104). These ideas legitimized residential segregation and naturalized nativist hostilities toward non-Anglo-Saxon immigrants, as well as racial prejudices toward African Americans. "Society," Giddings wrote, "is a means to a definite end—namely, the survival and improvement of men through a continuing selection of intelligence and sympathy" (1922:226). Through its mechanisms of social control and constraint, society worked in tandem with the processes of selection to produce stronger and more adaptive forms of social organization and institutions (Calhoun 2007). With the growing need for collective action, Giddings argued, systems of social organization developed internal complexity and took on hierarchical form.

Giddings's theory of consciousness of kind was consistent with formulations of environmental determinism that were used to legitimize racism and imperialism, and well-worn climatic theories of European racial superiority. Although Giddings emphasized the role that "intelligent action" played in adapting to the environment through ever more effective forms of social cooperation and action, consciousness of kind and the typologies that Giddings deduced from them (e.g., "motor," "emotional," and "intellectual" types) remained tethered to the nativist and racist prejudices of the day.[1] Like many Progressive Era social scientists and reformers, Giddings's Lamarckian view of human history, which maintained that adaptations to the environment were heritable, his theory of consciousness of kind held open the possibility for "race improvement" (Fredrickson 1971; Stromquist 2006). Despite recognizing the potential mutability of human behavior, Giddings held that there were limits, both sociological and biological, to the social improvement of the lesser races and ethnic groups.

Although Giddings's writing on race were scattered, he shared the Nordic, white supremacist views espoused by scientific racism and social Darwinism—views that stressed the innate incapacity of some groups to adapt and survive, as well as the role of whites in the project of civilizational progress: "Another race with little capacity for improvement is the surviving North American Indian. Though intellectually superior to the negro, the Indian has shown less ability than the negro to adapt himself to new conditions. The negro is plastic. He yields easily to environing influences. Deprived of the support of stronger races, he still relapses into savagery, but kept in contact with the whites, he readily takes the external impress of civilization, and there is reason to hope that he will yet acquire a measure of its spirit" (1896:328–29).

Giddings's sociology naturalized hierarchies of race and ethnicity, leveraging intellectual authority by identifying uniformities of conduct consistent with statistically derived norms. Giddings believed that the root of poverty was social disintegration—those who strayed from the norm needed to be corrected. This portion of society, he opined, "can be made useful, comfortable, and essentially free, only by being under bondage to society and kept under mastership and discipline until, if ever, they acquire power to help and govern themselves" (1922:243–44). As for the social elements and groups that deviated from the norm, Giddings reasoned, "Life is made so difficult for the variates that stray too far from type that they go down in the struggle. Society, in a word, creates artificial conditions of existence which affect selection as natural conditions do, by determining a selective death rate" (1922:204).

The "selective death rate" that Giddings's sociological science identified—like his analysis of poverty—allowed for systematizing the prevailing nativist, racist, and eugenicist ideologies and practices of the period. Giddings's students applied these ideas in their research, further cementing sociology's legitimacy in the academy, while simultaneously demonstrating the discipline's practical application to social problems. My analysis of Howard Woolston's Manhattanville study demonstrates that this practical application was rooted in power-laden nativist and racist doctrines of the time, informed by and informing Progressive Era strategies of limited ameliorative reform.

The new discipline of sociology created generalizable knowledge that appeared as both ahistorical and utterly natural. Its students gathered data and produced statistics, as did such offices as the US Census Bureau; elite philanthropies took on the work, as did Giddings's students, in their efforts at the Speyer School and Settlement. This mutually constituted network rendered the status quo palatable, placing the blame for poverty upon those very social groups whom the elite excluded and marginalized. It was this normative subject that needed to be examined through sociological analysis and safeguarded through disciplinary institutions and their mechanisms of social control. Knowledge, power, and sociological theory had become, as Ruth Wilson Gilmore puts it, "a means to produce more where there is already most" (2022:66).

The Manhattanville Study

Howard Woolston, like others in his cohort at Columbia, took up the question of social adaptation and adopted Giddings's speculative system of classification to assess the varied capacities for social integration of Manhattanville's ethnic and racial groups. Woolston maintained that a study of Manhattanville's neighborhood life and the social and inherited capacities of its residents would provide data for "a scientific program of social education" at the Speyer School and Settlement—one that would prepare its poor and working-class students for "effective citizenship" (1909:6). Woolston began with a well-researched chapter on the history of Manhattanville, followed by a statistical analysis of its population. Using data from the 1900 federal census and the Department of Health, as well as Rodenstein's 1865 sanitary survey, Woolston produced a block-by-block tabulation of population numbers and densities, an analysis of household composition, age and sex distributions, ratios of the native- and foreign-born, and an enumeration of Manhattanville's racial and ethnic groups. This statistical analysis provided a veneer of scientific authority for Woolston's highly deductive application of Giddings's social typology in the next and pivotal chapter, "The Social Temper."

Woolston adopted his mentor's premise that social types evolve in response to stimuli in the social environment and biological inheritance—"types," Woolston wrote, "that can be distinguished by traits and mannerisms peculiar to the group" (1909:8). These types provided the theoretical criteria for classifying temperament and behavior. Since the social units that he assessed were defined a priori as racial and ethnic groups, his empirical data was trumped by the adoption of Giddings's speculative categories. His text did little more than catalog well-worn stereotypes in the guise of a putatively scientific system and terminology.

Woolston's classifications were based on a hodgepodge of published sources, appeals to common knowledge, and anecdotal observations. For example, when classifying the "motor reaction type" of the Irish as "prompt but intermittent," Woolston pointed to their fondness for handball and other sports requiring speed and dexterity and their corresponding aversion to lectures and other activities requiring self-restraint (1909:55).

The origin of modern handball was in Ireland, where it had been played for centuries. Manhattanville boasted electrically lit handball courts at 131st Street and Amsterdam Avenue, just blocks away from the Speyer School, and supported a handball club that competed with like clubs in Brooklyn, Jersey City, and elsewhere. "The best handball players in the world," the *New York Herald* noted, "are Irishmen. It requires an Irishman's dash and vivacity and strength to follow the wild flights of the ball" (April 14, 1895:4). Here, as elsewhere, Woolston's appraisal of ethnic-cum-racial temperaments tracked depictions of these social groups in the press and in popular culture and often superseded his empirical facts. Du Bois criticized the contempt showed by Spencerian-influenced sociologists like Giddings for facts (i.e., descriptive sociology) and their "teleological purpose," observing, "Their data were imperfect—woefully imperfect: depending on hearsay, rumor and tradition, vague speculations, traveler's tales, legends and imperfect documents, the memory of memories and historical error" (2000:39).

Woolston pointed out that the traits of the Irish predisposed them to certain political loyalties and behaviors—that is, their "clannish" tendencies, fondness for personal bonds, and choleric nature inclined them to support the political style and tactics of the Democratic Party and its Tammany Hall political machine. This observation suggests the degree to which the wider societal context or scientific field influenced academic research and theory building. The notion—and anxiety—that Irish immigrants and other groups constituting the "submerged tenth" were unprepared to assume the responsibilities of democratic citizenship was shared by many Progressive Era reformers and academics. This view echoed contemporaneous ideas of the incapacity of Black freedmen to self-govern, associated with the work of, among others, Columbia historian and political scientist William A. Dunning and other members of his School of Reconstruction at Columbia (Stromquist 2006; Morris 2015).

Having addressed the other "naturalized sub races"—that is, immigrants and their immediate descendants—Woolston turned to native-born whites. Conceding that the category was difficult to define, he characterized it nevertheless:

He is traditionally prompt and persistent in his activities; serious and practical in his thoughts; with strong revulsions of emotion. He is ambitious, ingenious and adaptive. . . . Though not noted for the subtler qualities, the "American" is shrewd in reasoning and firm in his belief. He is above all a moneymaker and an organizer. Freedom is the breath of his nostrils, but opinion forms the atmosphere in which he lives. (1909:77)

In short, the native-born white American was the model capitalist, worker, and citizen, equipped with the intellectual, emotional, and organizational capacities needed to advance industrial society and Western civilization, and preserve the social order. This was the same subject interpellated through the normative frame of the federal census and sanitary surveys of public health officials, which similarly contrasted deviancy with the statistical norm.

Woolston left for last "another native race": Manhattanville's population of 1,300 African Americans. Again, Woolston appealed to the reader's "familiar" knowledge, fashioning a racial profile that was the inverse of the industrious, disciplined, and even-tempered native-born white American and congruent with the caricatures of the rural "Sambo" and "urban coon." "They are as a whole, slow and intermittent in their activities, impulsive and imitative in reaction. Their lives are steeped in emotion, which colors all their intellectual processes. Consequently, an ordinary negro's judgment is apt to be less clear and objective than a white man's. The African is proverbially credulous and easy-going. He has strong appetites and rather poor control over them. . . . Such a temperament and character might be classed as a primitive variety of the sanguine and convivial natures" (1909:90).

Unlike the naturalized sub-races, African Americans could not be naturalized (due to their very *natures*) but instead required constraint and, as Giddings put it, the "support of the stronger races" (1896:329). As Turner has pointed out, the studies produced by Giddings's students tended to be descriptive but shared his theoretical language and classificatory schema (1991). In his characterization of the "Negro type," Woolston reiterated the racist tropes and stereotypes prevalent in the academy and "blackface" performances and coon songs of the minstrel stage. Curiously, in a footnote to his section on the Negroes, Woolston referred the reader to Du Bois's *The Souls of Black Folks* (1903), along with Frederick Hoffman's racist text *Race Traits of the American Negro*, but there is little reason to believe that the former had any influence on his appraisal of the race traits of the American Negro.

Woolston's more descriptive account of Manhattanville's Black population recognized educational, occupational, and class differences within Black communities that, logically, contradicted his portrayal of the Negro type. For example, Woolston contrasted the African Americans living on West 130th and 131st Street (blocks enumerated by Alexander Lockwood in 1900) to those on Lawrence and 126th Streets in the vicinity of the Speyer School. Whereas the former lived in poorly maintained tenements and were largely employed in unskilled occupations, those living on Lawrence and 126th Streets were better housed and included persons engaged in commerce, the professions, and small businesses. The Speyer School and Settlement, where Woolston and his wife were employed, was located in the heart of this small and relatively prosperous area of Black settlement, referred to in some press accounts as "Little Africa," along Lawrence and West 126th Streets (*New York Times* 1902:2).

On Lawrence Street, African Americans were initially concentrated in three adjacent tenements (numbers 6, 8, and 10) that had been constructed in the 1870s, if not before.[2] Like those in the settlement on 130th and 131st Streets to the west, the majority of Black residents on Lawrence and West 126th Streets had been born in the upper South, primarily Virginia, and lived in almost exclusively Black buildings. However, unlike those to the west, the Black people living on Lawrence Street were employed in a range of skilled and semiskilled occupations.

In 1891, Black settlement on Lawrence Street had been given a boost when white realtor William Malone constructed two apartment buildings, the Garrison and the Sumner, at 21 and 23 Lawrence Street, respectively, for African American tenants. "Every apartment," Malone's February 21 ad in the *New York Age* boasted, "has got [a gas] Range, Stationary Tubs and Pier Glass Mirror." The *New York Age* praised Malone for "having been among the first to place desirable tenements at the disposal of Afro-Americans," and quoted the builder as explaining, "I suffered a good deal when I built the first house I owned in this city and put colored people in it. It was not as pretentious as the Garrison or Sumner, but it was the first in this city, and I can assure you that I take much pride in having done so."

Malone's tenements were advertised as suitable for "first class families," and the 1900 census confirms the relative prosperity of their Black occupants. For example, 21 Lawrence Street housed ten comparatively small households (five persons being the largest), eight of which consisted only of couples with children. None of the eight married women enumerated were working outside the home—at least, in regular wage labor—and their spouses were employed in semiskilled occupations as waiters, express men, porters, and bicycle repairmen. Most notably, none of the households had taken in boarders. Emma Wharton, a thirty-five-year-old laundress and native New Yorker, lived alone in a three-room apartment—rare, indeed, in the working-class districts. Woolston's description of the area emphasized elements congruent with the "Negro temperament":

> It has its own saloon, restaurant and pool room. There are more servants and persons engaged in commercial lines in this section. Formerly a few professional people (clergyman and teachers) lived in this settlement, but now they have moved on to better quarters. A group of men may be seen at almost any time in front of the saloon. The irregular nature of their employment may account for the leisure of some, who are draymen, waiters, barbers, etc. (1909:90–91)

What Woolston missed is that across the street, 7 Lawrence Street housed the offices of the Manhattan Colored Republican Club, incorporated in June 1900 near the completion of the census (*New York Times* 1900a). All seven of the club's directors lived in the Lawrence Street district. In 1890 the community had also organized a chapter of the Afro-American League, a civil rights and self-help organization that was cofounded by T. Thomas Fortune, the influential editor of the *New York Age*. The political life of "Little Africa" escaped Woolston's gaze even though such associational behavior was the bread and butter of Giddings's theory. In his characterization of the "Negro temperament," men hanging out in front of a saloon were more significant to Woolston's theory building than Black associational life.

This incongruence between Woolston's empirical observations and his application of Giddings's speculative system of classification—a tension or "fatal antithesis" that Albion Small criticized in Giddings's work (1896:296)—highlights the fact that the nativist and racist applications of Giddings's thought found authority and legitimacy, as well as practical application, well beyond the university and among social reformers, public officials, philanthropists, and a growing urban middle class. As Bourdieu has argued, "Epistemological conflicts are always, inseparably, political conflicts" (1975:21). Woolston's appeal to innate racial and ethnic types, despite his evidence to the contrary, enjoyed authority and legitimacy within the wider Progressive Era community and among economic and political elites, representing what Bourdieu termed a "foreclosing strategy"—that is, a strategy "intended to mark a decisive separation between the scientific problematic and profane, public debates (still present, but only as 'ghosts in the machine')" (1975:39).

One of the clearest statements of this foreclosing strategy is to be found in the introduction to Thomas J. Jones's study *The Sociology of a New York City Block*, where Jones expressed dissatisfaction with previous sociological research that employed the social survey method but failed to "give unity to the whole." By contrast, Jones wrote of his own "distinctly sociological" approach:

> It is an attempt to study a New York City street according to a complete system of social principles. *Even if the system were proved to be arbitrary,* the work would be more valuable, the writer believes, than an unsystematic attempt, however long continued, for the reason that the investigator has a basis for search and an order for arranging in his mind the innumerable impressions made by the unit considered. Without a system the study of a people is but a wild goose chase, and this, indeed, is the nature of too many of the so-called sociological investigations now carried on. (1904:8; emphasis added)

Jones's assertion that an arbitrary system is better than descriptive sociology is dubious at best, especially if that system is based on a priori racist and nativist dogmas, rather than on a critical analysis of the messier "mass of facts." An analysis of those facts, for Jones and for Woolston, would have led unavoidably to questions of sociopolitical and economic inequality and change that were well beyond the pale for Giddings and his students, as well as for most Progressive Era reformers and philanthropists (D. Ross 1991; cf. Du Bois 1899).

For despite the contextual autonomy claimed for Jones's "system of social principles" (and Giddings's "consciousness of kind"), the latter, rooted in the power-laden nativist and racist doctrines, were both informed by and, in turn, informed Progressive Era strategies of limited ameliorative reform aimed at rendering the status quo palatable to those very social groups that it excluded and reduced to poverty. The Speyer School and Settlement provides a useful case study demonstrating how these constructions of ethnic and racial types and their social evolutionist underpinnings informed strategies for "social education" and the fashioning of docile citizens resigned to the status quo.

Making Productive and Docile Citizens: The Speyer School and Settlement

Every year thousands of people from foreign countries, with very different standards of life and divergent conceptions of personal and public responsibility, are brought to our shores. In the South, over eight millions of people of a different race and a lower stage of civilization are settled in our midst. Not only is the body politic invaded by alien elements; within our own society we see a growing differentiation of social status.
—Howard Woolston

First opened in 1903, the Speyer School was designed to be an experimental school, or "laboratory school," providing students at Columbia University's Teachers College with practice teaching opportunities and serving as a laboratory for researching and testing new methods in public education. The school was intended to complement the college's Horace Mann School, a tuition-funded "demonstration school," where students observed best teaching and school management practices. When James Earl Russell became dean of Teachers College in 1898, he worked to both expand the Horace Mann School and differentiate its function as a private alternative to the public schools from the college's need to provide practice student teaching experience and promote research and experimentation in a public school setting (Toepfer 1966).

In the late nineteenth century, differentiated education—that is, the system that treated the children of poor and working-class immigrants and racial minorities differently from "mainstream" children in common schools—was gaining support, particularly among wealthy philanthropists and industrialists. The influx of non-Anglo-Saxon immigrants and African American migrants to rapidly growing urban industrial cities, coupled with the passage of child labor laws and compulsory school attendance, dramatically increased public school enrollments and stoked concerns that the traditional, uniform curriculum would not prepare students from these groups for subordinate roles in the economy as disciplined workers (Tyack 1974). Many, if not most, progressive educators believed that Black people and immigrants from Eastern and Southern Europe were mentally inferior and lacked the capacity to pursue an academic track and perform non-manual labor (Johnson 2000). Without vocational training and discipline, many argued, the children of these groups faced unemployment and pauperism, and, worse, posed a threat to the stability of the social order. Moreover, teaching vocational skills to students who were headed for unskilled and semiskilled jobs would increase their efficiency and discipline as future workers and lower training and management costs to their employers.

Frederick Bonser, a Teachers College professor and advocate of vocational or differentiated education, identified four biopolitical goals for the education of future workers in the public schools: "(1) the preservation of health, (2) the development of practical efficiency, (3) preparation for responsible and effective citizenship, and (4) training in the wise use of leisure" (1916:65). As director of the Speyer School, Bonser played a key role in developing its curriculum. He argued that public schools should play an aggressive role in "sifting" or tracking students for vocational training by the seventh grade.

A leading proponent of differentiated or specialized education was Teachers College graduate Ellwood P. Cubberley, who argued that schools should be adapted to the existing class structure and division of labor:

Our schools are, in a sense, factories in which the raw materials (children) are to be shaped and fashioned into products to meet the various demands of life. The specifications for manufacturing come from the demands of the twentieth century civilization, and it is the business of the school to build its pupils to the specifications laid down. (1916:337–38)

The Speyer School began as a joint venture with St. Mary's Episcopal Church in Manhattanville when its rector, the Reverend H. R. Hulse, invited Teachers College to take over its kindergarten class. Russell agreed, and the college rented a house on Lawrence Street within ten minutes' walking distance from the college to accommodate both a kindergarten and first grade class. The school began operation in fall 1899 and, in addition to its kindergarten and elementary school curriculum, established extension classes in the industrial and domestic arts for adults. Moreover, in keeping with the founders' vision of the public schools also serving as community or "social centers," a free library was created and the school's teaching staff made efforts to cultivate relationships with parents through school meetings and home visits.

This effort to engage the community at large though adult extension classes, lectures, and home visits was a controlling idea of the Speyer School as it expanded. It presupposed, as had Grace Dodge and the founders of the Kitchen Garden Association two decades earlier, that the conditions of poverty facing Manhattanville's children and their largely immigrant, working-class parents were the result of their inability to properly socialize their children and organize the household.

The Speyer School, Teachers College professor F. M. McMurry wrote,

should study the home environment and habits of the child with reference to the mechanical surroundings of the home. It should instruct the parents so that the home may provide, so far as it can, for the proper clothing, for proper food, shelter, eating, drinking, sleeping, bathing, care of the teeth, and for medical attention which the child needs, even when those conditions which demand attention are first discovered in the school. (1902:33)

This approach was consistent with the view that poverty and pauperism were the result of personal failings and the ameliorist position, shared by many Progressive Era reformers and social scientists, that social problems were best solved through the reform of individuals rather than significant societal changes.

Appraising the school's first year of operation, its acting principal, Jesse Burks, characterized its working-class and immigrant student body. Burks's comments highlight the degree to which the condition of immigrant and racially marked students and their parents was understood, a priori, to be the result of a defect in character:

> The pupils at the beginning were not all of a promising character. . . . Some were sickly; some feeble-minded; some were backward children from public schools. There were many applications for the admission of defective children whose proper place was in special institutions. Some children of a stronger type would have entered the school, but for the objection of their parents to the half-day session which was the arrangement of the first year. (1903:8)

Burks's assessment mimicked the medicalized nativism of the sanitary reformers and the racial and ethnic stereotypes and tropes cataloged by Woolston and other students of Giddings. Moreover, these dividing practices, both discursive and institutional, reiterated the class-cum-racial distinctions, inscribed in space, that characterized the relationship between the elite institutions and residents of Morningside Heights and surrounding poor and working-class communities, and provided the rationale for the Speyer School's pedagogic stress on training in the industrial and domestic arts (preparation for semiskilled and unskilled occupations that the students would one day occupy), as well as on hygiene, health education, and corporeal discipline.

As a tuition-free school, Speyer was fully supported by Teachers College, but despite the trustees' enthusiasm for the experiment in principle, it suffered from financial and administrative problems during its first two years of operation. Burks, for example, wrote that the school building was only "meagerly furnished with odds and ends no longer useful at the Horace Mann School" (1902:8). Moreover, in its first year of operation, only eight students from Teachers College used it for practice teaching, and four of these were attached to the domestic arts department (Toepfer 1966). In making the case to the trustees for additional funding, Russell stressed the need to encourage neighborhood children to develop occupational interests in the industrial and domestic arts, observing that, with sufficient funding, the school could develop into a college-sponsored settlement school, where the relationship between public education and social services could be examined.

In an essay on industrial training in American education, Russell praised the practical training programs at Tuskegee and Hampton Universities for "equipping the southern negro to earn a livelihood under adverse social conditions" and lamented the fact that white students in the public schools received training of the "head" but little of the "hand" (1905:61). Although Russell acknowledged that, as a social democracy, America designed its schools to provide equal opportunity to all, he maintained, echoing Giddings's view, that such a uniform educational system risked inciting social unrest and, more to the point, class conflict:

> How can a nation endure that deliberately seeks to rouse ambitions and aspirations in the on-coming generations, which in the nature of events cannot possibly be fulfilled? If the chief object of government be to promote civil order and social stability, how can we justify our practice in schooling the masses in precisely the same manner as we do those who are to be our leaders? . . . Is it any wonder that we are beset with labor troubles, or that the socialistic vote in the recent presidential election should make statesmen fear for the consequences? (1905:64)

The experimental school's financial problems were resolved for a time when James Speyer, a prominent Jewish banker and philanthropist, and his wife agreed to donate $100,000 for the erection of a new school building, and $12,000 annually for its support for a period of at least five years. Speyer, a Teachers College trustee and treasurer of the University Settlement Society, made the donation on the condition that the experimental school hire two trained settlement workers, nominated by the University Settlement Society, to ensure that the school was useful to the community beyond the classroom instruction of children. As Russell observed, "School work designed for children is really only a small part of it. Whatever tends to elevate the people of a community, to inspire them with higher ideals, to help them to better living, is educational.

Surely the public school falls far short of what it might do for the public welfare" (Russell 1902:4).

Education had been a key component of the settlement movement's strategy of assisting the poor and enlightening the general public. Settlements typically held classes in literacy, childcare, household management, and vocational education, and some settlements sponsored clinics, playgrounds, and social clubs. Jane Addams, the social worker, suffragist leader, and cofounder of Chicago's Hull House in 1889, was appointed to the Chicago School Board in 1905, where she advocated incorporating the educational and social service programs found in the settlement houses into the public school system (Luetkemeyer 1985). Addams's innovative work at Hull House and her social philosophy had a substantial impact on progressive school reformers.

On April 23, 1903, the new building housing the experimental school, now called the Speyer School and Settlement, opened at 94 Lawrence Street (West 126th Street), across the street from St. Mary's Episcopal Church. The school building included classrooms for 290 students in kindergarten through the eighth grade, a library, a gymnasium and shower baths, and rooms for cooking, sewing, and manual arts training open to both Speyer students and the general public. In addition, the school building included apartments for the settlement staff.

In addition to classroom teaching in the day school, the Speyer School held after-school extension classes in the domestic arts (e.g., sewing and decorative arts), domestic science (e.g., cooking, hygiene, and thriftiness), and the manual arts, such as carpentry, that were open to both Speyer and public school students in the neighborhood. Moreover, the school's staff made the building and its facilities, such as the gymnasium, available for use by boys and girls clubs, and parents' groups not always connected to the day school. For example, a group of twenty German immigrant women organized a reading club to discuss German-language materials. A Mothers' Club, composed of about sixty women, many the mothers of Speyer students, held bimonthly meetings to discuss child health, school policy, and other issues, and to host lectures and sponsor evening social events and entertainments (Kent 1904).

A central, though not always successful, goal of the school's settlement work was to establish relationships with neighborhood parents through school meetings and home visits. The home visits were intended both to

THE SPEYER SCHOOL, LAWRENCE STREET, NEW YORK, N. Y.
Edgar A. Josselyn, Architect.

Photograph of the Speyer School, 1906. From the architectural periodical *The American Architect*.

identify potential problems in the home (e.g., poor hygiene, food handling, and "excessive coffee drinking") that needed to be addressed in
the curriculum, and to assess the degree to which Speyer students were
applying lessons learned in the classroom to the home.

The work of the mature Speyer School had been influenced by philosopher John Dewey's Laboratory School, which he created at the University
of Chicago in 1896. Charles Richards, the director of the Department of
Manual Training at Teachers College, and Frederick Bonser, who directed
the Speyer School after 1910, were both leading interpreters of Dewey's
work, and central figures in developing the school's curriculum published
in 1913 (Luetkemeyer 1985). Union Settlement, founded on 104th Street in
East Harlem in 1895 by alumni of the Union Theological Seminary (prior
to its affiliation with Columbia University), may have also influenced the
manner in which settlement activities were developed at Speyer.

Dewey was troubled by the growing social divisions in American society resulting from laissez-faire industrial capitalism, specifically, the
incompatibility of democratic ethics with entrenched class inequalities,
which he believed prevented the working classes from achieving self-
realization through their labor (Westbrook 1992). Appointed to chair
the University of Chicago's philosophy department and direct a new department of pedagogy, Dewey grappled with the problem of creating a
pedagogy that promoted social reforms and advanced the cause of industrial democracy. In Chicago, Dewey encountered a second influence
that shaped both his philosophy and the work of the Laboratory School.

Dewey, like many Progressive Era reformers, had been influenced by
the settlement work and writings of Jane Addams. Charlene Seigfried
has noted that Dewey's pragmatist philosophy was shaped by his involvement in two communities: that of Addams's Hull House Settlement
and his Laboratory School (1999). Upon his arrival at Chicago, Dewey
became a regular visitor to Hull House, founded in 1889 by Addams and
Ella Flagg Young, and he developed a close, personal friendship with the
former. Dewey also served on the first board of trustees at Hull House,
where he occasionally lectured on social psychology.

Addams shared Dewey's pragmatist view that economic exploitation and powerful special interests subverted democracy and that the
dominant, liberal model of democracy was deeply flawed insofar as it
presupposed the self-interested and autonomous individual as the sub-

ject of rights (Seigfried 1999). And in contrast to many Progressive Era reformers and commentators, Addams identified capitalist relations of production—the antagonism between labor and capital—and their top-down structures of decision making as the central threats to democracy.

Dewey and his colleagues at the Laboratory School developed a curriculum that centered on the study of the "social occupations" (sewing, shop work, cooking, and so on) that corresponded to the activities and occupations that children encountered beyond the classroom. Influenced by the German philosopher Friedrich Froebel, Dewey held that learning through the social occupations provided children with concrete incentives to study reading, writing, mathematics, and other subjects in the traditional curriculum (Durst 2010).

In *The School and Society* Dewey wrote,

> The fundamental point in the psychology of an occupation is that it maintains a balance between the intellectual and practical phases of experience. As an occupation it is active or motor; it finds expression through the physical organs—the eyes, hands, etc. But it also involves continual observation of materials, and continual planning and reflection, in order that the practical or executive side may be successfully carried on. (2010:133)

For Dewey, occupational training was not an end in itself—that is, education primarily for a trade—but rather a means to encourage "growth that comes from the continual interplay of ideas and their embodiment in action, not in external utility" (2010:133). Although the Speyer School adopted Dewey's pedagogic emphasis on the social occupations, it redirected their instruction to a very different purpose—the preparation of Manhattanville's largely poor and working-class students for low-skilled and semiskilled jobs as housekeepers, teamsters, janitors, and policemen (Lagemann 2000). Whereas Dewey's focus on the social occupations was primarily a means to teach students—many the children of University of Chicago faculty—lessons in cooperation and participatory democracy and to enhance the teaching of academic subjects, the Speyer School focused on vocational training, coupled with a program of education in health and hygiene, civics, and physical fitness that was intended to produce docile bodies well adapted to their future roles at the bottom rungs of the social hierarchy and division of labor. As F. M. McMurry, the Speyer's supervisor of instruction, put it, "Since a school is a miniature community preparing for life in the larger community called society, the aims of a school should correspond with those of society" (1902:35).

This was a far cry from Dewey's vision, however circumscribed, of the Laboratory School as both an experimental school *and* aspirational model for an industrial democracy that did not yet exist but would have to be created through fundamental societal reforms. As Ellen Santora noted, the implementation of Dewey's vision by many of his contemporaries like Bonser and McMurry was "unsystematically fragmented and often hybridized with traditional school and classroom structures" (1999:4). Progressive rhetoric was often no more than a smoke screen to give traditional, scientifically guided schooling a humane face. In the case of the Speyer School, the problem of industrial democracy, central to the philosophy and work of Addams and Dewey, was subordinated to a pedagogy that aimed to shore up and deconflict social and economic inequalities. For example, in stark contrast to the Speyer School's gender-segregated classes, the Laboratory School's domestic and manual arts workshops were coeducational: both boys and girls, for example, learned cooking, sewing, and woodworking (Menand 2001).

In an article reviewing the experimental work being done in elementary schools, McMurry minimized the value of Dewey's philosophy in favor of educational innovations guided by "scientific" methods:

> Types of the best discussions of educational themes in the last ten years are Dr. John Dewey's *Interest as Related to Will* and his *Ethical Principles Underlying Education*. But each of these is a more philosophic than a scientific treatment; each is largely an *ex cathedra* statement, a proclamation of the truth, which readers accept, reject, or lay on the table—as though they might decide what is true by voting. (McMurry 1904:2)

Unsurprisingly, the Speyer School placed considerable emphasis on instruction in health, personal hygiene, and physical fitness and maintained that, beyond being screened for infectious and parasitic diseases as was required by the public schools, Speyer pupils should receive a "careful biologic examination," using the methods of anthropometry, medical examination, and sensory and motor skills testing. McMurry explained, "A complete motor education is one of the most necessary factors in the training of the child. It is important that he be trained in as many different forms of activity as possible, for this tends to give him self-control, an improved will power, and at least certain kinds of courage." McMurry argued that as children grew older, "there should be structured physical exercises given to command, so that the child may learn obedience and quick response" (1902:58–59). This had little to do with the training of the "head" and everything to do with preparing children for manual and domestic work and the varied forms of discipline and obedience that they required. One is reminded of the "motor reaction types" defined by Giddings and described by Woolston among Manhattanville's diverse population.

Michel Foucault's account of disciplinary power sheds light on the Speyer School's pedagogic philosophy and practice and, more generally, Progressive Era reformist strategies aimed at removing the rough edges of social inequalities and improving the governability of laissez-faire capitalism. As Foucault put it,

> Discipline increases the forces of the body (in economic terms of utility) and diminishes these same forces (in political terms of obedience). In short, it disassociates power from the body; on the one hand, it turns it into an "aptitude," a "capacity," which it seeks to increase; on the other hand, it reverses the course of the energy, the power that might result from it, and turns it into a relation of strict subjection. If economic exploitation separates the force and the product of labour, let us say that disciplinary coercion establishes in the body the constricting link between an increased aptitude and an increased domination. (1995:138)

Perhaps nowhere was the Speyer School's biopolitical mission of producing docile workers and citizens more apparent than in its 1904 staging of "Speyer City," an ongoing activity that was celebrated in the city's newspapers. The staff divided the school's building and grounds into five wards, each governed by one of the youth clubs. Each club selected a political party from among Republican, Socialist Labor, Tammany, Prohibitionist, and Populist Parties. Basing the municipality on the New York City charter, the school's staff organized elections for mayor, controller, board of aldermen, chief of police, and so on, and convened a police court and court of appeals to prosecute young offenders. In its first case, the police court sentenced two children (one identified in newspaper accounts as "a negro") to fifteen-cent fines for damaging a gym door (*New York Times* 1904).

The voting franchise in Speyer City was restricted to male citizens over the age of ten who, according to the *New York Times*, had not been apprehended "in the act of using profane language or expectorating from windows above the first floor." As chance would have it, the mayoral race was won by the Republican candidate, Edward Lockwood, the fifteen-year-old son of 1900 census enumerator Alexander Lockwood.

However, these restrictions on the voting franchise did not go uncontested. "So far no serious breach of the peace has occurred," the *New York Times* reported, "and no act of great political folly committed. Repeated attempts on the part of the girls' clubs of the Speyer School to gain the coveted franchise have been met with decisive refusals on the part of the male citizenship, and no relief in the immediate future seems probable" (February 8, 1904:7).

In this theater of the status quo, students were encouraged to identify with the elected officials, prosecutors, and police who governed their lives and enforced their compliance. And young girls—despite their protests—were given a mini-lesson in patriarchal political power. The Speyer School was a demonstration school that demonstrated obedience to its students and sought to inculcate them—and by extension, their parents—with the attitudes, values, and mores of responsible citizens, attitudes viewed to be wanting, if not absent, among poor and working-class immigrants and African Americans.

Although the Speyer School and Settlement attracted considerable attention and enjoyed qualified success in developing and testing new teaching methods and curricula, it suffered from a persistent lack of funding that affected its settlement work in particular. The school's extension classes and neighborhood work, key to its mission, received only limited support from the University Settlement Society, which made these activities dependent, in the absence of funding from the college, upon the transient and unpredictable efforts of volunteers from the community and student body of Teachers College (Toepfer 1966). However, these difficulties were not only financial. In a sober appraisal of the school's relationship to the community, Ernest Kent, an elementary education assistant, lamented the teaching staff's lack of "local knowledge" of neighborhood conditions, which both hindered the matching of classroom work to community needs—critical to social education—and led to the failure to get adequate support from school parents. "It is the exceptional teacher," Kent observed, "who has the knowledge of the interests, ideals and problems of the locality, gained from actual participation in neighborhood life" (1904:45). Though Kent attributed this lack of local knowledge to the onerous demands placed on the teaching staff and the distance that teachers lived from the school, his analysis suggested a more foundational problem.

The lack of local knowledge meant that Speyer School staff and volunteers knew little or nothing about the complex and conflictual social reality on the streets of Manhattanville and Harlem in the opening decades of the twentieth century. The strains of poverty and marginalization were protested in the form of widespread consumer activism and labor unrest. For example, in May 1904, eighty families living in four tenements on East 100th Street organized the Tenants Protective Association of Harlem and went on a rent strike to protest rent increases. Amid a tight housing market, the landlord of the adjacent buildings had increased rents from eight or nine dollars to as high as fifteen dollars; tenants unwilling or unable to pay the increases were evicted. "The women by day and the men by night," the New York Times reported, "are picketing the houses and, mounting guards on the stoops, are warning away possible renters. The situation became so acute yesterday that the police of the East One Hundred and Fourth Street Station were called on to preserve order" (May 17, 1904:1). Such rent uprisings, often inspired by similar protests on the Lower East Side, continued throughout the decade and received support from the organizers and lawyers of the Socialist Party's Anti-Rent Agitation Bureau (Day 1999).

Women also played leading roles in the "meat strikes" that swept Manhattan in the early twentieth century. In May 1902, the Women's Branch No. 2 of the Workmen's Circle (Der Arbeter Ring)—a Jewish mutual aid, educational, and pro-labor organization—joined their sisters on the Lower East Side and launched a campaign to reduce meat prices through a boycott of Harlem kosher meat markets. In the following month, the women of Branch No. 2 opened an ad hoc cooperative butcher shop in Harlem, offering a low-priced alternative to the high-priced kosher butchers. They were joined by gentile women, who extended the ongoing strike to non-kosher butchers (Gurock 2016). Women picketed and disrupted butcher shops to force their closing and, in cases, sprayed kerosene on the meat purchased by persons who crossed the picket line. The *New York Times* captured these women's militancy during a later meat strike that led to the arrests of eleven women:

> Housewives on the east side, just below the Harlem line, were not so gentle in their demonstrations against the kosher butchers as were their Harlem sisters. Under the leadership of a woman about 6 feet in height, determined in manner and speech, and clad in a dark dress with a red cap [a Socialist symbol], about 300 women residents of the blocks on Seventy-fourth and Seventy-fifth streets, between Avenue A and First Avenue, visited several shops in their neighborhood and forced the proprietors to close up. (April 10, 1910:1)

This same period also witnessed widespread labor actions and strikes that mobilized workers in Manhattanville, Harlem, and elsewhere. In July 1907, garbage collectors employed by the city's Street Cleaning Department went on strike, raising fears among physicians and public health authorities that the "evil odors" and filth resulting from the uncollected garbage led to epidemics of typhoid, typhus (or "prison fever"), and other infectious diseases. One physician, echoing both the still widely held miasmatic theory of disease and nativist anxieties, warned,

> Streets filthy with decaying matter in hot weather form just the condition that prison fever needs in which to flourish. Why, I shouldn't be surprised if Asiatic cholera and bubonic plague should follow, for there are many foreigners in the crowded districts, where the garbage situation is at its worst. There will be plenty of stomach troubles, and it is certain the death rate will increase mightily unless the streets are cleaned at once. (*New York Tribune*, July 1, 1907:1)

That same year, West Harlem and other sections of the city that still relied on gaslights were thrown into obscurity when members of the Lamplighters Union went on strike for higher wages against the privately owned gas companies. "There were perhaps 25,000 lights out in

West Harlem at 8 o'clock," the *New York Times* reported. "It was dark in the streets between Amsterdam Avenue and the Hudson River, from 130th to 100th Street, except for the incidental lighting that came from stores and flat windows. The blackness was most pronounced in the side streets. Morningside Avenue was fit for lovers and unfit for policemen" (April 15, 1907).

These varied forms of resistance to laissez-faire industrial capitalism, as well to patriarchal gender norms, did not find expression in the Speyer program of social education and community outreach. Although Howard Woolston served as resident director of night classes and neighborhood work at Speyer from 1904 to 1906, his research provided few, if any, insights into the culturally diverse households, ethnic foodways, and economic livelihoods of Manhattanville's residents. In Giddings's evolutionary positivist sociology, these socioeconomic and cultural deviations from supposed white middle-class norms were defects to be policed or corrected.

Kent noted the problems encountered by school staff members when, during home visits, they tried to encourage mothers to allow their daughters in Speyer's sixth grade cookery class to prepare dishes that they had learned in school.

> About half of the mothers were visited [by staff] during school hours, and all were glad to discuss the subject. It appeared that one girl—and only one—had reproduced nearly every dish at home. Most of the others had made no pretension of doing it regularly. All the mothers agreed that it would be a good thing to encourage the home application, several suggesting of their own accord the great difference between cooking one dish and preparing a meal, and the one-sidedness of experience derived only in the former way. . . . In most cases the real obstacle to such home work by the girls seemed to be the fact that it was more "bother" than doing it oneself, and this the mothers readily admitted was not a valid one. A further difficulty, however, was the small number of meals, which could be conveniently turned over to the children. (1904:49)

To imagine that poor and working-class households had the luxury of permitting sixth graders to make practice dishes at home or, for that matter, were unable to teach cooking themselves, suggests a disregard for the lives and conditions of poor and working-class people. More-over, neither the Speyer School's curriculum nor its neighborhood work engaged, acknowledged, or provided venues for addressing the pressing workplace, consumer, housing, and other issues that were of concern to poor and working-class people.

Nor was the experimental side of the Speyer School's work more suc-cessful. As Ellen Lagemann pointed out, although many Teachers Col-lege faculty members were engaged in research, few were interested in school-based experimentation in the lower grades and among poor and working-class students (2000). Finally, the Speyer School building was too small to accommodate the practice teaching needs of the growing number of Teachers College students.

In 1913 Dean Russell began discussions with the New York City Board of Education to explore the possibility of using the public schools for practice teaching and experimentation. After consulting with his fac-ulty, several of whom favored closing the Speyer School, Russell recom-mended to the trustees that the experimental school be discontinued (Toepfer 1966). As per Russell's agreement with the Board of Education, the school building was taken over by the city in 1915 as an annex to Manhattanville's Public School 43 for the purpose of pursuing collab-orative experiments agreed upon by Teachers College and the city. Four years later, Teachers College severed all connection to the school and leased the building to the Board of Education (Cremin et al. 1954).

This did not signal the end to Teachers College's involvement in ex-perimental education. In 1916 Teachers College began negotiations with the General Education Board (GEB), a philanthropy funded by John D. Rockefeller to support higher education, modernize agriculture, and promote rural education among Black people in the South. Inspired by the proposal of its executive secretary, Abraham Flexner, to modernize education and create a laboratory school, the GEB agreed to provide Teachers College with partial funding for a new, tuition-based school. The school, called the Lincoln School of Teachers College, opened in 1917 on the Upper East Side of Manhattan. "The tuition fees necessary to operate such a school," Cremin et al. noted, "all but precluded stu-dents from other than fairly well-to-do families, and the mores of such families dictated that their children should go on to college" (1954:111). The Lincoln School quickly became a training ground for the city's elite, and one of the most closely watched experimental schools in the nation. Four of John. D. Rockefeller Jr.'s children attended the school.

Though short-lived, the Speyer School and Settlement was a critical nexus of power/knowledge between Columbia University, the Progressive movement, and Manhattanville's poor and working-class population, a significant proportion of which consisted of recent immigrants and members of racialized groups. The Speyer School stressed training in the domestic and industrial arts, civic virtues, and bodily discipline, preparing students for roles as responsible citizens and laborers in an industrial economy and social order that were perceived to be threatened by class conflict and by increasing demands for greater ethnic, gender, and racial equality. This short-lived experiment influenced public education in the city and beyond, reiterating, along with the work of Columbia sociologists, the inherited inferiority of immigrants and racialized populations. As Giddings preached, social and economic inequality were inevitable and, indeed, necessary.

The case of the Speyer School and Settlement also demonstrates the complex way the development of sociology and allied disciplines were influenced by the wider scientific field. Disciplinary discourses were also sociopolitical practices lending legitimacy and scientific authority to Progressive Era strategies that addressed the labor question and increasingly diverse industrial cities. Giddings's sociological theories, applied by many of his students, were not only speculative, as Du Bois and Albion Small argued, but they also systematized the prevailing nativist, racist, and eugenicist ideologies and practices of the period.

Finally, the work of Howard Woolston exemplifies the way in which the application of other investigative technologies influenced strategies of reform. Together, these sharpened the boundary, both symbolic and spatial, between the institutions and community of Morningside Heights and Manhattanville and Harlem to the north and east. Racial and class segregation were driven by racism and the logic of capitalist development and other factors that limited the mobility of working-class populations. Giddings's sociology, along with other investigative technologies of the period, conflated the allegedly innate dispositions of immigrants and racialized people with the places and conditions in which they lived, lending enduring, yet spurious, scientific authority to hierarchies of race and class materialized in the landscape.

4

Spatial Politics and the Policing of the Color Line

I am overdetermined from without. . . .
"Look, a Negro!"
—Frantz Fanon

On December 20, 1910, white tenants living at 239 West 135th Street in Harlem waved brooms from their windows when a prospective Black tenant parked his moving van in front of the building. The four-story tenement, previously managed by a Black real estate agent, had been purchased by the Property Owners' Protective Association of Harlem, one of a number of white neighborhood associations that had been formed to reverse the "Negro invasion" of Harlem's white areas. John G. Taylor, the association's president and a retired policeman, explained the broom waving symbolism to a reporter: "A clean sweep of negroes from the white resident districts of Harlem." A policeman who had been posted in front of the apartment building refused to allow the Black man to unload his belongings from the van. The only African American tenant, the *Baltimore Sun* reported, "promised to vacate before the end of the week and, this done, the entire block will be free from negro residents" (*Baltimore Sun* 1910a). Taylor had moved to West 136th Street from 152 Waverly Place in Greenwich Village in 1903, where he and his wife, Agnes, had operated a rooming house in a leased four-story brick building (US Census Bureau 1900b:2). For the Taylors and other white people, the move to Harlem had been a step upward into a more affluent and higher-status community, and one that promised to remain exclusively white.

In 1910 Taylor had begun raising funds for a campaign to prevent African Americans living on the east side of Lenox Avenue—so-called "Little Africa"—from encroaching upon his solidly white and middle-class block, and to purchase properties at risk of being sold or rented to Black people. Taylor advocated for segregating the Ninth Avenue elevated railroad, barring Black people from the local public library, and building a twenty-four-foot-high wall, or racial "spite fence," along West 135th Street (M. Wallace 2017). In 1913 Taylor's organization, renamed the Harlem Property Owners Improvement Corporation, had convinced white property owners to sign restrictive covenants, excluding Black tenants from buildings between 129th and 136th Streets west of Lenox Avenue—an area that, since the 1880s, had been developing as an exclusively white middle-class community. "When," Taylor asked, "will the people of Harlem wake up to the fact that they must organize and maintain a powerful anti-invasion movement if they want to check the progress of the Black hordes that are gradually eating through the very heart of Harlem" (in Osofsky 1996:107).[1] Taylor's appeal was both a call to action and an evocation of a still unsettled conception of whiteness in a city rife with ethnic differences and divisions. Taylor evoked the spatial threat of a barbarian invasion and a virulent pathogen—a miasma—eating away at a normative construction of middle-class whiteness. Taylor's group, like other white protective associations—the Anglo-Saxon Realty Corporation and the Save-Harlem Committee, for example—maintained that the presence of people of African descent depreciated property values and undermined the integrity of whiteness.

The *New York Age*, the city's premier African American newspaper, challenged the veracity of the group's fearmongering and underscoring its irrationality:

> The most vile and vicious charges are made against Negroes—charges which are absolutely untrue and which could have their conception only in a depraved and distorted consciousness. That colored people are dangerous, that white women and children are in constant peril, that the Negro's mode of living is objectionable, that he is a growing menace and that white people cannot live on the same block with Negroes, were some of the wild and fantastic statements made. (August 7, 1913:1)

The *New York Age* report maintained that the white members of Taylor's organization were ignorant of the way Black people in Harlem actually lived and, therefore, their charges of Black vice, criminality, and immorality were "baseless fabrics of their perverted imaginations"—imaginations fed by the vaudevillian performances and imagery of the urban "zip coon." The *Age* published a list of names of prominent Black persons living in Harlem whose homes should be visited by the members of Taylor's association, including realtor Philip A. Payton Jr., the Reverend Adam Clayton Powell Sr., pastor of the Abyssinian Baptist Church, and the comedian and entertainer Bert Williams (August 7, 1913:7). The satirical invitation presented a demand for recognition grounded in an intersubjectively acquired understanding of the equal worthiness of human beings. Contemporary scholarly and popular cultural representations precluded this possibility through the exclusionary logic of racial segregation and dehumanization of the Black subject. Taylor's efforts, like those of other white protective associations, failed. By August 1920, when Marcus Garvey's Universal Negro Improvement Association (UNIA) paraded through Harlem's streets, the areas of Harlem west of Fifth Avenue to Eighth Avenue and from 130th to 145th Streets were predominantly Black.

In this chapter, I examine the transformation of Harlem from a mostly white middle-class neighborhood into the political and cultural mecca of Black life. My focus is on how the specter of a Negro invasion and attempts to draw the color line to shore up the exclusiveness of white areas—and of whiteness itself—drew upon spatiotemporal, symbolic, and epistemic distinctions. These distinctions fabricated Blackness as a zone of absolute abjection, peopled by unevolved pseudo-subjects, contrasted with an evolving normative construction of whiteness. W. E. B. Du Bois foresaw that this overdetermined and polysemous boundary was the central problem of the twentieth century. I investigate the multi-sited struggles over this boundary and over the meanings of its opposing terms as they occurred in the production of knowledge, in popular culture, and in spatial politics.

This "boundary work"—to adapt Thomas Gieryn's concept to a not-unrelated context—was not only foundational to the enforcement of racial subordination, but was also necessary for the constitution and reproduction of whiteness. Whiteness, in its turn, is a unifying fiction that because of its inherent instability had to be continuously produced, reiterated, and defended. This racial boundary work enlisted quotidian practices and symbolic violence associated with the enforcement of racial segregation and other exclusionary practices in Harlem in the early twentieth century. It mirrored an epistemological distinction prevalent in the academy and in popular culture, which denied co-presence and coevalness—that is, temporal coexistence—to people of African descent (see Fabian 2014). This denial enabled the projective constitution of Black subjectivity, agency, and sociocultural life—a perduring "savage slot" in American political culture (Trouillot 2004), creating a geography that is at once "demonic" and "deranged" (McKittrick 2006).

The Specter of "Negro Invasion"

At the turn of the twentieth century, a substantial population of African Americans and Black immigrants from the West Indies lived in Harlem, scattered from river to river in pockets of Black tenements in racially mixed communities like the Manhattanville enclave discussed in chapter 3. Many had relocated to Harlem from districts of Black settlement such as the West Village, Tenderloin, and San Juan Hill, where poor housing conditions, high rents, and white racial animosity and violence rendered the relatively sparsely settled Upper East Side and Harlem desirable. Moreover, the pre–World War I migration of African Americans from the South led to a sharp increase in the city's Black population. Between 1890 and 1910, Manhattan's Black population more than doubled, from 25,674 to 60,534. The majority of these newcomers had been born in the South (Osofsky 1996:220, n. 2). Many of these migrants settled in Harlem and nearby tenements along with Irish, Italian, and Eastern European immigrants.

Black settlement in Harlem was facilitated by a real estate bust fueled by overspeculation coupled with the inability of protective associations, such as Taylor's Harlem Property Owners Improvement Corporation, to unify white property owners against Black newcomers. In 1878 the Third Avenue El opened, linking South Ferry in lower Manhattan to 129th Street in East Harlem; that same year, a second elevated line was completed along Second Avenue from Chatham Square to 129th Street (Manhattan East Side Alternative Study 1999). Finally, in 1879 the Ninth Avenue elevated railroad reached 135th Street and Eighth Avenue on Harlem's west side. Property values soared, particularly in western areas of Harlem where developers and speculators vied with each other to purchase tracts of farmland and former estates upon which to build apartment buildings and townhouses designed for middle- and upper-middle-class whites.

The upper-middle-class housing stock being developed west of Fifth Avenue contrasted sharply with the tenements to the east, where Eastern European Jews, Italians, Irish, and, in lesser numbers, Black people found relatively affordable housing. Harlem's "Little Italy" extended roughly from 100th to 125th Streets, east of Third Avenue—a tenement district that had been developed on marshy land during the 1890s. Since the late 1880s, a sizable African American population had lived on blocks between East 97th and 107th Streets in the area of Second and Third Avenues (*Real Estate Record and Builders' Guide* 1900). However, by 1905, overspeculation in Harlem had led to exorbitant increases in land and property prices, now inflated beyond most people's financial means (Osofsky 1996). Property owners strapped for cash not only reduced rents, but also often offered several months rent-free to attract white tenants. To make matters worse, real estate speculators and builders had misjudged the completion date of the IRT subway and had built too many townhouses and high-rent apartment buildings in the years leading up to the second bust.

As a result of this over-building glut and correspondingly high vacancy rates, the city's financial institutions cut back on loans to speculators and developers, and foreclosed on delinquent mortgages. Desperate to fill their vacancies and stabilize rental incomes, some white property owners broke ranks with their pro-segregationist peers and rented or sold their properties to Black people, who typically paid considerably more than whites. A real estate agent explained to the *New York Times*, "When a real estate agent cannot rent a tenement to a white tenant for any purpose whatsoever he adds from 25 to 50 percent to the rents and throws it open to colored tenants" (*New York Times* 1889). The agent went on to laud the merits of Harlem's Black renters, but was quick to propound that these positive qualities were themselves the results of innate and inferior racial characteristics:

> They are an imitative race, and they have an inborn love of display. They naturally, therefore, try to imitate their betters in the decoration and adornment of their homes. They are a servant class, and have opportunities of observation in the residences, hotels, and sleeping cars where they are employed that the white people in their economic condition do not enjoy.

In short, African Americans could be incorporated into the body politic through the mindless imitation of whites in the context of subordinate relations of servility. In the dominant social evolutionist views of the period, people of African descent lacked the capacity to independently evolve toward a higher state of civilization and therefore were seen to be arrested in an earlier stage of racial development. As Edward Said observed, there is no knowledge of the Other that is not also a temporal act (1995). Racial segregation, like the stages of the social evolutionists, secured a sociospatial *and* temporal distance. The white real estate agent, appealing to widely held racist tropes, displaced Black tenants to an *other*, earlier time and evolutionary stage of development.

Spearheading the efforts to secure decent housing for Black people in Harlem were Black realtors and "race men" such as Philip A. Payton, John E. Nail, and John Royall. Payton was born in Westfield, Massachusetts, and moved to New York City in 1899 after graduating from Livingston College in North Carolina. Payton found work as a porter in a real estate office, where, as he told Booker T. Washington, "I conceived the idea of going into the real estate business" (Washington 1907:201). Payton's first foray into the real estate business with a partner failed, but after he moved in 1900 with his wife to West 134th Street in Harlem, his luck changed:

> One fine day I made a deal that netted me nearly $1,150. I could hardly believe it true. My wife refused to credit it, until I showed her the checks. From that time on things grew better. I opened an office on 134th Street. . . . I bought the flat house in which I was living. I bought two more flats and kept them five months when I sold them at a profit of $5,000. I bought another, kept it a month, and made $2,750 . . . and so on. (Washington 1907:203–4)

In 1903 Payton founded the Afro-American Realty Company, a partnership of African American investors that included James C. Thomas, a prominent undertaker and property owner, James Gardner, owner of a successful janitorial business, and Wilford H. Smith, a civil rights activist. Future officers and investors included Fred R. Moore, owner and editor of the *New York Age*, and Charles W. Anderson, an influential Black Republican and later the collector of internal revenue for the Second District of New York City. James C. Thomas, who served as Afro-American Realty's president, had prospered as an undertaker in the Tenderloin. With his earnings Thomas had purchased two buildings on Seventh Avenue that, due to their location near the site of the proposed Pennsylvania Station, he was able to sell for $202,000 (*New York Tribune* 1910). In May 1910, Thomas and his wife and business partner, Ella Thomas, moved their funeral home from 493 Seventh Avenue near 36th Street to West 134th Street in Harlem and into a new $25,000 building. The *New York Age* announced the move uptown and described the new facility: "The chapel will be very attractive. It will be ninety feet long and capable of seating six hundred persons. It will be built of white maple and the furniture will be of oak, including the organ and pulpit. The windows of the chapel will be decorative in design, portraying Scriptural characters. Both electricity and gas will be used from lighting purposes" (April 21, 1910:1). Thomas, reputed at the time to have been "the richest man of African descent in New York," also served as a member of the executive committee of Washington's National Negro Business League and as second vice president of the Colored Republican Club, founded by Charles Anderson in 1903 (Washington 1907:104).

Astutely aware of the cash-strapped predicament of white landlords, Payton's company began to buy and lease Harlem properties. Gilbert Osofsky observed that Payton would lease Harlem buildings from white owners "and assure them a regular annual income. He, in turn, would rent these homes to Negroes and make a profit by charging rents ten percent above the deflated market price" (1996:93). Payton shrewdly exploited the tension between the short-term interests of typically highly leveraged white property owners in securing stable rental incomes, and the long-term strategic interests of the real estate industry in preserving racial segregation and maintaining inflated property values.

In 1904–1905 the Afro-American Realty Company sparked controversy when it contested the Hudson Realty Company's attempt to control the racial composition of West 135th Street and its environs west of Lenox Avenue, which was considered to be the racial "deadline" separating Harlem's white areas from "little Africa."[2] Highly capitalized at $1 million, the Hudson Realty Company was directed by prominent members of the city's elite, including Maximilian Morgenthau, the company's president and brother of Henry Morgenthau Sr. (ambassador to the Ottoman Empire), and Joseph Bloomingdale, a philanthropist and cofounder of Bloomingdale's Department Store.

In April 1904, Payton's company had sold three buildings on West 135th Street (numbers 40, 42, and 44) to the white-owned realty company, which, intent on boosting the value of seventeen vacant lots it owned on West 135th Street, began evicting Black tenants and renting exclusively to whites. The imminent opening of the IRT subway's Lenox Avenue line provided white property owners in surrounding areas with a strong incentive to dispossess Black tenants in anticipation of rising property values. The *New York Times* reported that the Black tenants who had received the eviction notices "got together and, with Payton as their leader, obtained the leases of two substantial flat houses on 135th Street near those from which the negroes had been evicted" (December 17, 1905:12). In fact, Payton had bought the two buildings (numbers 30 and 32) from Black undertaker James C. Thomas and, one month later, transferred them to the Afro-American Realty Company (McGruder 2015).

Deeds in hand, Payton evicted the white tenants living at 30 and 32 West 135th Street and rented their units to the Black households dispossessed earlier. With the Hudson Realty Company's strategy of whitening 135th Street and environs foiled, Payton repurchased the original three apartment buildings and repopulated them with Black households. In the *New York Age*, Payton advertised the availability of four- and five-room apartments in the buildings at rents of $18 and $20, highlighting their "hot water supply and heated halls" (December 14, 1905:8).

The *New York Times* underscored Payton's role in undermining the racial deadline, and reported that the Afro-American Realty Company had "brought a negro invasion close enough to the doors of a white neighborhood to make the property owners willing to sell out to save their own holdings from depreciation" (December 17, 1905:12). In a pamphlet used to solicit investors for the newly incorporated Afro-American Realty Company, Payton linked the contest over the future of West 135th Street to the wider struggle for Black housing in Harlem: "When the movement was started to put the colored people out of West 135th street, this co-partnership, being unable to lease any houses on this street, voted to buy and did buy two 5-story flats valued at $50,000 and thereby stemmed the tide, which had it been successful on West 135th street would surely have extended to West 134th street, which is almost entirely given over to our people" (in McGruder 2015:54). Payton, along with other Black realtors and political and cultural activists, were crafting what Katherine McKittrick has called an "oppositional geography" amidst the racially exclusionary practices of the real estate industry, white property owner resistance, and the ever-present threat of white mob violence (2006). Yet Black people were able to carve out spaces of freedom, opportunity, and empowerment within the carceral geography of residential segregation and anti-Black violence.

Property owners who did rent, lease, or sell to Black people incurred the wrath of protective associations and landlords. In 1903 a furor erupted when Louis Frankel rented units in a building that he leased at 36 West 116th Street to African American households. Frankel had leased the apartment building for two years from Harry Goodstein, a major Harlem property owner and later president of the anti-Black West Harlem Property Owners' Association. The *New York Times* reported that the dispute had nearly resulted in bloodshed when Goodstein and his supporters confronted Frankel at the Harlem Police Court on 125th Street and added cryptically, if not menacingly, "The recent discussions in the papers following negro lynchings have had their effect on the controversy."

Goodstein owned buildings on the opposite side of West 116th Street and maintained that Frankel's actions had precipitated a decline in the area's property values. He made a failed attempt to cancel Frankel's lease. "At no time," Goodstein stated to the *New York Times*, "did Mr. Frankel complain to me about the lease . . . and owing to the fact that the lease was drawn without reference to colored tenants, and not dreaming that the lessee would resort to anything of this kind, my hands were tied." However, the building's janitor explained to the reporter, "Negroes are willing to pay more than the whites and pay more promptly," and she added that the white tenants who had preceded the African Americans in Frankel's building were "dressmakers who couldn't, and bookmakers who wouldn't pay" (August 23, 1903:10).[3]

Harry Goodstein reappeared in the newspapers three years later, when a Black realtor purchased an apartment building on 119th Street, behind a building that Goodstein owned, and rented its apartments to Black households. When white tenants living in Goodstein's building protested the Black tenants and "the sounds that accompanied the new invasion," Goodstein decided to "erect a fence that would not only separate his property from that occupied by the negroes, but [also] shut off the light and air from the negro tenement." Although by day, the *Baltimore Sun* reported, the construction of the sixty-six-foot-high iron spite fence—the highest of its kind in the city—was under police guard, "at night, with the aid of poles, the framework constructed during the day has been pushed down by persons from the windows of the negro tenement" (August 10, 1906:11). Citing Goodstein and his tenants, the *Times* also interpreted the efforts of Black tenants to raze the spite fence not as a conscious act of resistance to a potent symbol of white supremacy but as "the drumming of nightly tattoos." This interpretation effaced the agency of the Black tenants and reiterated their allegedly innate musicality popularized in the "coon songs" and other racist propaganda. The spite fence served to reduce the Black subject to mute physicality beyond the pale of *Aufklärung*, or enlightenment. As in Fanon's account of experiencing ontological dissolution when confronted with the words of a French boy, "*Look, a Negro*," the Black tenants were always already there in the minds of white racists.

The spite fence secured a spatial displacement—a denial of co-presence—and it was also a temporal displacement—that is, a denial of what Johannes Fabian has termed "coevalness" by relegating Black people to an anterior and inferior position on an evolutionary scale of racial progress (2014). By "spatializing time," as Fabian put it, the spite fence and other quotidian structures and practices of racial exclusion secured a spatiotemporal distancing of Black people. This symbolically and materially created the conditions of possibility for a unifying fiction of whiteness—that is, the constitution of a normative construction of whiteness through the splitting off and projection of alterity onto the epistemological field of Blackness.[4] Ethnic differences among white immigrants were muted and incorporated into an unmarked category of whiteness, constituted as the antithesis of the socio-symbolic field of Black abjection. "To put it bluntly," William D. Hart noted, "the objecthood of Blacks underwrites the subjecthood of white people" (2018:23).

Harry Goodstein's construction of the spite fence also evoked a logic of contamination and containment consistent with the cordons sanitaires imposed by public health authorities. Like the cordons sanitaires,

Music sheet drawing of "Dandy Jim from North Carolina," a minstrel song, c. 1843.

the racial spite fence spatially materialized a logic of difference that conflated the imputed characteristics of subaltern racial and ethnic groups with invasive contagions, whether infectious disease, immoral behavior, sound, or other supposedly race-linked pathologies (cf. Shah 2001). If the quarantine served to insulate white upper-income districts from disease-carrying miasmas and, more generally, sociobiological adulteration, Goodstein's spite fence insulated his white tenants from the sights, sounds, and signs of Black subjectivity, agency, and social normalcy— capacities that were degraded, if not negated, in the scholarly and popular cultural representations of the era. In this logic, Black people and other lesser races lacked the capacity of enlightenment and could, at best, only simulate its characteristics—hence, the white fear and loathing of imagined acts of Black *dissimulation* through racial passing, miscegenation, and the mindless imitation of whites. The Black dandy—like the Reagan-era trope of the "welfare queen" nearly a century later—was the embodiment of excess, who could at best only simulate social normalcy through clownish imitation.

Equally important, this displacement by means of the spite fence, racial deadline, and other space-time dividing practices, precluded possibilities for communication between people. Physical separation allowed racial dogma to substitute for actual knowledge and experience. This recalls Woolston's relatively nuanced description of Manhattanville's occupationally diverse Black population, direct knowledge superseded in his text by use of Giddings-inspired racial traits of the Black subject; that is, an epistemology wall both separated and subordinated his ethnographic account to "racial type." To paraphrase Fabian, the Black person was a *category* and not an object of thought and, therefore, as Fanon put it, had "no ontological resistance in the eyes of the white man" (1967:110).

Black Urbanism in the White Imagination

The specter of an invasive Black threat or infestation found legitimacy in the view that African Americans were incapable of adapting to the challenges of urban and industrial life. More broadly, they were portrayed as unable to manage the conditions of freedom following emancipation. As geographer Clyde Woods points out, "Slavery and the plantation are not an anathema to capitalism but are pillars of it" (2017:6). This view of Blackness, championed in literature, popular culture, the press, and, perhaps most significantly, the academy, shaped the spatial politics of racial segregation, the way Black people in cities such as New York were incorporated into the white popular imagination, and also their objectification through the policies and programs of philanthropic, educational, and other urban institutions. Academia was part and parcel of these constructions and processes aimed at community destruction (Woods 2002).

The writings of Columbia historian and political scientist William A. Dunning and his students had much in common with Columbia sociologist Franklin H. Giddings and his students, discussed in chapter 3. The Dunning School of Reconstruction dominated academic and popular views of the Black freedmen in the early decades of the twentieth century, and held that Reconstruction had been an atrocity visited upon the white South by northern carpetbaggers, southern "scalawags," and their African American allies, and that the Black freedmen had proven themselves to be incapable of self-government—a claim soundly critiqued by W. E. B. Du Bois in his groundbreaking essay "Reconstruction and Its Benefits" (1910).

Dunning had been influenced by John W. Burgess, his advisor and, later, colleague at Columbia, whose writings on Reconstruction and belief in the superiority of the Teutonic race and the inferiority of people of African descent sketched the outlines of Dunning's position. For example, in *Reconstruction and the Constitution, 1866–1876*, Burgess reasoned, "From the point of view of a sound political science the imposition of universal negro suffrage upon the Southern communities, in some of which the negroes were in large majority, was one of the 'blunder-crimes' of the century. There is something natural in the subordination of an inferior race to a superior race, even to the point of the enslavement of the inferior race, but there is nothing natural in the opposite" (1903:245).

Released from the paternalistic bonds of slavery, the Dunning School argued, African Americans would revert to a state of savagery and deviancy—a looming urban menace and potent source of angst-ridden mockery and humor that was elaborated and disseminated through the era's coon songs, racialized visual culture, and blackface performances. Black people were perceived as uniquely incapable of adapting to the discipline of the industrial workplace and unfit for the civic and political responsibilities of democratic citizenship. As David Roediger has demonstrated, this view was critical to the formation of the white working class (1991). European immigrants, equipped with industrial and civic training along the lines of the Speyer School and Settlement, could be assimilated to subordinate stations within the political economy and whiteness. Conversely, African Americans were viewed as anti-citizens and "the gravitational *black hole* around which white American identity revolves" (Hart 2018:23). The historiography of the Dunning School of Reconstruction, like the speculative theories of the evolutionists, legitimated constructions of Black urban subjects in popular culture and the wider public sphere.

With the hardening of the color line and heightening of attendant anxieties regarding Black transgressions of white-controlled public and residential space, the perceptions of northern whites toward urban Black people shifted (Dormon 1988). White anxieties were only intensified with the passage of the New York State Civil Rights Act of 1895, the so-called Malby Law, which banned discrimination in public facilities on the grounds of race, creed, or color. Newspapers railed against the civil rights law, maintaining that its enforcement would only heighten white antipathy and violence directed against people of African descent:

> Hotel guests, patrons of sleeping cars, patrons of the theatre, and customers of leading restaurants are likely to be provoked to tumult and violence by compulsory association with negroes. . . . The inadvisability of the agitation precipitated by the Malby law will be at once apparent. (*New York Times* 1895)

The mere co-presence of Black people in any but subservient public contexts was seen as sufficient to incite social disorder and white violence, as well as threaten the ontological integrity of whiteness. Charles Anderson, the influential Black Republican who had been a proponent of the law, led a "testing tour" for the purpose, as he told the *New York Tribune*, of "advertising and insuring compliance with the law" (August

8, 1895:4). Anderson was dismissed by the *New York Times* as being "plainly ignorant of the condition and needs of his race." The reporter went on to opine,

> Access to the privileges of fashionable restaurants and theatres on the footing of the most favored would be of no benefit to the colored people. If Mr. Anderson wishes to improve their condition, let him seek out some way of defending them against their besetting vices of idleness, vanity, and immorality. . . . Indeed, a little abatement of their present tendency to forwardness, especially in public conveyances, would be commendable. It is manifestly unwise for negroes and mulattoes to be self-assertive and swaggering in places where Italians, Scandinavians, English, Irish, and Americans bear themselves with habitual quietness and humility. (June 18, 1895:4)

What is striking about this passage is not only its erasure of white ethnic differences and rejection of Black heterogeneity—a binary classification formalized in the 1900 federal census—but also the contrast drawn between the "habitual quietness" of white people and Black "swaggering" and self-assertiveness. Whiteness here is ethnically unmarked, unobtrusive, silent, and disembodied. By contrast, Blackness is represented as conspicuous, disruptive and, as in the Black sonic transgressions discussed in the Goodstein case, LOUD. Blackness is reduced to the body and to mindless physicality—what Hortense Spillers has called a "pornotrope" (1987).

Indeed, the vaudevillian stage and widely disseminated iconography of the urban Black coon and dandy, crafted in New York City from the late 1880s through the early twentieth century, played a key role in shaping white views and prejudices toward Black urbanites, particularly those hailing from the South (Sacks 2006). The figure of the urban coon portrayed Black urbanites as violent and lascivious criminals, gamblers, and drunkards, and as vulgar, pretentious dandies intent upon violating the racial status quo through miscegenation, racial passing, and the flouting of the conventions of racial exclusion. The white violence enacted in the ubiquitous race riots of the period was incited by the efforts, both real and imagined, of Black people to assert racial equality. Such violence was symbolically projected onto the spectral figures of the urban coon and dandy. The lyrics of the popular 1904 Tin Pan Alley ditty "I'm the Toughest, Toughest Coon," documented in Dormon (1988), exemplified this projection of white animosity, violence, and angst onto the dehumanized Black subject:

> I'm the toughest, toughest coon that walks the street;
> You may search the wide, wide world, my equal never meet;
> I got a razor in my boot, I got a gun with which to shoot,
> I'm the toughest, toughest coon that walks the street.

This potential for violence, exploitation, and abuse was portrayed both in song and on the stage as directed against other Black people—oftentimes Black women—rather than at whites. This sublimated practices of Black self-defense and resistance to white violence. To concede *conscious* Black resistance to white structural racism weakened claims that racial inequalities were the result of innate inferiorities. By contrast, newspaper accounts of Black resistance to white mob violence rarely left any doubt as to its provocation and provocateurs.

For example, on Christmas Day in 1901, a riot erupted in Manhattanville after a group of white boys taunted and threw stones at two Black girls as they crossed Broadway. The girls reported the assault to neighbors, who, after confronting the boys and "boxing their ears," were set upon by some forty white men. The *New York Times* reported,

> The negroes were armed with revolvers, razors, and other weapons, and the whites with stones and clubs. There were a hundred fighters on each side. The negroes were at first victorious, but the police drove them back into their tenements, after they had charged the whites with pistols and razors. Fourteen negroes were arrested. Four whites, including a policeman, were badly shot and cut. (December 26, 1901:3)

As Eric Lott noted of blackface performances, "the white subject could transform fantasies of racial assault and subversion into riotous pleasure, turn insurrection and intermixture into harmless fun—though the outlines of the fun disclose its troubled sources" (1992:31). When the figure of the dandified bully coon did encounter white people, neither he nor his guns and razors were a match, as narrated in the second verse of Irving Jones's popular 1901 song "St. Patrick's Day's a Bad Day for Coons":

> Just then a high-toned yellow darky came cake-walking down the street,
> He had on a pair of yellow gater tops on his feet.
> He had on swell yellow gloves, also a yellow vest,
> And when those Irishmen saw that coon, I guess you know the rest.
> They quickly grabbed this darky, and he began to fight,
> They took his gun and razor, then he tried to pass for white!
> They shaved him with his razor, and they fanned him with his gun,
> If you show him a shamrock now, that yellow coon is always sure to
>   run! (Glibertarians, n.d.)

The song's narrator is a Black man who, after being accosted by a group of Irish revelers in a bar on St. Patrick's Day with cries of "Let's massacre the coon," is coerced into "drinking something Irish" and obligingly orders a crème de menthe. The target of the revelers' violence is a phenotypically ambiguous, "high-toned, yellow darky," dressed in yellow finery and taking on airs that blurred the boundaries between whiteness and its constitutive other—a borderlands occupied by the Irish revelers, who themselves held a tenuous grasp on whiteness. The yellow darky, like the "Black Irishmen," triggered such anxiety and violence because he destabilized the conflation of race, ethnicity, and skin color.

The menacing bully coon was handily disarmed—indeed, his own weapons were turned against him—but, in the midst of the fracas, he attempted to pass for white. Disarmed, humiliated, and put in his place, the yellow darky is transformed into a target for mockery, mirth, and pleasure. Far from mere entertainment, the ditty is a cultural rite of incorporation, situating the Irish (a sizable part of vaudevillian audiences) unambiguously within the socio-symbolic field of whiteness. Recorded on cylinder by the celebrated performer Lew Dockstader, the song ended with a chorus that drives its message home:

> St. Patrick's day's a bad day for coons,
> The only safe plan for us is balloons,
> Yellow coons must not be seen,
> If you drink, drink something green.

As Marcy Sacks has noted, New York's coon song craze reached both working- and upper-class audiences "interested in the consumption of racist material for pleasure" (2006:49). The Columbia University Glee Club performed coon songs and "plantation melodies" both on and off campus, including at the Speyer School in 1903 (Balakirsky 2017). The coon song craze occurred at a time when the popular music industry, with the publication of sheet music, development of recording technologies, and the rise of New York City's Tin Pan Alley, was reaching its zenith (Dormon 1988; Morrison 2017). Sheet music for German immigrant Fred Fisher's 1905 song "If the Man in the Moon Were a Coon" sold over three million copies and was recorded on wax cylinder by Ada Jones, one of the first popular singers to record with Thomas Edison's new technology.

The profile of the urban coon, aestheticized in popular culture and legitimized in the social sciences and press, provided license for white animosity and violence directed against people of African descent. Police Commissioner William McAdoo, a former congressman, described the "type of negro" that had been the relentless target of white mob violence and police persecution—a type that conflated the figure of the bully coon and dandy into an archetypal figure of excess, amorality, and insubordination:

> One of the most troublesome and dangerous characters with which the police have to deal is the Tenderloin type of negro. In the male species this is the over-dressed, flashy-bejewelled loafer, gambler, and, in many instances, general criminal. These fellows are a thorough disgrace to their race and have a very bad effect on decent colored people who come here from the South and other parts of the country. They never work, and they go about heavily armed, carrying, in addition to the indispensable revolver, a razor. When in pursuit of plunder, or out for revenge, or actuated by jealousy, they use both weapons with deadly effect. (1906:93)

The Black female type shared the same characteristics as her imagined male peer—drunkenness, promiscuity, and weapons use—but what especially galled McAdoo was their alleged exploitation of white upper-class men: "These women rob white men with impunity, especially those who look respectable and well-dressed, because they know the chances are that the man will not care to disgrace himself by appearing in court against them" (1906:99). Such women were to be found, McAdoo asserted, in the "creep joints," or brothels, and "Black and tan" saloons in the Tenderloin, where the two races mingled freely. Like the figures of the Black urban coon and dandy, the male and female Tenderloin types, as denizens of an interzone, were viewed as flauntingly transgressing the spatiotemporal logic of racial segregation. Once again, white violence, in this case sexual exploitation, was projected onto the body and person of the Black woman. "Black women," bell hooks wrote, "were naturally seen as the embodiment of female evil and sexual lust. They were labeled jezebels and sexual temptresses and accused of leading white men away from spiritual purity into sin" (2014:33; cf. Roberts 1997).

Furthermore, McAdoo maintained that the failure of "the better educated and progressive members of the negro race" to repudiate this Tenderloin type accounted for white antipathy and violence. "If one of these negro ruffians gets into trouble, either with the police or a white citizen," McAdoo reasoned, "he is apt to appeal to the better class of negro, on the grounds that he is being made the object of race hatred and prejudice in order to excite their sympathies; and it is in this wise that some of the riots and fierce outbreaks which have disgraced the city have been brought about in recent years" (1906:97). As in the case of the African American tester of the Malby Law, the appeal to racial justice was, in and of itself, an incitement of and justification for white racial violence—a perduring leitmotif in the defense of white supremacy.

In July 1905, during McAdoo's tenure as police commissioner, a race riot broke out in San Juan Hill, a predominantly Black section of the Upper West Side, when a Black man came to the assistance of an elderly white rag-collector who was being harassed by a mob of white youths. The Black Samaritan was then attacked by the white mob, provoking Black onlookers to defend him. In the ensuing riot, the police not only failed to protect Black residents, but also participated in their brutalization, joining white mobs in accosting Black people in restaurants, in saloons, and on streetcars (*New York Age*, July 27, 1905:1).[5]

The police assault made clear that it was the humanity of the African American community, variously distorted as "swagger," "forwardness," "boldness," and "self-assertiveness," that was the target of police violence. In this respect, the members of the "better class of negro" who were excited to sympathy and civic action, as McAdoo put it, were equally deserving of being reduced to mute physicality and a bloody pulp of flesh.

The spouse of a Black carpenter who had been fatally injured in the riot-ing accompanied a delegation of African Americans to the district attor-ney's office, charging that McAdoo's police force had colluded with white rioters. "She said that Christopher had endeavored to run away from the scene of hostilities," the *New York Times* reported, "but, being Black, was promptly pursued by some white rioters. Exhausted, he clung to a fence when he was clubbed by one policeman and shot by another, despite his cries that he wasn't a rioter" (July 20, 1905:12). No, but he was Black.

Racial Hegemony and the Constitution of the "Scientific Field"

The academic reputation and far-flung influence of the Dunning School established Columbia University as the leading center for the study of southern history during the early decades of the twentieth century (Humphreys 2013). In the last of a series of articles on Reconstruction published in the *Atlantic Monthly*, Dunning summarized his views on slavery, race relations, and the prospect of racial equality for African Americans in northern cities:

> The ultimate root of the trouble in the South had been, not the institution
> of slavery, but the coexistence in one society of two races so distinct in
> characteristics as to render coalescence impossible; that slavery had been
> a *modus vivendi* through which social life was possible; and that, after its
> disappearance, its place must be taken by some set of conditions which,
> if more humane and beneficent in accidents, must in essence express the
> same fact of racial inequality. The progress in the acceptance of this idea
> in the North has measured the progress in the South of the undoing of
> reconstruction. (1901:449)

The alleged failure of southern Reconstruction provided evidence of the impossibility of northern racial equality and coexistence. For Dun-ning, the coexistence of the races is impossible because two races that occupy distinct, ranked temporal positions in the evolution of civiliza-tion cannot also co-occupy space. Racial exclusion was the necessary condition of possibility for the constitution and reproduction of white-ness in the demographically dense, multiethnic, and multiracial cities of the North. Like the quotidian practices of ritualized subordination associated with racial exclusion and the dramaturgy of the vaudevillian stage, Dunning's view naturalized the Manichaean relations of mastery and servitude, constitutive of chattel slavery, enshrining the denial of coevalness and enforcing the deadline.

The precarity of this unitary conception of whiteness was demonstrated in the interethnic conflicts; white identity had to be continuously *re*constituted, performed, and defended through the racial spite fence and other technologies of racial exclusion, intimidation, and violence. These set Black people apart as the constitutive outside of an imagined white normativity. Although European immigrants suffered housing and other forms of discrimination, in contrast to people of African and Asian descent—most notably, the Chinese—they were deemed assimilable. European immigrants could be incorporated into a flexible and ever-expanding conception of whiteness by shedding their cultural differences from the imagined norms of white Anglo-Saxon society. In contrast, an imagined Blackness was fixed through the binary racial classification of the 1900 federal census and the ascendant one-drop rule (see Ignatiev 1995; Jacobson 1999; Roediger 1991). Furthermore, white European immigrants, through the discipline of differentiated education—notably, through the "social studies" curriculum advanced by Thomas J. Jones—and the discipline of the industrial workplace, could shed their differentness. During their leisure, these white European immigrants could re-encounter their racial others as disavowed sources of pleasure on the vaudevillian stage (Roediger 1991).

Richmond Mayo-Smith, professor of political economy and social science at Columbia and a celebrated authority on statistics, explained the innate incapacity of people of African descent to assimilate to American society or coexist within the same spatiotemporal frame:

> The negroes are by birth and race and previous condition of servitude incapable of representing the full American capacity for political and social life. They have neither the tradition of political life nor the practical experience in self-government. The presence of this numerous body of people, who will never fully amalgamate with the white population, will always be a problem for us. The tendency will be for them to remain in a position of inferiority, unable to meet the demands on their intelligence and virtue which our system of political liberty and equality make. (1898:64–65)

Mayo-Smith's prognosis was little more than a self-fulfilling prophecy—a tautology—since the ubiquitous practices of racial segregation precluded amalgamation in any but the most servile of social settings. Once again, the instability of whiteness as a lived social fiction required an obsessive, ritual-like disavowal of, and spatiotemporal distancing from, its imagined Other to sustain the "magic circle." In this sense, as Pierre Bourdieu has observed, "epistemological conflicts are always, inseparably, political conflicts," and Mayo-Smith's claim, dressed in the garb of science, was no more than a rationalization of the status quo—one in which Mayo-Smith and his peers were active participants (1975:21).

To suggest that the politics and symbolic economy of racial segregation and exclusion shaped and, in turn, were shaped by paradigm building in the social sciences—that is, defining the ontological and epistemological status of Black people—is to extend Bourdieu's conception of the "scientific field" beyond a focus on competitive struggles for scientific authority within the academy. Although Bourdieu noted the "two-fold" relation of science to the "relatively autonomous world endowed with its own rules of functioning," characteristic of the disciplines and the wider sociopolitical milieu within which scientific practices are embedded (1990:298)—a relation expressed by his eclectic conception of the "anti-political politics" of the intellectual (Pels 1995)—his emphasis remained largely on the internal agonistic dynamics of the academy (Camic 2011).

Karin Knorr Cetina and others have taken issue with Bourdieu's internalist emphasis and focus on specialist communities, which treat scientists "as though they were isolated in a self-contained, quasi-independent system" (1981:72–73). By contrast, Knorr Cetina noted, "Scientific work displays itself in the laboratory as traversed and sustained by relationships and activities which continually transcend the site of inquiry" and that scholars "frame their scientific work in terms of their *ex situ* involvements" (1982:117). Knorr Cetina referred to these locations and relationships beyond the academy as "transepistemic arenas of action." These heterogeneous *ex situ* fields of action include professional associations, government agencies, the press, and private foundations, as well as university administrations. For example, Progressive Era social scientists frequently served on government commissions and on the boards of charities, settlement houses, and other private groups; gave lectures before academic and lay audiences; and published in newspapers, magazines, and other venues accessible to diverse publics. Scholars simultaneously engaged in struggles for scientific competence and authority within the academy and deployed—and found validation and rewards for—their professional expertise, authority, and reputations well beyond its borders (Pels 1995).

After receiving his PhD in sociology from Columbia in 1902, Thomas J. Jones took a position as the associate chaplain and instructor of economics at the Hampton Institute, where he developed a new industrial education curriculum that included a social studies component based on the racial doctrines of Giddings. The resulting Hampton social studies curriculum advanced the claim that Native Americans and African Americans were disadvantaged by an evolutionary lag and by historical circumstances that, unrelated to oppression, could be remediated, if only partially, through industrial training, civic education, and practical economics. "Slavery and the tribal form of government," Jones reasoned, "gave the Negro and Indian but little opportunity to understand the essentials of a good home, the duties and responsibilities of citizenship, the cost and meaning of education, the pace of labor, and the importance of thrift. The origin and development of these institutions—social, economic, and religious—were hidden by the mysteries of superstition" (T. Jones 1906:111).

Jones argued that African Americans must avoid political activism or opposing the status quo since, in his view, only a prolonged process of social evolution, firmly guided by white educators, social workers, and philanthropists, could advance their social condition. In a nutshell, as Aldon Morris noted, "Jones instructed people of color to accept their subordination as a natural outcome" (2015:203). After leaving Hampton in 1909, Jones joined the US Census Bureau to supervise the collection of Black population data for the 1910 census. Jones's Hampton Institute curriculum, criticized by Du Bois as "subordinate training," became the model for social studies public school curricula nationwide, thus teaching immigrants and racial minorities to accept subordinate roles in the political economy and class structure. Jones's career illustrates the transepistemic circulation of knowledge between academics, philanthropic elites, and government officials.

In 1912 Jones was hired by the federal Bureau of Education as an authority on the education of non-white racial groups; he was also hired by the Rockefeller-funded General Education Board (GEB) to conduct a major study of African American education in the South, funded by the Phelps-Stokes Fund. In 1917 he published the results of his research in a two-volume study, *Negro Education: A Study of the Private and Higher Schools for Colored People in the United States*.

In *Negro Education*, Jones contended that Black colleges were placing too much emphasis on a liberal arts education (teaching, for example, Latin, science, and mathematics) at the expense of more "practical" instruction in subjects tailored to the needs—or, more to the point, supposedly limited abilities—of their students. Jones expressed doubts concerning the capability of Black institutions of higher learning. Unsurprisingly, Black educators and activists were outraged, and Du Bois wrote withering critiques of *Negro Education* in the *Crisis*, the official publication of the NAACP, where he described Jones as "that evil genius of the Negro race" (1919:9). Although Jones conceded the possibility of Black progress, albeit limited, it was to be contingent upon white expertise and patronage.

In a short essay published in the *Journal of Negro History* on the occasion of Jones's death in January 1950, the African American historian Carter G. Woodson addressed the extraordinary power and influence that Thomas J. Jones had exercised in the philanthropic community and among political and economic elites during his decades-long tenure at the Phelps-Stokes Fund. Pointing out that during a 1917 conference in Washington, DC, to discuss *Negro Education*, Jones had described African American schools as unworthy of financial support, Woodson observed,

> This fault in Jones' judgement led most Negroes to consider him an evil in the life of the Negro; but he was nevertheless, catapulted into fame among the capitalists and government officials supporting the education of Negroes. They made Jones the almoner of the despised race with the title of Educational Director of the Phelps Stokes Fund, which he served from 1913 to 1946. When he said do not give here and do not help yonder, the "philanthropic" element heeded his biddings. He became immediately successful as the most advanced agent of Negro control. (1950:107)

Thomas J. Jones's influential career demonstrates the epistemological symmetry between the quotidian, *ex situ* politics of Black exclusion and degradation in society at large and in paradigm building within the social sciences and philanthropy. Dunning, Giddings, and Jones exemplify the way in which whiteness was a critical and convertible form of social capital on par with academic competence and authority. The professional reputations and authority of scholars, the formation of their disciplines, and the institutional politics of their universities shaped and were shaped by the policing of racial, gender, and other social hierarchies in ways that were hegemonic and overdetermined.

Dick Pels has argued that "the scientific struggle is characterized by an 'essential duality' in which intrinsic intellectual and extrinsic material interests, intellectual and material strategies, and epistemological conflicts and power conflicts are indissolubly joined" (1995:85). Noting the "epistemological fusion" of knowledge production and politics, Pels stressed the practico-political effects of acts of scientific classification in a critical response to Bourdieu:

> Despite a deep sensitivity to the classifying effect of social and social-scientific classifications, which definitely sets him apart from the crowd of his fellow-sociologists, Bourdieu still underestimates the extent to which every codifying representation of social likenesses and differences, of frontiers and domains, articulations, and instances, *functions to create the same social universe that it claims objectively or realistically to mirror.* The defining sociologist engages just like any ordinary actor in the struggle for the imposition of legitimate classification, and classifies others in order "to tell them what they are and what they have to be." (1995:90; emphasis added)

For example, Robert McCaughey wrote of John Burgess, dean of Columbia's School of Political Science, "Burgess held fast to the idea of the university as a place reserved for 'the best men,' which is to say well-familied, white, Anglo-Saxon, Protestant males. Not only did Burgess oppose the entry of women into the university, at any level, he saw no reason to open its doors to African Americans or 'new' immigrants or to be welcoming to Jews" (2003:163). Burgess and his peers did more than reflect dominant ideologies; their racism and sexism demonstrate that intellectuals have been active in the constitution and policing—both in theory and in practice—of these differences across a wide range of institutional and societal contexts. The spatiotemporal logic of the racial spite fence was similarly the logic, inter alia, governing the assessment of competence and scientific authority within the academy.

Resistance at the Margins of the Scientific Field

George Edmund Haynes challenged claims of the innate inferiority of Black people and its logic of spatiotemporal exclusion. A protégé of Du Bois, Haynes wrote his doctoral dissertation in sociology at Columbia University on the economic pursuits and progress of Black people in New York City. He was the first African American to earn a PhD from Columbia, and his dissertation, *The Negro at Work in New York City*, was published in 1912. While studying jointly at Columbia and at the New York School of Philanthropy, Haynes cofounded, together with Ruth Standish Baldwin (a social reformer and the widow of Long Island Railroad magnate William Baldwin), the Committee on Urban Conditions Among Negroes (CUCAN), a precursor to the New York Urban League, and he served as the latter's first executive secretary (Reed 2008).

Haynes's career highlights the fact that the scientific field—its rules, transepistemic fields, and constitutive politics—is shot through with antagonisms, conflicts, and resistant practices that mirror or instantiate those of the larger society. Haynes, like Du Bois and other African American social scientists of his generation, was "denied," as Aldon Morris put it (2015), both as a human being entitled to social equality and as the purveyor of epistemological commitments that, rooted in the best practices of the nascent social sciences, challenged the racist dogma propagated both in the academy and society at large.

Haynes was born of modest origins in Pine Bluff, Arkansas, in 1880, and grew up as the Reconstruction-era gains of African Americans were being reversed and replaced by the racial politics and violence of Jim Crow. In 1898 Haynes enrolled at Fisk University, where he developed a close relationship with Du Bois, who was both a mentor and formative influence on his sociological research and social activism (Morris 2015). After earning his bachelor's degree in 1903, and with the support of Du

Bois, Haynes entered Yale University, earning a master's degree in sociology in 1904. After attending summer sessions at the University of Chicago in 1906 and 1907 while working with the YMCA, Haynes enrolled at the New York School of Philanthropy (NYSP) in 1908.

The NYSP had been created in 1898 by the Charity Organization Society (COS) of New York to provide training in philanthropy that combined academic coursework in sociology and related disciplines with practical social work experience, as was advocated by proponents of the "New Philanthropy." To that end, the NYSP partnered with Columbia University. In 1905 a chair endowed by banker and philanthropist Jacob Schiff was created, whereby the NYSP's director, Edward T. Devine, was appointed professor of social economy at Columbia (Berkman and Maramaldi 2001). In 1906 Schiff endowed a second chair in social legislation, which, at Devine's recommendation, was occupied by Samuel McCune Lindsay, a sociologist. NYSP courses were accepted toward the fulfillment of one minor for the MA and PhD in the Faculty of Political Science at Columbia. Students at the NYSP could enroll in courses at Columbia, Barnard, and Teachers College tuition-free (and vice versa) (New York School of Philanthropy 1909).

Haynes was one of twenty-four students out of a predominantly female student body of eighty-five who in 1909 were registered at both the NYSP and Columbia (New York School of Philanthropy 1909). Devine was impressed by Haynes's coursework and research at the NYSP and advocated for his admission to Columbia's doctoral program in sociology (F. Wilson 2006). Given Giddings's white supremacist beliefs and politics, it is unlikely that Haynes would have been admitted directly to the PhD program in sociology.

At Columbia, NYSP students primarily took courses taught by Devine and Lindsay, and the two men also co-taught the Seminar in Social Economy, which examined social reform efforts in New York City. "Social economy" served as a euphemism for applied, or "practical," sociology (in contrast to general, or "theoretical," sociology), which was viewed as the intellectually subordinate reserve of female scholars (Breslau 2007). This deeply gendered division mirrored the division between the science of education and its charity-related applications at Teachers College. In fact, the appointments of Devine and Lindsay not only added much-needed faculty to Giddings's fledgling Department of Social Science, but also released the latter from the burden of teaching and supervising fieldwork in practical sociology (R. Wallace 1989).

Lecturers at the NYSP included Franz Boas, Columbia professor of anthropology and critic of social evolutionism and scientific racism; Charles Loring Brace, abolitionist and founder of the New York Children's Aid Society; Lewis W. Hine, sociologist and photographer of social reformist causes; Florence Kelley, general secretary of the National Consumers League, founder of the National Labor Committee, and an NAACP organizer; Booker T. Washington, president of the Tuskegee Institute; and Mary Kingsley Simkhovitch, adjunct professor of social economy at Barnard and founder of the Greenwich House Settlement (New York School of Philanthropy 1909).

NYSP lecturers, along with Mary White Ovington, Columbia economist Edwin Seligman, Victoria Earle Matthews, and Boas, were also members of the Greenwich House Committee on Social Investigation (later the Social Science Research Council), which conducted research on housing conditions, child labor, and other poverty-related topics (Williams and MacLean 2015). Boas's stress on the significance of environment, culture, and, importantly, racial discrimination in explaining social differences informed and lent critical scientific authority to the relatively liberal views of the NYSP on race, although, as Vernon Williams has noted, Boas remained tethered to discussions and debates in physical anthropology regarding the significance of heredity in shaping the intellectual abilities and achievements of people of African descent (1996).

The NYSP's seminar American Race Problems was directed by Carl Kelsey, a sociologist at the University of Pennsylvania. Kelsey had previously held the Lamarckian view that acquired social characteristics could be inherited across generations—a perspective that was compatible with the evolutionists' claim of a hierarchy of superior and lower races. However, by 1909 he believed, echoing Du Bois and Boas, that social attributes resulted from environmental and cultural influences, not biological heredity (Degler 1991). In *The Physical Basis of Society*, Kelsey declared, "Until someone is able to put his finger upon some physical difference which can be shown to have some connection with the degree of culture or the possibility thereof, we have no right to assume that one group of human beings is either superior or inferior to any other"

(1916:292). Lecturers in Kelsey's course included Boas; Henry Moskowitz, philosopher, reformer, and co-organizer of the NAACP; Kate Holladay Claghorn, sociologist, legal scholar, and NAACP cofounder; and David Blaustein, a former rabbi and superintendent of the Educational Alliance, an educational organization and settlement serving Lower East Side Jewish immigrants (New York School of Philanthropy 1909).

African American scholars and progressive whites published in the COS magazine, *Charities and the Commons*, edited by Devine. An October 1905 special issue of *Charities* focused unprecedented attention on the social problems, needs, and experiences of African American migrants from the South in northern cities and included contributions by Du Bois, James Weldon Johnson, Booker T. Washington, Boas, Mary White Ovington, and the African American educator and women's rights advocate Fannie Barrier Williams.

Although John Recchiuti (2007) has described Franklin Giddings as "one of the stars at the School of Philanthropy," he served only on the Advisory Council and as an *ex officio* member of COS's Central Council. Giddings was not listed as an NYSP lecturer, nor were his courses at Columbia listed in the School of Philanthropy's bulletins (New York School of Philanthropy 1907–1912). Giddings's evolutionary positivism, Anglo-Saxon supremacist views, and anti-Semitism were incompatible with the NYSP's mission of social reform, emphasis on empirically grounded research, and environmental-cum-cultural approach to understanding human differences.

Haynes was awarded a fellowship at the Bureau of Social Research, the research unit of the NYSP, funded by the Russell Sage Foundation. Haynes conducted his study of Black migration and economic life under the auspices of the bureau. However, Haynes's formation as a scholar and social activist was strongly influenced by Du Bois's Atlanta School and by the vibrant, pre-Renaissance intellectual and political culture of Harlem, where he lived during his tenure at NYSP-Columbia. Haynes lived in Harlem at the peak of its racial real estate wars, when white protective associations were mobilizing against Black residential inroads. Harlem's Black population—10 percent of central Harlem in 1910—was concentrated in the area of 135th Street and Lenox Avenue, already a center of Black intellectual, artistic, and political life. That year, Haynes graduated from the NYSP, and in July a white mob went on a violent rampage in the area of Eighth Avenue and 135th Street after Jack Johnson's knockout victory over white pugilist Jim Jeffries. The mob dragged Black people from the streetcars along Eighth Avenue, savagely beating them to cries of "Let's lynch a nigger." Haynes's development as a scholar and reformer was deeply influenced by the often violent spatial politics incited by the presence of Black Harlemites and their struggles for racial justice.

Census records confirm Harlem's oppositional geography. In April 1910, Haynes was living as one of six boarders at 219 West 134th Street in an apartment rented by an African American caterer in an all-Black building and on a racially mixed block. Haynes's lodging was down the street from the real estate office of Philip A. Payton at 67 West 134th Street and directly across the street from St. Philip's Episcopal Church at 204 West 134th Street, then under construction.[6] Elizabeth Ross, whom Haynes married in December 1910, lived two doors away, boarding in the residence of Alexander Walters, a civil rights activist and bishop of the AME Zion Church. In the 1910s, Walters became a member of both the NAACP and the New York Urban League, where Haynes served as executive secretary (US Census Bureau 1910c:19B).

Bert Williams, the Bahamian American comedian and entertainer, lived not far away, at 2309 Seventh Avenue, near 135th Street. In 1908 Williams had founded, together with undertaker and realtor James C. Thomas and businessman Frank Wheaton, the Equity Congress. Each of the founders, along with the Irishman Michael Doyle, contributed $100 to the new organization, which later included among its officers Du Bois, Black realtor John M. Royall, and Barbados-born Isaac B. Allen, a longshoreman, realtor, and later president of Marcus Garvey's UNIA. In 1910 the Equity Congress successfully advocated for the hiring of the city's first African American police officer, Samuel J. Battle, and was instrumental in the formation of the 15th New York National Guard Regiment, later reorganized as the 369th Infantry Regiment, or "Harlem Hell fighters," the first Black unit to serve in World War I, although under assignment to the French Army (A. Browne 2015).

In 1908 George W. Walker, the vaudevillian comic and performance partner of Bert Williams, had founded the Frogs, a group organized to advance the economic position and prestige of Black actors and performers. The group took its name from the comedy by the Greek playwright Aristophanes, and club officers included J. Rosamond Johnson, the singer and composer of "Lift Every Voice and Sing" and brother of James Weldon Johnson; Bob Cole, the actor and playwright; and James Reese Europe, the composer, arranger, band leader, and director of the regimental band of the 369th Infantry Regiment (Forbes 2008).

While studying at the NYSP and Columbia University, Haynes lived at the residential center of Harlem's emerging Black intellectual, cultural, and political elite. His network of associations consisted of, to recall Pels's phrase, an "epistemological fusion" of the work of the leading Black figures, including Du Bois, Payton, Anderson, Walters, and Bishop Allen, and the racially progressive white social workers and academics who were affiliated with the NYSP. Haynes occupied a diverse and multi-sited scientific field that challenged the normalizing social science of white universities like Columbia.

Haynes's intellectual and social reformist influences were firmly grounded in the Du Bois-led Atlanta School—what Aldon Morris has called the "erased generation"—and not in the racist, evolutionary positivism of Giddings and those in his circle of influence (2015). As Morris wrote, "The first generation of Black graduates from white sociology departments looked toward Atlanta, where Du Bois was engaged in pioneering empirical research not being conducted elsewhere and valued Du Bois's approach over that of white sociologists. . . . They also embraced Du Bois's activism and the ways he utilized his scholarship to inform social change work" (2015:71–72). Whereas sociology at Columbia was going through the processes of separating the theoretical from practical applications of the discipline, the Du Boisian school necessarily fused the two.

In the opening chapter of *The Negro at Work*, Haynes challenged the prevailing view that African Americans were uniquely lacking in the capacity to adapt to urban conditions and that Black people, as Mayo-Smith had reasoned, would "never fully amalgamate with the white population" (1898:65). Haynes argued that the challenges faced by Black migrants from the rural South in cities were no different from those confronted by white migrants from rural regions of Europe or the South. Accordingly, Haynes maintained, "the problems that grow out of [the Black rural migrant's] maladjustment to the new urban environment are solvable by methods similar to those that help other elements of the population" (1912:14). This theoretical position challenged the claims of the Dunning School and die-hard social evolutionists like Giddings.

Haynes, like Du Bois, underscored the methodological weaknesses of speculative theory building, and his views shaped his methodology. In addition to analyzing data from the 1900 federal census, Haynes selected a sample of 2,500 families from the unpublished schedules of the 1905 New York state census for intensive investigation. Haynes also conducted a personal canvas of seventy-three African American households (as had Du Bois for *The Philadelphia Negro*), and interviewed Black wage earners and business owners at their workplaces and at one of the city's night schools. Of the 475 Black business owners listed in a 1909 city directory, Haynes interviewed 332 (Perlman 1972). The result was a rigorous, empirically grounded, and statistically sophisticated study of the occupational structure of Manhattan's Black population and a groundbreaking critical analysis of the ruinous consequences of racial discrimination, as practiced by white employers, trade unions, and financial institutions, for Black wage earners and entrepreneurs.

Although residential segregation was a relatively minor theme in *The Negro at Work*, he advanced a trenchant critique of the consequences of residential segregation in a 1913 article, "Conditions Among Negroes in the Cities." Underscoring the frustrated attempts of African Americans to secure decent and affordable housing and, by extension, access to better public facilities and amenities, Haynes stressed the contrast in residential mobility between African Americans and white immigrants, arguing that the "sequel of segregation" was substandard schools, inadequate police and fire protection, and "unpaved streets, the absence of proper sewerage, and lack of other sanitary supervision and requirements" (1913:116).

In 1910 Haynes and Ruth Standish Baldwin held a meeting at the New York School of Philanthropy that led to the founding of the Committee on Urban Conditions Among Negroes (CUCAN). Haynes recognized that the few philanthropic agencies that were addressing the needs of the city's Black population—such as the Committee for Improving the Industrial Condition of Negroes (CIICN) and the National League for the Protection of Colored Women (NLPCW)—were largely governed by upper-class white philanthropists whose ameliorist programs of reform did not address racial segregation, discrimination, and the need for societal change (Perlman 1972). For example, the NLPCW, founded by Frances A. Kellor, a social worker and NYSP graduate, sought to discourage southern Black women from migrating to the North and, for those who did, provided help in securing decent housing and "respectable employment." Chief among the NLPCW's objectives was to address the sources of Black crime and vice—notably, prostitution—which Kellor believed to be the consequence of the ignorance and vulnerability of southern women (Reed 2008).

Although Kellor rejected biological accounts of Black criminality and vice, the NLPCW, like many other white-led philanthropic organizations, pursued a paternalistic agenda that discounted the intelligence, agency, and capacity for self-guided progress of Black people and the manifold consequences of racial exclusion. "They failed to address," Cheryl Hicks observed, "the discriminatory employment practices that precluded Black women from non-personal-service jobs or the labor exploitation these women faced as domestic workers within everyday households. Instead, they sought to regulate working women's behavior by inculcating Victorian virtues and middle-class values with the purpose of improving their morals, employment prospects, and efficiency" (2010:121).

By contrast, Haynes maintained that "the problem alike of statesman, race leader, and philanthropist is to understand the conditions of segregation and the oppositions due to race prejudices that are arising as a sequel to this urban concentration" (1912:33). Haynes understood that in relegating Black people to poor housing, public services, and employment opportunities, racial discrimination established and sustained the spatiosymbolic conditions for constituting the ideology of white supremacy and reproducing racial prejudices. Racial desegregation, then, constituted an attack on the coherence and privilege of whiteness.

Although CUCAN's goals—improving housing and community conditions and addressing Black employment needs—overlapped with those of the NLPCW and the CIICN, the committee stressed the role that racism played in both shaping and aggravating "the Negro problem" (Perlman 1972). At its first meeting, CUCAN underscored the role that racism played in restricting access to labor markets: "Negroes are ill prepared to grapple with an intensive industrial competition and, except in domestic and personal service, meet a race prejudice which is insurmountable" (Wood 1910). Moreover, Haynes maintained that the race- and power-evasive paternalism characterizing white-governed philanthropic organizations could best be overcome by training Black social workers at Black colleges and universities, preparing them for leadership roles in urban centers (Reed 2008). Once trained, these social workers could be placed as equals in existing or new philanthropic and social service organizations. In 1911 Haynes's committee merged with the CIICN and the NLPCW to form the National League on Urban Conditions Among Negroes, renamed the National Urban League in 1917.

George Edmund Haynes's formation as a scholar and social activist underscores the ways the scientific field articulates with arenas of social practice well beyond the university. The politics and poetics of racial exclusion, at play in Harlem's real estate wars, in popular culture, and in society at large, informed, and were also legitimized in, the emerging social sciences. The racial spite fence was among the practices of racial exclusion serving to shore up whiteness through the debasement of Black humanity. So too, the work of Haynes, Du Bois, and other Black scholars was marginalized and fenced off within the academy. Scholars within the Acropolis such as Dunning, Giddings, and Jones produced authoritative accounts justifying racial exclusion and contributing to popular projective fantasies of Black people and Black culture. The spectral figure of the dandified, urban "bully coon" continued to rear its head throughout the twentieth century in studies of the Black ghetto and "tangled pathology" of Black inner-city life, as well as in the spatio-political imaginaries of American society into the twenty-first century.

5

Philanthropy, Race Liberalism, and Racial Containment

It is very easy to establish oppositions . . . such that on one
side lies the "productive," "forward looking," "lively," "positive" part of the epoch, and on the other side the abortive,
retrograde, and obsolescent. The very contours of the positive element will appear distinctly only insofar as this element is set off against the negative.
—Walter Benjamin

On December 26, 1926, John Coss, director of Columbia University's
summer session and a professor of philosophy, sent a memorandum to
Nicholas Murray Butler, the university's president, calling attention to
the expansion of Harlem's Black population (Coss 1926). Coss attached
a New York Urban League map showing Harlem's Black population in
1913, 1920, and 1926. The memo expressed concern that Harlem's Black
population continued to expand. Coss's message was simple, concise,
and actionable: "*Look, a Negro!*" And it is this projective and debased
Black subject, overdetermined by the tropes, discourses, and specters
constitutive of the Negro problem, that was the target of study and
exclusion in the decades to follow, as the institutions inside the American Acropolis mobilized to defend its imagined borders against Black
invasion and urban blight.

Only two years before, Marcus Mosiah Garvey's Universal Negro Improvement Association (UNIA), on the occasion of its 1924 international
convention, had paraded from its headquarters in the heart of Black
Harlem at 135th Street and Lenox Avenue, passing through still predominantly white sections of Harlem, to as far south as 110th Street. The *New
York Herald* described the magnificent spectacle:

Accompanied by eight blaring brass bands, the embodiment of the Republic of Africa paraded yesterday through the negro-crammed streets of

Harlem. Gilt-braided and uniformed, it invaded Carnegie Hall last night. The shining light of both occasions was Marcus Aurelius Garvey, known as the President General of the Republic, Supreme Potentate of the Nile, and Generalissimo of the African Legion. Garvey's army mobilized just before 2 o'clock near Lenox Avenue and 135th Street. A dozen negroes, mounted on smart horses and wearing red-striped Black uniforms with fat ropes of gilt-braid, cantered up and down 135th Street, bringing into order the massed troops and the Black Cross nurse contingents. (August 3, 1924:7)

The *Herald*'s use of militaristic language to describe the parade—"Garvey's army," "the massed troops," and "Generalissimo"—captured an important performative theme of the Garvey movement, while also magnifying the threat of the "Negro invasion." The 1924 Garveyite parade, as a spectacle in motion, transgressed the imagined geography of whiteness, loudly and militantly overwriting the well-worn iconography of Black inferiority and deviancy.

By 1926, the Harlem Renaissance had crystalized into a social movement of Black artists, intellectuals, and activists and, like the Garvey movement, had proclaimed the existence of a new subject, a "New Negro," untethered from the cultural politics of white supremacy. The year before, Alain Locke had published *The New Negro: Voices of the Harlem Renaissance* (1925), a groundbreaking anthology of fiction, poetry, and essays on African American and African art, literature, and life. In the opening paragraph of his essay, Locke proclaimed a radical rupture with the racist status quo and its transepistemic bulwarks, including "the Sociologist, the Philanthropist, and Race-Leader" (probably an allusion to supporters of Booker T. Washington). These captured the foundational and interlinked fields of scholarly and sociopolitical practices that defined the "Negro problem," for whom Black people were at best unevolved quasi-subjects requiring the firm guidance and patronage of white experts and elites. At worst, Black people were biologically inferior *non*-subjects—anti-citizens incapable of being productively incorporated into the body politic. In this chapter, I examine how institutions of the American Acropolis responded through philanthropy, the production of knowledge, and the politics of spatial control to the expansion of Black Harlem in the years leading up to and beyond the Great Depression.

As Coss proposed in his memo, a key strategy in resisting Black en-croachment from Harlem and the expansion of Manhattanville's mul-tiethnic working-class population would be spatial containment and exclusion through the control of real property and, further, the built environment. I begin by examining two of John D. Rockefeller Jr.'s real estate ventures in Harlem: the first, an effort to create a whites-only cordon sanitaire around Teachers College's Lincoln School, which had relocated to West 123rd Street from the Upper East Side; the second, an unsuccessful attempt to demonstrate the viability of a cooperative, moderate-income housing model in Harlem—namely, the construction of the Paul Laurence Dunbar Garden Apartments. Rockefeller believed that the Dunbar Garden Apartments would demonstrate to private in-vestors the profitability of unsubsidized middle-income housing, seek-ing also to instill in its Black tenant-owners virtues of responsibility, morality, and pride in homeownership, which were taken to be tenu-ous, if not absent, in Black communities. Inextricably tied to this poli-tics of spatial control was the simultaneous production of knowledge. As was the case earlier with the Speyer School, this knowledge was put into practice via the provision of ameliorative educational and social relief services aimed at mollifying the racialized working-class popula-tions of Harlem and Manhattanville. Finally, I examine New College, a progressive but short-lived experimental undergraduate college within Teachers College. In contrast to the Black racial containment pursued by Rockefeller and institutional elites on the Hill, New College aimed to redefine the civic role and responsibilities of educators by partnering with communities toward the co-development of curricula and the just reconstruction of society.

From Defending the Color Line to Racial Containment

Rockefeller, like the principals of other philanthropic foundations cre-ated in the early twentieth century—the Russell Sage and Carnegie Foundations and the Phelps-Stokes Fund—rejected palliative solutions to urban poverty and other social problems associated with Progres-sive Era charity organizations. Instead, he favored centralized and "scientifically managed" philanthropic efforts aimed at redressing their root causes. "The best philanthropy," John D. Rockefeller Sr. had observed, "is constantly in search of the finalities—a search for cause, an attempt to cure evils at their source" (1909:177). This emphasis on the rationalization of social control through scientific philanthropy led these foundations to embrace the eugenics movement. "After all," William Schambra wrote, "eugenics had begun to point the way to a bold, hopeful human future through the application of the rapidly advancing natural sciences and the newly formed social sciences to human problems. By investing in the progress and application of these fields, foundations boasted that they could delve down to the very roots of social problems, rather than merely treating their symptoms" (2013:4). Rockefeller and his foundations provided support to the American Eugenics Society and to Margaret Sanger, the militant feminist, suffragist, and proponent of "negative eugenics." Through his Bureau of Social Hygiene, created in 1913, Rockefeller provided funding to the Eugenics Record Office, a clearinghouse and training center for eugenics. During the 1920s, the Rockefeller Foundation supported eugenics research in Weimar Germany through contributions to the Kaiser Wilhelm Institute for Anthropology, Eugenics and Human Heredity, and the Kaiser Wilhelm Institute for Psychiatry—research that laid the pseudoscientific foundation for Nazi eugenics and genocide (Franks 2005).

This emphasis on the root causes of social deviancy shaped Rockefeller's Harlem experiment in profit-making middle-income housing, notably through his imposition of strict tenant selection criteria and paternalistic building management policies. "The people make the slums," Rockefeller had written in a note to the American Eugenics Society in 1925. "Moral people are born, not made; the criminal is a defective human, also born and not made; the intelligent will be successful anyway" (in Franks 2005:38). In this view, the solution to the Negro problem rested in the engineering, through natural and social selection, and policing of a compliant and normative subject, resigned to a subordinate station in American society and to the sociospatial logic of racial exclusion.

Rockefeller's first entrée into Harlem's real estate market was a defensive measure aimed at forestalling Black encroachments into Morningside Heights; it was an effort to prevent the American Acropolis in its future-leaning singularity from being tainted by Black abjection and particularism. In 1927 Rockefeller began buying up tenements surrounding the Lincoln School to create a "white protective zone" surrounding the Lincoln School, which had moved to Harlem in 1922 (Schwartz 1993). The new $1.5 million, five-story facility, funded by Rockefeller's General Education Board (GEB), brought the experimental school to within a few blocks of Teachers College. Four of Rockefeller's sons—Nelson, Winthrop, David, and Laurance—attended the Lincoln School.

The area immediately surrounding the new location was predominantly white and consisted of five-story Old Law tenements. However, as Coss had pointed out to President Butler in 1926, Black settlement was rapidly projecting west toward Morningside Park and beyond. By the end of the decade, Rockefeller owned most of the tenements along West 124th Street between Morningside and Amsterdam Avenues, and had begun purchasing buildings on West 123rd Street and Morningside Avenue to further buttress this exclusion zone. The buildings around the Lincoln School occupied a key corridor that, if controlled, would remain white, serving as a barrier to further Black encroachments.

By the mid-1930s, Harlem's Black population had begun to extend west of Morningside Avenue along the 125th Street corridor, prompting Rockefeller's real estate advisor to explain, "Of course we have held to white occupancy but our rents have had to be reduced 40% and we still have many vacancies" (in Schwartz 1993:65). In 1938 Rockefeller's real estate committee, facing continuing Black encroachments and declining rental income, recommended demolishing the tenement properties on 123rd and 124th Streets and Morningside Avenue in order to reduce their property tax burden. Rather than desegregate the tenements and stabilize their rental income, Rockefeller elected to demolish the buildings to prevent the Lincoln School from being sullied by the co-presence of Black residents. Rockefeller's efforts at defending the color line provide important context for his sponsoring of racially segregated housing within Harlem.

Rockefeller's depredations did not go unchallenged. During the Depression, the Communist Party (CPUSA) helped mobilize Harlem's tenants to fight exorbitant rent increases, deplorable housing conditions, and tenant evictions through Unemployed Councils and through its affiliate, the Black-led Harlem Tenants League (HTL). Beginning in the late 1920s, the CPUSA had placed the Black struggle for social equality and justice at the fore of its political agenda, following the Soviet Comintern's resolution in 1928 recognizing African Americans as an oppressed nation with rights of self-determination. Recognizing that the party's organizing efforts in Black communities had been hindered by "white chauvinism," the CPUSA resolved to train and empower a cadre of Black leaders, educate its white members on race-related issues, and confront problems facing African Americans that stretched beyond the workplace, such as racial discrimination, residential segregation, and housing conditions.

During the Depression years, the Harlem Tenants League, along with the CPUSA-backed Unemployed Councils, conducted rent strikes and eviction resistance actions during which activists returned the possessions of evicted tenants to their apartments while encouraging neighbors and onlookers to resist the marshals and police enforcing the eviction orders (Naison 1984). At its peak, the League boasted a membership of well over one thousand, the majority non-communists and Black working-class women.

Although the Harlem Tenants League dissolved by the mid-1930s due to inter-factional disputes among its CPUSA leadership, it catalyzed tenant activism among both community-based groups and tenants living in buildings organized by the Unemployed Councils. For example, in 1937 Berman Fernandez, a Puerto Rican-born organizer with the Harlem Unemployed Council, was charged with felonious assault after he led an anti-eviction protest at 213 East 114th Street in East Harlem, following the eviction of a family. The *Herald Tribune* described the ensuing melee, highlighting the council's formidable base of support in Harlem: "Police were forced to draw guns and Blackjacks to cope with a crowd of 1,000 that carried the Cicarellis' possessions back into their flat after they were evicted" (*New York Herald Tribune* 1937). Richard Wright, the African American novelist, poet, and social critic, wrote numerous articles on Harlem's deplorable housing conditions and rent strikes during his tenure as a journalist with the Harlem bureau of the CPUSA's newspaper, the *Daily Worker* (Bryant 2015). This CPUSA-organized tenant activism quickly spread to Black middle-income residents of Harlem across political affiliations.

Racial Containment and Racial Improvement

The Lincoln School and its collateral buildings were not the only or most notable of Rockefeller's forays into Harlem real estate and philanthropy. In October 1925, James H. Hubert, executive secretary of the New York Urban League and a graduate of the New York School of Philanthropy, submitted a plan to Rockefeller for promoting affordable housing in Harlem by attracting private investors and providing mortgage assistance.[1] In the following year, Charles O. Heydt, Rockefeller's real estate advisor, met with Urban League officials to consider the construction of model garden apartment buildings in Harlem, and to discuss the option of cooperative ownership (*Opportunity* 1926:263). Also attending the meeting were Arthur C. Holden, chairman of the New York Urban League, and sociologist George Edmund Haynes, serving at the time as executive secretary of the Commission on Church and Race Relations of the Federal Council of Churches. Haynes's understanding of the consequences of segregation and his advocacy for Black middle-income housing no doubt contributed to the Urban League's assessment of Harlem's housing needs. Holden, a Columbia University-trained architect and urban planner, was a veteran of the settlement movement and an early critic of slum clearance projects.

Rockefeller had previously experimented with the construction of affordable garden apartments for middle-income people in Bayonne, New Jersey—"good homes for low rents," as he put it—and in 1925 had completed the five-building Rockefeller Garden Apartments on Manhattan's Upper East Side, intended for the employees of the Rockefeller Institute, located next door (*New York Times* 1925b). Rockefeller's projects sought to develop and demonstrate a housing model that would make the construction of unsubsidized cooperative housing profitable for private investors. This goal dovetailed with the Urban League's interest in attracting private capital to improve Harlem housing.[2] Rockefeller's chief real estate advisor had encouraged involvement in housing development to influence public policy. There was growing pressure for the government to intervene in housing markets, whether by providing tax exemptions, offering subsidies, or constructing public housing (Rose 2008).

Given the rising tide of tenant activism, growing influence of Black communists, and the transformation of Black political culture associated with Garveyism and the Harlem Renaissance, a successful experiment in middle-income co-op housing in Harlem would have leveraged considerable attention, influence, and support among public policy makers, as well as among a broader public worried over the Negro problem. Moreover, the construction of segregated middle-income housing that was profitable to private investors in communities such as Harlem would also serve to contain the Black middle classes in segregated ghettos.

In May 1926, Rockefeller purchased sixty largely vacant lots comprising an entire city block from William Vincent Astor for $500,000. The property was occupied by an athletic field, garages, and a handful of wood frame buildings (*Amsterdam News*, May 12, 1926:3). In October, Andrew J. Thomas, Rockefeller's chief architect, filed plans with the city for the construction of six model apartment buildings containing 511 units at a cost of $3.5 million. Thomas, a self-trained architect, was a key figure in the development of the New York garden apartment movement, which advocated the building of U- or H-shaped buildings around a large garden court—the so-called "indented perimeter plan"—in order to maximize light, ventilation, and open space (Pommer 1978; Punz 2016). Heydt, Rockefeller's real estate advisor, was appointed president of the new Dunbar Apartments Corporation.

As construction of the Dunbar Garden Apartments (named after African American poet Paul Laurence Dunbar) began in October 1926, Rockefeller purchased five city blocks of largely unimproved land just north of the Dunbar site, creating the possibility of replicating similar apartment complexes (*New York Tribune*, October 30, 1926:19). The Dunbar was completed in February 1928 on the eve of the Great Depression. As a staunch conservative, Rockefeller had refused tax abatements that were available to the development under the state's 1926 Limited Dividend Housing Companies Act (Lasner 2016). Acceptance of the tax abatements would have lowered costs to tenant-owners, but the value of the Dunbar as a demonstration of the viability of privately financed middle-income housing and Rockefeller's patronizing mission of Black racial improvement would have been undermined. As an advertising brochure for the Dunbar touted, "With $3,939,000,000 worth of real property in the State of New York exempt from State and local taxation, the Dunbar Cooperative Community rejoices that it has not been called on to sacrifice its own self-respect by foisting upon others its due proportion of the burden of taxation. In this matter we pull our own weight in the boat" (*Monthly Labor Review* 1932:126). The brochure implied that Black people needed to be schooled in self-respect and self-reliance. Furthermore, it tied self-respect to proper citizenship via property.

As tenant-owners of the cooperative apartments, Dunbar residents were required to make an equity down payment of at least $150 (plus an additional $50 per room in the case of four-, five-, and six-room apartments) and pay a monthly fee averaging $14.50 per room, covering principal and interest, property taxes, and maintenance costs (Landmarks Preservation Commission 1970). For a four-room apartment, this required a down payment of $350 and a monthly maintenance fee of roughly $58—or $5,219 and $867, respectively, in 2020 dollars (US Bureau of Labor Statistics, n.d.). An Urban League study had found that the average monthly wage of a Harlem head of household was only $85 in 1928; a four-room Dunbar apartment accounted for 68 percent of the average household head's monthly wage. As Touré Reed has pointed out, the Dunbar at first prohibited the taking in of boarders. This "would have automatically eliminated Harlem's least privileged members from consideration for residency" (Reed 2008:55).

Only months before the Dunbar was completed, the Urban League's executive secretary, James Hubert, and the Dunbar's newly appointed resident manager, Roscoe Conkling Bruce, "were the targets of heated verbal attacks" at a meeting of housing activists and community groups (*Amsterdam News*, October 12, 1927:5). James Middleton, president of the North Harlem Community Council, a tenants' rights and community development organization, argued that the Dunbar's monthly fees violated New York state's rent laws, which set limits on the amount of rent that could be charged per room. As co-op apartments, the Dunbar was not subject to the state's rent laws, but protests at the meeting raised credible concerns about its affordability and accessibility—concerns borne out as the Depression set in.

Rockefeller also imposed strict tenant screening procedures (at least three letters of reference were required to confirm an applicant's moral character and financial capability) and disciplinary management policies aimed at monitoring and eliminating undesirable conduct and limiting the power of tenant-owners. As Matthew Lasner noted,

In practice he kept a tight grip by imposing rules at whim and selecting property managers who reported directly to his office. At Dunbar this meant no private resales, no playing on lawns, no taking in boarders, and a Harvard-educated manager who, despite being African American, saw the owners more as wards than clients. (2016:54)

The entrances to the Dunbar's six buildings faced the landscaped and patrolled interior courtyard, insulating the development from nearby tenements and street life. The courtyard and its playground were enclosed by a panopticon-like array of buildings. Moreover, the Dunbar offered few large apartments (the average unit size was only three and a half rooms), which, taken together with its rule against boarders and small room sizes, interpellated a small nuclear family limited to close kin. For example, when Du Bois inquired about purchasing an apartment in the Dunbar in 1927, he noted that a six-room apartment was insufficient for his purpose. "I realize," Du Bois wrote, "that the building is aimed at the working class of people and that their demands should prevail" (Du Bois 1927). The Dunbar's small apartment size and prohibition against boarders (non-kin, who were believed to exercise an immoral and disruptive influence on families) promulgated a middle-class ideal of domestic respectability and order that privileged heteronormative nuclear families. Further, regulations prohibiting loud music, parties, immoral behavior, and other undesirable conduct subjected residents to constant surveillance and the threat of eviction.

Roscoe Conkling Bruce was a Harvard-trained African American educator and the son of Blanche Kelso Bruce, a former slave and US senator from Mississippi during Reconstruction (1875–1881). The Bruce family had long-standing ties to Rockefeller interests and to Booker T. Washington. Washington had hired Roscoe Bruce in 1902 to lead Tuskegee's Academic Department, where he was charged with limiting its academic curriculum in favor of industrial or manual education. This emphasis on industrial training at the expense of academics was consistent with Washington's philosophy, the funding priorities of the Phelps-Stokes Fund's program of Black education, directed by Thomas J. Jones, and the Rockefeller-funded General Education Board's support for southern education (see Gates 1916).

In May 1927, while Rockefeller's Harlem development was still under construction, Bruce applied to be resident manager at the Dunbar with a weighty letter of recommendation from Mary Van Kleeck, director of the Russell Sage Foundation. Charles Heydt, president of the Dunbar Apartments Corporation and vice president of Rockefeller's Empire Mortgage and Trust Company, was impressed by Bruce's credentials—his Black aristocratic pedigree, Phillips Exeter and Harvard education, and previous position as the superintendent of Washington's Colored Schools. Bruce stressed that he would be best suited to socially select appropriate Black residents. "Fill the Harlem apartments with unselected Negro tenants," Bruce wrote to Heydt in July, "and the beautiful structures would soon become filthy, disorderly, a bad example to the new Harlem, a disgrace to the city of New York" (in Graham 2009:341). Bruce's paternalism resonated with the views of Progressive Era philanthropists, such as Anson Phelps Stokes (controlling member of the Phelps-Stokes Fund), Thomas J. Jones, and Rockefeller. As Eric Yellin noted, "Intrinsic to the apparent physical problems, [philanthropists] argued, was the decay of morality among people living in the tenements. The 'saving' of the tenements involved, therefore, the preservation and improvement of the personal character of humans" (2002:321). This "civilizationist" view, as Kevin Gaines put it, held that the problems facing Black people were the result of a deficit in cultural, social, and mental development (1996). This perspective found legitimacy and authority in the social sciences, still under the spell of social evolutionism, and in the Social Gospel movement, which emphasized moral uplift at the expense of societal change. In this view, Black progress, both in the United States and in Africa, required the guidance of white educators, philanthropists, and other purveyors of Western civilization. Racial improvement, the *mission civilisatrice* of benevolent whites, was a precondition for limited racial equality, rather than the converse. This view, shared by educational and philanthropic elites, emphasized the role that scientific philanthropy, managed by social experts, should play in racial improvement and in addressing social problems. This view also disparaged charity organizations that remained unenlightened by "the great historic movements of civilization" because they were community, ethnically, and religiously based. Thus, the Dunbar was to be a potentially replicable experiment in scientifically informed racial improvement.

In August, Bruce was hired as the Dunbar's resident manager and his wife as assistant manager. Bruce, assisted by the Urban League, had made an extraordinary effort to recruit prominent Black tenant-owners, who he maintained would serve as role models for—or guardians of— the Dunbar's less virtuous residents. Its residents would include Countee Cullen, A. Philip Randolph, Paul Robeson, Du Bois, and the Arctic explorer Matthew A. Henson. A spacious Madam C. J. Walker beauty salon occupied the Dunbar's retail space. However, the majority of the Dunbar's tenant-owners were working-class people employed as clerks, teachers, porters, and domestic servants. Bruce's snobbism, paternalistic attitude toward the Black working classes, and autocratic manner quickly drew the antipathy of the Dunbar's tenant-owners.

Not only was Roscoe Bruce's wife employed as assistant manager, but three of his children—Clara, Burrill, and Roscoe Jr.—had all been hired to the Dunbar's management staff, along with two longtime family friends. "This condition of affairs," cautioned the *Amsterdam News*, "portends subversion of the rights and reasonable demands of the tenant subscribers. The Bruces cannot afford, for the safety of their $18,000 in [aggregate] salaries, to contend strongly against Mr. Rockefeller on behalf of the tenant-owners" (January 9, 1929:1). That same month, the *Amsterdam News* published a series of editorials charging, among other things, that the Dunbar's tenant-owners had not yet received copies of leases signed the year before, that Bruce had made little or no effort to form a residents' advisory council or tenants' organization, and that the residents were being treated like children. All three criticisms, the editorials maintained, undermined the tenants' much-touted status as cooperative owners.

Within days of the publication of the second editorial in the series, Bruce struck back and served a dispossess notice to William M. Kelley, a tenant-owner and the editor-in-chief of the *Amsterdam News*. Kelley had been ten days late on his January installment and his certified check had been refused by the Dunbar's cashier. At the same time, a dispossess notice was also served to the secretary of the editorial office, also a tenant-owner (January 16, 1929:1). Two weeks later, perhaps under pressure from Heydt and the continuing bad publicity, Bruce relented and instructed his attorney to accept payments from both tenant-owners, which ended the harassing actions against the newspaper's staff.

To cultivate thrift and financial responsibility among tenant-owners and Harlem residents, Rockefeller created the Dunbar National Bank, which, located within the complex, opened in September 1928. To minimize investor risk, the bank's deposits were invested largely in government securities, rather than in real estate or in loans to Harlem businesses (Baradaran 2017). Although the bank's avoidance of real estate lending insulated it, to some degree, from the economic ravages of the Depression, its reluctance to provide financial services to Harlem residents only reinforced the systematic, race-based redlining of the community. Rockefeller maintained a tight grip on the bank, installing an all-white management team and board of directors, and retaining 75 percent of its stock despite his promise to make at least 50 percent of the bank's stock available to Harlem investors. "A few weeks ago," lamented the *Amsterdam News*, "it was understood that several Negroes had been tentatively selected to serve on the board of directors of the Dunbar National Bank but this hope has now been blasted" (*Amsterdam News* 1928). In the end, the only Black member appointed to sit on the bank's board was Roscoe C. Bruce.

If the bank's conservative investment policies spared it from financial ruin during the Depression, the Dunbar fared less well. Faced with unemployment and underemployment, many tenant-owners fell behind on their monthly installments and the project reported a deficit of $12,765 in 1930. To maintain cash flow, Rockefeller relaxed the rule against the taking in of boarders, and began allowing new tenants to rent rather than buy. Moreover, controversy swirled around the Dunbar and its management team from its opening.

The final blow to Rockefeller's experiment in profit-making affordable housing was delivered by the New Deal era's public housing initiative carried out by the Public Works Administration (PWA). In 1934 Langston W. Post, the city's tenement house commissioner and chairman of the recently created New York City Housing Authority, approached Rockefeller to buy four of the five still unimproved blocks that he owned north of the Dunbar Apartments. With funding made available through the PWA, Post hoped to construct low-income public housing. During the negotiations, Rockefeller's agent offered to sell the four blocks of vacant land together with the ailing Dunbar Garden Apartments. Rockefeller's experiment in cooperative housing was failing to generate profit, nor could its rental apartments compete with the proposed development's publicly subsidized rents. When Rockefeller's asking price far exceeded federal guidelines for land acquisition under the PWA, the negotiations collapsed (Radford 1996). The Harlem-based Consolidated Tenants League, which had advocated on behalf of the public housing project, organized protests together with Harlem's Unemployed Councils and distributed leaflets exhorting, "TENANTS OF HARLEM, WAKE UP!!! $7,000,000 from the Federal Government is knocking at your door to build houses to rent from $5 to $7 a room, per month, but the monied interests won't sell the land" (in Schwartz 1986).

In July 1935, facing escalating community demands, Post announced that the city would acquire the Rockefeller land through eminent domain, and that the PWA had allotted $4.7 million for slum clearance and construction (*New York Times* 1935). With negotiations still at an impasse, the city seized the Rockefeller land at a price of $1 million. In the following year, construction began on the nine-acre Harlem River Houses, celebrated as one of the city's first and most successful public housing developments.

In November 1937, one month after the opening of the Harlem River Houses, Rockefeller sold the Dunbar to a consortium of investors. Rockefeller's exit from the Dunbar marked the failure of his private, profit-making experiment in unsubsidized housing, along with its civilizing mission, in the face of economic depression and, equally important, a racially segregated housing market. "The Standard Oil heir," Gail Radford observed, "wanted his Harlem apartment complex to demonstrate his conviction that good housing for low-income people could be provided entirely through the private sector. When this proved impossible, he lost interest" (1996:159). On May 31, the Dunbar National Bank closed its doors. The *Amsterdam News*, in a blistering editorial, underscored the bank's failure to support Harlem businesses and its patronizing and inept leadership: "The time is long past when hand-picked stooges of rich white men should rule the race and help to keep it pauperized. Maybe the failure of the Dunbar Bank is a blessing in disguise" (April 23, 1938:12).

In the case of the Dunbar Garden Apartments, the construction of racially segregated middle-income co-op apartments in the heart of Harlem should be viewed as part of an effort to contain the Black working and middle classes within a carceral geography at a time when increasing demands were being made for residential desegregation by such organizations as the Urban League, NAACP, and Consolidated Tenants League. For Rockefeller and his peers, Black people were expected to *earn* the right to be treated as equals by submitting to racial segregation and the patronizing guidance of white elites. His scientific experiment in civilizational progress lasted less than ten years.

"The Finger of God": The Riverside Church in the City of New York

The dangerous elements of our civilization are each multiplied
and all concentrated in the city. Do we find there the conservative forces of society equally numerous and strong? Here
are the tainted spots in the body-politic; where is the salt?
—Reverend Josiah Strong

On the night of December 21, 1928, only months after the Dunbar National Bank opened, a fire raged through the largely Rockefeller-financed Riverside Church, then under construction on Morningside Heights. Hundreds of police reserves staved off the throngs of onlookers, estimated by police to have been in the thousands. During the five-alarm fire, the soaring neo-Gothic tower served as a flue for the stiff northerly wind, setting the interior scaffolding ablaze. "Flames ate up the woodwork like matchwood," the *New York Times* reported, "shooting a pillar of fire and smoke hundreds of feet into the air and showering sparks onto the roofs of the Union Theological Seminary and Columbia University buildings" (December 22, 1928:1). Damage from the fire—the third in as many months—was estimated to be over $1.7 million (R. Miller 1985). Despite these setbacks, the neo-Gothic cathedral would be completed within the next two years.

John D. Rockefeller Jr. and his sons—most notably David—would have a profound and lasting impact on the American Acropolis, providing funding to many of its existing institutions—for example, the Cathedral of St. John the Divine, Columbia University, and the Union Theological Seminary—and founding new ones, such as International House, the Riverside Church, and the Interchurch Center. After World

War II, banker David Rockefeller played a leading role in fighting the so-called "war on blight" in Morningside Heights in the face of Harlem's continued postwar expansion and the increasing presence of poor and working-class people of color in the Heights proper. David Rockefeller would help create and serve as president of Morningside Heights, Inc., a nonprofit consortium of institutions on the Hill tasked with stemming the tide of urban decline in the Heights. During the 1950s, MHI sponsored a major urban renewal project intended to shore up the Hill's northern border with Harlem. In short, Rockefeller's philanthropy in the Heights aimed at promoting the supposedly universal well-being of humanity had, as Balibar wrote, to "empty this singularity of any particularistic feature or mode of being and to fill it with universalistic elements" (Balibar 1989:11). The population of Harlem, overdetermined by the logic and practices of racial subordination and exclusion, was taken to be incapable of expressing the universal and was therefore inimical to the mission of the American Acropolis.

For Rockefeller, the Riverside Church was the materialization in space of this universal singularity—the culmination of an effort to reimagine and retool American Protestantism in the face of religious sectarianism and a growing secularism that many believed threatened to undermine the religious foundation of the civil order (Schenkel 1990). By the opening decades of the twentieth century, demographic changes, coupled with the increased influence of secular philosophies associated with modernism, had undermined Protestantism's role as the nation's common and hegemonic religion. In New York City, although Protestants remained the largest religious community in 1900, they no longer constituted the majority. Catholics alone exceeded one million persons in 1900, or roughly 30 percent of the population (Rosenwaike 1972).

The Riverside Church was the iconic symbol of and instrument for achieving this totalizing vision, for unifying Protestantism under an ecumenical banner and modernist theology, and for reconciling religion with an increasingly secular humanism. Morningside Heights, raised high above the city and already home to a constellation of elite educational, religious, and cultural institutions and constituencies, was the perfect location. Not included in this universalist vision were the Catholics, Jews, and various African American denominations of Manhattanville and Harlem. At the same time, Rockefeller preached religious tolerance and, as Schenkel observed, viewed "Catholicism, Judaism, and other religious traditions as co-belligerents in the fight to save America" (Schenkel 1990:60).

John D. Rockefeller Jr., his father, and other members of his family had attended the Park Avenue Baptist Church, which, under the leadership of Pastor Cornelius Woelfkin, had taken a liberal and modernist direction at a time when fundamentalism was gaining ground among Presbyterians and Northern Baptists. As Woelfkin neared retirement, Rockefeller and others began courting Harry Emerson Fosdick, a graduate of Union Theological Seminary, a liberal, and a vocal proponent of ecumenism (Schenkel 1990; Hudnut-Beumler 2004). Rockefeller had been so impressed by Fosdick's 1922 liberal sermon "Shall the Fundamentalist Win?" that he paid to distribute it among 130,000 pastors. After first declining Rockefeller's offer, Fosdick agreed in May 1925 (Hudnut-Beumler 2004).[3]

On May 1, 1925, Rockefeller's real estate holding company purchased an entire block on Morningside Drive (*New York Times* 1925b). This site was located adjacent to Columbia University, only a few blocks from the Cathedral of St. John the Divine. In February of that year, Rockefeller had donated $500,000 to the building fund of the still unfinished St. John the Divine, with the nonbinding qualification that the Episcopal church nominate Protestants from non-Episcopal denominations, including Rockefeller himself, to sit on its board of trustees.[4] Although the Episcopal bishop, William Manning, paid lip service to ecumenism, he rejected Rockefeller's proposal to open the cathedral's board as premature, infuriating the latter (*New York Times* 1925c; Dolkart 1998). Andrew Dolkart has suggested that it was Manning's rejection of Rockefeller's proposal that convinced him to fully commit to the new cathedral pastored by Fosdick, one that, if located on Morningside Drive, "would stand not only as a theological challenge but also, with its proposed tall carillon tower, loom as a visible challenge to the still incomplete Episcopal cathedral" (1998:73).

To the north of the new cathedral was public parkland, but also the multiethnic working-class neighborhood of Manhattanville and the still-expanding Black mecca, Harlem. In the imagined geography of the American Acropolis, these communities were beyond the pale of universalist modernity. The plateau's elevated topography, natural barriers, and class-cum-racial social geography assured, at least in the minds of its stakeholders, that the Heights would remain untainted by alterity "indefinitely."

The final design, made public in late 1926, was inspired by the Chartres Cathedral in France and included a sanctuary seating 2,500, a 392-foot-high tower, and a 72-bell carillon memorializing Laura Spelman, Rockefeller's mother (Dolkart 1998). Architect Charles Collens wrote in the *Church Monthly*, "It is not planned to consider this building as of a temporary character. Forty years is the average life of a New York church building. Stone, steel and concrete will all be so designed and assembled as to create a structure whose enduring qualities will far outlast its more temporary neighbors. For many generations to come, the tower should symbolize the finger of God pointing upward and the carillon celestial music" (*New York Times* 1926:3).

Verticality still mattered. Moreover, in this temporal narrative, the Riverside Church was untethered from time, universal, and future-oriented, in sharp contrast to its ephemeral, contingent, and implicitly obsolete religious neighbors. This contrast between universal and particular, modern and obsolete, future and past defined the imagined boundary between the American Acropolis and surrounding racialized, working-class neighborhoods, and also structured the discourses and tropes of urban preservation and the future "war against blight."

The new cathedral was designed in keeping with the institutional church tradition. Cities were viewed by Protestants as locations where religious influences were weak, vice and corruption were rampant, and immigrants spread diseases, intemperance, socialism, and "Romanism" (see Josiah Strong 1885). In the face of these urban perils, some churches sought to retain, expand, and insulate their congregations by providing vocational training, lectures, reading rooms, gymnasia, bathing facilities, and other social services and facilities (Boyer 1978). The completed neo-Gothic cathedral was an institutional church par excellence—a "total institution," in sociologist Erving Goffman's terms (Goffman 1961). The twenty-one usable floors in the church's tower housed a men's library and reading room, church offices, a sewing room, K-12 classrooms, a young people's meeting room, a women's lounge and classroom, and a kitchen. On the two floors below the church auditorium were a multipurpose assembly room, choir rooms, showers, bowling alleys, and a gymnasium (*New York Times* 1926; Riverside Church 1931).

Although Riverside's facilities and social activities, like its benevolent giving, were intended to serve a larger parish community, its members were understood to be the predominantly white middle- and upper-class population on the Hill—a population of comparatively liberal, modernist, and secular-leaning professionals that both Rockefeller and Fosdick aspired to engage. A 1956 church self-study clearly expressed this founding church mission: "The move from Park Avenue twenty-five years ago was a bold, deliberate decision to establish a liberal, dynamic Christian enterprise where the preaching ministry and the progressive program of the Church could influence the faculties, students, and residential neighbors of a group of important institutions" (in Weisenfeld 2004:119).

Early on the Riverside Church's benevolent giving adopted an approach, as Judith Weisenfeld put it, that was often "paternalistic and tended to keep the congregation safely insulated from difficult issues like urban poverty and racism" (Weisenfeld 2004:118). When the Reverend Egbert Ethelred Brown, pastor of the Harlem Unitarian Church and a longtime civil rights activist, appealed to Riverside's Benevolence Committee for support in 1941, the church's associate minister, Eugene Carter, informed the committee,

> I cannot imagine that the philosophy of the Benevolence Committee leaves an opening for such an appeal as this and am assuming that it will get no financial response. This is a local church—probably no better and possibly much worse than any one of the scores of local congregations in Harlem. My own opinion is that a response in money to any local congregation to pay expenses is outside our perview [sic]. (in Weisenfeld 2004:126)

By contrast, Riverside's Benevolence Committee did provide financial assistance to predominantly white congregations on Morningside Heights (including St. John the Divine) and to churches elsewhere that provided services to poor multiethnic neighborhoods, such as the Church of All Nations on Manhattan's Lower East Side (Weisenfeld 2004).

Fosdick, like other race liberals of the 1930s, embraced racial equality in principle, and the church hosted speakers and events that spotlighted interracial cooperation, Black achievement, and his own liberalism. Fosdick denounced de facto racial segregation in the North as unchristian, was a vocal supporter of anti-lynching legislation and the movement to abolish the poll tax, and was a member of the sponsoring committee of the Scottsboro Defense Committee (R. Miller 1985). In 1933 Fosdick convinced Ruby Bates, one of the two accusers of the nine Scottsboro boys, to return to Alabama and recant her false testimony given at an earlier trial. Bates had fled her home in Huntsville weeks before the new trial and had ended up in New York City, where, as Fosdick wrote in his autobiography, she "crept into my study at the Riverside Church and confessed to me that she had lied. . . . I appealed to her troubled conscience, and sent her back to confess her perjury at the second trial, lest she be in effect a murderer of the innocent" (Fosdick 1956:283). Bates had seen Fosdick's photograph in the newspaper and judged him to be honest.

However, as Schenkel noted, Fosdick's race liberalism was compromised by his elitism, or more accurately, by his "call for 'a genuine moral aristocracy,'" capable of reviving the spiritual foundations of society (1990:53). As Schenkel noted, Fosdick also often made condescending, if not outright racist, comments and jokes about typically poor and uneducated African Americans and other people of color—quips all too familiar to vaudevillian audiences. Schenkel highlighted the seeming paradox: "The moral aristocracy was to be mobilized against prejudice and oppression while being reassured of its difference from racism's downtrodden victims" (1990:67).

However, Fosdick's racism had roots firmly planted in social evolutionism and in the belief of the innate superiority of the Anglo-Saxon race. In a 1920 sermon, for example, Fosdick stated,

> Races are not equal. I no more know why than I know why one son of a family will be a genius, and another a dunce. Only here is the fact: you put the Anglo-Saxon people almost anywhere on earth, and before very long they will be running the government. The African people after unimpeded tenure of a whole continent for unnumbered ages have never, unaided, been able to establish a settled government. There is no need in blinking our eyes to these plain facts. (in R. Miller 1985:452–53)

Reverend Fosdick was also among a handful of liberal religious leaders to serve on the Advisory Council of the American Eugenics Society, whose appeal to modern science may have served to distance him from the anti-scientism of the religious fundamentalists (Rosen 2004). "Few matters are more pressingly important," Fosdick wrote, "than the application to our social problems of such well-established information in the realm of eugenics as we actually possess" (in Rosen 2004:116). And like John D. Rockefeller Jr., his benefactor, Fosdick was a supporter of Margaret Sanger's planned parenthood movement and voluntary sterilization, and he lent his support to the Sterilization League of New Jersey (R. Miller 1985).

Unsurprisingly, the membership of the Riverside Church remained almost exclusively white well into the 1950s; in 1956 only 10 percent of its members were people of color. As Lawrence Mamiya observed, "The social and psychological distance was great between the largely elite, white congregation in the towering cathedral structure and the Negro masses in the Valley below it" (2004:175). When asked why Black membership at the Riverside Church was so low during his pastorship, Fosdick managed to couch their absence as the result of a paternalistic act of Christian charity:

> In answer to your question as to whether we have made any definite attempt to get the people of Harlem to attend the Riverside Church, the answer is distinctly negative. We should have thought that an invasion of the membership of the colored churches. If we succeeded in winning away their loyal people, it would have been the most well-to-do and the best educated, and the ablest who would have come to us. That would have been a distinct disservice to the cause of Christ in Harlem, where intelligent workers in the colored churches are so desperately needed. (in R. Miller 1985:462)

The church's charitable work focused on the nearby multiethnic population of Manhattanville, which, located on the northern border of Morningside Heights, posed the gravest and most immediate threat to the racial stability of the institutions of the Acropolis, its upper-class white residents, and Fosdick's vision of "thoughtfully purposed, wisely planned homes." Moreover, the fact that the district was multiracial, albeit far from integrated, meant that financial donations could be construed as promoting interracial understanding and cooperation—that is, winning the hearts and minds of the unenlightened one soul at a time.

"Waiting for the Barbarians": Preparing for Threats to Come

In April 1933, representatives of the educational, religious, and cultural institutions on the Hill assembled in the trustees' office at Columbia University to announce the formation of the Neighborhood Association of Morningside Heights and Manhattanville and launch a "vast program of sociological research and relief work" (*New York Herald*, April 26, 1933:16). Among the institutions represented were the Riverside Church, Union Theological Seminary (UTS), the Lincoln School, Teachers College, the Juilliard School of Music, the Cathedral of St. John the Divine, the Jewish Theological Seminary, and Columbia University. Included on its executive committee were Herbert E. Hawkes, dean of Columbia College, sociologist Robert S. Lynd and labor economist Paul Brissenden, both at Columbia, Philip M. Stimson, a deacon at Riverside Church, and Teachers College professors F. Ernest Johnson and Patty Smith Hill. A pioneer in the kindergarten movement, Hill was one of the founders of the Institute of Child Welfare Research at Teachers College and a long-time advocate for greater university involvement in community services and development. The meeting had been convened by President Butler after he had been approached by a group of faculty, based at Teachers College and UTS, with the suggestion that the university and peer institutions play a more proactive and responsible role in studying and addressing the development needs of surrounding working-class areas. Butler had chosen the institutions participating in the new research and development association (Lucero 2009).

All the persons involved in the new organization were affiliated with the major institutions on the Hill, although its target areas for study and services were Manhattanville and southern sections of Central and West Harlem. Notably absent from the consortium was the Harlem-based New York Urban League, an organization with the experience, research capability, and professional staff to contribute significantly to such an effort. The project quickly fizzled out, and no comprehensive study or service plan was ever produced.

Nevertheless, the aborted effort did create a framework for inter-institutional collaboration on the Hill, and some institutions—notably Teachers College, UTS, and the Riverside Church—did make efforts during the Depression to address the needs of poor and working-class people. In 1930 students and faculty at Union, led by Professor Arthur Swift, established the Union Neighborhood Center in the heart of the "La Salle Street slum." The neighborhood center provided recreational services for youth and adults, sewing and arts and crafts classes, and a meeting room for clubs; later it hosted meetings and social gatherings of Local #9 of the Workers Alliance of America, a Popular Front organization founded in 1935 to mobilize unemployed workers. Most of the Black people involved in the neighborhood center were affiliated with the interracial Workers Alliance (Snyder 1936a).

The Riverside Church provided modest donations to the Union Neighborhood Center through the 1930s; for example, in 1935 the Women's Bible Class provided funding to send thirteen African American boys to the New York Urban League's summer camp; the Benevolence Committee provided funding for the center's recreational activities, along with Barnard College, Fosdick, and Mrs. John D. Rockefeller Jr. However, the Benevolence Committee also sharply criticized the center's lack of professionalism, numerous programs, and poor bookkeeping in a report that, even if deserved, suggests that the committee and church were intent on exercising a firm, if not patronizing, control over the community-based organizations that it supported (Weisenfeld 2004). This pattern of paternalistic governance, coupled with race liberalism at a distance, characterized the Hill's relationship to Harlem over the longue durée.

"Area No. 14": An Experiment in Radical Educational Reform

Dare the school build a new social order?
—George S. Counts

In September 1936, New College, an experimental undergraduate college created at Teachers College in 1932, released a report entitled *Area No. 14: A Study of an Urban Area*. The area included all of Manhattanville and areas of Harlem bordering on Morningside Heights.[5] The survey report, prepared by Agnes Snyder, compiled research that had been conducted by student committees during the previous year, including data on and a brief analysis of the area's population, housing conditions, juvenile delinquency, educational resources, and recreational facilities.

In the introduction to the report, Snyder underscored the importance of training teachers to understand and participate in the communities in which they worked:

> The teacher's work in the classroom is not carried on in isolation but is planned and carried forward as a contributing force to the growth of the community. Instead of living apart in an academic world consisting largely of co-workers in his own profession, he associates with men and women representing all the vocational and social interests of the community. (1936a:1)

This community approach marked a radical break with the limited and patronizing terms of engagement imposed by the American Acropolis upon neighboring working-class and increasingly racialized communities. Advancing a critical pedagogy anticipating Brazilian educator Paulo Freire's "pedagogy of the oppressed," New College's founders stressed the co-production of knowledge between educators and the communities that they served. Reforming schools was inseparable from promoting fundamental socioeconomic and political changes (Freire 1970).

Snyder, a leading figure in the nursery school movement, was a professor at Teachers College and had been among the faculty group that had urged President Butler to involve the institutions on the Hill in community research and development. Snyder and other New College faculty members were associated with the social reconstructionist movement at Teachers College, which, during the 1930s, maintained that schools and teachers should play an active role in reconstructing society toward greater socioeconomic equality. Among its proponents were Snyder, William H. Kilpatrick, George S. Counts, Harold Rugg, and philosophy professor John Dewey, whose book *Democracy and Education* (1916) had inspired the social reconstructionists (Welton 2002; McCarthy and Murrow 2013).

In his book *Dare the School Build a New Social Order?*, George Counts criticized earlier, progressive school reformers whose efforts served the interests of the middle and upper classes—for example, the Lincoln School—and who, as he phrased it, "wish to guard their offspring from too strenuous endeavor and from coming into too intimate contact with the grimmer aspects of industrial society" (1932:6). By contrast, Counts offered a community-engaged pedagogy, influenced by Dewey's instrumentalist philosophy, that stressed the practical consequences of ideas and, more to the point, education.

The more theoretically oriented faction of the social reconstructionists established the journal the *Social Frontier* in 1934. In contrast to the mainstream educational journals of the period, the *Social Frontier* exhorted educators to use schools as agents of societal change. Snyder, Thomas Alexander, and Florence Stratemeyer, founders of New College, were associated with the "methodological" wing of social reconstructionism. They focused on teacher training, curriculum development, and community engagement projects like the Area No. 14 study.

The proposal for New College had been developed by Alexander, who had been an early proponent of John Dewey's progressive education movement. William F. Russell, who had succeeded his father, James E. Russell, as dean of Teachers College, had been interested in creating an experimental school, or laboratory school, to boost the college's reputation for innovation and distinguish his deanship from his father's thirty-year tenure. The school opened its doors on September 15, 1932, on the fifth floor of the Russell Hall Library at Teachers College (Lucero 2009).

By August 1932, sixty-five students were enrolled at New College. Among the admitted group, fifty-three were women and, although Alexander had hoped for a student body representative of the nation, 40 percent of the admitted students were from New York City. Although New College did not document its students' race, only two Black students were known to have attended: Mercer Ellington, son of composer and bandleader Duke Ellington, and Ruth Ellington, the latter's younger sister (Lucero 2009). In this respect, New College perpetuated a well-established pattern of Black racial exclusion. The college did record students' religion and, in stark contrast to Columbia College—notorious for its Jewish quota—over 30 percent of the initially enrolled group were Jews.

New College's curriculum was organized around a series of seminars and internships. The seminars engaged students and faculty in the study and investigation of social issues and problems and in the analysis and dissemination of findings. The internships involved students in research and work activities at a variety of locations, such as a rural farm in North Carolina, an industrial factory, and schools and settlement houses. "In these settings," Mary Rose McCarthy and Sonia Murrow wrote, "students were encouraged to envision the social reconstruction of American society as including improvements in the social and economic circumstances of immigrants, the poor, and people of color" (2013:25).

The Area No. 14 seminar was organized by Agnes Snyder and built upon the work of her colleague and friend Patty Smith Hill, who, with funding from the Federal Emergency Relief Administration (FERA) and the New York Foundation, had opened the Hilltop Nursery School in 1933 on West 123rd Street in Harlem, one block west of the Lincoln School. By 1936, Hill was working closely with Snyder and New College, and Hilltop's services had expanded beyond its FERA nursery school to include an after-school program that offered recreational programs and classes in art, drama, music, home nursing, and foreign languages for all grade levels; an adult night school that provided instruction in public speaking, typing, and academic subjects; and teacher training for New College and Teachers College students. Hilltop's programs served the ethnically and racially diverse populations of Manhattanville and sections of Harlem.

During the summer of 1936, the students in Snyder's Educational Seminar I—sixty-five in all and divided into research committees—continued their work on the Area No. 14 study, visiting and conducting interviews at community schools, health clinics, municipal agencies, neighborhood associations, and political meetings, and compiling population, educational, housing, and other quantitative data. Representatives from municipal agencies and community-based organizations were also invited to meet with the student committees (Snyder 1936a). Based upon the yearlong research project, combining ethnographic research with the analysis of quantitative data, Snyder's seminar produced a comprehensive survey of neighborhood conditions, and generated four principles defining the role of the school in community development, which stressed the importance of collaborating with the community in developing curricula and addressing social problems:

1. It is the responsibility of the school to study the environment both physical and social and, in cooperation with other agencies, to define the problems of the community, set goals of achievement, and carry its share in the development of the community.

2. The school has the further responsibility of shaping its curriculum with reference to community needs.
3. The curriculum of the school must take into account the educational needs of all ages from infancy through adulthood.
4. The specific contributions of the school are: (1) The selection and organization of materials from all fields of knowledge with reference to their use in solving the problems of living; (2) the teaching of the use of such materials in solving the problems of living.

The phrase "problems of living" was a critical concept in New College's philosophy of education and referred to criteria for assessing the relevance of the curriculum to addressing the social needs and lived experiences of students and, by extension, their communities (Stemple 1949). These problems or, perhaps better, challenges included achieving economic and political security; adjusting to and cooperating with people; maintaining physical and mental health; and acquiring and transmitting social heritage. Less a final report than a blueprint for ongoing social research and praxis, the Area No. 14 study was a tool for determining how these evolving problems of living might be collaboratively addressed and resolved.

The survey report tangentially raised the issue of race relations by documenting individual attitudes about race and casual observations concerning group interactions. However, it did not address or identify structural issues of racial discrimination and segregation as "persistent problems of living." The absence is striking, given that the 1935 Harlem riot, which was well within Area No. 14, had taken place only the spring before Snyder's seminar. Moreover, in 1935–1936, the riot commission appointed by Mayor La Guardia to investigate the causes of the unrest convened well-publicized public hearings to investigate police misconduct, housing conditions, health and educational inequities, and other problems. The mayor's commission was headed by African American sociologist E. Franklin Frazier and included Countee Cullen, A. Philip Randolph, and Judge Hubert Thomas Delany. Although the commission's report was never officially released, a pirated copy was published by the *New York Amsterdam News* in July 1935. At a community meeting addressing the state of Harlem's schools, held while the Area No. 14 study was in progress, the Reverend John W. Robinson, a member of the commission, discussed the impact of racial inequality on Harlem's Black students: "The conditions of our public schools and treatment accorded the children contributed . . . to that violent outburst of last March 19th. . . . Practices of racial discrimination, overcrowded classrooms, antiquated facilities, and dilapidated buildings must all be reckoned as contributing elements. Harlem is part of New York City—it is not in Dixie" (*Amsterdam News*, March 28, 1936:3).

Snyder's seminar, like Fosdick's race liberalism, was limited by its focus on opportunities for interracial understanding and cooperation and, as a consequence, disregarded power-laden structures and practices of racial inequality and exclusion. The Area No. 14 study described disparities in the condition of the district's housing stock, detailing variations in age, maintenance, density of occupation and costs, but ignored the impact of residential segregation on these outcomes. By contrast, the riot commission's report revealed what George Edmund Haynes and the Urban League had argued for decades:

> All of the figures which we have cited tend to prove that the Negro tenants of Harlem pay relatively higher rentals than tenants in other sections of the city. Moreover, they show that the high rentals require Negro families to surrender an exorbitantly large part of their meagre incomes for the privilege of living in dwellings, many of which are unsanitary and dilapidated, and some totally unfit for human habitation. That the landlords of Harlem are able to exercise such autocratic power over the lives of 200,000 people is due to the fact that Negroes cannot move about freely in the city and live where they please. (New York City Mayor's Commission 1936:70)

The variations in rental costs, housing conditions, and household size that Snyder's group documented in 1935–1936 were strongly conditioned by racial segregation. Black people lived on racially and ethnically mixed blocks in Manhattanville, but they lived in racially segregated, all-Black buildings. By focusing narrowly on individual and group interactions, Snyder's seminar failed to address the structural engines of American racism, racial inequality, and racial violence.

The striking contrast between the two studies illustrates the distinction between a power-evasive race liberalism and a structural critique of racism; it also underscores the epistemological gulf that existed between African American scholars and urban experts on the one hand, and progressive white educators ensconced within the rarified precincts of the Acropolis on the other. That Mayor La Guardia "insistently refused" to release the riot report, as the *Amsterdam News* put it, and Snyder's seminar ignored it suggests a systemic refusal, both political and epistemological, to recognize the intellectual authority of Black experts, a refusal indexing the deeply entrenched nature of American racism.

Racial inequality—or, for that matter, gender inequality—was virtually absent from New College's framing of the "persistent problems of living" and from the planning documents for Snyder's Area No. 14 seminar. If New College's critical pedagogy and praxis sought to achieve the reconstruction of society, it was a project that, at best, addressed the interests of Black people only collaterally or, at worst, ignored them. In neither case were Black people regarded as autonomous agents of social transformation (cf. McCarthy and Murrow 2013:30).

Only weeks after the Area No. 14 study had been completed, Dean Russell convened a meeting of New College's Administrative Board, asking it to consider disbanding the college. Russell's unanticipated request occurred amidst intense student activism at New College (for example, in support of the unionization of teachers and loyalists during the civil war in Spain), and accusations that the school had been infiltrated by communists—red-baiting that intensified in the coming years (Lucero 2009). Dean Russell had also raised concerns to Alexander and others regarding New College's annual deficit, though during the Depression such deficits were not unusual. Moreover, some Teachers College faculty questioned the efficacy and generalizability of New College's community-based approach to school reform and social change—a criticism that had been leveled at the Speyer School and Settlement years earlier.

In the summer of 1938, a controversy erupted at Teachers College surrounding the publication of a doctoral dissertation criticizing the American Legion. Written by William Gellermann and supervised by George Counts, "The American Legion as Educator" argued that the Legion, known for its anti-labor vigilantism and red-baiting, pursued the interests of corporate and military elites, and that its educational activism propped up an obsolete and harmful status quo (Laats 2015). The book's publication by the Teachers College Press triggered a quick response from the Legion's national commander, Daniel J. Doherty, who declared in a press release that "many of our institutions of higher learning are hotbeds of communism for the dissemination of theories and philosophies of government which are entirely alien to the American concept." In another press statement, the Legion's state commander suggested that Gellermann and Counts "emigrate to that utopia of Soviet Russia where they will find no free enterprise nor private ownership of property."

Dean Russell, perhaps alarmed by the widespread press coverage of the controversy, invited Doherty to speak at a conference sponsored by the Advanced School of Education at Teachers College in July. After defending the Legion against Gellermann's thesis, Doherty asked, "Why not rid this institution of such baleful influences? . . . It is time that Columbia, through the actions of its trustees or other authorized body, differentiate between educators and propagandists. Do you like having it called 'the big red university'?" Some in the audience, which included New College students and faculty attending the summer session, hissed in reaction to Doherty's remarks. Russell expressed his contempt for the hissers, and then tellingly assured the gathering otherwise:

> Some say that Teachers College is a Red institution. I know better than anyone else does and I say it is not a Red institution, it is a conservative place. I have gone over the list of 151 members of the faculty and I say there are seven who might be considered a little extra liberal and that the three most radical of these are less radical than the British Labor Party. We think that we have one Communist among us, but I haven't been able to find out who he is, so I couldn't fire him if I wanted to. Teachers College is not Red. It is red, white and blue. (*New York Times* 1938)

However, well before the American Legion controversy erupted, the fate of both New College and the Hilltop project had been sealed. Since Hilltop had expanded its activities beyond its FERA nursery to include an after-school program, adult night school, and teacher training program for New College and Teachers College students, Snyder and Patty Smith Hill had struggled to raise money to renovate its overused and dilapidated building on West 123rd Street, the former home of the Jewish Theological Seminary. With no funds forthcoming, Hilltop was reorganized as an independent parents' cooperative. The school moved to a new location at 1125 Amsterdam Avenue. New College continued to play an advisory role, but students and faculty were required to become members of the association (Lucero 2009).

In February 1938, Thomas Alexander, founder and chairman of New College, was replaced by Dean Russell with Donald Tewksbury, former dean of Bard College. On November 9, 1938, only months after the American Legion brouhaha, Tewksbury sent a memo announcing a special assembly (Lucero 2009). At the assembly, Russell began by praising the innovative work of the college, its professional subject matter, seminar approach, internships, and community-based work, which, he stated, were "securing wide recognition and incorporation in other institutions for the education of teachers." Then came the bad news:

> We have . . . recommended the discontinuance of New College as an experimental unit of Teachers College as of June 30, 1939; and this recommendation has been approved by the President of the University and by the Board of trustees. (in Lucero 2009:475)

New College had become a lightning rod within Columbia for conservative red-baiting and, more generally, criticism of progressive activism during the Depression. For President Butler, a staunch critic of socialism and the Marxian thesis of class struggle, the label "big red university," the activism of New College's students, and the foundational tenets of social reconstructionism likely rendered the continued existence of the experimental college untenable.[6]

Equally threatening was the critical pedagogic praxis of New College, as evidenced by Agnes Snyder's Area No. 14 project and Patty Smith Hill's Hilltop school. By emphasizing community engagement and the co-production of knowledge between educators and a variety of community-based actors in the development of curricula and strategizing social change, New College's faculty and students challenged—indeed, transgressed—the sociospatial, symbolic, and epistemic boundaries that set apart the institutions of the American Acropolis from adjoining racially and ethnically diverse working-class communities.

As Harlem's Black population continued to expand after the Second World War, Columbia University and other institutions on the Hill adopted another strategy for preserving the American Acropolis: racial dispossession, or, in the words of Baldwin, "Negro removal." Only a few years after the closing of New College and in the midst of world war, Harlem again exploded in rioting and social unrest, adding critical urgency to efforts on the Hill to arrest the expansion of the Black and brown populations of Manhattanville and Harlem and create an interinstitutional alliance with the wherewithal to do so.

6

Waging the War Against Blight

A few hours after my father's funeral, while he lay in state in
the undertaker's chapel, a race riot broke out in Harlem. . . .
The day of my father's funeral had also been my nineteenth
birthday. As we drove him to the graveyard, the spoils of injustice, anarchy, discontent, and hatred were all around us.
—James Baldwin

On the night of August 1, 1943, Private Robert Bandy and his mother,
Florine Roberts, entered the lobby of the Braddock Hotel at the corner
of 126th Street and Eighth Avenue, around the block from the Apollo
Theater. Roberts had traveled to Harlem from Connecticut to spend
the weekend with her son and his fiancée. Bandy was in uniform; Roberts had gone to a movie and restaurant with the young couple, then
returned to the hotel to pick up her luggage. When Roberts and her
son approached the front desk, a young woman, Marjorie Polite, was
involved in a heated argument with a white police officer. James Collins, a rookie policeman, had been assigned to the hotel lobby on what
was referred to as "raided premises duty"—that is, the stationing of uniformed police at hotels that had been previously raided for prostitution
or other vices (Brandt 1996). When Collins manhandled Polite as he
attempted to arrest her for disturbing the peace, either Roberts or her
son intervened, and a fight ensued between the soldier and the police
officer. When Bandy managed to get hold of the policeman's nightstick
and hit him on the head, Collins shot the soldier in the back. Both were
taken to the hospital.

Although Bandy was not seriously wounded, rumors began to spread
through Harlem that the soldier had been killed by the rookie policeman. Thousands gathered outside the Braddock Hotel, Harlem's 23rd
Precinct, and Sydenham Hospital, where Bandy had been admitted. By
ten o'clock that night, rioting had broken out along West 125th Street

and on the avenues between 110th and 145th Streets. Mayor La Guardia mobilized six thousand police officers—roughly one-third of the city's force—and dispatched them to Harlem, along with military police, air raid wardens, and a Black civilian force. Eight thousand National Guard members were placed on standby. La Guardia declared a 10:30 p.m. curfew, closed bars and liquor stores, banned vehicular traffic, and suspended the wartime dim-out of lights in the curfew-affected areas. When order was restored on August 2, six African Americans were dead, over five hundred arrested, and some six hundred persons injured, the majority of whom were Black. Business owners, primarily white, estimated their losses at $4 million (Capeci 1977:163).

In radio broadcasts on August 2, Mayor La Guardia declared that the rioting was not racially motivated but was instead the work of thieves and young hoodlums. However, the uprising had everything to do with racial injustice. The Reverend Adam Clayton Powell Jr., pastor of the Abyssinian Baptist Church and a City Council member, issued a statement attributing the rioting to "blind, smoldering and unorganized resentment against the Jim Crow treatment of Negro men in the armed forces and the unusually high rents and cost of living forced upon Negroes in Harlem" (*New York Herald Tribune* 1943c). In fact, Powell had argued before the City Council only weeks before the riot that, if the police did not address the widespread police brutality against Black people in Harlem, rioting would take place as it had in Detroit in June (*New York Times* 1943a). Powell's point was reiterated by Arthur G. Hays, a renowned civil rights attorney and a former member of the 1935 Mayor's Riot Commission. In a letter to the *New York Times*, Hays pointed out that the suppressed commission's report had emphasized policing injustices and abuses, which had subsequently been ignored and, as a result, remained flashpoints for the 1943 unrest: "After reciting violations of the civil rights of people by the police, our report of 1935 said: '. . . the insecurity of the individual in Harlem against police aggression is in our judgment one of the most potent causes of the existing hostility to authority.'" Hays went on to extensively quote recommendations that had been made by the Frazier-led commission, including the formation of a civilian complaint committee to review cases of police brutality and abuse, educating police in the rights of citizens and appropriate use of force, and the investigation and prosecution of police officers who broke the law, "just as vigorously as where any other person is charged with a crime" (*New York Times* 1943b).

The La Guardia administration had come under fire for its anti-Black surveillance and policing of Harlem and other discriminatory policies. Only months before the uprising, Harlem's famed Savoy Ballroom was closed by the police and its license revoked on vice charges. The ballroom had allegedly allowed, if not promoted, prostitution, which the authorities claimed had led to the infection of white active-duty soldiers with venereal diseases. Syphilis had long been viewed as disproportionately affecting Black people due to their alleged sexual promiscuity and moral laxity (J. Jones 1981).

The charge that the Savoy Ballroom and Harlem's other entertainment venues were responsible for the spreading of venereal diseases among white soldiers and civilians—hence undermining the war effort—masked deeper anxieties over racial miscegenation, white racial degeneration, and the spatial ordering of racial difference. Harlem's music clubs and ballrooms, as well as hotels such as the Braddock, had been subjected to a prolonged campaign of intensive surveillance and harassment. Young Black men, clad in drape-shape, pleated zoot suits, were also a target of police repression for their flaunting of wartime fabric restrictions and hep-cat slang and style that constituted "a subversive refusal to be subservient" (Kelley 1996:166). Mexican American and other non-white youth had been the target of rioting white servicemen during the "zoot suit riots" in Los Angeles in June 1943 (Mazón 2010; Kelley 2009). In a telegram to Mayor La Guardia, Walter White, president of the NAACP, countered that the real reason for the Savoy's closing was that its management had refused to prohibit interracial dancing. White pointed out to La Guardia that the deputy police commissioner had repeatedly demanded that the Savoy cease advertising in white newspapers, hiring white bands, and permitting "mixed dancing," all of which, it was feared, attracted white patrons to its legendary dance floor (*Amsterdam News* 1943a; *Chicago Defender* 1943).

In an October interview with the *Afro-American*, Mayor La Guardia blamed conditions in Harlem and the riot on southern migrants, deploying a well-worn evasion of urban racial inequalities:

So many uneducated masses have come up from the South, I'm frankly worried. It's hard to assimilate some of them. They are not accustomed to education, mixed schools, decent housing or personal cleanliness. They are not even willing to send their children to school. Their life habits are simply not like ours. We are getting a higher percentage of venereal disease. These people have never had the opportunity to use free clinics, or free nursing services. They don't understand them and they don't use them. (*Afro American* 1943)

Echoing the historiography of the Dunning School and John D. Rockefeller's paternalistic philanthropy, Harlem *had* suitable housing, schools, and health services; southern migrants were just not prepared or sufficiently evolved to take advantage of them. The solution was to focus on the segregated assimilation of Black migrants, not substantive social change.

A second lightning rod for criticism of the administration's race-related policies was its support for the construction of the racially seg-regated Stuyvesant Town housing development on the East Side. The sixty-seven-acre project was sponsored by the Metropolitan Life Insur-ance Company, using the city's power of eminent domain and benefit-ing from a twenty-five-year tax exemption. At a May 1943 City Council meeting, Adam Clayton Powell Jr., together with Councilman Stanley Isaacs, introduced a resolution calling on the Board of Estimate, poised to vote on the $50 million project, to bar housing developments that ra-cially discriminated from receiving tax exemptions (Stern, Mellins, and Fishman 1995). "We cannot allow domestic fascism," Powell declared, "to score victories at home while our men are dying abroad" (*Baltimore Afro-American*, May 29, 1943:5). On the day before the Board of Estimate vote, urban development tsar Robert Moses, who had brokered the deal with Metropolitan Life, wrote a letter to the *New York Times*, rebutting point by point the myriad criticisms that had been leveled against the project—every criticism, that is, save its discriminatory policy. Fred-erick Ecker, chairman of the board of Metropolitan Life, when asked about the exclusion of Black tenants, explained, "Negroes and whites don't mix. Perhaps they will in a hundred years, but they don't now. If we brought them into this development, it would be to the detriment

of the city, too, because it would depress all the surrounding property"
(*Amsterdam News* 1943b).

The Board of Estimate approved the development on June 3 by an 11–5
vote. Only days later, at a freedom rally held at Madison Square Garden
against the poll tax, racial discrimination in the military and in the defense industries, and approval of Stuyvesant Town, Councilman Powell called for the impeachment of La Guardia before a crowd of some
twenty thousand, arguing that it and similar projects "will build here in
the heart of Manhattan a Southern town with all the worst elements of
Hitlerism in it" (*New York Herald Tribune* 1943d).

The La Guardia administration's support of segregated housing was
unacceptable to Powell and the many Harlemites who remained bitter over Rockefeller's aborted experiment with the Dunbar apartments
and bank. Moreover, they were still suffering from the Depression-era
housing crisis. The contradiction between fighting fascism abroad while
tolerating racism at home rendered the shooting of a Black soldier by
a white policeman a potent symbol of racial injustice and Black anger,
indexing perduring issues of police brutality, housing segregation, and
broader issues of economic injustice and racial discrimination in American society.

Perhaps no one better captured this postwar challenge than did Richard Wright in his introduction to the landmark study of Chicago, *Black
Metropolis*, where he linked the future of the nation to the resolution of
the "Negro problem" and to lessons learned from the rise of fascism and
anti-Semitic violence in Europe:

> What benefits will accrue to our country if this problem is solved? Will it
> so unify our moral duality as to permit the flowering of our political and
> cultural expression? (Some politicians have estimated that the presence of
> rigid anti-Negro feeling in our country has retarded our political devel-
> opment by more than fifty years!) Or will America, when she is brought
> face to face with the problem of the Negro, collapse in a moral spasm, as
> did Europe when confronted with the problem of the Jew? (1945:xxxi)

In the aftermath of the 1943 Harlem riot, the *Columbia Daily Spectator* published two articles presenting statements from faculty members
on the events. All four of those interviewed recognized that "the Negro

issue" needed to be addressed after the war; none spoke to the issues that had incited the uprising. Professor Ralph Linton, chair of the anthropology department, denied that race had been a factor, yet worried that the Harlem riot would be used by Axis powers as propaganda to expose the hypocrisy of America's defense of democracy. "It was apparently an entirely Negro show," Linton observed, "except for the fact that the stores that were looted were operated by whites. I think that the causes were simply rising prices, and resentment against alleged mistreatment of Negro soldiers." James Gutman, a professor of philosophy, reiterated Linton's curious denial:

> I was in Harlem that morning at nine o'clock. Little, excited groups of people, both white and Negro, were standing together on the streets discussing the disturbance, apparently very much sobered by what had occurred. There seemed to be no signs of racial antagonism whatsoever. (*Columbia Daily Spectator*, August 13, 1943:1, 4)

Linton and Gutman echoed the La Guardia administration's denial that structural racism had been at the heart of the uprising. Gutman's misplaced anecdotal certainty indicated not only the heuristic limits of racial liberalism, given its narrow focus on interpersonal understanding, but also the abstract notion of the social contract. Stunning, too, is a seeming lack of awareness of the events, personages, social issues, and living conditions of a community—the Black mecca of the Western Hemisphere—located less than a mile from the university (Mills 2008).

To deny that racism was at the crux of the riot and similar unrest requires the erasure of the words and deeds of Harlemites, as well as of the work of Black researchers and civil rights activists; in short, and to paraphrase Fabian once again, it requires treating Harlem and its residents as a category and not an object—or *subject*—of thought. The significance of the Harlem riot, its "Negro show," could be filled in with casual observations, callow opinions, and commonsense knowledge, delineating an epistemological and spatiotemporal divide between Harlem and the Heights. The lackluster efforts of the institutions on the Hill to improve postwar conditions in nearby Manhattanville—by 1950 a predominantly Black and Puerto Rican neighborhood—were initially dominated by an ameliorist or, better, biopolitical approach that framed structural racial and class inequalities as problems of education, social work, and mental health.

In February 1943, months before the riot, the Reverend James Robinson—the man who had been chosen to direct the Union Neighborhood Center over the objections of the laity of the Riverside Church—denounced racial discrimination in the military and defense industries at a conference held at Teachers College. "The Negro soldier," he declared, "hears platitudes about democracy but can see no adequate demonstration of them here." Robinson cautioned the audience that if the nation did not address the race problem with frankness and courage following the war, there would be social unrest and perhaps violence, since the Black soldiers who had been taught to kill for democracy abroad "are not going to discriminate between a German and American who does the same thing" (*New York Herald Tribune* 1943e). Robinson continued that he still believed that education was essential to advancing the cause of racial justice, but charged that universities continued to discriminate in the recruitment of students and faculty and thus only reinforced existing inequalities. Robinson's words were prescient on both accounts.

In this chapter, I examine the postwar efforts of institutional elites to stem the tide of Black and Puerto Rican migration into Morningside Heights by fortifying its northern border with Harlem. The provision of social welfare services was directed at mollifying the non-white population of Manhattanville. It was also a biopolitical strategy of containment. In addition, these elites prosecuted a policy of racial dispossession, using slum clearance tools made available by Title I of the 1949 Housing Act, to forcibly remove low-income people of color from Manhattanville and the Hill.

The Biopolitics of Racial Containment

I am inclined to believe that there is less of a chance of any members of Teachers College receiving a personal injury from an atomic attack than from daily crossings of Amsterdam Avenue.
—William F. Russell

In November 1946, Harry Emerson Fosdick, recently retired from the pastorate, convened a meeting of representatives from institutions on the Hill at the Riverside Church to address neighborhood conditions in postwar Manhattanville. Among those present were Harry Carmen, dean of Columbia College, Rabbi Moshe Davis of the Jewish Theological Seminary, Charles White of Union Theological Seminary, Stanley Isaacs, city councilman-at-large for the borough of Manhattan, and Father George Ford, rector of Manhattanville's Corpus Christi Church and Columbia University's Catholic chaplain (R. Miller 1985). The gathering realized a purpose that had eluded President Nicholas Butler a decade earlier: the creation of an inter-institutional alliance tasked with arresting and reversing the spread of urban blight from the valley below—an anxiety that had been sharpened by the 1943 Harlem riot.

Morningside Heights, like other urban communities that were receiving, or proximal to, Black and Puerto Rican populations, had experienced a loss of white working- and middle-class people after the war. Fosdick and other elites on the Hill worried that this population loss, together with an increase in lower-income Black and brown residents, made it difficult for the institutions in Morningside Heights to attract and retain employees, and discouraged additional institutions from joining the Acropolis. Though Fosdick and other elites publicly bemoaned the area's deteriorating physical conditions, their actions disclosed long-standing racially based anxieties that this changing demography degraded the socioeconomic and cultural structures of white privilege associated with the Hill and its residential community. Like the white residents who fled the city for the suburbs after the war, the institutions of the American Acropolis had a "possessive investment in whiteness"—that is, in preserving Morningside Heights as a center of Western civilization, untainted by racialized class differences and deviations from putatively white middle-class norms (Lipsitz 1995).

The Riverside Church meeting led to the creation of the Manhattanville Neighborhood Center, a social welfare center focused on providing services to the area's youth, believed to be threatening the Heights with crime and juvenile delinquency. Fosdick was chosen as chair of the center's board of directors. In his autobiography, Fosdick narrated witnessing the decline: "When the crowded tenements overflowed southward," Fosdick recollected, "it became evident that unless something were done about it, Columbia University and all the rest of our institutions would be located in a slum" (1956:314–15). It was this fear of the Heights becoming a racialized slum, rather than "humane care for the helpless," that drove the Hill's neighborhood preservation agenda for decades to come.

Planning for the Manhattanville Neighborhood Center (MNC) had begun as early as 1944, when Fosdick and other principals in the Heights launched a campaign to raise funding for renovation of the former Speyer School on West 126th Street, which, vacant for years, had been turned over to the MNC by Teachers College. Approximately $60,000 was raised from Hill institutions and private sources, along with a donation of $100,000 from John D. Rockefeller Jr. The renovated building included a gymnasium, an auditorium, a theater, a woodworking shop, and a homemaking unit for the teaching of home economics (*New York Times* 1948). Although Fosdick denied that the MNC was simply another settlement house, the emphasis of the center's programming was on cultivating responsible, productive, and docile citizens, much like the Speyer School decades earlier. Noting the poor schools, housing conditions, and recreational facilities nearby, Fosdick opined, "Juvenile delinquency will be an inevitable feature of such a neighborhood, but we have conquered it elsewhere and we believe we can convert the Manhattanville gangs into useful citizens with time. In all these efforts, however, the neighbors themselves must take the initiative. The institutions on the hill will furnish the social workers and the psychological guidance where necessary" (*New York Herald Tribune* 1948). In this socio-therapeutic model, emphasis was placed less on addressing the area's substandard conditions—for example, by advocating for stricter building code enforcement, school reforms, and desegregated housing—than on constituting docile subjects willing and able to adjust to the circumstances that immiserated them. This approach contrasted sharply with the philosophy of the social reconstructionists during the Depression and with the work, albeit flawed, of Agnes Snyder's Area No. 14 seminar group, which viewed Manhattanville's heterogeneous population as co-equals and potential active participants in defining and pursuing change.

By the 1930s, social work had become increasingly reliant on psychiatry for its professional status and legitimacy, reinforcing individualistic approaches to what were diagnosed as "personal problems." David Soyer, a social worker with the MNC during the 1950s, wrote of the advantages of delivering social services to Manhattanville's "hard-to-reach" residents in a more accessible, community-based setting like the center:

Suffice it to say that the [MNC] clients under discussion are not victims of refined neurotic conflicts. Primitive in ego development, they are quickly overwhelmed by outside pressures and anxieties of the moment, and seek the [case] worker out in their pain and panic; but once some kind of equilibrium is attained, they do not stay to "work through" their problems in order to avoid future crises. They seek quick and tangible help. Over and over again one senses, beneath a hostile veneer, an oral character; a client who never stops demanding, a mother who cannot give emotionally to her children but can only drain those around her of emotional sustenance. (1961:36)

Unlike the middle-class and presumably white subject of therapy, suffering from "refined neurotic conflicts," the Manhattanville resident was easily overwhelmed by her circumstances, was demanding and dependent, and sought out short-term fixes to her crises. The solution, then, in this deeply gendered discourse was to bring social welfare services—the exercise of biopower—into closer proximity to the client, and insinuate their normalizing functions, classifications, and interpretations of experience into her quotidian social activities, relationships, and process of subjectification. Moreover, psychiatry, it was believed, could provide ready solutions to problems that had eluded earlier social welfare workers, who framed issues of poverty and tenement housing, for example, in broader societal terms and requiring more substantive institutional reforms (Abbott 1988).

Stephen Webb, addressing the contribution of Italian philosopher Roberto Esposito to critical social work pedagogy, applied the latter's "immunity paradigm" to the normalizing role played by social workers in the biopolitics of urban governance:

A central feature of the biopolitical function of social work is found in the processes of immunization: that is, the immunization of those sectors of society that are perceived to be the most vulnerable, dangerous, risky, and in need of protection. The logic at work is to protect them from themselves, in order to protect others from any contamination. The host (variously described normatively as the modern state, the capitalist system, the community and the family) must be protected from infection. (2020:263)

When Manhattanville's most vulnerable or "at-risk" residents were "immunized" through social work interventions and other ameliorative services, structural, socioeconomic problems and injustices were individualized, or embodied in the service-user. Within the administrative apparatuses of the community center, school, and allied institutions, "antisocial" behaviors, associated with juvenile delinquency, rioting, and political resistance, could be surveilled and contained— much like the dot mapping and interventions of the nineteenth-century sanitarians. Such social work interventions cultivated and channeled the client-patient's capacity to self-govern in compliance with the dominant society norms of conduct.

Soyer recounted the case of a young Puerto Rican couple, a "Mr. and Mrs. B," who were recent migrants to New York City from Puerto Rico, to illuminate this process of biopolitical immunization. When Mr. B lost his job, the couple and their children were left without money, food, and medicine and were at risk of losing their Manhattanville apartment. When the family's Department of Welfare investigation (required for public assistance) was stalled, Mrs. B appealed to the MNC for help. "Mrs. B struck us as most primitive," Soyer wrote of her intake visit, "not only in her personality and ego development, but also in her cultural outlook. Her attitude toward religion, health, and even death reflected the peasant culture from which she came" (1961:40). The MNC staff assigned a Spanish-speaking social worker, who visited Mrs. B at home and diagnosed the alleged source of the family's problems:

> A real crisis arose when it was learned that the reason welfare help was so slow in coming was that Mrs. B was defying the Department of Welfare, noisily and angrily refusing to bring them information needed to complete their investigation. Then the worker took on the role of the firm mother that Mrs. B was so obviously seeking and told her decisively, "You have no choice. You must go see your investigator." The histrionics ended abruptly and Mrs. B followed the worker's directions. With the help of the Department of Welfare the situation improved. (Soyer 1961:41)

In short, the actual source of the family's problems, which Soyer argued could best be discovered through the intimacy of a home visit, was Mrs. B's *defiance*—the putative result of a cultural deficit and psychological need for a "firm mother," a role played by the expert caseworker. The social worker gave Mrs. B a shot in the arm, as it were, immunizing her, not from her husband's unemployment, racial discrimination, or other circumstances aggravating her socioeconomic precarity, but from her own cultural and psychological deficiencies. Soyer's account asserts that Mrs. B was transformed—or as Fosdick had put it above, "converted"—from a defiant and histrionic woman into a compliant subject of governmentality. The biopower exercised by the social worker—"You have no choice. You must go see your investigator"—was the power to "foster life," but only on the condition that Mrs. B submit and adjust to the normalizing administrative procedures, classifications, and judgments of the Department of Welfare (Foucault 2003). This "blame the victim" approach had been the stock-in-trade of nineteenth-century evangelical social reformers, who viewed the problems of the slums as arising from vice and sin. Moreover, the view that the poor were largely responsible for their own poverty resurged in the "culture of poverty" theories of the 1960s and 1970s and perdure in American political culture into the twenty-first century.

The new center provided a variety of social services, including childcare, recreational facilities, clubs for youth, and delinquency prevention efforts targeting neighborhood youth. The MNC, like its predecessors, was intended to serve as a laboratory for Columbia students. When teenagers wrecked the center's dining hall in 1949, the MNC embarked on a "street club project," which targeted neighborhood gangs for intensive intervention. The 1943 Harlem uprising, which La Guardia, the police, and others had attributed to young hoodlums, contributed significantly to a postwar concern, if not fixation, in the city with juvenile delinquency and street gangs among city agencies and community-based service organizations like the MNC (Suddler 2019). In the Hill's liberal-inflected discourse of community preservation, street gangs were a thinly veiled euphemism for the presence and incursions of Black and brown people into the Heights, stoking white fears of violence and criminality. As Henry Taylor Jr. et al. put it, referring to postwar slum clearance efforts at the University of Chicago and at Columbia, "progressive institutions, such as universities, could not use strong-arm, openly racist tactics to achieve their ends. Instead, they had to employ democratic and racially neutral methods to seize Black neighborhood lands and to displace 'undesirable' population groups" (Taylor et al. 2018). The Manhattanville Neighborhood Center provided the appearance of democracy and racial neutrality, but not the substance (Taylor et al. 2018).

The specter of roving gangs of delinquent youth invading Morningside Heights added to the Hill's sense of urgency to contain the expanding slum to the north. A 1949 *New York Times* article titled "New System Copes with Street Gangs" spotlighted the MNC's novel approach to working with street gangs, which included sending teams of social workers into the neighborhood to fraternize with gang members in bars and poolrooms and on street corners. Jules Schrager, the MNC's director, contrasted his approach with that of other community centers that simply ejected disruptive and antisocial youth. "When boys are sent away now," Schrager explained, "the agency's social workers go too, and contact is maintained between the agency and his club [i.e., gang]." As in the case of Mrs. B, Schrager believed that the intimacy of the intervention was critical to inoculating the gang member with normative values and conduct, as well as enabling social workers to function *in loco parentis*. Intimacy facilitated a transformative penetration of subjects, their agency, and quotidian behaviors—what Sam Binkley has termed "the government of intimacy" (2012). Binkley associated the origins of this systematized government of intimacy with the emergence of secular practices of welfare provision in the early years of the Progressive Era. "Broadly speaking, these efforts combined the social objectives of the welfare state—centering on the enforcement of social cohesion, the reduction of conflict between labor and capital, and mobilization of labor power itself—with the biopolitical objectives of a professional medico-institutional complex" (2012:559).

A few years later, in 1955, the *New York Herald Tribune* published a series of articles by Margaret Parton, a well-known novelist and journalist and graduate of the Lincoln School, addressing juvenile delinquency. One report in this "Our Lawless Youth" series featured the MNC's street club project and echoed the immunization and *in loco parentis* logic of Soyer's narratives. An MNC social worker, Roy Kurahara, attributed the delinquency of youth in Harlem and Manhattanville to dysfunctional families and deviant, negligent parents:

Alcoholism, drugs, over-breeding, broken homes, imbecility—around here they usually all have it in their backgrounds. So we do the things that parents are supposed to do. . . . Sure, we're acting as substitute parents. We've given up on trying to work with the parents because the parents have already rejected the kids. (Parton 1955)

Reminiscent of later discourses of "ghetto pathology," Kurahara cast Manhattanville as a zone of biopolitical exception, inhabited by *homines sacri*, who were irredeemable, cast off, and no longer savable from themselves (Agamben 1998). From the standpoint of elites in the Heights, the biopolitics of immunization—or as Fosdick had put it, "humane care for the helpless"—could not insulate Morningside Heights from the toxic miasmas of urban blight. "We try to get them out of this neighborhood," Kurahara concluded, "because there is *nothing* good here." Kurahara's comments use the language of dispossession, not rehabilitation. Manhattanville was *terra nullius*, bereft of civilization and ripe for slum clearance. One year after the MNC's dedication, its Hill-dominated board of directors signaled an important change of direction—a redirection enabled and expedited by the passage of the Housing Act of 1949 and its Title I slum clearance provisions.

On July 1, 1949, Clyde E. Murray was hired as executive director of the Manhattanville Neighborhood Center. One key objective was to develop the MNC's capacity to conduct community-based research, lending community legitimacy to a slum clearance project that displaced nearly half of Manhattanville's residents. As the area's population became increasingly Black and brown during the 1950s, biopolitical strategies of racial immunization and containment gave way to the slow sovereign violence of racial dispossession. For as Joy James has argued, noting Foucault's failure to attend to the role of anti-Black racism in the formation of the disciplinary society, "some bodies cannot be normalized no matter how they are disciplined, unless the prevailing social and state structures that figuratively and literally rank bodies disintegrate" (1996:27). Black and brown bodies that could not be normalized—such as gang members and their deviant families—were instead cast out or "banned" from the body politic and protection of the law. Biopolitics did not supersede the exercise of sovereign power, the power over life and death, as Foucault has suggested; rather, as Thomas Lemke wrote of Giorgio Agamben's analysis of sovereignty, "the constitution of sovereign power assumes the creation of a biopolitical body. Inclusion in political society is only possible . . .

through the simultaneous exclusion of human beings who are denied full legal status" (2011:54). Socio-therapeutic intervention and racial dispossession were both strategies casting Manhattanville's residents of color as abject, dependent, and unable to define or act effectively to address their social, economic, and political needs (cf. Alves 2018). The MNC had thus become a Trojan horse within the spatiotemporal boundaries of a soon-to-be razed multiracial, working-class community.

Urban Renewal and Racial Dispossession

> Of all the blights that can overtake a community, one of the worst—because of its effects on people as well as on the buildings—is what town planners call "creeping obsolescence." Planners usually mean this in terms of houses, buildings, street structures becoming old and neglected. But of equal importance is the "creeping obsolescence" of the human community spirit.
> —Gertrude Samuels

With this familiar salad of metaphors, Gertrude Samuels began her feature article in the Sunday magazine section of the *New York Times*, announcing a major initiative to arrest neighborhood decay in Morningside Heights-Manhattanville. Samuels, a veteran journalist, photographer, and member of the paper's editorial board, had spent the war years covering displaced populations in Europe and, soon after, the birth of the state of Israel (Saxon 2003). The hazy notions of "creeping obsolescence" and "urban blight" reiterated both the spatiotemporal boundary separating the Hill from its neighbors to the north and east, and the miasma-like infestation of a pestilence, reminiscent of the nineteenth-century sanitarians who conflated urban conditions with the dispositions of the poor.

Contrary to Samuels's claim, by the postwar period the concept of "obsolescence" had expanded beyond its earlier, more narrow references to neighborhood physical conditions to include an array of socioeconomic elements that were associated with the future viability of urban districts. As Daniel Abramson has noted, the concept of obsolescence took hold early in the twentieth century as real estate assessors sought increasingly sophisticated methods to determine land and property values. These valuations were used by businesses—brokers, banks, insurance companies, and owners of commercial real estate—to maximize profits and minimize risks, and by governments to estimate tax revenues (2012). By the Great Depression, the real estate industry was using detailed checklists to assess socioeconomic conditions that were believed to affect property values. As Abramson observed, "Their rubrics measured area factors such as economic stability, racial composition, family income, and adequate transportation. Whole districts that scored poorly were deemed in total to be economically deficient and thus obsolescent—regardless of the condition of individual properties—and so ineligible for lending, cut off from the capital market for investment and improvement purposes" (2016:40). Similar criteria for assessing neighborhood obsolescence were used by the New Deal–era Home Owners Loan Corporation to develop "residential security maps" and in the appraisal methods developed by the American Public Health Association to assess housing quality (American Public Health Association 1945). In these schemata the mere presence of people of color—Black people in particular—was taken to be an indication of obsolescence and neighborhood decline. Like the discourse of urban blight, the concept of obsolescence racialized the assessment of urban decline and conflated urban revitalization with elite-driven strategies of economic redevelopment.

Samuels's feature article also spotlighted a nonprofit organization that had been formed five years earlier on the Hill: Morningside Heights, Inc., directed by banker and former secretary to Mayor La Guardia, David Rockefeller. As a Lincoln School alumnus and president of the board of trustees of both International House and the Riverside Church, Rockefeller was well acquainted with the Acropolis, its principal actors, and their decades-long efforts to contain the valley below. Noting the threat posed by Manhattanville's slum conditions to the Hill's institutions, Rockefeller added a novel, Cold War spin on the problem of neighborhood deterioration: "As I see it, the future of the freedoms of Western civilization is determined more than anything else by education, culture, religion, of which there is a constellation here in the Heights. It's important that we not only live in that freedom but also radiate it into our whole community. If we succeed here, it could reverse the trend of obsolescence everywhere." In short, Manhattanville's slum and its residents posed a threat to Western civilization itself. The

American Acropolis was not only to be a citadel of learning, culture, and spirituality, but also a civilizational bulwark against the spread of communism and obsolescence (Samuels 1950:39). Samuels's feature article was reprinted in full in *Columbia College Today*, the alumni newspaper (December 1955:10).

Morningside Heights, Inc. (MHI) had been founded the same year that the Manhattanville Neighborhood Center was being organized and funded in the valley below, and its board of directors represented the same constellation of institutions and, to some extent, personnel as the MNC, including Reverend Fosdick, Father Ford, Dean Millicent McIntosh of Barnard and, in 1950, Dwight D. Eisenhower, Columbia's new president. For this reason the activities of the MNC and MHI are best viewed as a coordinated and mutually reinforcing effort, with the former stressing palliative social welfare services and research, and the latter slum clearance, or "urban renewal."

The seeds for MHI had been planted in May 1946, when David Rockefeller and other members of the board of trustees of International House hired William C. Munnecke, a social scientist and vice president at the University of Chicago, to conduct a survey study of the area surrounding the residence for students and visiting scholars. International House was located on Riverside Drive and blocks away from the well-publicized La Salle Street slum. In his report, Munnecke argued against the use of restrictive covenants, zoning, and similar "negative" measures to exclude undesirable land uses and social groups. These negative measures were not only ineffective, Munnecke maintained, but also undemocratic, since they violated the principles of tolerance and internationalism to which International House and other institutions in the Heights, at least in theory, aspired (Zipp 2012). Instead, as Joel Schwartz wrote,

> Borrowing from his Chicago experience, Munnecke recommended what he called "horizontal restrictions," which he explained were "positive actions" designed to keep worthy neighbors and discourage undesirables. With coordinated incentives, including city and state programs, mortgage subsidies, and tax relief, a disciplined effort over the next twenty-five years could create "a self-sustaining Community which is the spiritual, cultural, and intellectual center of the world." Within a planning document that soared with One Worldism, Munnecke urged International

House, New York, to plan a wholesale redevelopment, starting with a campaign against local rooming houses. (1993:153)

Munnecke called on Columbia to take the lead in the redevelopment process since the university owned considerable property in Morningside Heights and an endowment greater than any of its peer institutions. Accordingly, on November 8, 1946, acting president Frank Fackenthal held a meeting of institutional leaders on the Hill, including David Rockefeller, to discuss the Munnecke report. The meeting led to the formation of a planning committee, led by Columbia's vice president for finance, Joseph Campbell, and including Lawrence M. Orton, a member of both the City Planning Commission and the Regional Plan Association, John L. Mott, a trustee of the Riverside Church, and Otto Nelson, a vice president of the New York Life Insurance Company (Schwartz 1993).

Nelson, a retired major general, held the view that slum clearance and the decentralization of cities—or "defense dispersal"—were "a necessary course of treatment" when planning for survival after a nuclear attack (Abramson 2016; *New York Times* 1953). The decentralization of industry was understood to be critical to recovering economically and militarily from an attack; the high-density, infrastructurally impaired slums—like Paris before Baron Haussmann—were seen to pose a threat of panic, social disorder, and mob violence in the event of nuclear attack and would impede civil defense and post-attack recovery efforts (T. Davis 2007). Perhaps more important, as a vice president at the New York Life Insurance Company in charge of development, Nelson had been involved in the early efforts of Marshall Field and Company, the Illinois Institute of Technology, and other private groups to rebuild the Loop area of downtown Chicago using slum clearance. In 1948 New York Life, represented by Nelson, committed to providing financing for the Lake Meadows urban renewal project on the Near South Side of the city, one of the first in the nation (Hirsch 1983).

The Campbell committee recruited Ernest M. Fisher, economist and director of the university's newly created Institute for Land Use, to estimate the cost of preparing a study and long-range redevelopment plan for the Morningside-Manhattanville area. Fisher, together with sociologist Robert K. Merton, economist Raymond Saulnier, and other faculty, concluded that the preservation of the Heights required the redevelopment of nearby slum areas, recommending that the Campbell committee create a corporation with the technical staff for that purpose. Morningside Heights, Inc. was incorporated on July 4, 1947 (Schwartz 1993).[1] The creation of MHI also made it possible for Columbia to separate its academic policies and liberal ideology from its real estate practices—a strategy previously deployed by the University of Chicago in its effort to stabilize nearby Hyde Park-Kenwood during a similar urban renewal initiative (Hirsch 1983).

In its first years, MHI focused on the preservation of Morningside Heights. Although MHI's board also expressed concerns about the area of Central Harlem to the east of Morningside Park, the steep cliffside along the eastern edge of the plateau still provided a natural barrier with residential sections east of the park that had become predominantly Black and Puerto Rican by the mid-1950s.

However, the substantial reconstruction of the threatened border areas of Morningside Heights displaced their predominantly Black and brown residents at a time when affordable housing was in short supply. Accordingly, in January 1949, David Rockefeller, MHI's president, met with Robert Moses, chairman of the Mayor's Committee on Slum Clearance, to explore possibilities for building public housing at the Height's northern border with Harlem. Rockefeller had known Moses since his days working in the La Guardia administration. The plan was to build middle-income housing at the northern end of the Heights that buffered it from Harlem (Munnecke's "horizontal restrictions"), provide housing for employees of MHI-member institutions, and dovetail that private development with a public housing complex still further north. Moses expressed interest and, on March 7, 1949, Lawrence M. Orton, MHI's director and a member of the City Planning Commission, reported to the board that the city's Housing Authority, dominated by Moses, had given assurances that two superblocks in Morningside-Manhattanville were included in the city's urban renewal plan under Title I of the 1949 Housing Act, which was expected to be passed that summer (Hepner 1955; *Amsterdam News* 1950).

The matching of privately financed middle-income housing under Title I with public housing killed two birds with one stone: low-income residents displaced by the private housing project could, in theory, be relocated in nearby public housing; Title I financing could be used to acquire and demolish the site of the private development and thereby defray its costs and make it attractive to private sector sponsors. "Moses liked the idea," Rockefeller wrote in his memoirs. "He had been looking for a reliable, not-for-profit group to manage the City's first urban renewal site and expeditiously ushered our proposal through the maze of federal and city bureaucracies" (2003:386). The fact that MHI's executive director, Lawrence M. Orton, had retained his seat on the City Planning Commission, a clear conflict of interest, no doubt also helped MHI quickly negotiate that maze.

In October 1949, MHI incorporated Remedco, a real estate investment company, for the purpose of providing mortgages and construction financing to promote the purchase and rehabilitation of abandoned and declining residential buildings in Morningside Heights. Although it was funded by MHI's nine member institutions, few property owners and investors took advantage of Remedco's mortgages, which prompted Columbia and other institutions to begin buying the at-risk properties. Robert McCaughey explained the university's motives for purchasing real estate:

> Columbia offered two explanations for doing this. The first, essentially defensive, was that buying abandoned buildings and deteriorating SROs kept them from being trashed by squatters or used for illegal and locally disruptive purposes such as prostitution and drug dealing. The second, although this was not said openly, was that buying up these buildings precluded their use as dumping grounds by the city of its large and growing population of welfare and mental health clients. (2003:407)

Together with buttressing its border with Harlem, the rehabilitation of Morningside Heights through property acquisition would make it possible for the university and other Remedco members to not only evict undesirable, low-income tenants and attract and hold middle-class residents, but also hold these properties in reserve for future institutional expansion.

MHI's executive board decided in late 1949 to expand the organization's initial scope, focusing on Morningside Heights as far north as 135th Street and including all of Manhattanville (Hepner 1955). This expansion was a response to the emphasis placed in the Title I slum clearance legislation on community-wide planning, and the Housing Authority's requirement that funding for public housing promote racial integration. In the redevelopment plan presented by the Committee on Slum Clearance to Mayor Vincent Impellitteri and the Board of Estimate in 1952, Moses recommended approving two adjacent superblock projects: one, a middle-income private development, consisting of 981 apartments constructed through the urban renewal program; the second, a 1,600-unit public housing development to be built by the Housing Authority. The middle-income development, intended largely for employees of Hill institutions, would occupy two city blocks between West 123rd Street and La Salle Street, and from Broadway to Amsterdam Avenue, thereby razing the La Salle Street slum. The public housing development, occupying two superblocks, would be located northeast of the middle-income housing development.

In 1951 Father George Ford, rector of Corpus Christi Church and MHI's secretary, explained to the *Herald Tribune* how the proposal promoted racial and economic integration. "When we build one project and this is for the poor," Ford opined, "and then build another and say that this is intended for the more well-to-do, we are creating ghettos. This is a form of segregation, and it does not help our democracy one bit. The two projects should be close together so that the people of the community can live together." However, the fact that the two superblocks were near—indeed, adjacent to—each other would not promote integration or social porosity, as Jane Jacobs later argued (1961). Instead, the high-rise, high-density superblocks would create what Jacobs called a "border vacuum," reinforcing socioeconomic contrasts and buttressing the physical and polysemous barrier—not unlike a racial spite fence—between Harlem and the Heights. Urban renewal provided the American Acropolis with that which geography had not—a social *and* physical barrier at the northern edge of the Morningside plateau.

MHI obtained a grant from the Rockefeller Brothers Fund to conduct a study of the enlarged redevelopment area in order to document housing conditions (rents, apartment sizes, appurtenances, and so forth), household composition and income, and tenants' satisfaction with their existing accommodations. To that purpose, MHI opened a field office at the Manhattanville Neighborhood Center in March 1950. In a later report on the renewal project, MHI research director Elizabeth Hepner explained, "The Manhattanville Neighborhood Center, was to cooperate in all phases of the work, especially in interpreting both the survey and total redevelopment to the community, while Morningside Heights, Inc. was to concentrate on the more technical aspects of the survey" (1955:6). In addition, an MNC-sponsored Community Advisory Committee was created to raise community interest in the housing survey and publicize the redevelopment plan. Father Ford, both MHI's secretary and an MNC board member, served as chairman of the advisory council. Hepner noted that, along with representatives of schools, libraries, and other community groups, "outstanding community leaders participated as individuals" and "reflected the ethnic composition of the community" (1955:7).[2]

However inclusive the advisory council was—neither the Harlem-based New York Urban League nor the NAACP was represented on the council—the MNC had become both advocate and instrument for an urban renewal project that served not the needs of Manhattanville's residents for affordable housing and community stability, but rather the need—or, better—desire of institutional elites on the Hill to preserve Morningside Heights as white, middle class, and encapsulated. "The City will only endorse a plan," the MNC's executive director wrote to John D. Rockefeller Jr., "which has the full approval of local inhabitants. Through its close contacts with the people living there, [the MNC] is in a position to learn the wishes of the neighborhood, to interpret their needs to the planners, and then to 'sell' the plan to the neighborhood" (in Schwartz 1993:185).

To design the questionnaire, train interviewers, and process the data, MHI retained Columbia University's Bureau of Applied Social Research and, through an arrangement with Teachers College, trained 250 graduate students to conduct the interviews for course credit. Roughly one-third of the eleven thousand households living in the area between 122nd Street and 135th Streets and from Riverside Drive to Convent Avenue were canvassed during the summer of 1950, using questionnaires in English and Spanish.

The survey's findings showed not an immiserated, overcrowded slum, but a stable, multiracial working-class neighborhood. For example, the survey found "no exceptional incidence of crowding," though 23 percent of the households shared their apartments with boarders, and families with few children "were the rule" (Hepner 1955:8). Moreover, half of Manhattanville's residents had lived in the neighborhood between five and fifteen years; one-quarter for over fifteen years. The survey also found that rents in the study area were "almost uniformly low," with 64 percent of households paying less that forty dollars a month, significantly lower than the citywide average of sixty dollars. Significantly, nearly 50 percent of the area's residents walked to work. Finally, although half of residents told researchers that they were dissatisfied with their current housing—not uncommon in a city like New York—two-thirds did not plan to leave the neighborhood.

The disparity between MHI and press accounts of Manhattanville as a blighted slum, suffering from "creeping obsolescence," and the survey's findings that housing in the area was comparatively affordable and uncongested, and that two-thirds of residents had no intention of leaving the area, exposed a tension in the blight assessments. Themis Chronopoulos has pointed out that the arguments made by Robert Moses and others about the existence of blight and need for slum clearance relied heavily on visual signs of disorder—for example, children playing in the streets, vacant lots, clothesline mazes—that had little or no bearing on the viability of the housing stock or socioeconomic stability of communities (2014a). When preparing the site-specific brochures promoting slum clearance projects, Moses limited the amount of explanatory text in favor of photographs, diagrams, and other visual material that he believed would be universally understood and accepted. "The paradigm that was highlighted in the brochures of the 1950s," Chronopoulos wrote, "defined the problem as physical disorder in need of physical solutions" (2014a:208).

As Wendell Pritchett has demonstrated, the vagueness of the rhetoric of blight enabled far more than a conflation of the physical condition of communities with the mores of their inhabitants. It also allowed urban renewal supporters to shape the jurisprudence of eminent domain and its "public use" requirement (2003). Beginning in the 1920s, Pritchett noted, there was growing recognition among urban renewal boosters that major changes in property law were necessary to prosecute slum clearance and redevelopment; specifically, for municipal and state governments to exercise eminent domain on a large scale, the concept of "public use," enshrined in the Fifth Amendment of the US Constitution, needed to be understood more expansively by the courts. Pritchett writes,

> To secure political and judicial approval for their efforts, renewal advocates created a new language of urban decline: a discourse of blight. Blight, renewal proponents argued, was a disease that threatened to turn healthy areas into slums. A vague, amorphous term, blight was a rhetorical device that enabled renewal advocates to reorganize property ownership by declaring certain real estate dangerous to the future of the city. To make the case for renewal programs advocates contrasted the existing, deteriorated state of urban areas with the modern, efficient city that would replace them. (2003:3)

By maintaining that the Morningside-Manhattanville renewal area exhibited signs of urban blight, MHI only had to demonstrate that it was heading toward slum conditions and consequently could be put to better and more profitable uses through privately sponsored redevelopment. In this wider interpretation of the public use clause, economic development, broadly conceived and pursued by private entities, was understood to be a legitimate public use. And those more profitable public uses, as discussed above, by definition excluded Black and brown people.

With the housing survey completed, MHI addressed the question of middle-income housing to replace the La Salle Street slum. MHI asked Shirley Boden, a founder of the United Housing Foundation, for a proposal exploring the possibility of building cooperative housing at the renewal site. Like Rockefeller earlier, Boden was an advocate of cooperative housing for revitalizing the market in middle-income housing. Tenant ownership, MHI officials believed, would lower the monthly maintenance costs for its tenant-owners, creating more stable residency than rental housing. MHI's board of directors passed a resolution approving joint sponsorship of the cooperative housing in the area south of 125th Street, and formed a committee of MHI's member institutions. In June 1951, the Committee on Cooperative Housing submitted a letter to Robert Moses officially stating the intent of its nine members to sponsor the cooperative housing, which, along with data from MHI's housing survey, was to be included in the city's Morningside-Manhattanville

Redevelopment Plan. On October 1, the Mayor's Committee on Slum Clearance announced the MHI-sponsored redevelopment project and released an official version of the report, which was submitted to the Board of Estimate. A second version of the report was simultaneously released for distribution to the community.

Soon after the release of the two reports, tenants in the project area began organizing to press for more information and, if need be, to organize protests. In mid-October, residents established the Committee to Save Our Homes under the leadership of Elizabeth Barker. Barker lived on West 123rd Street, only doors away from the Rockefeller-financed building that had once housed the Lincoln School and was now home to Public School 125. Described in 1952 by the *New York Post* as "an energetic Irish mother of three," Barker had graduated from Stanford University and lectured at the Jefferson School of Social Science, a CPUSA-affiliated adult school providing instruction in Marxist philosophy and other movement-related subjects (Gettleman 2002).

New York City's tenants movements had long operated under a predominantly female leadership, and many of these women—like Barker, Baldwin's friend Orilla Miller, and the Harlem Tenants League's Elizabeth Hendrickson—had been connected to networks of Popular Front organizations and activists, such as the CPUSA, the American Labor Party, and leftist labor unions, that had been active through the 1930s and 1940s. Urban renewal mobilized these grassroots activists against slum clearance in the 1950s, including Jane Benedict, Frances Goldin, and Esther Rand, who were among the founders of the Metropolitan Council on Housing (Gold 2009). This intergenerational network of women exercised what Roberta Gold has called "practical feminism":

> Battling landlords in city courtrooms and leading demonstrations in the streets, these women did not conform to the domestic model of femininity promoted by cold war pundits. Although the object of their struggles—people's homes—might count as "women's sphere," the terrain on which they fought lay squarely in the political arena. These women did not take up feminism explicitly, or as their primary political affiliation. But none of them doubted their fitness to take action in the "man's world of politics." (2009:392)

Moreover, these women activists deeply politicized the domestic sphere by defining decent and affordable housing as a basic human right that was inseparable from broader issues of racial, economic, and gender justice.

In a statement to the press, Barker's Committee to Save Our Homes (CSOH) explained its opposition to MHI's Title I urban renewal plan:

> We are fighting to save our homes and our interracial community. We don't want to be victims of a "slum clearance" redevelopment project in which the vast majority of people are cleared out with the slums. Practically none of us can afford to make down payments of $500 to $625 a room and then pay $19 or $23 a room for the proposed "cooperative" apartments. And, although 2,400 of our families might technically be eligible for the low-rent project, there will only be 1,536 units there even if we got them all. (in Van Dusen 1954:87)

Barker and the CSOH had recognized that a sizable segment of Manhattanville households earned too little to afford the co-ops yet too much to qualify for public housing. This eligibility gap sent MHI and its Committee on Cooperative Housing scrambling to reduce the costs of the cooperative development. Moreover, the number of apartments in the public housing development was insufficient to rehouse the thousands of households displaced by the three superblock projects. Unsurprisingly, project boosters attempted to discredit the CSOH, charging that Barker and other members of the committee were not local residents but communists and puppets of outside organizations. Moreover, except for the *Daily Worker*, the CPUSA's newspaper, and the Black-owned *Amsterdam News*, the city's newspapers ignored CSOH, its arguments, and its protest actions.

In fact, Elizabeth Barker lived at one of the two proposed sites for public housing and had converted one of Manhattanville's vacant lots— one created by Rockefeller when he razed a cordon sanitaire around the Lincoln School—into a kitchen garden for local residents. In the heat of the Cold War and on the eve of the McCarthy hearings, such red-baiting carried considerable political weight and recalled well-rehearsed charges of the influence of communists in Harlem during the Depression. Opponents often deprecated Black political consciousness and activism in Harlem and other communities by attributing their origins and effectiveness to communists and other "outside agitators," reinforcing racist views concerning the inability of Black subjects to autonomously imagine and advance their freedom.

Whether or not Barker was a member of the CPUSA (she would "take the Fifth" at her 1953 Senate grilling), she and other CSOH members were affiliated with the American Labor Party (ALP) and its postwar campaign to oppose slum clearance projects and tenant evictions. Manhattanville's CSOH was part of a wider coalition, United Community to Save Our Homes, which had been organized by the ALP-backed Manhattan Tenants Council to rally against Title I projects in Manhattanville and Harlem and on the Upper West Side that had been slated for renewal by the Mayor's Committee on Slum Clearance (Zipp 2012; Schwartz 1993). One of these urban renewal projects, Manhattantown, razed six blocks between 97th and 100th Streets, and Central Park West and Amsterdam Avenue—a predominantly Black and Puerto Rican community and one of the earliest Black residential areas in northern Manhattan outside Harlem. Joel Schwartz described the Manhattantown redevelopment as "a transparent strategy to force Blacks and Puerto Ricans [back] across 110th Street" (1986:156). Here again, John Cos's 1926 memorandum had been prescient, warning of the expansion of Harlem south along the eastern edge of the Morningside plateau toward 110th Street and beyond.

Barker and Manhattanville's CSOH, working out of a storefront on Amsterdam Avenue, prepared for the Board of Estimate (BOE) hearing on the cooperative housing project, which had already been approved by the City Planning Commission. On October 26, the BOE met to consider the project but, as Hepner put it, "some seventy individuals under the leadership of the Save Our Homes Committee created such a furor that consideration of the matter was laid over until November 15" (1955:14). At the meeting, CSOH activists questioned the city's commitment to building the public housing, arguing that, even if built, it could not rehouse the 1,584 households that would be evicted from the cooperative site alone. Henry Abrams, an ALP organizer, declared that approval of the plan was tantamount to "building a wall of snobbery and prejudice" and that publicly financed Title I subsidies should not be used to support privately sponsored middle-income housing. In a 1951 letter to the *Columbia Daily Spectator* after the BOE meeting, J. L. Breslow,

CSOH's pro tem chairman, rebutted the false claim that its members did not live in the area, and reiterated the CSOH's position on the co-operative's per-room costs argued before the Board of Estimate: "The Committee successfully opposed the proposal to erect $23-per-room cooperatives here and will oppose any other proposal that would erect an economic barrier against the return of the present residents, most of whom are Negroes, Puerto Ricans, and people of Asian backgrounds. Any such proposal would, in its effect, be discriminatory and would in-tensify segregation in housing." The project's critics were well aware of its racially discriminatory effect, if not intent, and of the symbolic violence resulting from the construction of a three-superblock border vacuum.

To address escalating opposition to the redevelopment project, members of the Morningside Committee on Cooperative Housing held a conference with Borough President Robert Wagner and representa-tives of the Committee on Slum Clearance. Bernard Segal of the Jewish Theological Seminary announced that the co-op committee was willing to sponsor a cooperative project with per-room fees averaging $19 or less. Also at the conference and speaking in favor of the renewal plan were Clyde Murray of the Manhattanville Neighborhood Center, Father Ford of the Community Advisory Committee among others, and Robert Daugherty, a trustee of the New Lincoln School and a representative of the Morningside Citizens Committee, a civic association based on the Hill that supported the Title I project (Hepner 1955). In effect, MHI had manufactured its own community support for the project, what Paul Piccone has called "artificial negativity" (1978).

To lower the per-room costs of the co-op apartments, the Morning-side Committee on Cooperative Housing and MHI began exploring op-tions for using public tax subsidies to underwrite the project and, with Moses's support, requested that the Board of Estimate lay over its review of the project beyond the November 15 meeting to an unspecified date. Meanwhile, the Hill-based Morningside Citizens Committee launched a campaign to dispel community concerns, publishing a brochure and releasing a statement in January 1952 praising the middle-income cooperative.

Only days later, on January 28, Save Our Homes held a meeting of residents living on the site of the proposed cooperative project to adopt a plan for a housing program that addressed the needs of all Manhattanville residents. The meeting was attended by over three hundred residents and by representatives of the borough president, the City Council president (both members of the Board of Estimate), Congressman Jacob Javits, and representatives of the NAACP, Urban League of Greater New York, churches, and other organizations. Congressman Adam Clayton Powell Jr., the NAACP's Jennie Johnson, Henry Churchill, professor of architecture at Columbia, and Paul Carpenter, a representative of the Social Action Committee at Union Theological Seminary, spoke in support of the CSOH's position on the Title I project. The list of representatives at the meeting suggested both the CSOH's political clout and the breadth of its outreach. For a major renewal project that was being legitimated as a tool for promoting racial integration, it is telling that neither the NAACP nor Harlem-based New York Urban League was represented on the boards of MHI and the MNC, nor on the latter's perfunctory Community Advisory Committee (*Amsterdam News* 1952b).

On January 29, the newly formed Manhattanville Civic Association held its first meeting at the Manhattanville District Health Office on 126th Street, not far from the Speyer School. The civic association had been created by the MNC only the month before to replace its Community Advisory Committee, which had been dissolved after the release of the renewal plan. The MNC-sponsored civic association was an effort to expand, or at least appear to expand, the base of community support for the redevelopment project to include all of Manhattanville and adjacent sections of West Harlem. Unsurprisingly, the omnipresent Father Ford convened the public meeting, attended by Congressman Javits and other public officials, and the MNC's Clyde E. Murray was to serve as the pro-tem chair. As the meeting was about to begin, some forty to fifty supporters of Save Our Homes insisted that an election be held first to select a chairperson who lived in Manhattanville. As a result, William Kelley, a resident of the area and CSOH supporter, was elected chair and the new association went on to agree on resolutions demanding better police protection, drug addiction services, and a post office for the area. However, when the meeting turned to housing, a resolution supporting the cooperative housing project was "violently condemned," as the *Amsterdam News* put it, and voted down by CSOH supporters, who insisted that low-income rental apartments be built in its stead. Harlem Councilman Earl Brown charged that the CSOH faction had behaved "like a bunch of Communists, more interested in raising Hell than in getting more housing." Elizabeth Barker countered that the CSOH did not represent any outside group but were local residents who did not want the new civic association to become a "Columbia front group" (*Amsterdam News* 1952b).

The Save Our Homes committee and its supporters had won significant victories, both in forcing delays in the Board of Estimate's approval of the renewal plan and in foiling the MNC's attempt to create a front group to lend legitimacy to the redevelopment project. The CSOH, with the support of the Manhattanville Civic Association, campaigned in 1952 to rally opposition to the redevelopment plan, distributing leaflets and conducting door-to-door petition drives, and organizing protests at myriad public hearings. Harry Gottlieb, the social realist painter and printmaker, and other local artists built a truck-borne float that depicted scenes in the city's tenants' struggles and toured the neighborhood, serving as a speakers' platform for activists (*Daily Worker* 1952). Barker and her supporters held bake sales, raffles, and dances that featured Latin-jazz great Machito and His Afro-Cubans and Elmo Garcia and His Orchestra (Glanz and Lipton 2003).

In the spring of 1952, MHI and the Committee on Cooperative Housing began preparing a resubmission letter to the Committee on Slum Clearance, reflecting lower costs for the nonprofit middle-income cooperative. With public tax subsidies, the estimated per-room charges in the development now ranged between $16 and $22. Despite continued protests, the BOE gave its preliminary approval of the project on May 8 and, in late 1952, the City Planning Commission approved both the revised cooperative and public housing plans. In the revised plan, the number of units in the public housing complex was increased from 1,720 to 1,950—in response to the CSOH's demands—and MHI provided survey data to the New York State Division of Housing for a possible state-funded low-income housing north of 125th Street. On January 15, 1953, over the continued opposition of CSOH supporters and the now community-led Manhattanville Civic Association, the Board of Estimate gave its final approval of the redevelopment plan (Hepner 1955).

Morningside Heights, Inc. and its member institutions had achieved a great victory by creating a symbolically potent, superblock buffer between West Harlem and the Heights, and by eliminating the notorious

"La Salle Street slum" (along with its predominantly Black and brown inhabitants), which posed the most proximal threat to Riverside Church, Union Theological Seminary, and other Hill institutions. Moreover, the cooperative complex, named Morningside Gardens, provided 984 units of middle-class housing suitable for institutional employees. The result at Manhattanville and at comparable urban renewal sites, such as Manhattantown, was that a racially mixed working-class community was replaced by middle-class and predominantly white-occupied housing, while the former residents were displaced to segregated housing in neighborhoods where conditions were no better than those that they had been forced to leave (Zipp 2012; cf. Hirsch 1983).

In 1953, a few months after the Board of Estimate vote, Richard Lincoln wrote a feature article in the *Amsterdam News* highlighting concerns that the city's slum clearance program would intensify "Jim Crow" racial segregation, also weakening Harlem's political power by diffusing its Black and brown population. "In effect," Lincoln noted, "this would mean that the new, isolated Negro and Puerto Rican communities— 'little Harlems'—can be easily cut up in political districting. The result could be a sharp cut-down in Negro and Puerto Rican representation in public office" (Lincoln 1953).

Lincoln also raised the problem of the relocation of displaced residents, pointing out, as had Save Our Homes activists, that many households removed from Title I sites neither qualified for public housing nor could afford the new middle-income housing. Moreover, the sheer numbers of persons and households being displaced by urban renewal amid a tight, racially segregated housing market were beyond the capacity of Title I sponsors and city agencies to rehouse. A June 1955 report, produced by a subcommittee of the Mayor's Committee for Better Housing, estimated that between April 1, 1953, and March 31, 1956, a total of 150,000 persons were displaced from Title I sites—40,410 families of two or more, and 15,710 single persons. Single persons (boarders, roomers, and household heads), irrespective of income, were ineligible for public housing. The report also revealed that only 40 percent of the families dislocated from slum clearance sites had been relocated in public housing. Among the remaining evicted tenants, "about 60 percent were simply identified as 'moved—address unknown'" (Mayor's Committee for Better Housing 1955:5).

Finally, the subcommittee's report affirmed the concerns that had been expressed by Lincoln and the CSOH that urban renewal was creating new ghettoes:

> There is evidence of widespread deterioration of old housing, and gross overcrowding of such tenements and other dwellings through the City. This has arisen from a combination of circumstances, but undoubtedly one factor has been the displacement of families at a rate which makes it impossible for them to be absorbed in the existing supply of satisfactory housing, new or old. This process may have already resulted in the creation of new slum areas. . . . If left uncorrected, such a process will result in the creation of new slums at a faster pace than old slums are being eliminated. (MCBH 1955:8)

On January 11, 1954, in the ceremony marking the start of demolition at the Morningside Gardens site, Millicent McIntosh, president of Barnard College, took a crowbar to the stoop of a brownstone at 68 La Salle Street, sending up a cloud of red dust. President McIntosh was also chair of the board of directors of the Morningside Heights Housing Corporation, a limited dividend corporation that had been set up to sponsor the project. Also speaking at the ceremony, which took place in the middle of a blizzard, were Robert Moses, Harry Fosdick, David Rockefeller, and Philip Cruise, chairman of the city's Housing Authority. Demolition was already underway at the adjacent site of the low-income public housing development. In his speech, Moses expressed his regret at the "tough problem" that residents of the redevelopment area had faced with evictions and resettlement (Gottlieb 2008).

Elizabeth Hepner, MHI's research director, concluded that fears that the evicted tenants would be forced to move into less desirable housing in worse slum areas was wrong, but relocation data presented in her 1955 report painted a far from sanguine picture. By June 15, 1954—one year after relocation activities had begun and six months after the start of demolition—only 37.9 percent of the site's 2,188 residential tenants had been relocated. By March 25 of the following year, site tenants had been offered 1,423 apartments in privately owned housing with rents under $75. Only 313 accepted. Given that, according to MHI's own housing survey, 64 percent of households in the redevelopment area had paid

$40 or less in rent, the low acceptance rate should have come as no surprise. Finally, by that same March—two years after the beginning of relocations—only 204 of the 2,188 displaced households had been relocated in public housing, though not necessarily in the redevelopment area; others languished on Housing Authority waiting lists (1955:24; see Zipp 2012). The fears and concerns that had been expressed by the Committee to Save Our Homes and Mayor's Committee for Better Housing had been realized; many, if not most, of Manhattanville's former residents had simply "moved—address unknown."

For the tens of thousands of largely Black and brown people evicted from urban renewal sites across the city, dispossession posed far more than a problem of rehousing. Although the challenges of finding decent and affordable housing in a tight, low-income, and racially segregated housing market were alone daunting, the dislocation of households from neighborhoods also resulted in a fracturing of ties with kith and kin and, as Mindy Fullilove put it, "the destruction of all or part of one's emotional ecosystem" (2004:11). Furthermore, for the Manhattanville households forced to move, many to other boroughs of the city, displacement severed critical ties to schools, houses of worship, social service providers, and often employers—ties that required an arduous and protracted effort to rebuild and that often disproportionately fell on the shoulders of women. Like the evacuation of Black residents of New Orleans's Ninth Ward in the wake of Hurricane Katrina, the eviction of tenants from Manhattanville and slum clearance sites across the city constituted a de facto "exclusion from the shelter of citizenship" (Shockley 2010:104).

In September 1955, as demolition was nearing completion at Morningside Gardens and construction underway at the General Grant Houses, Gertrude Samuels returned to the area to write a second feature for the *New York Times* Sunday magazine. After recounting the history of the redevelopment project, praising the cooperation between community leaders and elites on the Hill, and lauding MHI's "democratic vision," Samuels offered a romanticized, if not mystical, account of how the two superblock projects defied racial and class-based segregation: "With no barriers between the two buildings—when landscaped they will flow naturally into one another—the fairly comfortable and the poor, intellectuals, white-collar workers, truck drivers, porters, will be living side by side" (Samuels 1955:37).

By late 1958, most of the apartments in Morningside Gardens had been occupied, few if any, by former residents of the redevelopment area. With average equity costs set at $750 a room and maintenance fees averaging $21 per room, the new cooperative apartments were unaffordable for most working-class people. Of the original stockholders in Morningside Gardens, 75 percent were white, 20 percent Black, 4 percent Asian, and 1 percent Puerto Rican (Gottlieb 2008:18). For middle-income African Americans, Morningside Gardens did present an opportunity to secure cooperative housing outside historically Black and underserved communities, but experts associated with the project maintained that no more than 25 percent of its units—the racial "tipping point"—should be occupied by Black and Puerto Rican residents (Gottlieb 2008). By contrast, as in public housing in general, Black and Puerto Rican people constituted the vast majority of tenants in the Grant Houses (Zipp 2012). MHI officials had reportedly hoped that the Grant Houses would be 50 percent white, but 90 percent of its new tenants were Black and Puerto Rican (Chronopoulos 2011).

Like Harlem's Dunbar apartments, Morningside Gardens was designed in the garden apartment tradition with its six, twenty-one story buildings arranged around a nine-acre landscaped interior courtyard. The entrances to the buildings faced the interior garden and playground, which opened onto 123rd Street, facing the Jewish Theological Seminary and institutions beyond. Four of the buildings formed a gated wall facing La Salle Street and the adjacent low-income, public housing complex, providing little, if any possibility that the superblocks would, as Samuels put it, "flow naturally into one another." Moreover, the co-op apartment complex was patrolled by private MHI security guards.

The General Grant Houses consisted of ten, twenty-story buildings arranged in the Corbusian-inspired "towers in the park" tradition— that is, high-rise buildings set back from the sidewalks and separated from each other by open spaces. Although the public housing projects covered only 12 percent of the site, the fenced-off, poorly maintained open spaces were underutilized by residents. And in contrast to Morningside Gardens' landscaped and fenceless interior courtyard, the winding pathways that connected the ten building lacked benches, creating a maze of anonymous and "indefensible spaces" (Newman 1972; Jacobs 1961). The contrast between the high-rise co-op and the public housing complex was further sharpened by the latter's lack of balconies, small window size, and few public amenities. The claim that the proximity of the two complexes promoted racial integration was absurd; at best, it reinforced what ALP organizer Henry Abrams had termed "a wall of snobbery and prejudice." In testimony before the National Commission on Urban Problems in 1968, Roger Starr, the conservative urbanist who became the architect of the city's infamous policy of "planned shrink-age" during the 1970s, conceded as much (Wallace and Wallace 2001). Starr, whose nonprofit organization, the Citizens Housing and Planning Council, had supported the Morningside-Manhattanville renewal project, told the commission,

> I don't think there is any effective interaction between Grant Houses and Morningside Gardens at all. I think we originally thought there would be. We originally hoped that by building Morningside Gardens alongside General Grant Houses we could get white families to move into General Grant Houses and make it an integrated community. We said to ourselves, "This is near Columbia. It's a section of the city that should be very attractive. Let's see if by putting it next to the co-op, and by trying to develop interaction between the co-op and the low-rent public housing, we can't get white families to move into this when it's new." But the fact is today that there are 3 percent of white families in General Grant Houses. (National Commission on Urban Problems 1968:470)

7

Racial Dispossession and Rebellion

We are looking for a community where the faculty can talk
to people like themselves. We don't want a dirty group.
—Stanley Salmen

With its northern border with West Harlem secure, Morningside Heights,
Inc. and its member institutions focused on crime, housing deterioration, and "undesirable" population groups. During World War II, many
apartment buildings on the Upper West Side were converted into rooming
houses, or single room occupancy hotels (SROs), to absorb the rapid influx
of migrants from the South, Puerto Rico, and elsewhere, who were drawn
to jobs in the city's wartime economy. SRO conversions were profitable. For
example, a six-room $70 per month apartment could be subdivided into
three unregulated room units, each renting for $40 per month.

Middle-class norms of respectable domesticity privileged nuclear,
heteronormative families. SROs were viewed by elites as violating these
regulative norms, which were held to be critical to the formation of normative subjects. After the war, thousands were displaced from urban
renewal sites across the city; demand for low-income housing skyrock-
eted. Households "doubled up" in apartments, rented rooms in SRO
hotels, and took in boarders. Once again, in 1958 the *New York Times*
warned of the physical decline and social deviancy concealed behind the
gilded facade of the American Acropolis:

> From these buildings the cancer of slum living has spread through all
> of Morningside Heights, driving out the decent, dragging other hous-
> ing down to its level, despoiling the schools and turning side streets and
> parks into fearsome places. (Philips 1958)

At the heart of this imagined threat to Morningside Heights were supposedly deviant SRO households, viewed as lacking in domestic order,

moral discipline, and hygiene. In this deeply racialized and medicalized discourse, low-income people of color were reduced to virulent pathogens eating away at the social body and normative whiteness. Like the notorious La Salle Street slum, razed through urban renewal, SROs and their low-income residents of color were perceived as abject and irredeemable, requiring excision from the body politic. The Manhattanville Neighborhood Center's policy of biopolitical racial containment would be supplanted by a policy of racial dispossession.

The War Against the SROs

By the mid-1950s, Columbia University had launched an aggressive campaign to buy SROs and other buildings occupied by low-income Black and Puerto Rican tenants in order to evict undesirables and renovate them for other uses. Between 1954 and 1964, Columbia purchased seventy-one buildings and pursued a program of tenant harassment and eviction by, for example, failing to repair broken elevators or provide sufficient heating in winter (Chronopoulos 2011). In 1956 the university purchased a seven-story, thirty-unit apartment building at 431 Riverside Drive and, shortly thereafter, petitioned the city's rent commission for certificates of eviction. Claiming that a lack of housing had prevented some four hundred married students from enrolling at the university, the petition declared that the building would be renovated to accommodate eighty Columbia-affiliated couples (*New York Times* 1957).

In coordination with the university, Mayor Robert F. Wagner launched a campaign to inspect SROs in Morningside Heights for building code and occupancy violations (Morningside Heights, Inc. 1959). Teams of inspectors, representing the departments of buildings, sanitation, fire, and other city agencies were dispatched in a "mass attack" on the slums (*New York Herald Tribune* 1958). In December 1958, Bernice Rogers, deputy commissioner of the Department of Buildings, arrived at 380 Riverside Drive with her inspection team—a building originally designed with 72 apartments, now consisting of 301 rooms and 58 apartments. One seven-room apartment housed seventeen people from different households, who shared a common kitchen and bathroom. Commissioner Rogers assured the *New York Times* in 1958 that most of the problems the inspection team encountered were tenant-caused. In a response, Franz Leichter, representing the Riverside Democrats, wrote to the *Times* in 1958 arguing that landlord neglect and lax building code enforcement were the problem: "With the present housing shortage," he stated, "we must allow families of four and five to live in one room, sharing public facilities with some twenty other people. The only alternative would seem to be to put these people out into the streets." Leichter's conclusion was sobering but sound, given the thousands of households that were being displaced from Title I sites and the paucity of affordable units available to rehouse them. However, the real estate purchases made by Columbia were intended precisely to remove their Black and brown tenants—to drive them into the streets.

Stanley Salmen, hired in 1956 to head university planning at Columbia and serve as MHI's executive director, made it clear that the mere public presence of people of color was unacceptable to MHI and the university:

> These houses . . . are the houses of many who are drunk on the sidewalks and benches, who play cards on the stoops, who call from sidewalk to fifth floor windows, who clutter the streets with tons of rubbish of all kinds, and who congregate in noisy groups until late at night. It is the children of these families who learn to dismantle cars, snatch pocket books, dominate the streets with games which lead to drinking and gambling among spectators and participants. . . . Some of these children start to use narcotics by the time that they are twelve and start extorting money from other children and stealing by the age of seven. (in Chronopoulos 2011:43; Salmen 1961)

Salmen's description of Black and brown residents is rife with symbolic symmetry to nineteenth-century descriptions of the urban coon. In this racially coded rant, Salmen read visual signs of deviations from white middle-class norms of civility and public life—card playing on stoops, calling to a window, and street games—as evidence of vice and criminal behavior. In this discourse of racial pathology, people of color manifested an *excess*—in their densities, desires, and sociability—that leaked from their buildings and into the streets, transgressing the imagined boundaries between respectable domesticity and the public sphere, between the licit and illicit, between civilization and its exoticized others. *"Look, a Negro!"* Salmen's narrative also articulated a spatiality of anti-Black policing and dispossession, flagging modes of Black and brown embodiment in space that were inappropriate, if not criminal, and thus subject to intensive surveillance, policing, and violence—that is, the imposition of sovereignty as the power to define "who is disposable and who is not" (Mbembe 2003:27).

The Columbia and MHI strategy for redeveloping Morningside Heights was one of racial dispossession, aimed at eliminating the affordable units housing most of the Heights' Black and brown tenants. The racialized bodies and conduct subverted the regulatory norms of white middle-class society and the civilizational project of the Acropolis. Their disturbing presence and behaviors were signs of social alterity. Unruliness was evidence of what Athena Athanasiou has referred to as "the refusal to stay in one's proper place" (Butler and Athanasiou 2013:221). The allegation that Black and brown residents of the Heights had failed to properly occupy urban space was also a denial of coevalness—that is, a claim that people of color, like their nineteenth-century predecessors, were insufficiently evolved to inhabit the privileged temporal landscapes of urban modernity (cf. Kern 2016).

This notion that people of color were out of place on the Hill—what Jaime Amparo Alves has referred to as "ontological placelessness"—was reiterated in MHI's reference to them as "transients" who lacked a stake in the area (2018). A 1959 MHI report claimed, "It is normally difficult for these transients to make a positive contribution to the community and most of the [Hill's] leadership comes from the residents who have roots in Morningside Heights and a stake in its future" (MHI 1959:4). The assertion that Black and brown residents were rootless transients incapable of leadership mirrored settler colonial discourses that constructed Indigenous peoples as "aimless wanderers"—as in the case of the Aboriginal peoples of Australia—in order to undermine their connections to the land and legitimize settler sovereignty (Curthoys 1999; Konishi 2018). A discourse of dispossession, this claim privileged a propertied, normative subject and spatiotemporal relationship to place. "In the political imaginary of (post)colonial capitalist western modernity," Athanasiou observed, "and its claims of universal humanity, being and having are constituted as ontologically akin to each other; being is defined as having; having is constructed as an essential prerequisite of proper human being" (Butler and Athanasiou 2013). The consequence of this privileging of propertied urban subjects—those with "a stake in the future"—is that the social, cultural, and historical attachments of unpropertied people of color to place were discounted and erased in redevelopment planning and its legitimating narratives, rendering them once again "ungeographic" (McKittrick 2006).

In 1959 Morningside Heights, Inc. released a report entitled *Morningside Heights*, which presented data on land use, housing conditions, population densities, transportation, schools, and community facilities on the Hill. The report, addressed to Mayor Robert Wagner and Borough President Hulan Jack, hammered home the message that Morningside Heights was in trouble. In their introductory letter, David Rockefeller and Grayson Kirk, president of Columbia University and then MHI's president, summarized the case for a new urban renewal effort: "The report shows substantial overcrowding and shared facilities for the individual, the family, and larger community group. This does not contribute to a good neighborhood climate. We believe that improvement of these conditions is long overdue, if our people and institutions are to enjoy the normal opportunities to realize their potential in a balanced community" (1959:1). Once again, the area's African American and Puerto Rican residents—those living in the overcrowded and shared facilities—were targeted as the source of the community's deterioration and beyond the pale of normality. If, as Laura Pulido has argued, a neighborhood is a "constellation of opportunities," then low-income people of color were imagined to be excluded, a priori, from them (2000:30). The technical report provided little sociological data on these racially marked residents and their housing needs, or suggestions as to how their living conditions might be improved in a "balanced community." As in the urban renewal brochures, the focus on the physical conditions of the neighborhood and its problematic buildings effaced the agency and subjecthood of people of color through a representational strategy of negative ontologization (Yancy 2004; cf. Berti et al. 2013).

In a two-paragraph section of the report, simply entitled "People," MHI addressed the changing racial composition of Morningside Heights:

Fifty nationalities are represented in the area. The total number of people living in the area is practically the same as it was in 1950, but there has been a substantial shift in the composition of the population. Approximately 86% of all persons and households in 1950 were white, other than Puerto Rican; by 1957 this proportion had dropped to 73%. The minority populations had increased from 8,000 to 15,000. (1958:8)

The increase in the area's non-white population was sufficient to identify the source of the problem and the nature of its solution. The report provided no remedies, merely recommending that city agencies "take action to develop and implement an effective reclamation program" (1959:30). In a front-page *New York Times* article, Charles Grutzner reported that he had learned from reliable sources that MHI favored small slum clearance projects, public housing, and the rehabilitation of old buildings. In addition, Grutzner noted, MHI supported providing property owners with low-interest loans and rent *increases* to encourage them to maintain and upgrade their buildings and remove low-income residents (Grutzner 1959).

In 1961 the Morningside Renewal Council (MRC) was established by the Housing and Development Administration to coordinate urban renewal planning between neighborhood interests and city agencies. Composed of representatives of MHI (about one-third of its membership), community-based organizations, and elected officials, the MRC was tasked with representing the Heights' interests and needs for redevelopment to the city, and identifying specific sites for rehabilitation and rebuilding. Although the MRC generally supported Columbia's vision for Morningside Heights, as outlined in MHI's 1959 study, it opposed key Columbia and MHI initiatives, notably the university's aborted plan to build a gymnasium in Morningside Park.

During the 1960s, Columbia and its MHI-Remedco partners continued their campaign to purchase apartment buildings and SROs on the Upper West Side in order to evict low-income Black and brown tenants and upgrade the buildings for students and institutional employees. In September 1961, the university assumed the mortgage of the Devonshire Hotel, a ten-story SRO at 542 West 112th Street. Its landlord then issued eviction orders to its 350 residents. In the agreement with the building's owner, Remedco committed to invest $1.5 million to install a new roof, new elevators, and new air conditioning and heating systems, thus rendering the Devonshire suitable for the employees of MHI members. The Devonshire's tenants filed a complaint with the State Commission Against Discrimination, charging that the university had embarked upon a redevelopment campaign to drive Black and Puerto Rican people out of Morningside Heights. In response, a university spokesperson denied a discriminatory intent by making a curiously beside-the-point argument that erased the social locations of people of color who were being displaced: "None of the educational institutions," the spokesperson stated, "makes color or race a factor in the acceptance of qualified students. St. Luke's [hospital] accepts patients without regard for color or creed. International House is, in large part, made up of students from many lands. The policies of these institutions are reflected in Remedco" (Arnold 1961:39). Like later discourses of multiculturalism, Columbia substituted a defensive appeal to cultural diversity for the recognition of power-laden and racialized socioeconomic inequalities.

In January 1962, the Devonshire's remaining tenants won a tenuous victory when the State Rent Commission ruled that the building was subject to the rent control system. The ruling delayed further evictions by requiring that evictions not be allowed unless the Devonshire were to be demolished or its entire interior renovated, or gut rehabbed (*New York Times* 1962b:25). To overcome this new obstacle, Remedco purchased the building and pledged to conduct structural changes and attempt to induce the remaining tenants to relocate without further legal actions.

As evictions accelerated, resistance to Columbia University's expansion and policy of racial cleansing escalated. Tenant and neighborhood associations, many led by women, formed to fight the evictions and tenant harassment, demanding transparency from the university about its expansion plans. In a report addressing harassment complaints made by tenants in Columbia-owned buildings, the Morningside Renewal Council described what it found at one location: "Upon our first visit, we found tenants without heat or hot water, without properly functioning elevators, with broken windows and plaster in public and private areas, with unlocked doors . . . , with rat and roach infestation, with improper removal of refuse, and with other conditions hazardous to health and safety" (in Chronopoulos 2011:46).

When the tenants living in eight apartment buildings on Morningside Drive received eviction notices in 1961, they organized to fight back under the leadership of Marie Runyon, a single mother who had honed her skills as an organizer with the ACLU. Although the landlord identified on her lease was the 130 Holding Company, Runyon's research revealed that the eight buildings were owned by the Columbia College of Pharmacy, which was located downtown but planned to move uptown near the Morningside campus (Gold 2014). Through the courts Runyon and her group, known as the "Morningside Six," demanded proof that the college had the financial means to demolish and redevelop the site, as required by the rent control laws governing tenant evictions. Three years later, the College of Pharmacy was forced to concede that it was $3 million short in financing, but not after it had already razed four of the eight apartment buildings. Among the tenants evicted was Hannah Arendt, the German political philosopher and exile from the Nazis (*Berea College Magazine* 2004; Gold 2014).

As Runyon and the Morningside Six were fighting to save their homes, Columbia University announced a vast, six-year expansion plan, which included a new home for the Graduate School of Business, an international studies center, a Morningside Heights site for the School of Social Work, a graduate residence hall, and a new gymnasium. The graduate residence and International Affairs Building would join the Law School's Jerome L. Greene Hall, then under construction on the east side of Amsterdam Avenue, to form the new East Campus. This East Campus superblock was to be built on an elevated platform and connected to the main campus by a 100-foot-wide causeway over Amsterdam Avenue, demapping 117th Street and creating a street-level barrier that walled off the new campus from Amsterdam Avenue. In short, architecture mirrored and reinforced the university's fraught and asymmetrical relationship to the community (Hechinger 1961).

Columbia University sociologist Daniel Bell penned a feature article in the *New York Times* Sunday magazine section in 1964 that warned of a "crisis phase" in the northern civil rights movement triggered by militancy and direct-action protests. "New leaders are quickly 'thrown up,'" Bell declared, "as the movement spreads from civil rights to schools, to rent strikes, to claims for preferences in jobs." It is far from clear how civil rights might be disentangled from questions of fair housing, education, and employment opportunities. Nevertheless, citing the World's Fair protests and mocking Harlem's Black political leadership, Bell professed,

> The exacerbated climate is favorable to demagogues—in fact, some of the influential Negro leaders have quietly stepped back from overt involvement with immediate issues and are waiting for calmer times—and these have been quick to emerge, abetted by such wily politicians as [Harlem Congressman] Adam Clayton Powell who dreams of becoming "the grand old man of the 'Black Revolution.'" (Bell 1964)

Bell's power-evasive reasoning echoed the race liberalism of the 1930s, as well as the racial improvement policies discussed in chapters 5 and 6. His patronizing essay went on to argue that it was "foolish and illusory" to assume that all of the solutions to the problems of African Americans could be achieved by political means. Like his predecessors, Bell viewed racial inequalities as caused by cultural and moral deficiencies within Black communities—not structural racism or power. Citing Nathan Glazer and Daniel P. Moynihan's *Beyond the Melting Pot* (1963), Bell pointed to high percentages of female-headed households and "illegitimacy" in Black communities, which, he asserted, "sheds enormous light on the limited economic resources, the inadequate motivational patterns and other social handicaps of the Negro community" (1964:31).

Bell's position was representative of the culture of poverty literature that took shape during the 1960s, which stressed culture rather than socioeconomic inequalities as the leading factor reproducing the "cycle of poverty." Michael Harrington's influential book *The Other America* maintained that the poor were "internal exiles," whose cultural and psychological penchants led them "to develop attitudes of defeat and pessimism and who are therefore excluded from taking advantage of new opportunities" ([1962] 1997:179). Harrington's views had a profound influence on the War on Poverty then underway (Aksamit 2014).

A second critical influence on the shaping of the culture of poverty paradigm and War on Poverty was Stanley Elkins's highly contested study *Slavery: A Problem in American Institutional and Intellectual Life*, published in 1959. Elkins, a Columbia-trained historian, maintained that slavery as a "closed system" of total oppression had created distinct cultural and psychological traits, characterized by extreme dependency, docility, irresponsibility, and infantile personality features—traits that persisted among the internal exiles living in contemporary urban ghettos. Elkins associated this alleged trait complex with the racist "Sambo" caricature and asked whether *it* might be taken seriously:

> The [Sambo] picture has too many circumstantial details, its hues have been stroked in by too many different brushes, for it to be denounced as counterfeit. Too much folk-knowledge, too much plantation literature, too much of the Negro's own lore, have gone into its making to entitle one in good conscience to condemn it as "conspiracy." (1959:84)

As I suggested in chapter 4, the iconic figure of the urban coon and similar racist tropes were dialectically insinuated into discourses of policing, the press, and the social sciences. That the Sambo archetype was omnipresent, in Elkins's reasoning, meant that it was reliable. Although Elkins's "Sambo thesis" was soundly critiqued by historians and others on various grounds (see Rainwater and Yancey 1967; Lane 1971), it nevertheless had a critical influence on sociologist and War on Poverty architect Daniel P. Moynihan, whose influential report *The Negro Family: The Case for National Action* (1965) drew heavily on Elkins's thesis to make the case that the alleged "tangle of pathology" in Black communities had its origins in the collapse of the Black family during slavery.

It is not without irony that the removal of low-income people of color from Morningside Heights to segregated ghettos, such as Harlem and the South Bronx, only exacerbated the closed system of internal exiles that culture of poverty theorists argued was so destructive. By identifying the nexus of Black pathology—Bell's "cool world"—as fatherless Black boys, such accounts also focused anxiety, surveillance, and policing attention on the supposed menace posed by Black and brown youth. Morningside Heights, Inc. hatched its own academic study of the area's street gangs. Lewis Yablonsky, director of MHI's crime prevention unit and a sociologist, published an ethnographic study of youth gangs in Manhattanville, *The Violent Gang* (1962), based on research that he conducted while employed by MHI.

Policing was a critical component of MHI's community redevelopment program. As early as 1948, MHI's president, David Rockefeller, had called attention to the problem of crime in Morningside Heights, leading to the creation of a Committee on Law and Order. One of the committee's first initiatives was to develop a system for documenting "untoward happenings" (Van Dusen 1954). This crime monitoring data was then used to explore the possibility of coordinating protective services among MHI members and with police. Once again, MHI turned to the University of Chicago for expertise, arranging a meeting in New York with its chancellor, Lawrence A. Kimpton, a member of the law enforcement committee of the South East Chicago Commission (SECC). The SECC had been created by the University of Chicago in 1952 to address crime and housing deterioration in Hyde Park, a community adjacent to the University of Chicago with a sizable Black population (Hirsch 1983). In 1953 MHI hired Lewis Yablonsky, a twenty-eight-year-old criminologist, to head its public safety program. By 1961, MHI had created a private security force to man posts and walk beats throughout the Heights.

In *The Violent Gang*, Yablonsky drew a sharp contrast between Manhattanville's largely Black and brown gangs and the white "Norton Street Gang" studied by William F. Whyte for *Street Corner Society* (1943), his foundational account of Boston's North End. Yablonsky argued that whereas friendship, camaraderie, and cooperativeness were central norms for the Norton Street Gang, Manhattanville's Black and brown gangs were "cold killers," motivated by the psychological need to achieve "existential validation" through violence. They were, in short, "bully coons."

Like Columbia's policy of evictions, Yablonsky's approach called for the removal of supposedly sociopathic Black and brown youth (*homines sacri*) from normative, white middle-class society—an exercise of racial dispossession and carceral power. In the discourse of MHI's institutions, violent gangs were little more than a synecdoche for the area's Black and brown residents and their allegedly deviant modes of conduct. In a special issue of the *Barnard Alumnae* magazine, "Morningside Heights: A Portrait," Roselle Kurland linked Daniel Bell's angst concerning Black militancy to the alleged violent threat posed by Black and brown youth:

> There is evidence that racially-inspired tensions stemming from the present civil rights and civil liberties movements are increasing. This is a problem for the entire nation, but it indicates certain security needs

for Morningside Heights. Located next to Harlem, preventive measures are wise and security procedures mandatory, concerning possible racial violence in and about Morningside Heights. Police officials state that racially-based youth groups are forming and that irrational violence in group form is again possible, if not imminent, in the next years. (1966)

This conflation of Black political activism with crime and anti-white violence recalled the red-baiting of Save Our Homes the decade before. It served to delegitimize the opposition of Harlem-based groups, activists, and politicians to MHI's program of redevelopment, while eliding structural racism and police violence directed *at* Black and Puerto Rican youth. Less than two months after Daniel Bell's rebuke of Black direct-action politics, rioting once again broke out in Harlem following the killing of a fifteen-year-old Black boy, James Powell, by an off-duty white police lieutenant on the Upper East Side. After a peaceful rally organized by CORE, a crowd assembled in front of the 28th police precinct on West 123th Street and demanded the arrest of the lieutenant and dismissal of the police commissioner. The police cordoned off the entire block in front of the police precinct and charged the crowd, setting off six days of social unrest in Harlem and in the Bedford-Stuyvesant section of Brooklyn. When it was all over, one Black protester was killed, 200 injured, and 465 arrested (Flamm 2017).

As in the uprisings of 1935 and 1943, police violence and criminal justice system abuses were at the heart of the social unrest and wider civil rights agenda (Taylor 2013). In his weekly column in the *Chicago Defender*, baseball legend Jackie Robinson drew a parallel between the nomination of Barry Goldwater as the Republican Party's candidate for president in 1964 and the police shooting of James Powell. He then praised the role that James Farmer, the national director of CORE, had played in speaking out against the police violence: "He has refused to bite his tongue," Robinson declared, "about the Gestapo methods of the New York City Police. I do not have to be in Harlem to be familiar with the kind of frenzied and sadistic brutality that many of the New York City police force feel they can get away with when dealing with Negro and Puerto Rican citizens." Although Mayor Wagner implemented largely symbolic reforms in the wake of the Harlem uprising—for example, increasing the number of Black police officers stationed in Harlem—he responded aggressively to the alleged crisis of Black and brown undesirables in Morningside Heights.

In September 1964, only weeks after the Harlem riot, Mayor Wagner and the chairman of the Housing and Development Administration announced the release of a sweeping redevelopment plan for the Upper West Side. The proposal, entitled the Morningside General Neighborhood Renewal Plan (GNRP), mapped out a ten-year plan for the rehabilitation or clearance of a ninety-two-block area, extending from West 100th to 125th Streets, between Riverside Drive and Eighth Avenue-Central Park West. The GNRP targeted sections of the West Side that had been identified as problematic in MHI's report five years earlier, and additional sections for either conservation or slum clearance. Importantly, fourteen blocks surrounding Columbia were excepted from the GNRP's renewal area and set aside for institutional expansion, thereby exempting them from the public hearing requirements and other regulations (the anti-discrimination policy, for one) governing the city's urban renewal program (Drosnin 1964).

Tenant groups and activists in Morningside Heights and Harlem rallied to oppose the GNRP. In early 1964, over five hundred residents of Harlem and Morningside Heights rallied at the Riverside Church to protest the university's expansion activities. Speakers at the event included Congressman William Ryan, Jane Benedict, chair of the Metropolitan Council on Housing, and Marie Runyon, now leading the neighborhood-wide tenants' group Morningsiders United. Also present at the rally was Percival Goodman, a Columbia professor of architecture and an urban theorist, who lamented the lack of humanitarianism at modern universities. An early critic of Robert Moses's policies, Goodman contrasted the redevelopment policies of Columbia with Oxford University in the thirteenth century, when, according to Goodman, students had taken up arms to defend the local peasants from the bishop's army (Gold 2014; Alden 1964).

In March 1965, the Morningside General Neighborhood Renewal Plan was brought before the Board of Estimate. Black and Puerto Rican protesters gathered outside City Hall and in the hearing room. "You give money for everything else," William Stanley, an African American building superintendent and head of the Uptown Tenants Council, told the board. "How much will you give for a human life?" Estelle Edwards, representing the Tri-Community Organization, a coalition of tenant activists from Morningside Heights, Harlem, and Manhattan Valley, challenged the central premise of MHI's construction of the neighborhood's undesirables: "The institutions say [it is the] economic and social and cultural conditions of the community; [that] children of our type have nothing that can afford them anything; we are of low culture; we are not good housekeepers. Are we always going to be a collection of citizens, in a minority, categorized by what we haven't got? We want to be first-class citizens too" (O'Kane 1965). Here, one recalls Athanasiou's observation that in (post)colonial capitalist society, "having is constructed as an essential prerequisite of proper human being."

Speaking in support of the GNRP was the crème de la crème of the American Acropolis, including the presidents of Barnard and Teachers College, the chairperson of Columbia's board of trustees, the provost of the Jewish Theological Seminary, and the chairperson of the Morningside Renewal Council. Jacques Barzun, the noted cultural historian and Columbia's provost, reiterated the racist tropes that permeated MHI's discourses of dispossession and characterized the area's undesirables as "transient, footloose, or unhappily disturbed" (Kaplan 1965a:45). In a well-worn appeal to white fears, Barzun invoked the specter of the Black bully coon, terrorizing the white residents of Morningside Heights. "I have seen the streets become unsafe at night," Barzun averred. "Gangs have attacked some of my colleagues, muggers have assaulted their wives, snatched their purses, and held up students. . . . They must not be subjected to an environment that requires the perpetual *qui vive* of a paratrooper in enemy country." All that was missing in Barzun's characterization was mention of the bully coon's gun and razor.

Constance Baker Motley, the African American Manhattan borough president and member of the Board of Estimate, stated that she wanted firm safeguards in the GNRP that Black and Puerto Rican tenants would not be evicted to create a "white, middle-class enclave in the Heights." Motley, the first woman to occupy the seat, also wanted to ensure that residents dislocated from renewal sites would be adequately rehoused.

On April 22, the Board of Estimate approved a revised version of the ten-year renewal plan. In the revised GNRP, Columbia was barred from additional expansion initiatives within the renewal area for ten years, apart from some eleven projects already underway. The renewal area was expanded to include the fourteen-block area around the university that had originally been exempted (consequently covering them under the ten-year moratorium) and a ten-block section of West Harlem to the north of 125th Street and west of Broadway. Finally, the board adopted a declaration of intent that at least 25 percent of the new housing constructed in the university area be set aside for low-income families. Herbert Evans, chairman of the Housing and Development Administration, explained at the hearing that the ten-block section north of 125th Street, referred to as the "piers area," could be used to build moderate- and low-income housing (Kaplan 1965b:1). This piers area—the site of the original settlement of Manhattanville and located along the fault line valley—would presumably serve to relocate people uprooted from Morningside Heights, thereby pushing them north of 125th Street.

These minor revisions did little to quell community opposition to the GNRP. In May, nine members of the West Harlem Community Organization dropped in at Jacques Barzun's office in Low Memorial Library, as he was meeting with President Grayson Kirk, and demanded an apology for his characterization of Black and brown residents of the Hill as "transient, footloose, or unhappily disturbed people." The resulting exchange, documented by *New York Times* reporter Samuel Kaplan, is worth quoting at length:

"No one, especially an educated man like you, has the right to talk about people the way you did," said Mr. Stanley. "You insulted me."

Smiling, and talking in measured, cultured tones, Dr. Barzun replied that his statement had been misinterpreted.

"I was not talking about you good people," said Dr. Barzun, "but about addicts and prostitutes."

"How do you know what we are?" interrupted Mr. Stanley, sitting up stiffly. "You were talking about a part of our community. About Harlem. About colored people."

Dr. Barzun flushed. His smile disappeared, and with a sweep of his hand he slid out onto the table a book entitled, "Race, A Study in Superstition."

"I wrote this book in 1937, before most people were thinking about discrimination," he said.

"Then you should know better," replied Mrs. Margaret MacNeil, a housewife who had brought along her 3-year-old son. (Kaplan 1965a:45)

The exchange exposed the gulf that existed between the institutional elites of the Heights and the low-income Black and brown people living amongst them; between the theoretical ruminations of the professoriate and the spatial politics of the university. Barzun's statement, that his book was written "before *most people* were thinking about discrimination," presupposed the erasure of Black people from history and denied the subjecthood of the seven Black people sitting in his office. Stanley's query, "How do you know what we are?," cut to the heart of the matter: the university's appeal to the synecdochic tropes—drug addict, prostitute, transient—in its discourse of dispossession to characterize people of color as undesirable. In fact, this was an important but by no means original argument in Barzun's book *Race: A Study in Superstition*: "Race theories shift their ground, alter their jargon, and mix their claims," Barzun wrote, "but they cannot obliterate *the initial vice of desiring to explain much by little and to connect in the life of the group or individual some simple fact with some great significance*" (1965:114; emphasis added). Mrs. MacNeil's pithy response, "Then you should know better," was precisely correct.

Stanley's challenge, "How do you know *what* we are?," was a demand to restore the ontological void—"colored people"—that was produced by the racial tropes that cast people of color beyond the pale of modernity and the law itself. In this discourse of dispossession, the Hill's undesirables were constituted as *homines sacri*, as "bare life," ontologically reduced to carnal excess and excepted from the right to residential security, a stable community life, and, as in the killing of fifteen-year-old James Powell, the very protection of the law (Agamben 1998, 2005). If MHI and Columbia's policy of racial dispossession imposed a "state of exception" on low-income people of color in the Heights and environs, then police violence was its logical extreme—sovereign violence visited upon those deemed to be less-than-human.

Mrs. MacNeil made one last attempt to contest the logic of exception articulated in Barzun's offensive comments by declaring:

> "We want to help the addicts. They are part of the community. The University, with all its education, should also help the addicts."
>
> "That is a technical problem," said Dr. Barzun.
>
> "No!" shouted Mr. Stanley in a sharp voice, "that is a *human* problem."

Not bare life, but fully human. Less than a year after the revised GNRP was approved, Borough President Motley charged that the university had violated the GNRP by evicting 350 tenants from four Columbia-owned buildings not previously earmarked for expansion.

In March 1967, the Faculty Civil Rights Group (FCRG) released a report criticizing the renewal plan and urged the university to preserve racial diversity in the area (*Columbia Daily Spectator* 1966). The committee, chaired by Immanuel Wallerstein, charged that urban renewal projects often united government and private sector sponsors "in a drive to dispossess the poor and raze their buildings in order to construct gleaming new developments out of their financial reach" (Hardman 1967).

In a second report, released in November, the FCRG decried the failure of city government to mediate on behalf of community interests:

> There is no rational machinery with the authority to make decisions between the claims of the University and the community. Though the city government is looked to by the community to play this role, its legal powers are only indirect and dubious at best. . . . Thus, in the absence of a mediating authority, the decision is generally made on the basis of relative FORCE, financial in this case, by university administrators who see their responsibility as almost entirely defined by the educational institutions to which they belong. (FCRG 1967:13)

The FCRG supported other civil rights causes both on and off campus. When parents of children attending Harlem's PS 125 began a boycott to protest their lack of inclusion in school decision making, the faculty group issued a statement of support and asked the faculty to contribute money and time to support the West Harlem Liberation School, which had been created during the boycott. The FCRG also advocated for the recruitment of Black students and faculty, the addition of courses in Black history and culture, and the creation of a teacher exchange program with historically Black colleges and universities (Hardman 1967; Kopel 1969:1).

The discourses and practices of racial dispossession, exercised by Columbia and its allies, were grounded in the much earlier fabrication of the American Acropolis as an elite, capsular space and, as the *New York Times* editorialized in 1892, "a conspicuous center of civilization;

a city set on a hill and devoted to the things of the mind, where it will remain an impressive monument to those engaged in the material strife that will go on below it." Once defended from that strife and its underlying socioeconomic differences by geography, later by the modern technologies of power of the industrial city, this capsularity also relied on the construction of spatiotemporal, symbolic, and epistemological distinctions, radically differentiating white native-born educational, cultural, and religious elites on the Hill from the racially marked poor and working-class populations in the valley below. Although this spatiotemporal boundary was honed differently by various interests on the Hill, the notion of the American Acropolis defined as a unified, predominantly white and elite community of interest, engaged in the production of Western civilization, against a constitutive outside of racial, ethnic, and economic alterity endured. However, in 1968 that imagined singularity and the spatiotemporal distinctions upon which it rested were radically contested.

A Bridge Too Far: The "Crisis at Columbia"

The gymnasium is *the* Columbia issue *par excellence*.
—Eric Bentley

On the evening of May 17, 1968, members of the Community Action Committee occupied a Columbia-owned building at 618 West 114th Street. The university intended to raze the tenement and replace it with a new building for the School of Social Work. While members of the Action Committee took up positions inside and in front of the six-story structure, some eight hundred Columbia students marched from campus, where they had been attending a "monster rally" called by the student Strike Coordinating Committee. In a press statement, the Community Action Committee averred, "Columbia must be stopped. Since none of the prescribed methods of protest has succeeded, we are now taking back one of the buildings that Columbia has taken from us."[1] The students handed out statements, signed by remaining tenants in the building, condemning the university for its actions. "Blankets, cartons of food, mops, brooms, sponges and soap powder were brought into the new 'community-owned building,'" Robert Friedman wrote. "One vacant room was designated a meeting area, and the old and young activists worked together at sweeping and washing it. A bullhorn was brought over from Strike Central, and for the next several hours various students and community leaders gave speeches to the crowd outside" (1969:243).

From the stoop of the occupied tenement, Michael Golash, a leader of the Students for a Democratic Society (SDS), announced a press conference that evening and noted, "All press will be welcome, with the exception of the *New York Times* and CBS." Golash, who headed the SDS's committee on university expansion, explained that Arthur Ochs Sulzberger, president and publisher of the newspaper, and William Paley, president of the Columbia Broadcasting System, were both members of the university's corporate-heavy board of trustees. The week before, Columbia students had picketed Sulzberger's Fifth Avenue residence to protest the newspaper's biased coverage of the campus protests (*Columbia Daily Spectator* 1968c). As night fell, hundreds of students sat down in the street, lit candles, and sang "We Shall Not Be Moved." At 4:15 the next morning, some 175 police in riot gear marched down 114th Street and began making arrests. One hundred and twenty-one protesters were arrested, including Golash and the SDS's chairman, Mark Rudd, and twenty-seven members of the Community Action Committee (*New York Times* 1968). The arrested Columbia and Barnard students, as well as members of the Community Action Committee, spent the night in jail and were arraigned the next morning on charges of disorderly conduct (Friedman 1969).

At the campus rally the day before, students called on the university to relinquish all claims to Morningside Park, where the university was building a gymnasium; return College Walk (the closed road through campus connecting Broadway to Amsterdam Avenue at 116th Street) to the city for use by the public;[2] and cease all racist institutional policies. "Columbia and other institutions in our community," their statement read, "have deliberately forced the removal of almost every Black, Puerto Rican, and Oriental (except for those affiliated with the University) from Morningside Heights, thus turning it into a white ghetto" (Stern 1968).

During the spring of 1968, the Columbia campus was beset by student protests against the campus recruitment efforts of the Dow Chemical Company (the manufacturer of napalm), the university's ten-year affiliation with the Institute for Defense Analyses (IDA), the building of a gymnasium in Morningside Park, and the university's rule against indoor protests, which had led to the disciplining of six members of the SDS (Cox Commission 1968). The IDA had been created in 1955 by the Department of Defense and Joint Chiefs of Staff to coordinate university-based research on weapons systems and other Pentagon interests and projects. Columbia's involvement with the IDA, along with the recruitment activities of Dow Chemical, were lightning rods for student opposition to the war in Vietnam and the draft.

The Student Afro-American Society (SAS), founded in 1964, and a network of students and professors at the School of Architecture had focused critical attention on the university's expansion policies and institutional racism, on and off campus (Rosenkranz 1971; Slonecker 2006). In February, members of the SAS had joined Harlem-based groups, including the West Harlem Morningside Park Committee, CORE, and others, to protest against the gym at the construction site and in the campus vicinity. Some members of the SAS were also members of Harlem-based groups, such as CORE and the Student Nonviolent Coordinating Committee (SNCC), and student coalitions, such as the Black Student Congress, where they had gained experience in organizing and direct-action strategies. Black women at Barnard College had organized to demand transparency with respect to the university's expansion policies and to establish links with Harlem-based groups through the Barnard Organization of Soul Sisters, or BOSS (Bradley 2009).

For the SAS, BOSS, and community-based organizations, the gym project—dubbed the "Jim Crow gymnasium"—was a lightning rod for opposition to a host of issues, including campus expansion and racial inequities at Columbia, as well as the Hill's historically contentious relationship to Harlem. The design of the facility, which would span the hundred-foot cliff-barrier that separated Morningside Heights from Central Harlem, became a potent symbol, materialized in space, of the polysemous racialized boundary between the two areas, and of hierarchy itself. The gym featured two separate entrances and facilities: one for students at the top of the plateau on Morningside Drive, and another for members of the community in Morningside Park below. That vertical contrast, which had been foundational to imagining the Acropolis as an elite and capsular space and source of the contrastive monikers "Hill" and "Valley," epitomized the perduring power differentials between the two communities. The gym's significance as a potent "condensation symbol" of this fraught relationship was not lost on the press (Graber 1976).

In her article on the gym controversy, fittingly entitled "How Not to Build a Symbol," architectural critic Ada Louise Huxtable noted,

> There is a symbol going up right now in Morningside Park: the new Columbia University gymnasium. But this is not the kind of symbol anyone wanted. It stands for one of the more disturbing problems of our troubled times—the deep and bitter split and many-layered misunderstanding between a privileged urban university and an unprivileged community. (Huxtable 1968a)

In the mid-1950s, as demolition of the Morningside-Manhattanville renewal area was nearing completion, Columbia began developing parkland at the southeast corner of Morningside Park for use by students and neighborhood residents. In 1954 President Grayson Kirk had met with Park Commissioner Robert Moses and lamented the university's lack of recreational space. For his part, Moses expressed his concern that Morningside Park was not being utilized (in Stern, Mellins, and Fishman 1995:742). By 1957, the Columbia-Community Athletic Fields occupied five acres of public parkland and included two baseball diamonds and other athletic facilities. Spurred by the need for more recreational space for students and encouraged by the apparent success of the athletic fields, Columbia University officials began meeting with Moses to discuss the possibility of constructing a gymnasium in the Olmsted-designed public park. Soon afterwards, Kirk reached an agreement with Moses that if the university were to build a gym in the park for public use, the city would allow it to piggyback a student facility on top. In 1961, with the approval of the City Council and state legislature, Columbia signed a one-hundred-year lease for air rights over the 2.1 acres of public parkland at an annual rental fee of $3,000 (Cox Commission 1968).

In the design developed by the architectural firm Eggers & Higgins, the "vertical gym" would have two separate entrances: a Morningside Drive entrance at the level of the plateau at 113th Street with access to the campus, and a community entrance over one hundred feet below, at grade with Morningside Park. Inside the multilevel gymnasium, the two facilities did not communicate, preventing contact between Columbia students and Harlem residents. "The entire community gym," Michael Carriere noted, was "smaller than the student swimming pool alone by 5,440 square feet" (2011:18). In short, the vertical gym was the material expression of separate and unequal. As opposition among community-based groups and Harlem elected officials grew, the university agreed to build a swimming pool in the community facility, which only fanned the flames of outrage. At a June 1967 rally in Morningside Park, State Assemblyman Charles Rangel stressed the obtuse insensitivity of the pool concession: "There will be a colored pool and a white pool. Doesn't Columbia realize that to put in a colored pool is insulting rather than accommodating?" (Carriere 2011:5–29; *New York Times* 1967).

By the time that Columbia President Grayson Kirk announced groundbreaking for the project in 1966, community-based and student opposition to the vertical gym had ballooned. That same year, a coalition of community organizations, the Ad Hoc Committee for Morningside Park, was formed and demanded the cancellation of the city's lease with Columbia. The Columbia chapter of CORE, a member of the ad hoc coalition, introduced a resolution to the Student Council, demanding that the university suspend construction of the gym until it had reached an agreement with the community. The resolution passed. State Senator Basil A. Paterson and State Assemblyman Percy Sutton, Black Harlem Democrats, introduced bills in chambers, calling for the repeal of the 1960 act that had granted the city the right to lease public parkland to Columbia (Slonecker 2006; Carriere 2011).

The *Amsterdam News* denounced the plan in a January 29, 1966, editorial, declaring, "If Mayor Lindsay permits Columbia University to grab two acres of land out of Morningside Park for a gymnasium, it will be a slap in the face of every Black man, woman, and child in Harlem." Thomas Hoving, the newly appointed commissioner of parks, also opposed the gym project on the grounds that it would eliminate public parkland and that the mere 12 percent of space allotted for the community's use was not only insufficient, but also evidence that the project was little more than a "land grab" (Bradley 2003). Community and student groups protested in Morningside Park and, on the eve of the 1968 student occupations at Columbia, hundreds of protesters interrupted a campus event, ironically themed "The Urban Struggle for Power," which featured among its speakers Sargent Shriver, director of the War on Poverty's Office of Economic Opportunity (Carriere 2011).

An influential critic of the gym project and Columbia's expansionism was the Architects Renewal Committee in Harlem (ARCH). Founded in 1964 by architect C. Richard Hatch, ARCH was critical of the top-down approach of modernist urban planning and sought to advocate on behalf of low-income communities and provide planning and other services directly to residents (Goldstein 2017). Composed largely of Black architects, urban planners, and other experts, many working as volunteers, ARCH received funding from the War on Poverty's Office of Economic Opportunity and other sources (Bradley 2009). In 1964 the Tri-Community Organization, a coalition of tenant groups founded by the Reverend Eugene Callender, pastor of Harlem's Church of the Master, retained ARCH to review the Morningside GNRP. The ARCH analysis of the plan criticized the city's inadequate relocation assistance program, and argued against excluding the fourteen-block area around the university from the renewal area, which, as noted above, would have exempted Columbia's activities there from public review and regulation. For the Architects Renewal Committee in Harlem, the gym project, like the Morningside GNRP, prioritized the needs of elites over those of Black and brown residents of the city (Goldstein 2017).

Michael Carriere has argued that the reason that the gym became so powerful and unifying a symbol of protest for students and community activists was that both groups were able to tie the project to wider regional and international policies and events: "By linking Columbia's urban planning practices to the university's complicity in events in Vietnam (and by showing that both were the result of a certain undemocratic culture of expertise), the protesters were able to connect the university to the dark sides of both campaigns" (2011:20). In the political culture of the 1960s, such associations were commonplace, if not de rigueur, within Black communities, where activists linked the war in Vietnam, struggles against apartheid in South Africa, and anti-colonial conflicts in Mozambique and Angola to "internal colonialism" at home (Ture and Hamilton [1967] 2011; cf. Blauner 1969). The discourse and policy of dispossession exercised by Columbia and MHI mirrored those of settler colonial societies, where depopulation and coerced assimilation were used to assert settler sovereignty over land, while Indigenous populations were depicted as violent, hypersexualized, and "aimless wanderers." Patrick Wolfe's account of the relationship of colonized people to the settler society as one of dispensability holds true for the relationship of the undesirables in the Heights to the American Acropolis. As Wolfe observed, "Settler-colonization is at base a winner-take-all project whose dominant feature is not exploitation but replacement. The logic of this project, a sustained institutional tendency to eliminate the Indigenous population, informs a range of historical practices that might otherwise appear distinct—invasion is a structure not an event" (1999:163). Like the La Salle Street slum and SROs that housed low-income people of color in the Heights, the public parkland in Morningside Park was *terra nullius*.

However, opposition to the gym was not only galvanized by its separate and unequal design and its ready comparability to the Jim Crow South and spatial politics of settler colonialism; it also tied problems of racial justice affecting neighboring communities to racial disparities on campus with respect to the paucity of Black students, faculty, and administrators and lack of courses in African American studies, as the Faculty Civil Rights Group and Student Afro-American Society maintained (Cox Commission 1968). Race was *the* issue that cross-cut the town-gown divide and animated both. Here, as it had before, the denial of racism provided evidence of its centrality.

Roger Starr, writing for the neoconservative public policy journal the *Public Interest*, defended the gym project and blamed the linking of Columbia's internal and external racial difficulties on the Architects Renewal Committee in Harlem. Arguing that there was no intrinsic relationship between the on- and off-campus racial issues and that many Harlem residents supported the gym, Starr reached the curious conclusion that ARCH had seized on the gym controversy for its own purpose—that is, to woo Black clients for its urban planning services, ARCH stoked community opposition to the gym where there had been little (1968).

Starr was unable or unwilling to recognize Black oppositional agency as anything other than a cynical effort at self-promotion: ARCH needed Black clients, so it manufactured Black outrage. Starr himself clarified the connection between the on- and off-campus issues of racial injustice, concluding that both struggles were attacks on the academic standards and future of an urban Ivy League university—an all-too-familiar evasion of structural racism on college campuses:

> The question asked of the Columbia gymnasium by the most potent of its adversaries is whether a gymnasium incorporating the standards of Ivy League sport and physical training is *relevant* to the needs of the people who live nearest it. And if the gymnasium is not, as they put it, "relevant," can the institution itself be relevant? When Columbia faculty and administrators are asked why there are so few (reportedly, six) Negro faculty members, the answer comes back that it is hard to find qualified faculty. The militants then pose the questions as to whether the qualifications should not be adjusted to the human candidates, not merely by lowering the standards for acceptance, but by changing the taught subject matter, changing the student body, changing—perhaps entirely—the value system of the university. (1968:120)

Starr's mocking characterization of ARCH and the student protesters did capture precisely what Black students at Columbia and residents of Harlem were both fighting against *and* unified by: racial inequalities masquerading as calls for excellence and racial injustices dressed in the garb of progress. In this sense, Starr's defense of the Jim Crow gym was both a familiar denial of structural racism and a disclosure of its underlying premise—Black and brown people were insufficiently evolved to participate as equals in American society.

On April 22, the SDS called for a demonstration to protest disciplinary actions that had been taken against six students who had participated in a banned indoor protest against the IDA the month before. Since all six were members of the SDS, the action was viewed by many as an attempt to dismember the student organization. By noon the next day, some five hundred protesters had gathered around the sundial on College Walk, where representatives of campus organizations gave speeches; hundreds more milled around Low Plaza. Ted Gold and Nick Freudenberg, representing the SDS, spoke on the IDA and the university's disciplinary policies, and Cicero Wilson, president of the SAS, denounced the gymnasium under construction in Morningside Park (Cox Commission 1968; Bradley 2003).

When protesters attempted to enter Low Library, the central administration building, they were blocked by security guards and by roughly 150 conservative student counter-protesters. With prompting from the SAS's Cicero Wilson, some 300 protesters then marched to Morningside Park, where they uprooted a forty-foot section of the twelve-foot-high chain-metal fence surrounding the gym site. When the police arrived, fistfights broke out with the protesters; one student, Fred Wilson, was arrested on charges of felonious assault, criminal mischief, and resisting arrest. Following speech making and discussion, the demonstrators decided to return to campus, chanting, "The racist gym must go!" They marched into Hamilton Hall and demanded to see Dean Harry Coleman. When Dean Coleman returned to the building from lunch, he withdrew to his office, where he remained until late the next day (Stulberg 1968; Raskin 1985). Accounts of the occupation of Hamilton Hall differ as to whether Dean Coleman was a de facto hostage or, as Mark Rudd put it, an "invited guest" (Cox Commission 1968; Friedman 1969).

Ray Brown, an SAS leader, and Mark Rudd announced to the protesters that requests had been made to groups, both on and off campus, for support in the form of provisions and expertise in direct-action strategies. Later that afternoon, Tom Hayden, an SDS founder, came to Hamilton Hall. Hayden was one of the "Chicago Eight" arrested that summer after the police riot at the 1968 Democratic National Convention. Later in the evening, H. Rap Brown, leader of the Student Nonviolent Coordinating Committee, and representatives of the Harlem branch of CORE and the Mau Mau Society of Harlem, an anti-crime and self-defense group, joined the occupation. Harlem-based organizations, students, and other supporters brought blankets and food to the protesters. Rumors circulated claiming that armed Black militants had joined the occupation, which prompted the university's security office to announce that the "police have been notified and they can be called to campus at a moment's notice" (Raskin 1985; Cox Commission 1968; Barry 1968).

Early the next morning, the Black students occupying Hamilton Hall asked their white counterparts to leave the building. The SAS and SDS had disagreed over the tactics and goals of the occupation. Whereas the SAS and SNCC leader H. Rap Brown wanted to barricade the building and give students the power to control access to it, the SDS wanted to stage a sit-in, allow classes to continue, and use the occupation to convene discussions with administrators and faculty and politicize the student body. Black protesters maintained that the SDS was disorganized and lacked focus. "Discipline and organization," Stefan Bradley observed, "were of utmost importance to the Black protesters. To 'dramatize the situation' effectively, they had to do so in a manner that showed they were serious and focused on their goal" (2003:172). Equally important, the SAS maintained that a Black-led student occupation of Hamilton Hall strengthened the occupation's association with the gym controversy, campus expansionism, and other policies affecting Harlem. William Sales, an SAS leader and a graduate student in public law and government, addressed the SAS's reasoning behind the request that white students vacate the building in a 1968 interview in the *Partisan Review*:

> White students were asked to leave Hamilton Hall because Black students wanted to hold at least one building to focus the protest on community-wide issues: in other words, to forge an identification between what Black students were doing in Hamilton Hall and what the community was doing in Harlem in relation to Columbia University's racism. Many of the white students were not prepared to dramatize the issue through a confrontation with students and faculty. (Donadio 1968:377; Hamilton 1968)

Sales also noted that the white students were told that if they wanted their actions to be relevant to this wider struggle for racial justice, they should "take as many other buildings as they could hold." Led by the SDS, the white protesters did just that. Some 250 students entered Low Memorial Library, crossed the rotunda, and broke into the suite of President Kirk, where they searched the president's files for evidence of the university's collaboration with the military establishment. Although a small detachment of police arrived in response to a call from the Columbia security force, they only temporarily repossessed the executive suite, which allowed campus security guards to remove valuable art works. On Wednesday evening, the day after the occupation of Hamilton Hall, students in the School of Architecture took control of Avery Hall and barricaded its entrances. The next morning, students occupied Fayerweather Hall. Mathematics Hall soon followed.

The Cox Commission report concluded that the SAS's request that white students leave Hamilton Hall was critical to events, since it con-

verted a "somewhat unfocused, noisy, disorderly, and all-night demonstration into an unprecedented uprising involving the occupation of
five campus buildings" (1968:14). Furthermore, the commission's report
maintained that it was the university's reluctance to call on the city's
police to retake Hamilton Hall that spared the occupations of the other
four campus buildings: the administration feared that the removal and
arrest of Black students and their community-based supporters from
the building would trigger more widespread and perhaps militant conflicts with Harlem and organizations such as CORE, SNCC, and the
Mau Mau Society, which, led by Charles 37x Kenyatta, had marched
across the campus in support of the Black protesters and their demands
(Friedman 1969).

Immanuel Wallerstein, the world systems theorist and then associate
professor of sociology at Columbia and serving as the Ad Hoc Faculty
Group's representative to the Black students in Hamilton, reiterated the
commission's assessment and argued that issues of racial justice became
central to the crisis at Columbia:

> I don't believe for a moment that the SDS talking about the IDA could
> have escalated the University into the kind of crisis it found itself in. I
> think the fact is that when the Black students barricaded Hamilton Hall,
> *that* transformed the situation. *That* was the critical issue. That explains
> why the University didn't use force that first morning on the 24th. If it
> had just been Mark Rudd and his friends going into Low Memorial Li-
> brary, we would have had the police on campus in thirty minutes. (Cox
> Commission 1968:356)

The Ad Hoc Faculty Group (AHFG) was established by a group of
faculty that had been meeting informally in Philosophy Hall and was
concerned that the university's positions on the gymnasium and student amnesty were too rigid, and that consequently the police would
be called on to forcibly remove the occupiers. The AHFG drew up resolutions requesting that the trustees act to immediately cease excavation at the gym site; that a tripartite committee of students, faculty,
and administrators be delegated all disciplinary power over the student
protesters; and that students end all occupations pending a settlement.
The AHFG pledged, "Until this crisis is settled, we will stand before the

occupied buildings to prevent forcible entry by police and others" (Cox Commission 1968:117).

This pledge was soon tested. Two days after the occupation of Hamilton Hall, the AHFG learned that David Truman, Columbia's vice president and provost, had announced that the police would be called to end the protests; members of the faculty group left Philosophy Hall and took up positions around the five occupied buildings, intending to block police. At 2:30 in the morning, some twenty to thirty men pushed past the crowd gathered around Low Library and attempted to enter the southeast entrance, which gave access to the temporary offices that were being used by the administration. The men in plainclothes were mid-level police officers, who had been sent by their superiors to confer with Columbia administrators and prepare a plan for retaking the occupied buildings. Members of AHFG asked the officers for identification and blocked their entrance, leading to a skirmish. Richard Greeman, an instructor, received a serious head wound. Blood gushing from his head, Greeman withdrew into Low Library, where AHFG members, supported by George Fraenkel, dean of the Graduate School of Arts and Sciences, urged Truman to reverse his decision to call the police to campus. At 3:15 a.m., Truman left Low Library and addressed the crowd gathered outside, announcing that the AHFG had convinced the administration to postpone police action. Truman also stated, "At the request of the Mayor, and without prejudice to its continuation at a later time, we have suspended construction of the gymnasium pending further discussions" (Cox Commission 1968:123).[3]

The administration's restraint was short-lived. On or about Tuesday, April 29, President Kirk made the decision to bring the police to campus. Beginning at 2:00 a.m. the next morning, some one thousand uniformed and plainclothes police began clearing the five occupied buildings and arresting the protesting students. The first to be retaken was Hamilton Hall, where about thirty members of the city's Tactical Police Force approached the building's barricaded entrance and an underground access tunnel. The Cox Commission reported that the students in Hamilton Hall, advised by civil rights lawyers, had already come to an agreement with the police to nonviolently vacate the building. AHFG members who had locked arms in front of the building stood aside when they were informed that the Black occupants would not resist. However, neither the police nor the administration had been negotiating with the students and AHFG members supporting the occupation of the four other buildings. The police forcibly entered Low Memorial Library, Fayerweather, Avery, and Mathematics Halls. The *Spectator* described the violent melee at Fayerweather:

> The police moved in, some swinging radio aerials from walkie-talkies, whip-sawing faces. Several heads were pushed against the stone steps. . . . The faculty line toppled onto the steps. Plainclothesmen kicked, Black-jacked students trying to jump the hedge. Rabbi A. Bruce Goldman fell to the ground, rolling, as he was black-jacked. Professor James Shenton was bleeding, dazed. Uniformed cops here used no clubs, just fists. Students and faculty were then herded out to the gate onto Amsterdam [Avenue]. (1968d)

The numbers of persons arrested and injured provide evidence of both the scale of the campus uprising and the violence with which it was suppressed. In all, 692 arrests were made in and around the occupied buildings, 75 percent of whom were Columbia students; the remainder were alumni, students from other schools, and community residents. Almost 10 percent of the students enrolled in the School of Architecture were arrested at Avery Hall. Seventy-four students, faculty, and other staff were treated at local hospitals, and an additional thirty-five were treated at a makeshift infirmary in Philosophy Hall (Cox Commission 1968). The events of April 29–30 did not end the campus protests, which continued through the summer and into the next academic year. In August 1968, facing mounting criticism on campus and in the press over his handling of the crisis, President Kirk announced his resignation.

On taking office, acting President Andrew W. Cordier maintained that the gymnasium would not be built in Morningside Park without community support. In February 1969, Columbia's vice president for public affairs announced that it would conduct a mail poll of one hundred community leaders in Harlem and Morningside Heights to decide whether to proceed with the controversial gym. Victor Solomon, chairman of CORE's Harlem branch, described the gym poll as "a new outrage on the part of Columbia" and a crude measure of community sentiment that could be easily manipulated (Kopel 1969). Suspecting that the university was attempting to revive the plan, CORE, ARCH, and the West Harlem Community Organization held a rally and press conference on Morningside Drive, while students held a simultaneous demonstration on campus. The *Columbia Daily Spectator* had earlier criticized the administration for failing to meaningfully engage community organizations in discussions over the future of the gym, despite Cordier's assertion that it was in the university's interest to do so. The *Spectator* editorial pointed to Columbia's failure to participate in a meeting sponsored by the West Harlem Community Organization on the future of Morningside Park in October:

> Ironically, at the moment Dr. Cordier was discussing his lack of action on the gym issue, the West Harlem Community Organization and the Architects Renewal Council of Harlem were holding a press conference to reveal their plans for community recreational facilities to be constructed where Columbia had planned to build its gym; the University had been invited, but failed to attend. . . . Had the administration bothered to send someone to the meeting, it would have had a chance to see what type of buildings many community members would really like to see erected in the park. (1968b)

At the meeting and press conference, held at the West 113th Street offices of the West Harlem Community Organization, architect J. Max Bond Jr., executive director of ARCH, had presented a fifty-one-page report detailing an alternative plan for the gym site. In the ARCH plan, an amphitheater seating 1,200 people would occupy the gym site, along with a skating rink, swimming pool, and community arts center. The amphitheater would serve as a venue for professional and amateur concerts and theatrical performances. Evening performances and better lighting throughout the park, ARCH maintained, would improve public safety. State Senator Basil A. Paterson called on Columbia to categorically abandon all plans for the vertical gymnasium (Bird 1968).

On February 27, 1969, acting President Cordier announced that he was recommending that the university permanently abandon its plans to build the gym in Morningside Park. Less than a week later, the trustees unanimously affirmed Cordier's recommendation, directing the university to terminate its contracts with the city and its construction contractors (*New York Times* 1969).

The Jim Crow gymnasium was not the only casualty of the crisis at Columbia and escalation of community opposition to the university's expansion activities. In October 1968, the university canceled its plans to co-sponsor an urban renewal project in the "piers area," the ten-block section of Manhattanville between 125th and 135th Streets and west of Broadway that had been identified for redevelopment in the Morningside GNRP in 1964. Courtney Brown, dean of the Columbia Business School, explained that the university's co-sponsorship of the $241 million project would be perceived as another land grab in the wake of the gym defeat and continuing protests against its expansion activities. Instead, the university would serve only as a consultant to the Negro Labor Council, which then became the sole sponsor of the proposed housing development and industrial complex (Bird 1968; *Columbia Daily Spectator* 1968a).

In 1964 Percival Goodman, a Columbia professor of architecture, had developed a redevelopment plan for the piers area at his own expense for a community organization. As noted above, Goodman had spoken out against the Morningside GNRP at the Riverside Church earlier in the year and was a critic of Robert Moses. In his plan, Goodman proposed the construction of middle- and low-income housing, parkland, and an elementary and secondary school. The parkland and high school were to be built on a platform that extended out into the Hudson River to the pierhead line. The development also included a complex for science-based industries. Goodman had dubbed the redevelopment plan "Manhattanville-on-the-Hudson." However, Goodman's tenure as architect of the piers project was short-lived.

In May 1968, as Columbia grappled with student protests, the city's Housing and Development Administration announced that it was reviewing a proposal for the redevelopment of the piers area, which had been submitted by the university. In the plan, co-sponsored by Columbia and the Negro Labor Committee (a coalition of labor unions formed to advance the cause of Black workers), Columbia would build a commercial complex to house science-based industries and offices in the piers area at grade with the Hudson and Twelfth Avenue. The industrial complex would be topped by a platform at the level of the plateau and viaduct on which the Negro Labor Committee (NLC) would build three thousand units of middle-income housing, a third of which would be set aside for Columbia employees. In addition, the NLC-sponsored contribution would include a marina, a Black history museum, and other recreational and cultural facilities. The negotiations between the two sponsors had been led by Dean Courtney Brown of the Columbia School of Business and the executive director of the NLC, L. Joseph Overton. Although the NLC had previously presented the proposal to sixty groups represented by the United Council of Harlem Organizations, the Reverend Dwight Wood, chairman of the Morningside Renewal Council (the organization charged with representing community interests in urban renewal planning), stated that his directors had been presented with the Columbia proposal only fifteen days before it was prematurely announced by the city, and consequently played no role in its development (Bird 1968).

The public announcement of the Columbia proposal had been prompted by the publication of an exposé in the *New Republic* on Columbia's expansion activities and real estate holdings by James Ridgeway, an investigative reporter. In his article, Ridgeway recounted Columbia's history of expansion and tenant evictions, and the aborted gym project. He then addressed the relationship between the university's trustees and administrators and the real estate industry. Ridgeway's reporting disclosed that Dean Brown, who had negotiated the piers area project with the NLC, was a shareholder in the Uris Buildings Corporation, a major commercial real estate developer, and a member of its board. Percy Uris, chairman of Uris Buildings' board of directors, was a Columbia trustee (chairman of its powerful finance committee) and a special advisor to President Grayson Kirk for new construction (Ridgeway 1968; Price 1973). Uris Buildings had been slated to construct the piers project's industrial complex. For the striking students of the School of Architecture who had occupied Avery Hall in April, the university's failure to consult Columbia architects in the planning of new buildings had been an ongoing bone of contention. Faculty and students at the architectural school had criticized the designs of new buildings, such as Jerome L. Greene Hall and the International Affair Building, on aesthetic grounds and for not better integrating with the surrounding community. Professor Goodman had been replaced on the piers redevelopment by Percy Uris with a new set of architects and a novel plan. Asked about his replacement, Goodman pithily told the *New York Times*, "It's the usual procedure. They swipe your stuff and then tell you to turn up your bottom so they can kick it" (Huxtable 1968b).

Ridgeway concluded by arguing that although Columbia was a private university, its decisions—and those of its ancillaries, MHI and Remedco—had profound consequences for the general public; therefore, its trustees meetings should be public and, in order to receive public funds, required to publish detailed financial reports. Although Dean Brown denied that Uris Buildings would play a role in the piers project, Ridgeway's article intensified public scrutiny of Columbia's role and interests in the $241 million redevelopment project (Kihss 1968b).

Once Columbia had withdrawn, progress on the piers project stalled. In 1972 Walter Dukes, chairman of the King-Kennedy Foundation, an urban planning group, charged the city's housing and development administrator and City Planning Commission with delaying, if not obstructing, further review of the piers area project, since renamed the Academy Plan. "They have always been able to kill anything," Dukes maintained, "that started in Harlem with any Black in-put" (Simon 1972; *Amsterdam News* 1971). The King-Kennedy Foundation had worked with a consortium of Harlem organizations and planners to revise and revive the Negro Labor Committee's proposal. Thomas Sinclair, who had been counsel to the NLC in the 1960s, reiterated Dukes's accusation, stating that the Housing and Development Administration had "made our Committee get shot-gun-married to Columbia University. But even that forced wedding did not produce any results." The Academy Plan was never realized, but in 1976 a smaller development, consisting of a 1,250-unit moderate-income housing complex, sponsored by the Brotherhood of Sleeping Car Porters pension fund (a member of the since disbanded NLC), and a public school, was completed (L. Williams 1976).

The 1968 rebellion, by linking student and community opposition to the policies of racial dispossession pursued by Columbia University and its allied institutions, shattered the illusion of the American Acropolis as a unifying and universal singularity. Race erupted as *the* issue that cut across the imagined spatiotemporal frontier, dividing elite institutions on the Morningside plateau from their constitutive outside, and exposed the hypocrisy of their gestures to the principles of democracy, liberalism, and racial equality. The separate and unequal vertical gymnasium, spanning the hundred-foot drop in elevation between the plateau and Harlem flats, did not bridge the socioeconomic divide between the valley and the Acropolis, but instead materialized in space its foundational and racially exclusionary premise: that non-white populations—whether the immigrants debased by the social evolutionists in the nineteenth century or African American and Latinx populations in the next—were ill-equipped, by nature or by nurture, to fully participate in the crafting of civilization or inhabit the temporal landscape of urban modernity. Giving physical form to that exclusionary premise, the Jim Crow gymnasium also condensed, made explicit, and rendered subject to dispute a sedimented order of meaning, contrasting the elevated and lowly, universal and particular, enduring and obsolete, enlightened and benighted, and white over Black. In 1968 Columbia's expansion and practices of racial dispossession were brought to a halt at 125th Street. But it did not end there. In the twenty-first century, nearly forty years later, Columbia returned to the piers area with a new plan for campus expansion. Deploying the same racialized discourses of urban obsolescence and blight, and making the well-worn appeal to the need for civilizational progress, the university harnessed the state's powers of eminent domain to reorder the landscape of northern Manhattan, projecting the spatiosymbolic order and boundaries of the American Acropolis deep into West Harlem and the longue durée.

Epilogue

Plus Ça Change, Plus C'est la Même Chose

There is a quality even meaner than outright ugliness or disorder, and this meaner quality is the dishonest mask of pretended order, achieved by ignoring or suppressing the real order that is struggling to exist and to be served.
—Jane Jacobs

I've done everything I can to put the ghost of the gym behind us. Columbia is a different neighbor now.
—President Lee Bollinger

On June 10, 2006, opponents of Columbia University's Manhattanville campus expansion project joined with other anti-gentrification protesters to hold a rally at Marcus Garvey Park in Central Harlem. The 9:00 a.m. event had been organized by the Harlem Tenants Council (HTC), the Coalition to Preserve Community, and the Columbia Student Coalition on Expansion and Gentrification—the same groups that had rallied against the closing of Floridita restaurant and use of eminent domain in February.

An audience of about two hundred Harlem residents and students were seated in the park's amphitheater. "Why are we here?" Nellie Hester Bailey, the HTC's president, asked the assembly. "We are here today because, if we don't do something, if we don't organize, Harlem will cease to exist. It will become just a bus stop on tour buses from downtown. Columbia now wants to expand its campus into Manhattanville. And they don't want to work with the community. They have ignored all the proposals that were made by the Community Board and others. What they can't buy they are going to take using eminent domain. And we have to stop them!"

The demonstrators marched up Lenox Avenue to West 135th Street, along the route of Marcus Garvey's 1924 UNIA parade, and then west to Broadway. As we marched past the new, glass-encased condominium developments and chic sidewalk cafés on Lenox Avenue, I struck up a conversation with Rosalind, a middle-aged African American woman who, as a longtime resident of the Delano Village Apartments, was facing eviction. As the marchers chanted, "Hell no, we won't go!," Rosalind expressed her thoughts. "This is nothing new," she said. "Columbia has been running roughshod over Harlem for years. In 1968 they tried to build a gym in Morningside Park on public land! And the community stopped them. Now they want to take all this," she said, waving her arm in a wide arc. "And they don't want to give the community any say at all."

At Broadway and 135th Street, we joined another group that had been organized by Nos Quedamos (We Stay), an umbrella organization representing tenants' rights and anti-gentrification activists in the predominantly Dominican neighborhood of Washington Heights. Nos Quedamos had been founded earlier in the year by State Assemblyman Adriano Espaillat—the first Dominican American to be elected to the state legislature and, in 2016, to Congress—and the City University of New York Law School to assist tenants in northern Manhattan fight illegal rent increases, evictions, and landlord harassment. Shortly thereafter, other feeder marches arrived, representing Local 1199 of the Service Employees International Union, the Mirabal Sisters (a cultural and community service center), and youth groups from Washington Heights.

The combined rally on Broadway took place in front of the Riverside Park Community Houses, the 1,190-unit low- and middle-income housing development that had been sponsored by the Brotherhood of Sleeping Car Porters in the footprint of Columbia's piers area project, abandoned in 1968. The five-building complex was completed in 1976, using subsidies made available by the Mitchell-Lama program, a New York state affordable housing program created in 1955, which provided low-interest mortgages and property tax abatements to developers in return for their commitment to provide apartments at below-market rents. In 2005 the housing development's owner, Jerome Belson, prepaid the subsidized mortgages, enabling him to increase rents. As a result, the *New York Times* reported, "rents more than doubled to $1,800 a month from $755 for a one-bedroom apartment, and to $2,300 from $897 for a

Rally in front of an apartment building with Nellie Hester Bailey of the Harlem
Tenants Council, 2006. Photo by author.

two-bedroom" (T. Williams 2008a). Tenants who were unable to pay the
rent increases faced eviction. Housing activists and tenants agreed that
it was Columbia's expected campus expansion and the promise of rising
property values that triggered the landlord's decision (Hughes 2011).

By noon, when we were scheduled to begin our four-mile trek north
to Dyckman Street at the tip of northern Manhattan, the assembly had
grown to some six hundred persons. Along the Broadway route, by-
standers shouted their support, taking up the chant, "Aquí estamos, y
no nos vamos" (Here we are, and we're not leaving!). The march ended
at Post Avenue, where Latinx, African American, and other activists
made speeches addressing the range of housing and community development issues facing the residents of northern Manhattan, including Columbia's expansion plan. The rallies and march were reported in
the Spanish-language media, both broadcast and print; none of their
English-language counterparts took note.

The comments of Nellie Bailey and other protesters that day demonstrated how present the history of institutional expansion and racial

State Assemblyman Adriano Espaillat at Dyckman Street rally, 2006. Photo by author.

dispossession was in the memories of activists and vernacular culture of Harlem residents—an area that was undergoing rapid neoliberal redevelopment in the opening decades of the twenty-first century. In this epilogue, I demonstrate how Columbia University adopted discourses and strategies of racial dispossession and political disempowerment to secure its campus expansion that had been rehearsed for nearly a century.

Once again, the university asserted an imagined spatiotemporal contrast between the putative modernist universalism of the American Acropolis and a moribund temporality of racial difference of the people living and working in Manhattanville. As in the urban renewal projects prosecuted by Morningside Heights, Inc. during the 1950s and 1960s, Columbia assembled a growth coalition of public agencies and elected officials that collaborated in framing the university's private interests as those of the people of Harlem and city as a whole. The complicity and support of this growth coalition also enabled Columbia to harness the powers of the state—most notably, that of eminent domain—to achieve its objectives. Once again, when faced with widespread and well-organized community resistance to the expansion, the university and its allies attempted to manufacture their own community support to lend legitimacy to and advance their private interests while making few significant concessions to the needs, interests, and alternative land-use proposals of the people of Greater Harlem.

"The Same Old Song and Dance"

Columbia University announced its Manhattanville campus expansion plan in the fall of 2003. The seventeen-acre project footprint corresponded roughly to the boundaries of the piers area project, abandoned by the university in 1968. Manhattanville's potential for redevelopment had long been recognized due to its unique access to rail, road, and water transportation—the same locational advantages that had made Manhattanville attractive to its founders two centuries before.

As early as 1991, Community Board 9 (CB 9), a community-based advisory council representing West Harlem, Hamilton Heights, and Morningside Heights, had begun to prepare a comprehensive redevelopment plan for the area, pursuant to Section 197-a of the New York City Charter (Department of City Planning 2008).

Community boards develop 197-a plans in consultation with the Department of City Planning, the City Planning Commission, and the borough president. Once approved by the City Planning Commission and City Council, 197-a plans serve as guides for the future actions of city agencies in the city's fifty-nine community districts.

Community Board 9's 197-a plan called for the creation of a Manhattanville Special Purpose District and stressed the area's potential for creating jobs, businesses, recreational facilities, and affordable housing to benefit the residents of Greater Harlem.[1] The 197-a plan emphasized mixed-use development and contextual zoning that would "build on the strong social, economic, and cultural base of the district through a sustainable agenda that would recognize, reinforce and reinvigorate this ethnically and culturally diverse community" (Community Board 9, Borough of Manhattan 2008:3). CB 9's plan was modified on several occasions and approved by the City Planning Commission in the spring of 2008. Under the advice, if not pressure, of the City Planning Commission, CB 9's 197-a plan was substantially revised to accommodate

Columbia's campus expansion plan, which was independently being developed for an area roughly congruent with the board's proposed Special Purpose District. However, despite the revisions to the plan—for example, increasing the allowable floor-to-area ratio and maximum building heights—CB 9 adamantly opposed eminent domain, which the university maintained was necessary to achieve its purpose. As Jordi Reyes-Montblanc, chairman of CB 9, stated at a public hearing on the Columbia plan in 2007,

> The use of eminent domain or even the threat of eminent domain MUST be removed. Community Board 9 Manhattan stands firmly and unequivocally on that principle. We will support any owner of properties that refuses to sell and stand with them against eminent domain use for the private benefit of another private entity. Columbia's failure to meaningfully discuss and negotiate with CB9M regarding the land use issues that do not meet CB9M's 197-a Plan standards has been a lost opportunity to help develop the trust and partnership that Columbia indicated was their objective. (CB9M Blog archives 2007)

As Community Board 9 was developing its 197-a plan, the New York City Economic Development Corporation (EDC) was preparing its own proposal for the redevelopment of West Harlem. In August 2002, the EDC released the West Harlem Master Plan for Manhattanville. The EDC's master plan was developed in consultation with community organizations (including CB 9), public officials, and local businesses. An important, long-term objective of the plan was the creation of an intermodal transportation hub. The EDC's plan included extending bus service to Twelfth Avenue, reestablishing ferry service to the piers, and siting a Metro-North train station at 125th Street in Manhattanville, restoring the area's historic link to rail service along the Hudson River.

Although the master plan envisioned the growth of "multiple uses and a mixture of new and existing jobs"—a goal that suggested community participation during the course of the plan's implementation—soon after the release of the master plan, the EDC granted lead responsibility to Columbia for the institutional and economic redevelopment of the area, and joint lead responsibility with the EDC for rezoning required for campus expansion. In fact, the EDC had been meeting with Columbia staff as early as 2001 and, after the release of its master plan, stopped meeting with community groups and local business owners (Kaur v. Empire State Development Corporation 2009). Once again, the university harnessed the power of city and state agencies to advance its private interests.

In the Columbia expansion plan, the project required exclusive control of the seventeen-acre site in order to locate some campus facilities—parking, storage, energy plants, and mechanical facilities—below grade at depths of up to eighty feet in what came to be known as the "bathtub." This, in turn, required the use of eminent domain to secure properties that the university could not acquire through purchase.

Some argued that the project's location in a flood zone and along a geographic fault line rendered the bathtub and its facilities vulnerable to flooding. The Harlem-based group WE ACT for Environmental Justice warned that hazardous waste from the university's planned biological research laboratories posed a risk to the area and river in the event of flooding and/or seismic activity (West Harlem Environmental Action 2006). Columbia geophysicist Klaus Jacob, a renowned authority on urban environmental issues, warned Columbia officials that a storm surge, worsened by rising sea levels associated with climate change, could lead to a wide-scale disaster affecting the seven-story underground facility. According to Jacob, his misgivings went unheeded. "My original concern was to help Columbia solve its own problem," he told the *Village Voice*. "But for some reason, they weren't interested. I was naïve enough to think that by mentioning something, I could make something happen" (*Village Voice* 2008; Amzallag 2008). Only a few years later, Hurricane Sandy produced a storm surge with catastrophic results in the city's low-lying areas. Other critics argued that a contiguous, seventeen-acre self-enclosed bathtub was little more than an engineering pretext for justifying the use of eminent domain to gain control of the expansion site.

In 2004 the Empire State Development Corporation (ESDC), the state agency tasked with approving the taking of private and public property through eminent domain, began meeting with Columbia officials, lawyers, and consultants. Columbia also needed ESDC approval to override local law in order to amend the New York City map to build the bathtub and relocate a Metropolitan Transit Authority (MTA) bus depot, among other things. In June, Columbia hired the planning and engineering firm Allee King Rosen & Fleming (AKRF) to assist in the design of the below-grade bathtub and the preparation of an environmental impact study, and to act as its agent in securing agency approvals. In the following month, Columbia entered into an agreement with the ESDC to cover the latter's costs of preparatory work in connection with the expansion plan. Columbia agreed to fund a neighborhood blight study, required to provide the ESDC with grounds to determine that the project area was "substandard or insanitary"—a finding needed to approve eminent domain. The ESDC hired Columbia's consultant, AKRF, to conduct the study. Despite the apparent conflict of interest, the ESDC later contended that a "Chinese wall" had been erected between the AKRF team working on the blight study and the team working on behalf of the university (Tuck-It-Away v. ESDC 2009).

As Columbia was pursuing the use of eminent domain with the ESDC, it formed a Community Advisory Committee (CAC) to provide "feedback and guidance from a spectrum of community leaders concerning the Manhattanville in West Harlem Campus Project" (Community Advisory Committee 2004:2). Members of the CAC included representatives of not-for-profit organizations, community boards, churches, and other concerned parties in northern Manhattan. Peggy Shepard, director of Harlem-based WE ACT for Environmental Justice, chaired the committee on environment, and the Reverend Earl Kooperkamp, rector of St. Mary's Episcopal Church in Manhattanville, chaired the committee on economic development.

The committee's draft final report, issued on September 10, 2004, addressed a broad range of economic, sociocultural, and environmental issues and maintained that "community engagement must continue to be embedded in University development plans, recognizing that the University cannot be an island unto itself" (Community Advisory Committee 2004:3). The CAC report voiced community concerns about the exercise of eminent domain, as well as the project's potential negative impact on affordable housing, cultural diversity, and economic equity. In addition, the report underscored the impact that the Columbia expansion would have on surrounding areas already experiencing gentrification and cited the case of the Riverside Community Houses (3333 Broadway) (Gregory 2013). As the Reverend Earl Kooperkamp put it to me, "We tried to get Columbia to see the bigger picture. That Harlem is going through gentrification that is increasing rents and displacing people. And that what they build will affect people—poor people, people of color. And not just in the project area but for miles around."[2]

Columbia sought to decouple the campus expansion from a long history of socioeconomic exclusion and racial dispossession, eliding the pressing consequences that the campus expansion would have on Greater Harlem. In short, the needs of the university trumped those of the Black and brown residents of Harlem for affordable housing, small business opportunities, and sociocultural diversity. Once again, Columbia engaged in temporal and spatial decontextualization, this time presenting the public benefits, or "public purpose," of the project in abstract and future-leaning terms, where Columbia's researchers might find a cure for Alzheimer's and, more generally, as a signal contribution to the city's knowledge economy, unlike the moribund communities nearby. Needless to say, the CAC's role, like that of its 1950s namesake, fulfilled no more than the illusion of community participation. The CAC was dissolved after the completion of its final report.

Eminent domain remained a lightning rod for community opposition. Although Community Board 9 and the Community Advisory Committee recognized the university's right to purchase property to enlarge its campus, they opposed the latter's demand for exclusive control of the expansion site, which would lead to the loss of all existing jobs, businesses, and housing there. Both groups advocated mixed-use redevelopment and contextual zoning, preserving existing buildings and jobs, some through adaptive reuse, and allowing for new construction by Columbia.

Critics of the expansion plan also argued that Columbia's initiative served a private and not a public purpose, as required by the New York State Constitution for the use of eminent domain. For its part, the university argued that the scientific research and other activities planned for the new campus served a public purpose. For example, on the university's website Manhattanville in West Harlem, it was asserted, "This kind of smart growth will not only generate thousands of new local jobs for a diversity of people, but also result in maintaining Upper Manhattan as a world center for knowledge, creativity, and solutions for society's challenges" (Columbia Neighbors, n.d.). This notion of "smart growth" once again reiterated the perduring, racialized class boundary between the university and its constitutive outside. Harlem residents—their needs, livelihoods, and aspirations—were to be recognized and valued only to the degree to which they contributed to the Malthusian economics of "smart growth."

On March 8, 2006, just weeks before the ESDC-sponsored blight study was to begin, Lee Bollinger, president of Columbia University, appeared on the *Brian Lehrer Show*, a radio talk show broadcast on public radio station WNYC. The subject was the university's expansion plan. Midway through the interview, Bollinger was asked by Lehrer about the expected use of eminent domain.

> LEE BOLLINGER: First of all, eminent domain is itself a part of our constitutional system to help achieve public purposes and, if we want to build a national park and private property stands in the way, it's very important for the collective good that we be able to have eminent domain. Columbia is a nonprofit, public institution. It's not a private developer. We're not trying to make money, and if a party stands in the way of developing neuroscience work which may actually find a cure to Alzheimer's—the second gene to Alzheimer's was just discovered by a Columbia scientist—that is a proper use of eminent domain.
>
> BRIAN LEHRER: But let me just challenge you on that for a second, because you just called Columbia a *public* institution. [The State University of New York] is a public institution, the railroad is a public institution. Columbia is a *private* institution, isn't it, . . . a not-for-profit, private institution?
>
> BOLLINGER: It's a not-for-profit but it's a public institution in the sense that it—not in what we do for profit. We are funded by the federal government to do research on issues like . . . matters like Alzheimer's.

Bollinger's claim that the university was not a private developer was belied by the long history of Columbia and other institutions of the American Acropolis. It requires a stretch of the imagination to construe the university's decades-long campaign of property acquisition, expansion, and tenant evictions both in Manhattanville and Morningside Heights as serving a public purpose, let alone the public good. As investigative reporter James Ridgeway had put it in his 1968 exposé of the university's ties to the real estate industry, "Columbia ought to be recognized for what it is, a development corporation which exercises the prerogatives of a government in Morningside Heights." More to the point, discovering a cure for Alzheimer's disease and other research-related activities did not require a contiguous, self-enclosed campus. Rather, it was a "campus atmosphere" that this insularity was intended to achieve, as it had been for almost a hundred years. In an interview on the campus plan, Mark Wigley, dean of the Graduate School of Architecture, waxed philosophical on the need to create a self-enclosed campus:

> A University is a place where young people take a step back from the world so that when they re-enter, they do so with great intensity, care and responsibility. So the University must be a defined space. The fascinating challenge is how to make that as a space of withdrawal and reflection and at the same time integrate that space in the richest way possible in the vibrant New York City. (Eviatar 2006)

This pedagogic appeal to the need for monastic-like retreats—what Robert Friedman described as "medieval attempts to keep reflective thought separated from reality" (1969:4)—was belied by another narrative: a history of institutional expansion and dispossession that both buttressed and extended a racialized class boundary between the Hill and surrounding low-income communities of color. The outdated nature of Columbia's insistence on an insular campus in order to create a collegiate ambiance was not lost on its opponents. In a discussion with Renzo Piano, the new campus's architect, Earl Kooperkamp challenged Piano's claim that a public "piazza" at the center of the campus would attract Harlem residents and promote discourse: "You're talking about being a 21st century university," Kooperkamp said. "And this looks like 12th-century Christ Church in Oxford. It's a quad. That's not a piazza. That's not open space for a community. If it were, it would be a big lawn on 125th Street or Broadway" (Eviatar 2006).

As a member of the Harlem Tenants Council put it to me, "You know, this is just that same old song and dance. Jim Crow. That's all it is. They're just dressing it up in fine clothes and calling it progress." Another activist with the HTC, whose father had been the president of a Harlem block association that had fought against the Jim Crow gymnasium, told me, "They think that people in Harlem are stupid. That they can't figure out that none of this is for us. They talk about all these jobs they're going to create. They never gave us nothin'." History over the longue durée mattered.

The university's claim that the campus expansion served a public purpose was rooted in wider discussions in the academic literature and among public officials about the increasing importance of the "knowledge economy" in generating economic growth in postindustrial cities. Popularized by Peter Drucker in *The Age of Discontinuity* (1969), the knowledge economy generally refers to the use of knowledge-based technologies (i.e., information and communication technologies) and knowledge-intensive activities to spur job creation and economic development. Key to the concept is the assertion that, under postindustrial conditions, intellectual capabilities have become more important to producing economic growth than physical inputs and natural resources associated with the manufacturing sector (Powell and Snellman 2004). Critics have argued that the rise of the knowledge industry is a presumption rather than empirically established fact, since "the stock of knowledge embodied in production is difficult to measure and compare across time" (Chandrasekhar 2006). The appeal to the knowledge economy made it possible for the university and its supporters to construct the public good in abstract and future-oriented terms while discounting, if not ignoring, the challenges, needs, and aspirations of surrounding communities of color that were experiencing the marginalization, displacement, and symbolic violence associated with gentrification and neoliberal strategies of urban redevelopment.

In 2006, Community Board 9 and the city's Economic Development Corporation announced the formation of a local development corporation to negotiate a community benefits agreement (CBA) with Columbia. A CBA is a contract signed between a community and a real estate developer that requires that the latter provide amenities and/or mitigations to the areas affected by a development project. CBA agreements are legally binding but are often difficult to monitor and enforce. The West Harlem Local Development Corporation (LDC) included representatives of CB 9, local businesses, tenant groups (e.g., the tenant council of the Ulysses S. Grant Houses), and elected officials. Tom DeMott, head of the Coalition to Preserve Community and a staunch critic of

the expansion plan, sat on the LDC representing community associations. Nick Sprayregen, owner of the Tuck-It-Away Storage Company,
was seated as a spokesman for businesses within the project area. A rift
developed among the members of the LDC when it voted against making Columbia's rejection of the use of eminent domain a precondition
for negotiations. Opponents of the prerequisite argued that the university would use eminent domain with or without a benefits agreement
and so it would be better to have an agreement than not (Durkin 2006).

The following year, protesters demonstrated at an LDC public forum.
They wanted the LDC to require Columbia to reject eminent domain and
maintained that the LDC's deliberations lacked transparency. Speakers,
including some LDC members, argued that politicians had, as one put
it, "engineered what amounted to a coup by forcing their way onto the
board" (Durkin 2007). This rift within the LDC, and between the LDC
and the Community Board, escalated in September 2007, when a representative of City Councilman Robert Jackson unsuccessfully attempted
to remove Nicholas Sprayregen from the body. Although the motion
failed, all but one politician among the seven on the board voted in favor
of Sprayregen's removal, leading critics of the LDC to charge that the
politicians were working in cahoots with the university (Durkin 2007).
One month later, three members of the LDC—Tom DeMott, Sprayregen,
and Luisa Henriquez, a resident of the project area—resigned in protest.
"They were more interested in being friends of Columbia and big developers," Sprayregen scoffed, "than they were in truly representing the
community" (Durkin 2007). Three other resignations soon followed.

Looking for Urban Blight . . . Again

Space and light and order. Those are the things that men
need just as much as they need bread or a place to sleep.
—Le Corbusier

In September 2006, AKRF, the consulting firm hired by the Empire State
Development Corporation, began its neighborhood conditions study of
Manhattanville. The study involved a survey and analysis of the project
site, and included an evaluation of building conditions, land use, community infrastructure, and environmental conditions. Like the blight

studies conducted through the urban renewal program, the AKRF study focused on the physical conditions and mobilized a discourse of urban obsolescence. In the opening paragraphs of the executive summary, released in 2007, AKRF summarized its verdict on Manhattanville: "Physical conditions in the study area are mainly characterized by aging, poorly maintained, and functionally obsolete industrial buildings, with little indication of recent reinvestment to reverse their generally deteriorated conditions, particularly in industrial properties" (AKRF 2007:i).

The notion that Manhattanville's buildings and, more generally, the area as a whole were functionally obsolete was a leitmotif that played throughout narratives supporting the university's expansion. For example, in his interview with Brian Lehrer, President Bollinger had opined, "It's not realistic and it won't help the people who live there to think that, or to act on a policy that manufacturing will return. It's just not going to happen." Columbia officials typically referred to the area as "the old Manhattanville manufacturing area," as though it were stuck in the past, reasserting a spatiotemporal boundary that separated the people and institutions of Harlem from the future-leaning mission of the American Acropolis—an exercise of what Johannes Fabian has termed "chronopolitics" (1983). In fact, as noted above, Community Board 9 had produced a detailed and comprehensive 197-a plan for the redevelopment of the area, which proposed among other things the construction of affordable housing, the retention of existing jobs, and the "creation and development of job-intensive businesses to benefit local residents," none of which implied a return of manufacturing (CB9M 2008:44). For Bollinger to refer generically to "people in the Harlem area," rather than to Community Board 9, the defunct Community Advisory Committee, or other Harlem-based institutions, was indicative of the university's long-standing disregard of the needs, aspirations, and expertise of Harlem residents and their institutions—a disregard grounded not only in the Realpolitik of elite institutions, but also in the perduring metaphysics of anti-Blackness. For although the discourse of decay and obsolescence marshaled by Columbia and the AKRF study targeted the physical conditions of the area, it also suggested that the residents and workers of the area were stuck in a static past—an assertion typical of constructions of racial difference. To put it bluntly and to paraphrase Frantz Fanon, Black and brown communities had no ontological resistance in the eyes of the university and its allies.

This narrative of functional obsolescence was supported by the study's contention that the area was physically and visually isolated from surrounding neighborhoods. AKRF asserted that to the east, the elevated IRT subway viaduct and to the north, the MTA's bus depot impeded the flow of pedestrian and vehicular traffic into the project area. The claim was blatantly false. Manhattanville was not only the western terminus of West 125th Street, a major east-west artery, but also the site of entry and exit ramps of the Henry Hudson Parkway, a north-south highway with connections to the George Washington Bridge and Lincoln Tunnel.

This discourse of spatial isolation resonated with and found support in academic and mass-mediated constructions of the "ghetto underclass" during the 1980s and 1990s. Sociologist William Julius Wilson, arguing against both conservative and liberal views of concentrated urban poverty, held that inner-city communities had become increasingly socially isolated from mainstream society as a result of the economic recession of the 1970s and the spatial mobility of the Black working and middle classes in the aftermath of civil rights–era reforms. As a result, Black inner-city areas suffered a loss of institutions, opportunity-creating social networks, and exposure to normalizing role models. "Social isolation," Wilson wrote, "not only implies that contact between groups of different class and/or racial backgrounds is either lacking or has become increasingly intermittent but that the nature of this contact enhances the effects of living in a highly concentrated poverty area" ([1987] 2012:61; cf. Gregory 1998). Therefore, AKRF's characterization of Manhattanville as visually and physically isolated suggested that there were sociological effects of this isolation beyond the study's narrow focus on the physical deterioration and obsolescence of the area, not unlike the behavioral problems that Wilson attributed to the "ghetto underclass" (Wilson 1993).

Ironically, although neither topography nor the elevated subway viaduct created "dead end" border vacuums as described by Jane Jacobs, the contiguous and single-use seventeen-acre campus proposed by Columbia certainly would. In her book *The Death and Life of Great American Cities*, Jacobs used the alignment of single-use institutions in Morningside Heights to exemplify the concept of the border vacuum: "Morningside Heights in New York contains a long strip of neighborhood edged on one side by a campus and on the other side by a long waterfront park. This strip is further interrupted by the barriers of intervening institutions. Every place you go to in this strip brings you quickly to a border" (1961:260–61). The campus extension would simply extend that strip north to West 133rd Street in West Harlem. Community organizations understood that the border vacuum created by the campus expansion would obstruct access from Harlem to the piers area. The Harlem-based group WE ACT for Environmental Justice noted in its comments to the City Planning Commission that "with the University's notoriously heavy-handed security measures (including the heavy gates and guarded doors used at all its campus sites), [the campus plan] will likely deprive West Harlem residents of the use of the waterfront park" (West Harlem Environmental Action 2006:2).

This rhetoric of blockage and isolation was echoed in other planning and publicity documents associated with the campus expansion plan and gestured in part to an anxiety in modernist architecture and urban planning associated with obscure, illegible, and blocked urban spatial forms and relations—qualities of the built environment that formed the rhetorical foundation of AKRF's Manhattanville analysis.

By contrast, "transparency," achieved in modernist architecture through glass construction, was associated with a greater openness in society, the transcendence of archaic ways of thinking and, for the Swiss-born architect Le Corbusier, "the end of superstition and irrationality" (McQuire 2003:109). This preoccupation with glass had its roots in the Neues Bauen (New Building) movement in Weimar-era Germany and was closely associated with the designers Paul Scheerbart and Bruno Taut. Scheerbart envisioned a revolutionary glass culture that would yield a new transparent landscape and an enlightened civilization—one that would progress through modern technology and the transformation of the built environment. Taut, an architect and urban planner, was influenced by Scheerbart's glass vision and declared in 1930, "The old times can never be resuscitated, and it must be their atmosphere of mold and decay that exercises that strange power of suggestion which fogs the brains of the otherwise clear thinkers of the present. The resort to graveyards and the love of ghosts seems in truth to express a passion for the past" (in Jarosinki 2002:68–69).

This discourse of urban obsolescence and decay, reminiscent of the visual rhetoric of the slum clearance program, would serve as the foil for the university's marketing of the new campus through a discourse stress-

The bunker-like and far from "transparent" Forum at the northwest corner of West 125th Street and Broadway, April 2021. Photo by author.

ing transparency via glass architecture. In contrast to Manhattanville's obsolete, neglected, and obscure past-present, Columbia proposed the converse: a glass campus that would shepherd the university and city into a luminous future of scientific innovation and smart growth.

In contrast to Manhattanville's opaque past-present, the project's boosters held, the glass structures of the new campus would be more accessible and inviting to residents of Harlem and elsewhere. If the rhetoric of transparency promised deliverance from the area's murky industrial past toward a radiant economic future, then it also proposed a utopian and power-evasive ideal of community, "an urge to unity," as Iris Young put it, "in which the self is transparent to the self and to others" (1990:229). The widely held concern voiced by Harlem residents that the self-enclosed campus would constitute a white elite exclusionary zone—fears grounded in a history of racial dispossession—could be resolved through glass architecture in a metaphysical-like manner, not unlike the medieval belief in "visual communion." In that view, the visual perception and contemplation of the Eucharist could stand in for bodily participation in the rite (Sand 2020).

Moreover, as Michel Foucault noted, this mystical ideal of transparency, far from facilitating forthrightness, openness, and democratic communality, secured a "tyranny of transparency," rendering those seen subject to a disciplinary gaze. Like Bentham's quest for transparency through the carceral panopticon, the glass campus would render the campus walks and public spaces more vulnerable to surveillance than the research laboratories housed inside and on high. Far from welcoming, recognizing, and engaging sociocultural differences, this will to transparency "represses the ontological difference of subjects," as Young put it, eliding asymmetries in the vulnerability and effects of visibility between those who exercise power and those who are subject to its gaze (1990:230). For African Americans in particular, the stakes were especially high. As Simone Browne has demonstrated, "racialized surveillance" and the logic of the panopticon have been perduring technologies of social control and subordination for African Americans, rendering the Black body hypervisible and "reifying boundaries along racial lines" (2015:16–17). This lopsided transparency secured an ontological negation—a visual "spite fence" subjecting Black and brown bodies to an objectifying gaze.

Although the campus expansion plan promised openness and transparency, its progress through the complex process of public approval had been far from transparent. For example, the AKRF Neighborhood Conditions Study failed to report that the west side of Twelfth Avenue—the study excluded the west side of the avenue—had been undergoing an urban renaissance that demonstrated the economic potential of adaptive reuse. The AKRF claim that there was "little indication of recent reinvestment" was disingenuous at best, and deceitful at worst. Fairway, a 35,000-square-foot supermarket, opened in 1995 on the west side of Twelfth Avenue in a former meatpacking plant. A combination gourmet and wholesale food store, Fairway boasted a 250-car parking lot and drew customers from as far away as New Jersey and Westchester County. In fact, the *Columbia University Record* had celebrated Fairway's opening. In an article entitled "Fairway Brings Crowds to Harlem," the *Record* proclaimed, "On the sidewalks of Broadway and 125th Street, from the clogged West Side Highway off-ramp, in taxis and shuttle buses, people are heading toward Harlem's new sprawling discount supermarket on the Hudson River waterfront at 133rd Street" (*Columbia University Record* 1996).[3]

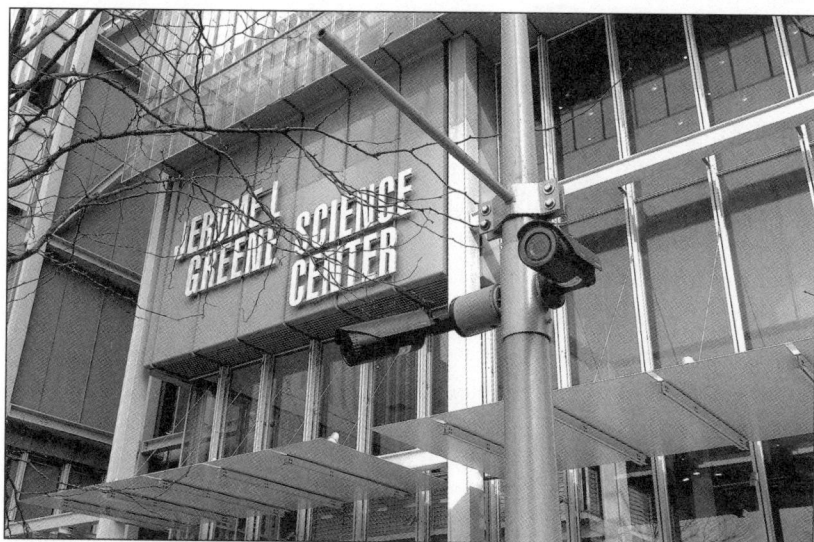

Surveillance cameras surrounding the Jerome L. Greene Science Center, April 2021. Photo by author.

Fairway's success attracted visitors, as well as other businesses to the area. In 2004 Dinosaur Bar-B-Que opened on the east side of Twelfth Avenue at 131st Street. The popular barbeque restaurant featured live music and attracted throngs of customers from Harlem, Washington Heights, and beyond. Soon after, a plumbing contractor bought an abandoned railroad freight warehouse on the west side of Twelfth Avenue, just north of the Columbia expansion area. Encouraged, in part, by the soon-to-be $18.7 million renovation of the Hudson River piers by the city, the new owner leased the 20,900-square-foot building to restaurateurs, prompting the *New York Times* to refer to the area as an emerging "restaurant row" (Gregor 2006). By 2008, the area had acquired the trendy moniker "ViVa," short for Viaduct Valley (Salkin 2008). AKRF's claim that pedestrian and vehicular traffic to the area was impeded by structures and geography and worsened by a lack of "significant destinations" was dubious at best. The AKRF team had simply ignored the west side of Twelfth Avenue and other signs of economic vitality, adaptive reuse, and street life.

Viewed from the perspective of Jane Jacobs, the redevelopment that was occurring in ViVa introduced new neighborhood uses—restaurants, a nightclub, artist studios, a major food market, and renovation of the waterfront as recreational space by the city—creating new "pools of use" that attracted diverse pedestrian traffic during the day *and* at night. Moreover, these new uses were taking place in old buildings—warehouses, former freight stations, and so on—due to their low rents and property values, confirming Jacobs's position that a mixture of old and new buildings was critical to sustaining both a mixture of uses and socioeconomic diversity (1961). Community Board 9's redevelopment plan for its "Special Purpose District" would have added to that diversity by promoting mixed uses, retaining some existing buildings and businesses, and building affordable housing. In stark contrast, the campus expansion using eminent domain would arrest that process of diversification by building a contiguous, seventeen-acre, single-use campus. Even if, as Columbia asserted, the new campus would include retail space, the high overhead costs associated with new buildings would place that retail space beyond the means of small community-based businesses. As Jacobs observed, "hundreds of ordinary enterprises, necessary to the safety of public life of streets and neighborhoods, and appreciated for their convenience and personal quality, can make out successfully in old buildings, but are inexorably slain by the high overhead of new construction" (1961:188).

"Thing Power": On Graffiti, Cracked Sidewalks, and a Dead Rat

My hunch is that the image of dead or thoroughly instrumentalized matter feeds human hubris and our earth-destroying fantasies of conquest and consumption.
—Jane Bennett

AKRF's contention that Manhattanville was visually and physically isolated and functionally obsolete provided evidence, albeit specious, of the need to redevelop the area to spur investment and create jobs—a finding that had already been reached by Community Board 9 and the Columbia-sponsored Community Advisory Committee. However, in order for the ESDC to approve the exercise of eminent domain, the AKRF study needed to demonstrate that the area was blighted, or "substandard or insanitary," requiring demolition. Definitions of blight are notoriously vague and elastic and can include such factors as the existence of building code violations, the underutilization of buildings, the presence of vermin, safety hazards, and graffiti, and other signs of decay and disuse. Moreover, definitions of blight are periodically reviewed and amended by the state legislature and reinterpreted through court decisions.

The blight study's reductive materialism, by evacuating all human agency, only obscured urban processes—that is, how people inhabit, adapt to, and shape urban landscapes, as opposed to how the landscapes *look*. Notwithstanding the study's omission of data on economic redevelopment that was occurring in ViVa, the AKRF study offered little or no substantive data or analysis of existing businesses in the study area, their employees, or the small residential community in the project's footprint. Many small businesses—including auto repair shops, wholesale meat distributors, and gas stations, as well as Floridita—were minority-owned businesses that benefited from the area's comparatively low commercial rents, zoning, and locational advantages, such as proximity to the Henry Hudson Parkway and the 125th Street corridor. Moreover, the majority of people employed in the area who would lose jobs were people of color—those most disadvantaged in labor markets. Equally important, the AKRF study failed to address the long-standing causes and agents responsible for Manhattanville's blighted conditions.

A critical component of the study needed to demonstrate that Manhattanville was underutilized, deteriorated, and obsolete was a detailed survey of its buildings. Thornton Tomasetti, Inc., a structural engineering firm, was subcontracted by AKRF to conduct a survey of building conditions. As chance would have it, the chairman and cofounder of Thornton Tomasetti, Richard Tomasetti, was an adjunct professor at Columbia in the Department of Civil Engineering and Engineering Mechanics while the study was in progress. The AKRF study noted that 72 percent of the properties surveyed were either already owned by or under contract to Columbia. Moreover, of the study's eighteen color photographs documenting building blight, all but two were taken in properties owned by the university at the time of its release on November 1, 2007. The coincidence of neglect, underutilization, and the presence of hazardous conditions with Columbia's stewardship prompted critics to charge that the university was itself responsible for the blighted conditions. As a member of Community Board 9 told me, "Columbia has basically blighted the neighborhood by buying it up and by keeping most of what they bought vacant. You know, the life was drained out of the neighborhood. A whole lot of what was going on in the footprint, economic activity, social life, is no longer going on. It's a dead zone." This suspicion was confirmed by a 2008 decision of the Appellate Division of the State Supreme Court in upholding a Freedom of Information Law petition filed by the West Harlem Business Group, a coalition of family-owned businesses that had organized to resist Columbia's planned use of eminent domain. The decision is worth quoting at length. Referring to the years preceding the AKRF study, the court found that "ESDC delayed making any inquiry into the conditions in Manhattanville until long after Columbia gained control over the very properties that would form the basis for a subsequent blight study" (Tuck-It-Away v. ESDC 2009, Appendix B, 60a.)

In short, the AKRF blight study served to conceal Columbia's role in producing blight, and to naturalize deterioration and disuse as ineluctable consequences of obsolescence. Moreover, like earlier blight studies, AKRF discounted, if not ignored, the viewpoints and appraisals of the residents, employees, and business owners of the district where they lived and worked.

In November 2006, the West Harlem Business Group filed an Article 78, Freedom of Information Law (FOIL) petition in the New York State Supreme Court. The petition alleged that the Empire State Development Corporation had colluded with Columbia by hiring AKRF, and sought the release of earlier withheld ESDC documents. The disclosure of documents attesting to AKRF's collusion with the university would undermine, if not obviate, an ESDC blight finding and approval of eminent domain to take the remaining properties not owned by the university. In June 2007, State Supreme Court Judge Shirley Kornreich ordered the ESDC to release 117 documents and correspondences that shed light on the ESDC's relationship to Columbia and AKRF, ruling that, "while acting for Columbia, AKRF has an interest of its own in the outcome of [ESDC's] action, as AKRF, presumably, seeks to succeed in securing an outcome that its client, Columbia, would favor" (Hartocollis 2007). The ESDC then appealed the court's decision to the Appellate Division, arguing, among other things, that a "Chinese wall" had been erected between the AKRF team working for the ESDC and the team working for the university.

In July 2008, the Appellate Division of the State Supreme Court upheld the lower court's ruling. Because the courts raised serious concerns about the ESDC's decision to hire AKRF to conduct the blight study, the ESDC hired a second engineering and environmental firm, Earth Tech, to support AKRF's finding and head off future court actions.

Two days after the appellate court's ruling, the board of the Empire State Development Corporation declared Columbia's project area blighted and approved the university's General Project Plan (GPP). At the meeting, Avi Schick, president and chief operating officer of the ESDC, also announced that the AKRF Neighborhood Conditions Study was not the sole basis for determining that Manhattanville was blighted and that a second study had been conducted by Earth Tech, a consulting firm not associated with Columbia, that confirmed ARKF's conclusions. The Earth Tech study had been completed in May 2008.

Completed only two months before the ESDC's approval of the university's plan, the Earth Tech report reiterated the claim that Manhattanville was isolated from Harlem and Hamilton Heights, and identified additional obstructions (e.g., Riverside Park and the Riverside Community Houses) that formed visual barriers between the study area and surrounding residential communities (Earth Tech Inc. 2008:2–7). To support its account of "visual clutter," "grimness," and deterioration, the study included photographs of, among other things, cracked sidewalks, graffiti, windowless building facades, and a dead rat (2008:2–20). Unsurprisingly, neither Earth Tech nor AKRF conducted pedestrian or vehicular traffic studies to support their conclusions. Both studies advanced a spatial ideology that defined old and mixed-use buildings as "streetscape clutter," and a lack of transparency as a telltale sign of neighborhood blight and obsolescence. "Although the majority of buildings are low-rise," Earth Tech surmised, "building heights vary, creating a discordant skyline and limit any perception of coherent design" (2008:2–11).

Don't Fear Columbia

As the campus expansion project wound its way through the courts and approval process, Community Board 9 held a public hearing on Columbia's 197-c application to rezone thirty-five acres of West Harlem and modify the city map, both of which were needed to advance the university's plan. The August 2007 hearing, held at the Manhattanville Houses Community Center, drew a crowd of about three hundred persons: representatives of the community opposed to the expansion plan and university officials and others who supported the plan, including President Bollinger and former Mayor David Dinkins, then a professor at Columbia's School of International and Public Affairs. A few months earlier, Dinkins had published an op-ed in the *New York Times*, aptly titled "Don't Fear Columbia" (Dinkins 2007).

Also attending were members of a recently formed pro-expansion group, the Coalition for the Future of Manhattanville. The coalition had been organized by Bill Lynch, a paid Columbia consultant (at an estimated $40,000 per month) and a deputy mayor under Dinkins (Gonzalez 2007). Bill Lynch Associates had, in turn, hired the public relations firm Sunshine, Sachs & Associates to drum up community support—or, at least, the appearance of such. The pro-Columbia coalition included Harlem residents, businesspersons, and others, such as Hazel Dukes, president of the NAACP's New York State Conference, and the Reverend Reginald Williams, pastor of a Bronx church and director of Addicts Rehabilitation Center in East Harlem. At the meeting, which I attended, a group of Black and brown men, some wearing hardhats as used in the construction industry, passed out flyers and held signs reading, "Columbia Creates Jobs." These men were patients at Reverend Williams's addiction center, who had been paid to simulate community support at the hearing (Durkin 2007; Astor 2008).

During the five-hour hearing, the *Columbia Daily Spectator* reported, twenty-two people testified in favor of the expansion plan and seventy-three against. The raucous crowd booed Bollinger, Dinkins, Dukes, and other expansion supporters. Opponents criticized the university's failure to engage CB 9's 197-a plan and its pursuit of eminent domain. After the hearing, Community Board 9's zoning committee voted 17–1 against the plan. Soon after, the general board adopted a resolution in a 32–2 vote, recommending disapproval of Columbia's rezoning application, citing familiar criticisms and concerns.[4]

Despite the opposition, on November 26, 2007, the City Planning Commission voted to approve the university's rezoning application with only minor modifications in what the *New York Times* described as a "raucous hearing." At the same meeting, the commission also approved

CB 9's 197-a plan, which, given its limited advisory power, was little more than a perfunctory gesture to community participation.

The modifications to Columbia's 197-c rezoning application addressed none of the central issues that had been raised by CB 9's August resolution and identified in its 197-a plan. In fact, the section of West Harlem that was approved by the commission in CB 9's revised 197-a plan excluded the university's project footprint—precisely the area that had been Community Board's 9's focus, the proposed Special Purpose District. Moreover, the modifications to Columbia's application were relatively minor and included replacing the research facilities planned for Broadway with faculty housing and academic buildings, lowering the maximum building height in areas of the footprint, and improving the accessibility of public spaces.

On December 18, less than a month after the City Planning Commission approved the university's rezoning application, the Empire State Development Corporation voted unanimously to approve eminent domain (Astor 2009). Under the ruling, the properties of the two remaining holdouts (Nick Sprayregen, owner of Tuck-It-Away Self-Storage, and the Singh family, owners of two gas stations) would be condemned and taken by the state in return for just compensation, then turned over to Columbia. The very next day, the last major hurdle in the approval process was removed: the New York City Council approved the university's 197-c rezoning application in a 35–5 vote, with six abstentions. Tragically, on the same day that the ESDC approved eminent domain, Jordi Reyes-Montblanc, the chairman of CB 9 who had led the fight for its 197-a plan, died of cancer (Astor 2008; Williams and Rivera 2007).

Ironically, one month after the ESDC approved eminent domain, the *Columbia Daily Spectator* announced that the university was planning a three-day series of events in March 2008 to commemorate the fortieth anniversary of the 1968 student rebellion. The year before, four alumni who had participated in the campus uprising wrote to President Lee Bollinger, lamenting the "hazy understanding" that students, alumni, and Columbia employees had of the period. Bollinger endorsed the commemoration. In a report written after a planning meeting with current students, the 1968 veterans observed, "[Students] deeply felt the lack of continuity with, and institutional memory of '68 and wondered why the way they feel now seems so different from the way we did back then" (Levi 2008a). However hazy the institutional memory of 1968 was, the university presented the campus expansion as decoupled from that history—a history of racial dispossession that required "characteristic amnesias," as Benedict Anderson put it, to elide and replace with a new narrative (1991:209).

By contrast, memories of the struggles of 1968 were very much alive in Harlem. Activists consistently linked the defeated gym project to the struggle over the new campus, and viewed the latter as a continuation of the university's practices of racial exclusion and dispossession—of "Jim Crow." Whereas Harlem activists refused to have those memories annulled—memories that were insinuated into the embodied spatial order and political culture of activists—the university sought to decouple the expansion from history and the politics of race. Unsurprisingly, Columbia officials denied that there was a historical link. For example, Senior Executive Vice President Robert Kasdin, a key figure in advancing the expansion, assured the *Columbia Daily Spectator* that the university's relations with Harlem in 2008 could not be compared to those in 1968: "I don't think the analogy is appropriate at all. There is [now] real community support" (Morais 2008a).

Although campus-based opposition to the Manhattanville project never reached the scale or scope of the 1968 protests, it was not insignificant. In February 2007, the Student Coalition on Expansion and Gentrification declared the university's South Lawn "blighted" and seized the green space for a day of protest with Harlem activists (Phillips 2007b). Later that year, five students went on a hunger strike against the expansion and for increased funding for the university's Center for the Study of Ethnicity and Race, pitching tents on South Lawn, supported by nightly candlelight vigils. As in 1968, student organizations worked closely with Harlem activists in planning and coordinating protests. For example, in November 2007, students met with activists and CB 9 board members at St. Mary's Episcopal Church, to march to Low Library and the president's residence. Along the route the demonstrators chanted, "West Harlem, Our Homes," behind a banner that read, "1968, 2007, Same Fight" (Schreiber 2007).

By contrast, local, citywide, and state politicians supported the expansion plan and the exercise of eminent domain. Congressman Charles Rangel, State Assemblyman Keith Wright, and City Councilman Robert

Jackson, all representing Greater Harlem, expressed their support for the project at critical stages in the public review process. Borough President Scott Stringer gave his support to the $6.3 billion campus expansion in 2007 after Columbia agreed to contribute $20 million to initiate a fund to build affordable housing and support local parks. Governor David Paterson, a former Harlem state senator and Columbia alumnus, emphasized the benefits that would accrue to Harlem, rehearsing the well-worn smart growth narrative: "The expansion of one of New York's oldest educational institutions will enhance the vitality of both the University and its neighboring community, while meeting the long-term needs of its residents" (Durkin 2007; BWOG 2009). The only elected official to voice strong criticism of the project and attend anti-expansion protests was Harlem State Senator Bill Perkins.

On January 20, 2009, Nick Sprayregen and the Singh family filed separate lawsuits in the New York Supreme Court, Appellate Division, challenging the ESDC's blight finding and approval of eminent domain. In this and other court cases, Sprayregen and the Singh family were represented by the eminent civil rights attorney Norman Siegel. In December, in a surprise decision, the appellate court ruled that, as "a private elite institution," Columbia could not claim a public purpose for its Manhattanville campus expansion and that the ESDC's actions violated the Takings Clause of the US Constitution and Article 1§7 of the New York State Constitution. The court also determined that the blight finding was made in "bad faith" and the ESDC's definition of blight was unconstitutionally vague.

However, on June 24, 2010, the New York State Court of Appeals unanimously overturned the Appellate Division's decision, arguing that a private university could serve a public purpose (Bagli 2010). The court of appeals also cited earlier precedent concerning the Brooklyn Atlantic Yards project, in which the ESDC had condemned and taken property on behalf of a private developer; the appellate court had ruled in favor of the ESDC and the private developer. In December 2010, the US Supreme Court refused to hear an appeal filed by Nicholas Sprayregen.

Although the university had signed a community benefits agreement with the West Harlem Local Development Corporation in 2009, activists questioned the degree to which it was legally binding. The agreement called for Columbia to provide a total of $150 million in benefits, including $30 million for a university-operated public school, $20 million for affordable housing, $4 million to provide legal services to tenants, and $20 million for in-kind services—namely, public access to certain "existing CU facilities, services, and amenities." In addition, $76 million in unencumbered funds was set aside for community programs to be identified by the LDC and implemented over a sixteen-year period.

Activists also questioned the degree to which the LDC and its process of negotiation represented the interests of residents. For example, Community Board 9, which authorized the formation of the WHLDC in 2006, had not intended elected officials or their representatives to be *voting* members. Walter South, a member of CB 9 who had participated in the creation of the LDC, noted,

> The idea was that we would have representatives from the politicians, but they would be advisers and not have any voting power—it would be a community-based organization, and it should primarily function to benefit the community. But [Congressman] Rangel said if he didn't have a vote, he was going to kill it, so they caved and gave them a vote. But by them all voting in a bloc, they were able to almost manipulate what the organization was all about. (Astor 2011)

State Senator Bill Perkins, the only elected official to consistently oppose the campus expansion, expressed his reservations about the LDC: "These community benefits agreements, you have to be very careful because all that glitters is not gold, especially from the perspective of the people who live in the community, the little people" (*Wall Street Journal* 2011). In 2011 members of Community Board 9 argued that the West Harlem LDC should be disbanded. As late as 2011, the LDC had no office, staff, contact information, or tax-exempt status, and had spent less than $700,000 in the two and a half years since the signing of the benefits agreement. "A serious problem with community benefits agreements is legitimacy," Vicki Been, a New York University law professor and expert on land-use regulation, told the *Wall Street Journal*. "What is the community, who represents it, how does the community hold the negotiators accountable, who enforces and how do they do that?" (*Wall Street Journal* 2011). Given Columbia's actions over the years, it is clear that these questions were not high in the minds of its administrators. Unsurprisingly, many Harlem activists viewed the control of the West Harlem LDC and its $150 million fund by politicians as little more than a quid pro quo for their support of the university's $6.2 billion campus expansion.

Whatever the credibility of Columbia's claim that the new campus would create thousands of jobs, contribute to the city's knowledge economy, and benefit the residents of Harlem, the critical issue was whether the interests of an elite, private university supersede the needs, aspirations, and right—however circumscribed—to self-determination of Black and brown communities. To recall, the bête noire was never the university's right to redevelop its own properties; rather, it was the university's intent to build a contiguous and insular campus by harnessing the state's powers of eminent domain. This, like the urban renewal program—James Baldwin's "Negro removal"—was an act of racial dispossession.

Surrounding communities were already experiencing the slow violence of gentrification in the form of increased rents, residential displacement, symbolic violence, and what Mindy Fullilove termed "root shock" (2004). In order to create and defend a "campus atmosphere," the university and its boosters decoupled the campus expansion from its wider sociospatial and macroeconomic context—and, equally important, from its long history of racial exclusion and dispossession. Like the Harlem spite fence, the theoretical frame of the evolutionists, and visual rhetoric of the urban renewal program, Columbia imposed an imagined spatiotemporal border that counterposed the future-oriented, modernist universalism of the American Acropolis against a moribund and particularistic temporality of racial difference.

If the longue durée provides critical context for understanding the logic of the self-enclosed campus and perduring role of racial chronopolitics in shaping the urban landscape and spatial politics, so too does it disclose how geography, or thing power, provided a material frame for articulating hierarchical spatial imaginaries, discourses, and social identities. The elevated topography of the Morningside plateau, along with natural barriers—for example, the cliffs edging Morningside Park—enabled the vertical secession of the American Acropolis from surrounding poor and working-class immigrant and Black and brown communities, giving rise to the moniker "the Hill" to capture the elite interests and concentrated power of its institutions. The symbolic and physical potency of this vertical hierarchy would come to the fore when, in order to build a gym on public parkland beyond its borders, Columbia adopted an architectural solution, a "vertical gymnasium," that would make public land available for the university's use, while securing a separation between student and community users of its unequal facilities—a division succinctly expressed by its opponents in the phrase "Jim Crow gymnasium." The symbolic potency of this vertical symbol of racial inequality galvanized the opposition of both campus and Harlem activists and led both to the cancellation of the gym and the university's first attempt at a "land grab" in West Harlem, the abandoned piers area project.

Geography also shaped the politics of land use in the Manhattanville Valley, which was located in a poorly drained fault line valley. Manhattanville's founders sought exception from the 1811 grid plan in order to ensure that its main avenues drained properly. However, as the district rapidly grew, apart from 125th and 126th Streets, the area was remapped to conform to the tyranny of the grid, which aggravated the area's drainage problems and contributed to the spread of infectious diseases. Louis A. Rodenstein's 1864 sanitary survey captured these insalubrious conditions and, as was the tendency during the period, conflated them with the allegedly innate, racial-cum-cultural dispositions of the immigrant poor. Thus, the contrast between the lowland valley and upland Acropolis was reinforced by a potent medicalized nativism and fear of transgressive miasmata, and was critical to the processes of racial and class formation.

However, Manhattanville's ready accessibility to river, rail, and road transportation had also made it an important entrepôt for the transfer and distribution of goods from the Hudson Valley, New Jersey, and beyond, and a filling site for manufacturing industries well into the twentieth century. The contrast between Manhattanville's economy and patterns of land use and the civilization-building missions of Columbia and its peer institutions would be seized upon by the university in the twenty-first century to reiterate the spatiotemporal boundary between the Heights and "the old Manhattanville manufacturing zone." Moreover, the valley's hydrological challenges would return as an important political factor in disputes over the need for, and environmental impact of, the subterranean "bathtub"—the lynchpin in the university's case for the use of eminent domain.

In 2011 Columbia began the demolition of structures in Manhattan-ville. From the fifteenth floor of the building where I lived (a Columbia faculty residence on the edge of the footprint), I watched buildings vanish, as if overnight—Sprayregen's Tuck-It-Away storage warehouses, the Singhs' gas stations, the assortment of car repair shops, the Eritrean social club, and Floridita, just to name a few. And in their places arose new Columbia buildings, some transparent and some not so, including the Jerome L. Greene Science Center, the Lenfest Center for the Arts, and the Forum, described on its webpage as "a unique community gathering place."

Hidden away between two of the completed buildings facing West 125th Street was Small Square, a pocket "piazza" bordered by saplings and supplied with brightly colored movable chairs. I have yet to see more than a handful of people using it, and most, if not all, of those users have been university employees from adjacent Columbia buildings. The piazza's lack of public use was quite predictable. It was set back from 125th Street along a seamless border vacuum, and there was little reason for residents of West Harlem to be there at all. Although insignificant in the larger scheme of things, Small Plaza is an architectural synecdoche of the new campus's relationship to West Harlem and its people—to *their* needs, interests, and aspirations. And this social, political, and cultural asymmetry has characterized the relationship of the institutions of the American Acropolis to working-class communities of color in the valley over the longue durée.

Coda: The Necropolitics of Smart Growth

I completed this book during the summer of 2020, when the long history of police violence against Black and brown communities had given rise to a nationwide and broad-based social movement under the stewardship of Black Lives Matter. It was also the final year of the Trump administration, which had aggressively pursued xenophobic and racist policies that, among its outrages, separated immigrant children from their parents at the southern border, purged transgender soldiers from the military, and appeased and encouraged white supremacy and anti-Black violence. These policies culminated in an insurrection that ended in the violent attack on the US Capitol on January 6, 2021, by a white and overwhelmingly male mob—a hateful horde that included white supremacists, Nazi sympathizers, southern redemptionists, and armed militias that advocated the overthrow of the "deep state" and murder of liberals. Similar mobs had lynched thousands of African Americans in the South and North after the Civil War; ran amok through the city's Black Tenderloin district in 1900, burning, looting, and killing; and destroyed the neighborhood of Black Greenwood in Tulsa, Oklahoma, in 1921 and massacred its African American residents.

If the Trump presidency, 2020 election, and Capitol riot revealed how deeply sewn racism and xenophobia were into the nation's populace and sacrosanct institutions, then the COVID-19 pandemic tragically demonstrated how deadly their consequences remain. The pandemic made clear that access to affordable housing, community resources (clinics, food pantries, well-equipped public schools, and so on), and empowered community institutions were not just disposable amenities that could be bargained over and sacrificed in the name of economic progress, but were matters of life and death. The virus sickened and killed those who lacked access to health care and to the vaccines that became available; it killed the homeless, the dispossessed, and those living in overcrowded and substandard housing; and it killed people who lacked community-based institutions that could inform, serve, and advocate on behalf of the low-income, elderly, immigrant, and working-class people who serve the public through thick and thin. In New York City the virus disproportionately sickened and immiserated Black and brown people who lived in underserved and disenfranchised areas, such as the South Bronx, Washington Heights, and Harlem—communities that had suffered the rough justice of neoliberal redevelopment and been denied the right to participate effectively in the urban planning decisions that most directly affected their neighborhoods, livelihoods, and well-being. This suffering and death could not be papered over with colorful architectural renderings of visually pleasing and neatly arranged glass buildings, open "view corridors," or

Small Square, April 2021. Photo by author.

tree-lined piazzas teeming with a diversity of publics. Nor could these consequences be muted or elided by cheery talk about cutting-edge scientific research, "smart growth," or vague, patronizing promises of trickle-down community benefits. This, then, is my conclusion: Black and brown lives matter; justice matters; and the right to the city for *all* matters, not just for a privileged, putatively enlightened, and, more often than not, white few. They are all matters of life and death.

NOTES

CHAPTER 2. MANHATTANVILLE VALLEY, CONSTITUTING THE OUTSIDE

1 A particularly good example of the use of census data during the period by academics is Richmond Mayo-Smith's 1890 text *Emigration and Immigration: A Study in Social Science.*

2 At the time of the 1920 census, James Goodlett, eighty-two and a widower, was living in the household of his sister-in-law, Eliza Morris, in New Rochelle. Morris had taken over her late sister's employment business and was housing eight boarders, all of whom were employed in service occupations. Three young men worked as waiters "at a college," possibly the College of New Rochelle nearby. James Goodlett's occupation was again recorded as "fish peddler."

3 Pre-law tenements were buildings that had been constructed prior to the passage of the Tenement House Act of 1879. The 1879 law required that all rooms in tenements built after the date of the legislation have windows facing the street, the rear yard, or an interior air shaft. Although the 1879 law was intended to increase the light and ventilation in new buildings, the interior shafts were generally too small to provide adequate ventilation or sunlight to apartments below the top floor and served, with tragic result, as air flues when the buildings caught fire (Dolkart 2007).

4 Lynch's provenience poses a puzzle: French-speaking parents, born in Ireland and Africa, and birthing a son in Dublin in 1830. While his parents' origins cannot be reconstructed, the data does confirm the mobility of people of African descent. The Irish were well represented in the conquest, settlement, and provisioning of Europe's circum-Caribbean colonies as seamen, soldiers, merchants, and indentured servants. It would not have been inconceivable for a French-speaking Irishman (a seaman, merchant, or sail rigger, for example) to marry a French-speaking free woman of color who had been born in Africa (slavery was abolished in the French colonies in 1794, reinstated in 1802, and abolished once again in 1826), relocate to Ireland's major port city, and then emigrate to New York, a city poised to become the maritime and financial capital of the Western Hemisphere. Lynch's enumerator in 1920 was perhaps trying to connect these dots—possibly at Lynch's request—when he appended "O.C." to his mother's place of birth, perhaps indicating "overseas colony" or residence in a French colony. Equally plausible, Lynch père and his African-born wife might have fled Saint Domingue during the Haitian Revolution (1791–1804).

CHAPTER 3. POWER/KNOWLEDGE AND THE CRAFTING OF CITIZENS

1 In a review of *The Principles of Sociology*, Albion W. Small at the University of Chicago criticized the limitations of Giddings's concept of "consciousness of kind," saying that "what we need, however, is not an a priori dogma about the part which 'consciousness of kind,' or recognition of likeness, has played in human association; but observation, arrangement and generalization of facts" (1896:295–96).

2 When these pre-law tenements were canvassed in the 1880 federal census, they were exclusively white, as was most of Lawrence Street and 126th Streets (US Census Bureau 1880).

CHAPTER 4. SPATIAL POLITICS AND THE POLICING OF THE COLOR LINE

1 Taylor assured a *New York Tribune* reporter, "Our organization has shown no discrimination against race or color. Its members have large sums invested in Harlem, and, naturally, they want to keep the earning power of the properties up to that mark, which will insure a fair return on their investment" (*New York Tribune*, August 31, 1913, D1).

2 Editor's note: The "deadline" was a spatial demarcation having life-and-death consequences. The origin of the word can be traced to the Civil War. The infamous Andersonville Prison at Camp Sumter was an internment camp for Union soldiers captured by the Confederacy. Unfenced, it was surrounded by a line that, if crossed by inmates, would lead to them being summarily executed by their Confederate captors. The term was in wide use by the 1900s but likely had particular resonance in the case of Harlem.

3 In another case, a landlord who was struggling to maintain full occupancy in a building with white tenants paying rents of $14 to $17 per month found that Black tenants would pay considerably more. "The owner decided," the *New York Times* reported, "to rent to colored tenants and the house is now filled with colored families paying from $20 to $24, and there is a long waiting list" (December 19, 1915, 21).

4 "In *projective identification*, parts of the self and internal objects are split off and projected onto an external object, which then becomes 'identified' with the split-off part as well as possessed and controlled by it. Its defensive purposes include fusion with the external object in order to avoid separation; control of the destructive, so-called bad object, which is a persecutory threat to the individual; and preservation of good portions of the self by splitting them off and projectively identifying them in the therapist for 'safe-keeping'" (Moore and Fine 1990:109).

5 Underscoring the role of the police in provoking renewed white violence following a period of calm, Mary White Ovington wrote, "The police, however, instead of keeping the peace, angered the Negroes, urged on their enemies, and by Monday night found that they had helped create a riot, this time bitter and dangerous. Overzealous to proceed against the 'niggers,' officers rushed in places frequented by peaceable colored men, whom they placed under arrest. Dragging their vic-

tims to the station-house they beat them so unmercifully that before long many needed to be handed over to another city department—the hospital" (1911:200).

6 John M. Royall's real estate office was at 21 West 134th Street, and James C. Taylor, the property owner and undertaker, had a funeral parlor at 89 West 134th Street.

CHAPTER 5. PHILANTHROPY, RACE LIBERALISM, AND RACIAL CONTAINMENT

1 At an earlier meeting with Rockefeller's architect, Andrew J. Thomas, Hubert was reportedly told, "Mr. Rockefeller isn't interested in Blacks or Jews" (Hubert 1970).

2 As his biographer, Raymond Fosdick, put it, "The need for housing was so great and the field so large that there was not enough private money in the United States to handle it unless it was handled on a business basis; and by a business basis [Rockefeller] meant adequate housing that would earn an investment return of somewhere in the neighborhood of 5 or 6 percent" (1956:409).

3 Andrew Dolkart has noted that it was Harry E. Edmonds, the founder of International House, who first proposed to Rockefeller considering Fosdick to lead a new, progressive Protestant church on Morningside Heights, as well as its eventual location at Riverside Drive and 122nd Street (1998).

4 In a letter accompanying the donation, Rockefeller wrote, "In making this gift the undersigned desires to express the hope that, if not now, in the near future, it may be deemed right and fitting to invite representatives of Protestant communions other than the Protestant Episcopal Church to share in the control and direction of the erection, maintenance and management of the Cathedral of St. John the Divine" (in Fosdick 1956:226). See also *New York Times*, 1925a, 1925c.

5 Area No. 14 included census tracts 209 and 211 and was bound by 135th Street in the north, 122nd Street in the south, the Hudson River in the west, and Eighth Avenue (Frederick Douglass Boulevard) in the east.

6 On Butler's anti-communism, see Rosenthal 2006.

CHAPTER 6. WAGING THE WAR AGAINST BLIGHT

1 MHI's member institutions included Barnard College, the Cathedral of St. John the Divine, Corpus Christi Church, International House, the Jewish Theological Seminary, the Juilliard School of Music, Teachers College, the Riverside Church, Union Theological Seminary, St. Luke's Hospital, and Columbia University.

2 Members of the Community Advisory Committee included Herman Lester, spokesperson for the Uptown Business and Civic Association, and B. F. McLaurin, a representative of the Brotherhood of Sleeping Car Porters, both African Americans.

CHAPTER 7. RACIAL DISPOSSESSION AND REBELLION

1 The Community Action Committee was a coalition of representatives from Morningsiders United, the Grant Parents-Community Associations, and various block associations.

2 In 1953 the university had purchased the right of way for 116th Street between Broadway and Amsterdam for a fee of $1,000 and turned it into a landscaped walkway; in 1967 gates were installed at either end of the closed street (Stern, Mellins, and Fishman 1995).

3 At an emergency meeting on Wednesday, presided over by President Kirk and Vice President Truman, the faculty of Columbia College had voted in favor of recommending "the immediate suspension of on-site excavation of the gymnasium facility in Morningside Park" (*Columbia College Today* 1968).

EPILOGUE

1 This Special Purpose District was bounded by West 135th Street to the north, West 122nd Street to the south, the Hudson River to the west, and Convent/Morningside Avenues to the east.

2 Author's interview with the Reverend Earl Kooperkamp, May 14, 2006.

3 More generally, as Tuck-It-Away's 2009 petition to the State Supreme Court against the ESDC argued, the AKRF report was bereft of any economic analysis of the area.

4 CB 9 had passed a resolution condemning the anticipated use of eminent domain in 2004.

REFERENCES

Abbott, Andrew. 1988. *The System of Professions: An Essay in the Division of Expert Knowledge*. Chicago: University of Chicago Press.

Abramson, Daniel. 2012. "Boston's West End: Urban Obsolescence in Mid-Twentieth Century America." In *Governing by Design: Architecture, Economy, and Politics in the Twentieth Century*, edited by Aggregate Architectural History Collaborative. Pittsburgh: University of Pittsburgh Press.

———. 2016. *Obsolescence: An Architectural History*. Chicago: University of Chicago Press.

Afro American. 1943. "You Have Got to Clean Up Harlem—La Guardia." October 30, 1943.

Agamben, Georgio. 1998. *Homo Sacer: Sovereign Power and Bare Life*. Palo Alto: Stanford University Press.

———. 2005. *State of Exception*. Translated by Kevin Attell. Chicago: University of Chicago Press.

AKRF (Allee King Rosen & Fleming). 2007. *Columbia Manhattanville Neighborhood Conditions Study*. New York: AKRF.

Aksamit, Daniel Victor. 2014. "'Absolutely Sort of Normal': The Common Origins of the War on Poverty at Home and Abroad, 1961–1965." Doctoral dissertation, Kansas State University.

Alberti, Benjamin, Severin Fowles, Martin Holbraad, Yvonne Marshall, and Christopher Witmore. 2011. "'Worlds Otherwise': Archaeology, Anthropology, and Ontological Difference." *Current Anthropology* 52(5):896–912.

Alden, Robert. 1964. "Neighbors Assail Columbia Growth." *New York Times*, January 18, 1964.

Allen, Anne Taylor. 1988. "'Let Us Live with Our Children': Kindergarten Movements in Germany and the United States, 1840–1914." *History of Education Quarterly* 28(1):23–48.

———. 2017. *The Transatlantic Kindergarten: Education and Women's Movements in Germany and the United States*. Oxford: Oxford University Press.

Alves, Jaime Amparo. 2018. *The Anti-Black City: Police Terror and Black Urban Life in Brazil*. Minneapolis: University of Minnesota Press.

American Iron and Steel Association. 1880. *Directory to the Iron and Steel Works of the United States*. Philadelphia: American Iron and Steel Association.

American Public Health Association, Committee on the Hygiene of Housing. 1945. *An Appraisal Method for Measuring the Quality of Housing: A Yardstick for Health*

Officers, Housing Officials and Planners. New York: American Public Health Association.

Amsterdam News. 1928. "Dunbar Bank Opens." September 19, 1928, 3.

———. 1943a. "Mixed Dancing Closed the Savoy Ballroom." May 1, 1943, 1.

———. 1943b. "Negroes and Whites 'Don't Mix!' Metropolitan Life President Says." May 29, 1943, 1.

———. 1950. "Housing Survey Made for Month." June 10, 1950, 36.

———. 1952a. "Housing Battle Is on Again." January 26, 1952, 1.

———. 1952b. "Housing on West Side Confusing." February 2, 1952.

———. 1971. "Housing Plan Said Ignored." September 18, 1971, C15.

Amzallag, Daniel. 2007. "Three Members Resign from LDC." *Columbia Daily Spectator*, November, 29, 2007.

———. 2008. "Experts Say M'ville May Pose Hazard." *Columbia Daily Spectator*, September 22, 2008.

Anderson, Benedict. 1991. *Imagined Communities: Reflections on the Origin and Spread of Nationalism*. London: Verso.

Anderson, Margo J. 1988. *The American Census: A Social History*. New Haven: Yale University Press.

Arno Press. 1969. *The Complete Report of Mayor La Guardia's Commission on the Harlem Riot of March 19, 1935*. New York: Arno Press and New York Times.

Arnold, Martin. 1961. "Tenants Accuse Columbia of Bias." *New York Times*, October 4, 1961, 39.

Astor, Maggie. 2008. "Former Chair of CB9, Jordi Reyes-Montblanc, Dies." *Columbia Daily Spectator*, January 20, 2008, 1.

———. 2009. "Eminent Domain Ruling Clears M'Ville Hurdles." *Columbia Daily Spectator*, January 20, 2009.

———. 2011. "Where Have the Benefits Gone?" *Columbia Daily Spectator: Eye Magazine*, February 17, 2011, 7.

Ayoub, Lea. 2009. "Public Air Space: Planning and Accessing Tall Buildings in London." In *Critical Cities*, edited by Deepa Naik and Trenton Oldfield. London: Myrdle Court Press.

Bagli, Charles V. 2010. "Columbia Wins Fight for West Harlem Campus." *New York Times*, December 14, 2010, A1.

Bailey, Nellie Hester. 2008. "Women, Gentrification, and Harlem." In *Feminism and War: Confronting US Imperialism*, edited by Robin L. Riley et al. London: Zed Books.

Balakirsky, Talia. 2017. "The Influence of Extracurricular Activities on Racism at Columbia University Through 1930." Columbia University and Slavery website. https://columbiaandslavery.columbia.edu.

Balch, William R. 1885. *Life and Public Service of General Grant*. Philadelphia: Aetna.

Balibar, Etienne. 1989. "Racism as Universalism." *New Political Science* 8(1–2):9–22.

Baltimore Sun. 1910a. "Negroes Given Clean Sweep." December 20, 1910.

———. 1910b. "Race Riots Follow Negro's Ring Victory." July 5, 1910, 1.

Baradaran, Mehrsa. 2017. *The Color of Money: Black Banks and the Racial Wealth Gap.* Cambridge: Belknap.

Barrows, Robert G. 1973. "The Manuscript Federal Census: Source for a 'New' Local History." *Indiana Magazine of History* 69(3).

———. 1978. "The 1900 Federal Census: A Note on Availability and Potential Uses." *Indiana Magazine of History* 74(2).

Barry, Kenneth. 1968. "Challenge to Administration Strongest in School's History." *Columbia Daily Spectator,* April 24, 1968, 1–3.

Barzun, Jacques. 1965. *Race: A Study in Superstition.* New York: Harper Torchbooks.

Bell, Daniel. 1964. "Plea for a 'New Phase in Negro Leadership.'" *New York Times Magazine,* May 31, 1964.

Bender, Barbara. 1993. Introduction to *Landscape Politics and Perspectives,* edited by Barbara Bender. Oxford: Routledge.

Bender, Thomas. 1987. *New York Intellect: A History of Intellectual Life in New York City from 1750 to the Beginnings of Our Own Time.* Baltimore: Johns Hopkins University Press.

Bennett, Nathan J., et al. 2017. "Conservation Social Science: Understanding and Integrating Human Dimensions to Improve Conservation." *Biological Conservation* 205:93–108.

Berea College Magazine. 2004. "For More Than 50 Years, Marie Runyon, '37, Has Fought to Ensure Harlem Is Home." 74(4):18–22.

Berkman, Barbara, and Peter Maramaldi. 2001. "Health, Mental Health, and Disabilities." In *The Columbia University School of Social Work: A Centennial Celebration,* edited by Ronald A. Feldman and Sheila B. Kamerman. New York: Columbia University Press.

Berti, Chiari, Monica Pivetti, and Silvia Di Battista. 2013. "The Ontologization of Romani." *International Journal of International Relations* 37(4):405–14.

Binkley, Sam. 2012. "The Government of Intimacy: Satiation, Intensification, and the Space of Emotional Reciprocity." *Rethinking Marxism* 24(4):556–73.

Bird, David. 1968. "Harlem Architects Urge Amphitheater for Morningside Park." *New York Times,* October 29, 1968, 18.

Blauner, Robert. 1969. "Internal Colonialism and Ghetto Revolt." *Social Problems* 16(4):393–408.

Blight, David W. 2002. *Race and Reunion: The Civil War in American Memory.* Cambridge, MA: Belknap.

Bonser, Frederick. 1916. "Education for Life Work in Non-Professional Occupations." *Annals of the American Academy of Political and Social Science* 67:64–76.

Bourdieu, Pierre. 1975. "The Specificity of the Scientific Field and the Social Conditions of the Progress of Reason." *Social Science Information* 14(6):19–47.

———. 1977. *Outline of a Theory of Practice.* Cambridge: Cambridge University Press.

———. 1986. "The Forms of Capital." In *Handbook of Theory and Research for the Sociology of Education,* edited by J. Richardson. Westport, CT: Greenwood.

———. 1990. "Animadversiones in Mertonem." In *Robert K. Merton: Consensus and Controversy,* edited by Jon Clark, Celia Modgil, and Sohan Modgil. London: Falmer.

Boyer, Paul. 1978. *Urban Masses and Moral Order in America, 1820–1920*. Cambridge: Harvard University Press.

Bradley, Stefan. 2003. "'Gym Crow Must Go!': Black Student Activism at Columbia University, 1967–1968." *Journal of African American History* 88(2):163–81.

———. 2009. *Harlem vs. Columbia University: Black Student Power in the Late 1960s*. Urbana: University of Illinois Press.

Brandt, Nathan H. 1996. *Harlem at War: The Black Experience in WWII*. Syracuse: Syracuse University Press.

Braudel, Fernand, and Immanuel Wallerstein. 2009. "History and the Social Sciences: The Longue Durée." *Review (Fernand Braudel Center)* 32(2):171–203.

Breslau, Daniel. 2007. "The American Spencerians: Theorizing a New Science." In *Sociology in America: A History*, edited by Craig Calhoun. Chicago: University of Chicago Press.

Brown, Mary. 2017. "Early Twentieth-Century Deportation and the Resistance." Center for Migration Studies, July 31, 2017. https://cmsny.org.

Browne, Arthur. 2015. *One Righteous Man: Samuel Battle and the Shattering of the Color Line in New York*. Boston: Beacon.

Browne, Simone. 2015. *Dark Matters: On the Surveillance of Blackness*. Durham: Duke University Press.

Bryant, Earle V., ed. 2015. *Byline, Richard Wright: Articles from the Daily Worker and New Masses*. Columbia: University of Missouri Press.

Burgess, John W. 1903. *Reconstruction and the Constitution, 1866–1876*. New York: Scribner's.

Burks, Jesse D. 1902. "History of the Speyer School." *Teachers College Record* 3(5):6–12.

Butler, Judith. 1993. *Bodies That Matter*. London: Routledge.

Butler, Judith, and Athena Athanasiou. 2013. *Dispossession: The Performative in the Political*. New York: Polity.

Butler, Nicholas Murray. 1939. *Across the Busy Years: Recollections and Reflections*. Vol. 1. New York: Scribner's.

Bwog: Columbia Student News. 2009. "Head Honchos Support Manhattanville." May 20, 2009. https://bwog.com.

Caledonian Research Trust. 2023. "Scottish Built Ships." www.clydeships.co.uk.

Calhoun, Craig. 2007. *Sociology in America: A History*. Chicago: University of Chicago Press.

Camic, Charles. 2011. "Bourdieu's Cleft of Science." *Minerva* 49(3):275–93.

Canguilhem, Georges. 1991. *The Normal and the Pathological*. New York: Zone Books.

Capeci, Dominic J. 1977. *The Harlem Riot of 1943*. Philadelphia: Temple University Press.

Carriere, Michael. 2011. "Fighting the War Against Blight: Columbia University, Morningside Heights, Inc., and Counterinsurgent Urban Renewal." *Journal of Planning History* 10(1):5–29.

CB9M Blog archives. 2007. "Activists Vow to Continue Fight Against University Expansion." http://cb9m.blogspot.com.

Centner, Ryan. 2008. "Places of Privileged Consumption Practices." *City & Community* 7(3):193–223.

Chandrasekhar, C. P. 2006. "Who Needs a 'Knowledge Economy': Information, Knowledge and Flexible Labor." *Social Scientist* 34(1–2):70–87.

Chauncey, George. 1995. *Gay New York: Gender, Urban Culture, and the Making of the Gay Male World, 1890–1940*. New York: Basic Books.

Chicago Defender. 1943. "Bigotry Charges Fly in Wake of Savoy Closing." May 8, 1943, 6.

Chronopoulos, Themis. 2011. *Spatial Regulation in New York City: From Urban Renewal to Zero Tolerance*. Oxford: Taylor & Francis.

———. 2014a. "Robert Moses and the Visual Dimension of Physical Disorder: Efforts to Demonstrate Urban Blight in the Age of Slum Clearance." *Journal of Planning History* 13(3):207–33.

———. 2014b. "Urban Spatial Mobility in the Age of Sustainability." In *Incomplete Streets*, edited by Stephen Zavestoski and Julian Agyeman. London: Routledge.

Clark, Nigel. 2017. "Politics of Strata." *Theory, Culture & Society* 34(2–3):211–31.

Clark, Nigel, and Kathryn Yusoff. 2017. "Geosocial Formations and the Anthropocene." *Theory, Culture & Society* 34(2–3):3–23.

Columbia College Today. 1968. "Six Weeks That Shook Morningside: A Special Report." Spring 1968, 15(3).

Columbia Daily Spectator. 1966. "Faculty Committee Formed to Study Civil Rights Plans." October 21, 1966, 3.

———. 1968a. "Brown Expresses Skepticism over Piers Project Future." October 1, 1968.

———. 1968b. "Gym Sight." October 30, 1968, 4.

———. 1968c. "Students Picket Sulzberger's Home." May 3, 1968, 1.

———. 1968d. "University Calls in 1,000 Police to End Demonstrations as Nearly 700 Are Arrested and 100 Injured." April 30, 1968.

———. 1969. "News Briefs." March 12, 1969, 1.

———. 2007. "Students and Locals Protest CU Expansion into M'Ville." November 12, 2007.

Columbia Engineering. n.d. "Richard Tomasetti—Adjunct Professor." Columbia University directory. Accessed June 30, 2011. www.columbia.edu.

Columbia Neighbors. n.d. "Columbia Neighbors." Accessed August 12, 2010. http://neighbors.columbia.edu.

Columbia University Record. 1996. "Fairway Draws Crowds to Harlem." February 23, 1996, 1.

Commission on Industrial Education. 1889. *Report of the Commission on Industrial Education Made to the Legislature of Pennsylvania*. Harrisburg: Edwin K. Meyers.

Community Advisory Committee. 2004. "Manhattanville in West Harlem Campus Project: Community Impact and Policy Recommendations." Manuscript copy. http://cb9m.blogspot.com.

Community Board 9, Borough of Manhattan. 2008. *197-A Plan for Community District: Hamilton Heights, Manhattanville, Morningside Heights*. New York: Department of City Planning.

Coss, John J. 1926. Memorandum to Nicholas Murray Butler, December 26, 1926. John J. Coss Papers. Rare Book and Manuscript Library, Columbia University.

Counts, George S. 1932. *Dare the School Build a New Social Order?* New York: John Day.

Cox Commission. 1968. *Crisis at Columbia: The Cox Commission Report.* New York: Vintage.

Cremin, Lawrence A., David A. Shannon, and Mary Evelyn Townsend. 1954. *History of Teachers College, Columbia University.* New York: Columbia University Press.

Croghan, Lore. 2005. "Affordable Housing Disappearing: Mitchell-Lama Woes." *New York Daily News,* August 2, 2005, 46.

Cubberley, Ellwood P. 1916. *Public School Administration.* New York: Houghton Mifflin.

Curthoys, Ann. 1999. "Expulsion, Exodus and Exile in White Australian Historical Mythology." *Journal of Australian Studies* 23(61):1–19.

Curtis, Bruce. 2002. "Foucault on Governmentality and Population: The Impossible Discovery." *Canadian Journal of Sociology* 27(4):505–33.

Daily Worker. 1952. "Manhattanville Tenants Mass at City Hall Today." April 24, 1952, 3.

Davis, Lennard J. J. 1995. *Enforcing Normalcy: Disability Deafness, and the Body.* New York: Verso.

Davis, Mike. 1999. *Ecology of Fear: Los Angeles and the Imagination of Disaster.* New York: Vintage.

Davis, Tracy C. 2007. *Stages of Emergency: Cold War Nuclear Civil Defense.* Durham: Duke University Press.

Day, Jared N. 1999. *Urban Castles.* New York: Columbia University Press.

Deaf-Mutes Journal. 1915. "Fanwood." February 4, 1915, 3.

Degler, Carl. 1991. *In Search of Human Nature: The Decline and Revival of Darwinism in American Social Thought.* New York: Oxford University Press.

Department of City Planning, City of New York. 2008. *197-a Plan for Community District 9: A 197-A Plan as Adopted by the City Planning Commission and the City Council.* Spring 2008. DCP# 08–03.

Dewey, John. 2010. *The Child and the Curriculum; including The School and Society.* New York: Cosmo Classics.

Dinkins, David N. 2007. "Don't Fear Columbia." *New York Times,* May 27, 2007, CY11.

Dolinar, Louis. 1968. "Columbia Abandons Piers Area Project." *Columbia Daily Spectator,* October 17, 1968.

Dolkart, Andrew. 1998. *Morningside Heights: A History of Its Architecture and Development.* New York: Columbia University Press.

———. 2007. *Biography of a Tenement House in New York City: An Architectural History of 97 Orchard Street.* Santa Fe: Center for American Places.

Donadio, Stephen. 1968. "Columbia: Seven Interviews." *Partisan Review* 35(3):366.

Dormon, James H. 1988. "Shaping the Popular Image of Post-Reconstruction American Blacks: The 'Coon Song' Phenomenon of the Gilded Age." *American Quarterly* 40(4):450–71.

Drake, St. Clair, and Horace R. Cayton. 1945. *Black Metropolis: A Study of Negro Life in a Northern City.* New York: Harcourt, Brace.

Drosnin, Michael. 1964. "New Life for Declining Morningside." *Columbia Daily Spectator*, October 5, 1964.

Du Bois, W. E. B. 1899. *The Philadelphia Negro*. Philadelphia: University of Pennsylvania Press.

———. 1910. "Reconstruction and Its Benefits." *American Historical Review* 15(4):781–99.

———. 1919. "Returning Soldier." *The Crisis* 18:9.

———. 1927. W. E. B. Du Bois to Paul Laurence Dunbar Apartments. October 18, 1927. W. E. B. Du Bois Papers (MS 312). Special Collections and University Archives, University of Massachusetts Amherst Libraries.

———. 2000. "Sociology Hesitant." *Boundary 2* 27(3): 37–44.

Dümpelmann, Sonja. 2014. *Flights of Imagination*. Charlottesville: University of Virginia Press.

Dunning, William A. 1901. "The Undoing of Reconstruction." *Atlantic Monthly*, October 1901, 437–49.

Durkin, Erin. 2006. "LDC Defers Land-Use Demands." *Columbia Daily Spectator*, October 31, 2006, 1.

———. 2007. "Expansion Fight Gets Personal." *Columbia Daily Spectator*, September 5, 2007, 1.

Durst, Anne. 2010. *Women Educators in the Progressive Era*. New York: Palgrave Macmillan.

Ealy, Lenore T., and Steven D. Ealy. 2006. "Progressivism and Philanthropy." *Good Society* 15(1):35–42.

Earth Tech Inc. 2008. "Manhattanville Neighborhood Conditions Study." www.documentcloud.org.

Elden, Stuart. 2013. "Secure the Volume: Vertical Geopolitics and the Depth of Power." *Political Geography* 34:35–51.

Elkins, Stanley. 1959. *Slavery: A Problem in American Institutional and Intellectual Life*. Chicago: University of Chicago Press.

Eviatar, Daphne. 2006. "The Manhattanville Project." *New York Times*, May 21, 2006, 33.

Fabian, Johannes. 2014. *Time and the Other: How Anthropology Makes Its Object*. Reprint, New York: Columbia University Press.

Faculty Civil Rights Group. 1967. "The Community and the Expansion of Columbia University." Christine C. Collins Collection of the West Harlem Coalition for Morningside Park and Urban Problems of Contiguous Communities: West Harlem, Manhattan Valley, Morningside Heights and Manhattanville, Sc MG 397, Box 1, Folder 7. Schomburg Center for Research in Black Culture, New York Public Library.

Fanon, Frantz. 1967. *Black Skin, White Masks*. New York: Grove.

Farrar, Margaret E. 2000. "Health and Beauty in the Body Politic: Subjectivity and Urban Space." *Polity* 33(1):1–23.

Farrell, Grace. 2009. *Lillie Devereaux Black: Retracing a Life Erased*. Amherst: University of Massachusetts Press.

Flamm, Michael W. 2017. *In the Heat of the Summer: The New York Riots of 1964 and the War on Crime*. Philadelphia: University of Pennsylvania Press.

Forbes, Camille F. 2008. *Introducing Bert Williams*. New York: Basic Civitas.

Fosdick, Harry Emerson. 1956. *The Living of These Days*. New York: Harper & Brothers.

Foucault, Michel. 1995. *Discipline and Punish: The Birth of the Prison*. 2nd ed. Translated by Alan Sheridan. New York: Vintage.

———. 2003. *Society Must Be Defended: Lectures at the Collège de France*. New York: Picador.

Fowles, Severin. 2010. "People Without Things." In *The Anthropology of Absence*, edited by Mikkel Bille, Frida Hastrup, and Tim Flohr Sørensen. New York: Springer.

Franks, Angela. 2005. *Margaret Sanger's Eugenic Legacy: The Control of Female Fertility*. New York: McFarland.

Fredrickson, George M. 1971. *The Black Image in the White Mind*. Middletown: Wesleyan University Press.

Freire, Paulo. 1970. *Pedagogy of the Oppressed*. New York: Herder and Herder.

Fried, Joseph P. 1968. "Columbia Softens Role in Huge Harlem Project." *New York Times*, October 17, 1968, 28.

Friedman, Robert. 1969. Introduction to *Up Against the Ivy Wall: A History of the Columbia Crisis*, edited by Robert Friedman. New York: Atheneum.

Fullilove, Mindy. 2004. *Root Shock: How Tearing Up City Neighborhoods Hurts America, and What We Can Do About It*. New York: One World/Ballantine.

Gaines, Kevin. 1996. *Uplifting the Race: Black Leadership, Politics, and Culture in the Twentieth Century*. Chapel Hill: University of North Carolina Press.

Gandy, Matthew. 2002. *Concrete and Clay: Reworking Nature in New York City*. Cambridge: MIT Press.

Gates, Frederick T. 1916. *The Country School of To-morrow*. Occasional Papers, No. 1. New York: General Education Board.

Gettleman, Marvin E. 2002. "No Varsity Teams: New York's Jefferson School of Social Science, 1943–1956." *Science & Society* 66(3):336–59.

Giddings, Franklin H. 1896. *Principles of Sociology: An Analysis of the Phenomena of Association and of Social Organization*. New York: Macmillan.

———. 1922. *Studies in the Theory of Human Society*. New York: Macmillan.

Gieryn, Thomas. 1999. *Cultural Boundaries of Science*. Chicago: University of Chicago Press.

Gilder, Richard Watson. 1886. "The Grant Memorial." *Century Illustrated Monthly Magazine* 31.

Gilmore, Ruth Wilson. 2022. *Abolition Geography: Essays Towards Liberation*. Edited by Brenna Bhandar and Alberto Toscano. New York: Verso.

Glanz, James, and Eric Lipton. 2003. *City in the Sky: The Rise and Fall of the World Trade Center*. New York: Times Books.

Glazer, Nathan, and Daniel Patrick Moynihan. 1963. *Beyond the Melting Pot: The Negroes, Puerto Ricans, Jews, Italians, and Irish of New York City*. Cambridge: MIT Press.

Glibertarians. n.d. "Drunk Belligerent White People Day." Accessed November 29, 2019. www.glibertarians.com.

Goffman, Erving. 1961. *Asylums: Essays on the Social Situation of Mental Patients and Other Inmates*. New York: Anchor.

Gold, Roberta. 2009. "'I Had Not Seen Women Like That Before': Intergenerational Feminism in New York City's Tenant Movement." *Feminist Studies* 35(2):387–415.

———. 2014. *When Tenants Claimed the City: The Struggle for Citizenship in New York City Housing*. Urbana: University of Illinois Press.

Goldstein, Brian D. 2017. *The Roots of Urban Renaissance: Gentrification and the Struggle over Harlem*. Cambridge: Harvard University Press.

Gonzalez, Juan. 2007. "Rage Building in Harlem." *New York Daily News*, June 1, 2007.

Gottlieb, Beatrice. 2008. *The Historical Background of Morningside Gardens*. New York: 50th Anniversary Committee, Morningside Heights Housing Corporation.

Graber, Doris. 1976. *Verbal Behavior and Politics*. Urbana: University of Illinois Press.

Graham, Lawrence Otis. 2009. *The Senator and the Socialite*. New York: Harper Perennial.

Graham, Stephen, and Lucy Hewitt. 2012. "Getting Off the Ground." *Progress in Human Geography* 37(1):72–92.

Gregor, Alison. 2006. "Square Feet: Along a Viaduct, a Restaurant Row Emerges." *New York Times*, June 7, 2006.

Gregory, Steven. 1998. *Black Corona: Race and the Politics of Place in an Urban Community*. Princeton: Princeton University Press.

———. 2013. "The Radiant University: Space, Urban Redevelopment, and the Public Good." *City & Society* 25(1):47–69.

Grutzner, Charles. 1959. "Slum Clearance Asked in Big Area Around Columbia." *New York Times*, October 15, 1959.

Gurock, Jeffrey S. 2016. *The Jews of Harlem*. New York: New York University Press.

Guttenplan, G. G. 1989. "Who Killed Bruce Bailey?" *Newsday*, July 16, 1989, 4.

Hacking, Ian. 1982. "Biopower and the Avalanche of Printed Numbers." In *Biopower*, edited by Vernon W. Cisney and Nicolae Morar. Chicago: University of Chicago Press.

Hall, Edward H. 1922. *A Guide to the Cathedral Church of St. John the Divine in the City of New York*. New York: Cathedral Church of St. John the Divine.

Hall, Stuart, et al. (1978) 2013. *Policing the Crisis: Mugging, the State, and Law and Order*. London: Red Globe Press.

Hamilton, Charles V. 1968. "Black Power: A Discussion." *Partisan Review* 35(2):204.

Hardman, Robert. 1967. "Faculty Group Hopes GNRP Will Save Local Integration." *Columbia Daily Spectator*, March 24, 1967, 1.

Harrington, Michael. (1962) 1997. *The Other America: Poverty in the United States*. New York: Touchstone.

Harris, Andrew. 2015. "Vertical Urbanisms: Opening Up Geographies of the Three-Dimensional City." *Progress in Human Geography* 39(5):601–20.

Harris, Leslie M. 2004. *In the Shadow of Slavery: African Americans in New York City, 1626–1863*. Chicago: University of Chicago Press.

Hart, William David. 2018. "Constellations: Capitalism, AntiBlackness, Afro-Pessimism, and Black Optimism." *American Journal of Theology & Philosophy* 39(1):5–33.

Hartocollis, Anemona. 2007. "Neutrality in Expansion by Columbia Is Questioned." *New York Times*, June 30, 2007, B2.

Haynes, George Edmund. 1912. *The Negro at Work in New York City*. New York: Columbia University, Longmans, Green.

———. 1913. "Conditions Among Negroes in the Cities." *Annals of the American Academy of Political and Social Science* 49:105–19.

Hechinger, Fred. 1961. "Columbia Plans Huge Expansion." *New York Times*, April 6, 1961, 1.

Hepner, Elizabeth R. 1955. *Morningside-Manhattanville Rebuilds: A Chronological Account of Redevelopment in the Morningside-Manhattanville Area*. New York: Morningside Heights, Inc.

Hermalyn, Gary. 1983. "The Harlem River Ship Canal." *Bronx County Historical Society Journal* 20(1).

Hevesi, Dennis. 1989. "Police Are Puzzled by Tenant Advocate's Slaying." *New York Times*, August 17, 1989, B5.

Hickman, Christine B. 1997. "The Devil and the One Drop Rule: Racial Categories, African-Americans, and the US Census." *Michigan Law Review* 95(5):1161–1265.

Hicks, Cheryl D. 2010. *Talk with You Like a Woman: African American Women, Justice, and Reform in New York, 1890–1935*. Chapel Hill: University of North Carolina Press.

Hirsch, Arnold. 1983. *Making the Second Ghetto: Race and Housing in Chicago, 1940–1960*. Cambridge: Cambridge University Press.

hooks, bell. 2014. *Ain't I a Woman: Black Women and Feminism*. New York: Routledge.

Hubert, James H. 1970. *Profiles of Adventure: Transcripts of Negro Heritage*. Introduction by Benjamin E. Mays. New York: Vintage.

Hudnut-Beumler, James. 2004. "The Riverside Church and the Development of Twentieth-Century American Protestantism." In *The History of the Riverside Church in the City of New York*, edited by Peter J. Paris, John W. Cook, et al. New York: New York University Press.

Hughes, C. J. 2011. "Hamilton Heights: Awaiting a Bounce." *New York Times*, June 10, 2011.

Humphreys, James S. 2013. "William Archibald Dunning: Flawed Colossus of American Letters." In *The Dunning School: Historians, Race, and the Meaning of Reconstruction*, edited by John David Smith and J. Vincent Lowery. Lexington: University Press of Kentucky.

Huxtable, Ada Louise. 1968a. "How Not to Build a Symbol." *New York Times*, March 24, 1968, D23.

———. 1968b. "Strike at Columbia Architecture School Traced to Anger over Exclusion from Planning." *New York Times*, May 20, 1968.

Ignatiev, Noel. 1995. *How the Irish Became White*. New York: Routledge.

Jacobs, Jane. 1961. *The Death and Life of Great American Cities*. New York: Vintage Random House.

Jacobson, Matthew Frye. 1999. *Whiteness of a Different Color*. Cambridge: Harvard University Press.

James, Joy. 1996. *Resisting State Violence: Radicalism, Gender and Race in US Culture*. Minneapolis: University of Minnesota Press.

Jarosinki, Eric. 2002. "Architectural Symbolism and the Rhetoric of Transparency: A Berlin Ghost Story." *Journal of Urban History* 29(1):62–77.

Johnson, Donald. 2000. "W. E. B. Du Bois, Thomas Jesse Jones and the Struggle for Social Education, 1900–1930." *Journal of Negro History* 85(3):71–95.

Jones, James H. 1981. *Bad Blood: The Tuskegee Syphilis Experiment*. New York: Free Press.

Jones, Thomas Jesse. 1904. *The Sociology of a New York City Block*. New York: Columbia University Press.

———. 1906. "Social Studies in the Hampton Curriculum: Economics and Social Welfare." *Southern Workman* 35(2):111–16.

———. 1916. *Negro Education: A Study of the Private and Higher Schools for Colored People in the United States*. Washington: Bulletin.

Kahn, David M. 1980. *General Grant National Memorial Historical Resource Study*. National Park Service History Electronic Library and Archive. http://npshistory.com.

Kaplan, Samuel. 1965a. "Angry Group of 9 at Columbia to Protest Morningside Allusion." *New York Times*, May 4, 1965, 45.

———. 1965b. "Uptown Renewal Given Go-Ahead." *New York Times*, April 23, 1965, 1.

Katz, Esther. 1980. "Grace Hoadley Dodge: Women and the Emerging Metropolis, 1856–1914." Doctoral dissertation, New York University.

Kaur v. Empire State Development Corporation. 2009. 892 N.Y.S. 2d 8, 15. Appellate Division.

Kelley, Robin D. G. 1996. *Race Rebels: Culture, Politics, and the Black Working Class*. New York: Free Press.

———. 2009. *Thelonius Monk: The Life and Times of an American Original*. New York: Free Press.

Kelsey, Carl. 1916. *The Physical Basis of Society*. New York: D. Appleton.

Kennedy, Albert Joseph, and Robert Archey Woods, eds. 1911. *Handbook of Settlements*. New York: Charities Publication Committee. http://archive.org.

Kent, Ernest B. 1904. "Interrelations of School and Neighborhood Work in the Speyer School." *Teachers College Record* 5(3):44–60.

Kern, Leslie. 2016. "Rhythms of Gentrification." *Cultural Geographies* 23(3):441–57.

Kihss, Peter. 1968a. "City Will Consult on Columbia Plan." *New York Times*, May 15, 1968.

———. 1968b. "Columbia Spurs Massive Renewal North of 125th Street." *New York Times*, May 14, 1968, 1.

King, Shannon. 2017. *Whose Harlem Is This, Anyway?* New York: New York University Press.

Knorr Cetina, Karin. 1981. *The Manufacture of Knowledge.* Oxford: Pergamon.

———. 1982. "Scientific Communities or Transepistemic Arenas of Research? A Critique of Quasi-Economic Models of Science." *Social Studies of Science* 23(1):101–30.

Konishi, Shino. 2018. "Crossing Boundaries: Tracing Indigenous Mobility and Territory in the Exploration of South-Eastern Australia." In *Indigenous Mobilities*, edited by Rachel Standfield. Canberra: ANU Press.

Kopel, Jerry. 1969. "Reaction to Poll on Gym Is Mixed." *Columbia Daily Spectator*, February 18, 1969.

Kristeva, Julia, and John Lechte. 1982. "Approaching Abjection." *Oxford Literary Review* 5(1–2):125–49.

Kurland, Roselle. 1966. "Morningside Heights: A Portrait." *Barnard Alumnae* 55(3).

Laats, Adam. 2015. *The Other School Reformers.* Cambridge: Harvard University Press.

Laclau, Ernesto, and Chantal Mouffe. 1985. *Hegemony and Socialist Strategy.* New York: Verso.

Lagemann, Ellen Condliffe. 2000. *An Elusive Science: The Troubling History of Educational Research.* Chicago: University of Chicago Press.

Lamb, Martha J. 1886. *The Guide for Strangers to General Grant's Tomb.* New York: J. J. Little.

Landmarks Preservation Commission. 1970. Report on public hearing. July 14, 1974. http://s-media.nyc.gov.

Lane, Ann J., ed. 1971. *The Debate over Slavery: Stanley Elkins and His Critics.* Urbana: University of Illinois Press.

Lasner, Matthew Gordon. 2016. "Paul Laurence Dunbar Apartments." In *Affordable Housing in New York*, edited by Nicholas Dagen Bloom and Matthew Gordon Lasner. Princeton: Princeton University Press.

Law, John. 2009. "Actor Network Theory and Material Semiotics." In *The New Blackwell Companion to Social Theory*, edited by Bryan S. Turner. Oxford: Blackwell.

Lefebvre, Henri. 1992. *The Production of Space.* New York: Wiley-Blackwell.

Lemke, Thomas. 2011. *Biopolitics: An Advanced Introduction.* New York: New York University Press.

Leone, Massimo. 2014. "Wrapping Transcendence: The Semiotics of Reliquaries." *Signs and Society* 2(S1):49–83.

Levi, Scott. 2008a. "Admin. Endorses 1968 Commemorations." *Columbia Daily Spectator*, January 22, 2008.

———. 2008b. "Money, Words Fly in Heated Public Relations Battle." *Columbia Daily Spectator*, January 22, 2008.

Lincoln, Richard. 1953. "Review Plan to Increase Jim Crow, Cut Negro Vote: Evict 150,000 Harlemites in 5 Years." *Amsterdam News*, April 11, 1953, 7.

Lipsitz, George. 1995. "The Possessive Investment in Whiteness." *American Quarterly* 47(3):369–87.

Locke, Alain, ed. (1925) 1999. *The New Negro: Voices of the Harlem Renaissance.* New York: Touchstone.

Lott, Eric. 1992. "Love and Theft: The Racial Unconscious of Blackface Minstrelsy." *Representations* 39:23–50.

Loukaki, Argyro. 1997. "Whose Genius Loci?" *Annals of the Association of American Geographers* 87(2):306–29.

Low, Seth. 1891. "Report to the Board of Trustees from the Committee on Site." December 3, 1891. Building and Grounds Collection, Series III, Box 4, folder 1. Columbia University Archives.

Lucero, George W. 2009. "New College, Teachers College, Columbia University: A Demonstration Experimental Teachers College, 1932–1939." Doctoral dissertation, Illinois State University.

Luetkemeyer, Joseph F. 1985. "The Social Settlement Movement and Industrial Arts Education." *Journal of Epsilon Pi Tau* 2(1):97–103.

Mahar, William J. 1988. "'Backside Albany' and Early Blackface Minstrelsy: A Contextual Study of America's First Blackface Song." *American Music* 6(1):1–27.

Mamiya, Lawrence H. 2004. "Congregations Within a Congregation: Contemporary Spirituality and Change at the Riverside Church." In *The History of the Riverside Church in the City of New York*, edited by Peter J. Paris, John W. Cook, et al. New York: New York University Press.

Manhattan East Side Alternative Study. 1999. *Major Investment Study/Draft Environmental Impact Study*. New York: US Department of Transportation and MTA/New York City Transit Authority.

Marx, Karl. 1963. *The Eighteenth Brumaire of Louis Bonaparte*. New York: International Publishers.

Mayor's Committee for Better Housing of the City of New York. 1955. "Report of the Subcommittee on Problems of Relocation of Persons Displaced by New Housing and Other Public Improvements." June 1955.

Mayo-Smith, Richmond. 1890. *Emigration and Immigration: A Study in Social Science*. New York: Scribner's.

———. 1898. *Emigration and Immigration*. New York: Scribner's.

Mazón, Mauricio. 2010. *The Zoot-Suit Riots: The Psychology of Symbolic Annihilation*. Austin: University of Texas Press.

Mbembe, Achille. 2003. "Necropolitics." *Public Culture* 15(1):11–40.

McAdoo, William. 1906. *Guarding a Great City*. New York: Harper and Brothers.

McCarthy, Mary Rose, and Sonia Murrow. 2013. "Racial Inequality and the Social Reconstructionists at Teachers College." *Journal of Negro Education* 82(1):20–34.

McCaughey, Robert A. 2003. *Stand, Columbia*. New York: Columbia University Press.

McGruder, Kevin. 2015. *Race and Real Estate: Conflict and Cooperation in Harlem, 1890–1920*. New York: Columbia University Press.

McKay, George L., Jr. 1943. "Spectator Survey Polls Faculty Opinion on Significance of Recent Harlem Riots." *Columbia Daily Spectator*, August 13, 1943, 1.

McKittrick, Katherine. 2006. *Demonic Grounds: Black Women and the Cartographies of Struggle*. Minneapolis: University of Minnesota Press.

McMurry, F. M. 1904. "Experimental Work in Elementary Schools." *Teachers College Record* 5(3):1–3.

McMurry, F. M., C. H. Farnsworth, and T. D. Wood. 1902. "Controlling Ideas in the Curriculum of Kindergarten and Elementary School." *Teachers College Record* 3(5):45–61.

McQuire, Scott. 2003. "From Glass Architecture to Big Brother." *Cultural Studies Review* 9(1):103–23.

Menand, Louis. 2001. *The Metaphysical Club: A Story of Ideas in America*. New York: Farrar, Straus and Giroux.

Miller, Alice Duer, and Susan Myers. 1939. *Barnard College: The First Fifty Years*. New York: Columbia University Press.

Miller, Robert Moats. 1985. *Harry Emerson Fosdick: Preacher, Pastor, Prophet*. Oxford: Oxford University Press.

Mills, Charles W. 2008. "Racial Liberalism." *PMLA* 123(5):1380–97.

Minutes of the Committee on Site. 1891. Building and Grounds Collection, Series III, Box 4, folder 1. Columbia University Archives.

Moga, Steven T. 2020. *Urban Lowlands: A History of Neighborhoods, Poverty, and Planning*. Chicago: University of Chicago Press.

Monthly Labor Review. 1932. "Housing." 34(1): 110–33.

Moore, Burness E., and Bernard D. Fine. 1990. *Psychoanalytic Terms and Concepts*. New Haven: Yale University Press.

Morais, Betsy. 2008a. "Columbia's Relationship to Harlem Then and Now." *Columbia Daily Spectator*, April 23, 2008, 6.

———. 2008b. "Strained Relationship with Community over Manhattanville Expansion Reminds Some of 1968 Controversies." *Columbia Daily Spectator*, January 22, 2008, 6.

Morningside Heights, Inc. 1959. *Morningside Heights*. New York: MHI.

Morris, Aldon. 2015. *The Scholar Denied: W. E. B. Du Bois and the Birth of Modern Sociology*. Los Angeles: University of California Press.

Morrison, Matthew D. 2017. "The Sound(s) of Subjection: Constructing American Popular Music and Racial Identity Through Blacksound." *Women and Performance* 27(1):13–24.

Morshed, Adnan. 2004. "The Aesthetics of Ascension in Norman Bel Geddes's Futurama." *Journal of the Society of Architectural Historians* 63(1):74–99.

Moynihan, Daniel P. 1965. *The Negro Family: The Case for National Action*. Washington, DC: US Department of Labor.

Muller, Edward K., and Paul A. Groves. 1979. "The Emergence of Industrial Districts in Mid-Nineteenth Century Baltimore." *Geographical Review* 69(2):159–78.

Naison, Mark. 1984. *Communists in Harlem During the Depression*. Urbana: University of Illinois Press.

National Commission on Urban Problems. 1968. *Hearings Before the National Commission on Urban Problems*. Vol. 4, September 1967. Washington, DC: Government Printing Office.

Nelson, George F. 1916. "Progress of the Cathedral's Development." In *Cathedral of Saint John the Divine*. New York: St. Bartholomew's Press.

Newman, Oscar. 1972. *Defensible Space: Crime Prevention Through Urban Design*. New York: Macmillan.

New York City Mayor's Commission of the Conditions in Harlem. 1936. *The Negro in Harlem: A Report on Social and Economic Conditions Responsible for the Outbreak of March 19, 1935*. New York: NYC Mayor's Commission of the Conditions in Harlem.

New York Herald Tribune. 1895. "Training at Handball: There Is a Good Court at Manhattanville and Exciting Games Are Played in It." April 14, 1895, 4.

———. 1900. "Cassidy and the Census: A Conscientious Effort to Aid the Enumerator." June 17, 1900, A1.

———. 1933. "Vast Relief Plan Formulated for Manhattanville." April 26, 1933, 16.

———. 1937. "Harlem Eviction Riot Jails One for Assault." February 21, 1937, 4.

———. 1943a. "Curfew in Harlem Relaxed to 11:30." August 4, 1943, 8.

———. 1943b. "Harlem Peaceful Again After Riots; Guard Mobilized: Quiet Is Restored." August 3, 1943, 1A.

———. 1943c. "Leaders Blame Trouble on Rise in Harlem Costs." August 3, 1943, 7.

———. 1943d. "Negro 'Freedom Rally' in Garden Draws 20,000." June 8, 1943, 21A.

———. 1943e. "Negro Pastor Says US Faces Post-War Peril of Race Conflict." February 25, 1943, 17.

———. 1948. "Manhattanville Neighborhood Center Moving to a New Home." March 19, 1948, 17.

———. 1958. "11 Buildings Show 1,000 Violations." December 4, 1958, 22.

New York School of Philanthropy. 1909. *Bulletin*, Summer Session, 58.

New York State Legislature. 1888. *Documents of the Senate of the State of New York*. Vol. 5.

New York Times. 1889. "Prejudices of Landlords." April 14, 1889, 10.

———. 1895. "Equality by Legislation." June 30, 1895, 20.

———. 1900a. "Census Count Soon Ends: Manhattan and Bronx Enumeration Must Be Complete by Friday." June 11, 1900.

———. 1900b. "Mrs. Eppright Humble Now." June 19, 1900, 9.

———. 1902. "Wife Jumped from Window." December 27, 1902, 2.

———. 1903. "Tenements—Average Earnings of Women Home Workers $3.20 a Week." February 23, 1903, 5.

———. 1904. "Boys Run Speyer City." February 8, 1904, 7.

———. 1905. "New York's Recreation Piers Well Worth Their Cost." June 25, 1905.

———. 1925a. "Propose Rockefeller Jr. as Cathedral Trustee." May 6, 1925, 1.

———. 1925b. "Rockefeller, Jr. Buys Plot Uptown." May 26, 1925, 8.

———. 1925c. "Rockefeller Seeks Union in Cathedral." February 7, 1925, 4.

———. 1926. "Baptists Approve $4,000,000 Plans for Fosdick Church." December 27, 1926.

———. 1935. "$4,700,000 Housing Planned in Harlem." July 3, 1935, 1.

———. 1938. "Doherty Says Reds Smirch Columbia." July 22, 1938, 1.

———. 1943a. "Negro Councilman Warns Mayor of the Danger of Race Riots Here." June 25, 1943, 8.

———. 1943b. "Riots in Harlem Analyzed." August 6, 1943, 14.

———. 1948. "Manhattanville to Dedicate Center." March 19, 1948, 27.

———. 1953. "Bomb Threat Cited in City Slum Areas." October 13, 1953, 50.

———. 1957. "Columbia Applies to Oust Tenants." July 12, 1957, 22.

———. 1962a. "Institutions Buy West Side Hotel." July 12, 1962, 25.

———. 1962b. "Ruling on Hotel Delays Eviction." January 11, 1962, 25.

———. 1967. "Columbia Offers Harlem a Pool, but Gym Proposal Is Assailed." July 30, 1967, 64.

———. 1968. "121 More Arrests at Columbia." May 19, 1968, 22.

———. 1969. "Columbia Trustees Scrap the Gym-in-Park Plan." March 4, 1969, 28.

New York Tribune. 1910. "Material Progress of the Colored Citizens of Gotham." August 14, 1910, 10.

Nixon, Rob. 2011. *Slow Violence and the Environmentalism of the Poor.* Cambridge: Harvard University Press.

O'Kane, Lawrence. 1965. "Morningside Tenants Protest Renewal at City Hall Hearing." *New York Times,* March 12, 1965, 17.

Olmstead, Dwight H. 1886. *Land Transfer Reform, or, The Free Transfer of Land.* New York: Evening Post.

Opportunity. 1926. "Survey of the Month, Housing." *Opportunity* 4(44):263.

Osofsky, Gilbert. 1996. *Harlem: The Making of a Ghetto, 1890–1930.* New York: Ivan R. Dee.

Ovington, Mary White. 1911. *Half a Man: The Status of the Negro in New York.* New York: Longmans, Green.

Park, Robert E., and Ernest W. Burgess, eds. 1925. *The City: Suggestions of Investigation of Human Behavior in the Urban Environment.* Chicago: University of Chicago Press.

Parton, Margaret. 1955. "Our Lawless Youth: A Picture of the City's Social Agencies at Work Trying to Substitute for Defaulting Parents." *New York Herald Tribune,* June 8, 1955, 1.

Pels, Dick. 1995. "Knowledge Politics and Anti-Politics: Towards a Critical Appraisal of Bourdieu's Concept of Intellectual Autonomy." *Theory and Society* 24(1):79–104.

Perlman, Daniel. 1972. "Stirring the White Conscience: The Life of George Edmund Haynes." Doctoral dissertation, New York University.

Pessen, Edward. 1985. *Jacksonian America: Society, Personality, and Politics.* Urbana: University of Illinois Press.

Peterson, Jon A. 1979. "The Impact of Sanitary Reform upon American Urban Planning." *Journal of Social History* 13(1):83–103.

Philips, Wayne. 1958. "Slums Engulfing Columbia Section." *New York Times,* June 9, 1958, 25.

Phillips, Anna. 2007a. "LDC Criticized at Public Forum." *Columbia Daily Spectator,* March 28, 2007, 1.

———. 2007b. "Students Declare South Lawn Blighted." *Columbia Daily Spectator,* February 20, 2007.

Piano, Renzo. 2017. "Manhattanville: Reflections on a 21st-Century Campus." *Columbia Magazine*, Spring 2017. https://magazine.columbia.edu.

Piccone, Paul. 1978. "Culture and Politics in the Age of Artificial Negativity." *Telos*, no.5:56–72.

Pommer, Richard. 1978. "The Architecture of Urban Housing in the United States During the Early 1930s." *Journal of the Society of Architectural Historians* 37(4):235–64.

Powell, Walter, and Kaisa Snellman. 2004. "The Knowledge Economy." *Annual Review of Sociology* 30:199–220.

Prager, Lois. 1967. "PS 125 Boycott Involves 1700 Pupils." *Columbia Daily Spectator*, March 14, 1967, 1.

Price, Robert E. 1973. "Columbia: Turning the University Around." In *The University and the City: Eight Cases of Involvement*, edited by George Nash et al. New York: McGraw-Hill.

Pritchett, Wendell E. 2003. "The 'Public Menace' of Blight: Urban Renewal and the Private Uses of Eminent Domain." *Yale Public Law and Policy Review* 21(1):1–52.

Pulido, Laura. 2000. "Rethinking Environmental Racism: White Privilege and Urban Development in Southern California." *Annals of the Association of American Geographers* 90(1): 12–40.

Punz, Richard. 2016. *A History of Housing in New York City*. New York: Columbia University Press.

Raab, David. 1973. "600 Heights Residents Join Union of Columbia Tenants." *Columbia Daily Spectator*, October 5, 1973, 1.

Radford, Gail. 1996. *Modern Housing for America: Policy Struggles in the New Deal Era*. Chicago: University of Chicago Press.

Rainwater, Lee, and William L. Yancey. 1967. *The Moynihan Report and the Politics of Controversy*. Cambridge: MIT Press.

Raskin, Eleanor. 1985. "The Occupation of Columbia University: April 1968." *Journal of American Studies* 19(2):255–60.

Real Estate Record and Builders' Guide. 1900. "The Distribution of the Negro." *Real Estate Record and Builders' Guide* 65(1677):762.

Recchiuti, John Louis. 2007. *Civic Engagement: Social Science and Progressive-Era Reform in New York City*. Philadelphia: University of Pennsylvania Press.

Reed, Touré F. 2008. *Not Alms but Opportunity*. Chapel Hill: University of North Carolina Press.

Reitano, Joanne. 2010. *The Restless City*. New York: Routledge.

Repko, Melissa. 2007. "CPC Approves M'Ville Plan." *Columbia Daily Spectator*, November 27, 2007.

Ridgeway, James. 1968. "Columbia's Real Estate Ventures." *New Republic*, May 18, 1968.

Riker, James. (1881) 1904. *Revised History of Harlem (City of New York): Its Origin and Early Annals*. New York: New Harlem Pub.

Rios, Jodi. 2020. *Black Lives and Spatial Matters: Policing Blackness and Practicing Freedom in Suburban St. Louis*. Ithaca, NY: Cornell University Press.

Riverside Church. 1931. *The Riverside Church in the City of New York: A Handbook of the Institution and Its Building*. Philadelphia: Franklin Print Co.

Roberts, Dorothy. 1997. *Killing the Black Body: Race, Reproduction, and the Meaning of Liberty*. New York: Pantheon.

Robertson, Nancy Marie. 2007. *Christian Sisterhood, Race Relations, and the YWCA, 1906–46*. Urbana: University of Illinois Press.

Rockefeller, David. 2003. *Memoirs*. New York: Random House.

Rockefeller, John D., Sr. 1909. "Some Random Reminiscences of Men and Events." In *A History of Our Time*, edited by Walter Hines Page and Arthur Wilson Page. New York: Doubleday, Page.

Rodenstein, Louis A. 1865. "Twenty-Eighth Sanitary Inspection District." In *Report of the Council of Hygiene and Public Health of the Citizens' Association of New York upon the Sanitary Condition of the City*. New York: D. Appleton.

Roediger, David R. 1991. *The Wages of Whiteness: Race and the Making of the American Working Class*. New York: Verso.

Rose, Kenneth W. 2008. "Partners in Housing Reform: The Apartment Developments of John D. Rockefeller, Jr. Charles O. Heydt, and Andrew J. Thomas." Paper presented at the conference on New York History, Cooperstown, NY.

Rosen, Christine. 2004. *Preaching Eugenics: Religious Leaders and the American Eugenics Movement*. Oxford: Oxford University Press.

Rosenberg, Rosalind. 2004. *Changing the Subject: How the Women of Columbia Shaped the Way We Think about Sex and Politics*. New York: Columbia University Press.

Rosenkranz, Richard. 1971. *Across the Barriers*. Philadelphia: Lippincott.

Rosenthal, Michael. 2006. *Nicholas Miraculous*. New York: Farrar, Straus and Giroux.

Rosenwaike, Ira. 1972. *Population History of New York City*. Syracuse: Syracuse University Press.

Rosenzweig, Roy, and Elizabeth Blackmar. 1992. *The Park and the People: A History of Central Park*. Cornell: Cornell University Press.

Rosner, David. 1982. *A Once Charitable Enterprise*. Cambridge: Cambridge University Press.

Ross, Dorothy. 1991. *The Origins of American Social Science*. Cambridge: Cambridge University Press.

Ross, Edward A. 1901. "The Causes of Racial Superiority." *Annals of the American Academy of Political and Social Science* 18(1):67–89.

Ruppert, Evelyn S. 2008. "'I Is; Therefore I Am': The Census as Practice of Double Identification." *Sociological Research Online* 13(4): 69–81.

Russell, James E. 1902. "The Purpose of the Speyer School." *Teachers College Record* 3(5):4.

———. 1905. "Discussion on How to Fit Industrial Training into Our Course of Study." *Department Bulletin*, No. 3. University of the State of New York. Albany: New York State Education Department.

Sacks, Marcy S. 2006. *Before Harlem: The Black Experience in New York City Before World War I*. Philadelphia: University of Pennsylvania Press.

Said, Edward. 1995. *Orientalism*. New York: Penguin.

Salkin, Allen. 2008. "Vital Signs Under the Viaduct." *New York Times*, October 19, 2008.

Salmen, Stanley. 1961. "Public Safety on Morningside Heights." April 17, 1961. Stanley Salmen Files. Central Files, Columbia University.

Samuels, Gertrude. 1950. "Community at Work: A Lesson for Others." *New York Times Magazine*, August 6, 1950.

———. 1955. "Rebirth of a Community." *New York Times Magazine*, September 25, 1955.

Sand, Alexa. 2020. "The Fine Art of Dying." In *Quid Est Sacramentum? Visual Representation of Sacred Mysteries in Early Modern Europe, 1400–1700*, edited by Walter S. Melion et al. Leiden: Brill.

Santora, Ellen. 1999. "Historiographic Perspectives of Context and Progress During a Half Century of Progressive Educational Reform." *Education and Culture* 16(1):1–15.

Saxon, Wolfgang. 2003. "Gertrude Samuels, 93, Photojournalist and Writer in Many Genres." *New York Times*, July 5, 2003.

Schambra, William A. 2013. "Philanthropy's Original Sin." *New Atlantis* 39:3–21.

Schenkel, Albert F. 1990. *The Rich Man and the Kingdom: John D. Rockefeller, Jr., and the Protestant Establishment, 1900–1960*. Cambridge: Harvard University Press.

Schramm, Katharina. 2011. "Landscapes of Violence." *History and Memory* 23(1):5–22.

Schreiber, Laura. 2007. "Six Students Begin Hunger Strike Today." *Columbia Daily Spectator*, November 8, 2007, 1.

Schwartz, Joel. 1986. "Tenant Power in the Liberal City, 1943–1971." In *The Tenant Movement in New York City, 1904–1984*, edited by Ronald Lawson. New Brunswick: Rutgers University Press.

———. 1993. *The New York Approach: Robert Moses, Urban Liberals, and Redevelopment of the Inner City*. Columbus: Ohio State University Press.

Schweik, Susan M. 2009. *The Ugly Laws*. New York: New York University Press.

Scott, James. 1999. *Seeing Like a State*. New Haven: Yale University Press.

Seavoy, Ronald E. 1972. "Laws to Encourage Manufacturing: New York Policy and the 1811 General Incorporation Statute." *Business History Review* 46(1):85–95.

Seely, Bruce. 1981. "Blast Furnace Technology in the Mid-19th Century: A Case Study of the Adirondack Iron and Steel Company." *Journal of the Society for Industrial Archaeology* 7(1):27–54.

Seigfried, Charlene H. 1999. "Socializing Democracy: Jane Addams and John Dewey." *Philosophy of the Social Sciences* 29(2): 207–30.

Sennett, Richard. 1996. *Flesh and Stone: The Body and the City in Western Civilization*. Rev. ed. New York: Norton.

Shabazz, Rashad. 2015. *Spatializing Blackness: Architectures of Confinement and Black Masculinity in Chicago*. Champaign: University of Illinois Press.

Shah, Nayan. 2001. *Contagious Divides: Epidemics and Race in San Francisco's Chinatown*. Los Angeles: University of California Press.

Shockley, Evie. 2010. "The Haunted Houses of New Orleans: Gothic Homelessness and African American Experience." In *Katrina's Imprint*, edited by Keith Wailoo et al. New Brunswick: Rutgers University Press.

Simon, Anekwe. 1972. "City, State Said to Team Up to Obstruct 125th St. Housing Plan." *Amsterdam News*, March 11, 1972, A5.

Slonecker, Blake. 2006. "The Politics of Space: Student Communes, Political Counter-culture, and the Columbia University Protest of 1968." Master's thesis, University of North Carolina.

Small, Albion. 1896. "Review of *The Principles of Sociology* by Franklin Giddings." *American Journal of Sociology* 2:288–305.

Snyder, Agnes. 1936. *Area No. 14: A Study of an Urban Area*. New York: New College.

Soyer, David. 1961. "Reaching Problem Families Through Settlement-Based Casework." *Social Work* 6(3):36–42.

Spillers, Hortense J. 1987. "Mama's Baby, Papa's Maybe: An American Grammar Book." *Diacritics* 17(2):64–81.

Stabler, Walter. 1905. "Development of the West Side." *Real Estate Record and Builders' Guide* 7(1921).

Starr, Roger. 1968. "The Case of the Columbia Gym." *Public Interest*, no 13:102–21.

Stemple, Forrest W. 1949. "Education." *Educational Forum* 13(2):242–43.

Stern, Michael. 1968. "Tenant Group Seizes 114th St. Apartment House in Protest Against Columbia's Expansion Policy." *Columbia Daily Spectator*, May 18, 1968, 1.

Stern, Robert A. M., Thomas Mellins, and David Fishman. 1995. *New York 1960: Architecture and Urbanism Between the Second World War and the Bicentennial*. New York: Monacelli.

Straus, Lina Gutherz. 1917. *Disease in Milk: The Remedy, Pasteurization: The Life Work of Nathan Straus*. New York: Dutton.

Stromquist, Shelton. 2006. *Reinventing "the People": The Progressive Movement, the Class Problem, and the Origins of Modern Liberalism*. Urbana: University of Illinois Press.

Strong, J. A. 1990. *The Cathedral of St. John the Divine in New York City*. Doctoral dissertation, Brown University.

Strong, Josiah. 1885. *Our Country: Its Possible Future and Its Present Crisis*. New York: American Home Missionary Society.

Stulberg, Robert. 1968. "Protesters Say They Will Not Negotiate Until CU Grants Disciplinary Amnesty." *Columbia Daily Spectator*, April 24, 1968, 1–3.

Suddler, Carl. 2019. *Black Youth and the Justice System in Postwar New York*. New York: New York University Press.

Swackhamer, Conrad. 1858. "Hon. Daniel F. Tiemann, Mayor of the City of New York." *United States Democratic Review*, n.s. 42:420–36.

Szajkowski, Zosa. 1978. "Deportation of Jewish Immigrants and Returnees Before World War I." *American Jewish Historical Quarterly* 67(4):291–306.

Szczygiel, Bonj, and Robert R. Hewitt. 2000. "Nineteenth-Century Medical Landscapes." *Bulletin of the History of Medicine* 74(4):708–34.

Taylor, Clarence. 2013. "Race, Class, and Police Brutality in New York City: The Role of the Communist Party in the Early Cold War Years." *Journal of African American History* 98(2):205–28.

Taylor, Henry Louis, Jr., D. Gavin Luter, and Camden Miller. 2018. "The University, Neighborhood Revitalization, and Civic Engagement: Toward Civic Engagement 3.0." *Societies* 8(4):1–21.

Thomas, Julian. 1993. "The Politics of Vision and Archaeologies of Landscape." In *Landscapes: Politics and Perspectives*, edited by Barbara Bender. Oxford: Berg.

Tilley, Christopher. 2006. "Introduction: Identity, Place, Landscape and Heritage." *Journal of Material Culture* 11(1–2):7–32.

———. 2017. *Landscape in the Longue Durée: A History and Theory of Pebbles in a Pebbled Heathland Landscape*. Los Angeles: University of California Press.

Toepfer, Kenneth H. 1966. "James Earl Russell and the Rise of Teachers College, 1897–1915." Doctoral dissertation, Columbia University.

Townsend, Mary Evelyn. 1954. *A History of Teachers College of Columbia University*. New York: Columbia University Press.

Trouillot, Michel-Rolph. 2004. *Global Transformations*. New York: Palgrave Macmillan.

Tuck-It-Away v. ESDC. 2009. Accessed February 21, 2021. www.cato.org.

Ture, Kwame, and Charles V. Hamilton. (1967) 2011. *Black Power: The Politics of Liberation*. New York: Vintage.

Turner, Stephen. 1991. "The World of the Academic Quantifiers: The Columbia University Family and Its Connections." In *The Social Survey in Historical Perspective*, edited by Martin Bulmer, Kevin Bales, and Kathryn Kish Sklar. Cambridge: Cambridge University Press.

Tyack, David. 1974. *The One Best System: A History of American Urban Education*. Cambridge: Harvard University Press.

US Bureau of Labor Statistics. n.d. CPI Inflation Calculator. https://data.bls.gov.

US Census Bureau. 1880. Census Place: New York City, New York, New York. Enumeration district 530. Roll 892.

———. 1900a. "1900 Census Instructions to Enumerators." June 1, 1900.

———. 1900b. Federal Census. Census Place: Manhattan, New York, New York. Enumeration district 0611. FHL microfilm 1241108.

———. 1900c. Federal Census. Census Place: Manhattan, New York, New York. Enumeration district 0851. FHL microfilm 1241119.

———. 1910a. "1910 Instructions to Enumerators." April 15, 1910.

———. 1910b. Federal Census. Census Place: Manhattan Ward 12, New York, New York. Enumeration district 0303. Roll T624_1013. FHL microfilm 1375026.

———. 1910c. Federal Census. Census Place: Manhattan Ward 12, New York, New York. Enumeration district 0536. Roll T624_1022. FHL microfilm 1375035.

———. 1910d. Census Place: New Rochelle Ward 1, Westchester, New York. Enumeration district 0079. Roll T624_1091. FHL microfilm 1375104.

———. 1993. "1860 Census Instructions to Enumerators." December 23, 1993.

Valverde, Mariana. 2011. "Seeing Like a City: The Dialectic of Modern and Premodern Ways of Seeing in Urban Governance." *Law & Society Review* 45(2):277–312.

Van Dusen, John G. 1954. "Morningside Heights, Inc." Senior thesis, Princeton University.

Village Voice. 2008. "Hurricane Klaus." October 1, 2008, 21–24.

Wallace, Deborah, and Rodrick Wallace. 2001. *A Plague on Your Houses: How New York Was Burned Down and National Public Health Crumbled.* New York: Verso.

Wallace, Mike. 2017. *Greater Gotham.* Vol. 2. New York: Oxford University Press.

Wallace, Robert W. 1989. "The Institutionalization of a New Discipline: The Case of Sociology at Columbia University, 1891–1931." Doctoral dissertation, Columbia University.

Wall Street Journal. 2011. "Pact's Benefits in Limbo." November 28, 2011, A19.

Washington, Booker T. 1907. *The Negro in Business.* Boston: Hertel, Jenkins.

Waugh, Joan. 2005. "'Pageantry of Woe': The Funeral of Ulysses S. Grant." *Civil War History* 51(2):151–74.

Webb, Stephen. 2020. "Resistance, Biopolitics, and Radical Passivity." In *The Routledge Handbook of Critical Pedagogies for Social Work*, edited by Christine Morley et al. New York: Routledge.

Weisenfeld, Judith. 2004. "Universal in Spirit, Local in Character: The Riverside Church and New York City." In *The History of the Riverside Church in the City of New York*, edited by Peter J. Paris, John W. Cook, et al. New York: New York University Press.

Weizman, Eyal. 2007. *Hollow Land: Israel's Architecture of Occupation.* London: Verso.

Welton, Burton. 2002. "Praxis Imperfect: John Goodlad and the Social Reconstructionist Tradition." *Educational Studies* 33(1):61–83.

Westbrook, Robert B. 1992. "Schools for Industrial Democrats: The Social Origins of John Dewey's Philosophy of Education." *American Journal of Education* 100(4):401–19.

West Harlem Environmental Action (WE ACT) for Environmental Justice. 2006. *Official Written Comments on Columbia's Proposed Manhattanville in West Harlem Zoning and Academic Mixed-Use Development Environmental Impact Statement.* January 6, 2006. http://old.weact.org.

Whooley, Owen. 2013. *Knowledge in the Time of Cholera.* Chicago: University of Chicago Press.

Williams, Joyce E., and Vicky M. MacLean. 2015. *Settlement Sociology in the Progressive Years.* Leiden: Brill.

Williams, Lena. 1976. "A Giant Looks Out over Harlem." *New York Times*, June 13, 1976, 1.

Williams, Timothy. 2008a. "Eviction Anxiety Rattles a Formerly Subsidized Upper Manhattan Building." *New York Times*, October 16, 2008, A37.

——. 2008b. "2 Gas Stations, and a Family's Resolve, Confront Columbia Expansion Plan." *New York Times*, September 21, 2008, A39.

Williams, Timothy, and Ray Rivera. 2007. "$7 billion Columbia Expansion Gets Green Light." *New York Times*, December 20, 2007, A1.

Williams, Vernon J., Jr. 1996. *Rethinking Race: Franz Boas and His Contemporaries.* Lexington: University Press of Kentucky.

Wilson, Francille Rusan. 2006. *The Segregated Scholars.* Charlottesville: University of Virginia Press.

Wilson, William Julius. (1987) 2012. *The Truly Disadvantaged: The Inner City, the Underclass, and Public Policy*. Chicago: University of Chicago Press.

———, ed. 1993. *The Ghetto Underclass: Social Science Perspectives*. New York: Sage.

Wirth, Louis. 1925. "A Bibliography of the Urban Community." In *The City: Suggestions of Investigation of Human Behavior in the Urban Environment*, edited by Robert E. Park and Ernest W. Burgess. Chicago: University of Chicago Press.

Wolfe, Patrick. 1999. *Settler Colonialism and the Transformation of Anthropology*. London: Cassell.

Wood, L. Hollingsworth. Papers. 1910. "Minutes of the First Meeting of the Committee on Urban Conditions Among Negroes Held at the School of Philanthropy." September 29, 1910. Box 5, Minutes folder, Rare Book and Manuscript Library, Columbia University.

Woods, Clyde. 2002. "Life After Death." *Professional Geographer* 54(1): 62–66.

———. 2017. *Development Arrested: The Blues and Plantation Power in the Mississippi Delta*. 2nd ed. London: Verso.

Woods, Margaret E., and Peter S. K. Chi. 1986. "Sanitary Reform in New York City in 1866 and the Professionalization of Public Health Services: A Case Study of Social Reform." *Sociological Focus* 19(4):333–47.

Woodson, Carter G. 1950. "Thomas Jesse Jones." *Journal of Negro History* 35(1):107–9.

Woolston, Howard. 1906. "Social Education in the Public Schools." *Charities and the Commons* 16:570–78.

———. 1909. "*A Study of the Population of Manhattanville*." Studies in History, Economics and Public Law. Doctoral dissertation, Columbia University.

Wright, Richard. 1945. "Introduction by Richard Wright." In *Black Metropolis*, by Horace R. Cayton and St. Clair Drake. New York: Harcourt, Brace.

Yablonsky, Lewis. 1962. *The Violent Gang*. New York: Macmillan.

Yancy, George. 2004. "Fragments of a Social Ontology of Whiteness." In *What White Looks Like*, edited by George Yancy. London: Routledge.

Yellin, Eric S. 2002. "The (White) Search for (Black) Order: The Phelps-Stokes Fund's First Twenty Years, 1911–1931." *Historian* 65(2):319–52.

Young, Iris Marion. 1990. *Justice and the Politics of Difference*. Princeton: Princeton University Press.

Zipp, Samuel. 2012. *Manhattan Projects: The Rise and Fall of Urban Renewal in Cold War New York*. New York: Oxford University Press.

INDEX

Page numbers in *italics* indicate Figures

INDEX | 303

ABOUT THE AUTHOR

STEVEN GREGORY was the inaugural Dr. Kenneth and Kareitha Forde Professor of African American and African Diaspora Studies at Columbia University. His work in Anthropology on the intersection of race, class, gender, and urban-based social movements unfolded in numerous books and articles, notably the volumes *Black Corona: Race and the Politics of Place in an Urban Community* (1998), *Santería in New York City: A Study in Cultural Resistance* (2000), and *The Devil Behind the Mirror: Globalization and Politics in the Dominican Republic* (2007), which received the Society for Urban Anthropology's Anthony Leeds Prize and the Caribbean Studies Association's Gordon K. Lewis Book Prize.

ABOUT THE EDITOR

ELIZABETH CHIN is an anthropologist and ethnographer with a varied practice that includes ethnography, performance, community collaboration, and art making. After thirty years in the academy, she pivoted to being an independent researcher and freelance developmental editor. She became editor-in-chief of *American Anthropologist* in 2020, continuing through 2028.